Steam Nostalgia

By the same author

Severn Valley Steam

'Clun Castle' heads the 'Cathedrals' Express' up Chipping Campden Bank
(From an original oil painting by Terence Cuneo)

Steam Nostalgia

Locomotive and Railway Preservation in Great Britain

Sir Gerald Nabarro, F Inst F MP

Routledge & Kegan Paul   London and Boston

First published 1972
by Routledge & Kegan Paul Ltd
Broadway House, 68–74 Carter Lane
London EC4V 5EL and
9 Park Street,
Boston, Mass. 02108, U.S.A.

Printed in Great Britain by
The Camelot Press Ltd, London and Southampton

Library of Congress Catalogue Card Number 72 81445
ISBN 0 7100 7391 7

Contents

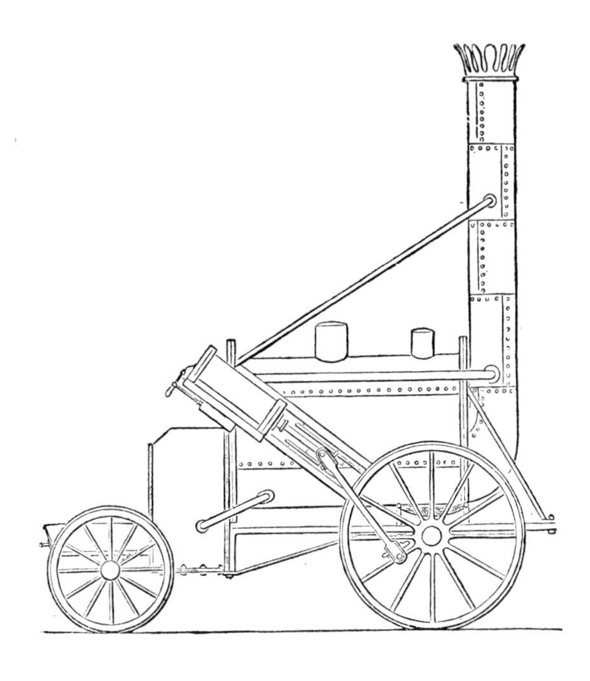

Stephenson's 'Rocket',
the Rainhill winner

Appendices

Plates

L&NWR 'President', one of McConnell's Bloomer class

Tables and maps

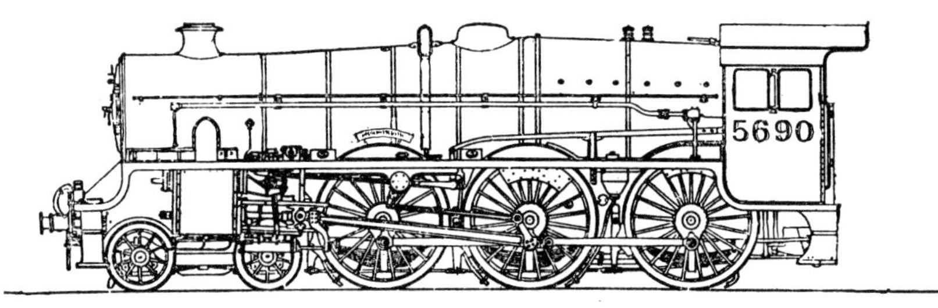

Jubilee class, no. 5690, 'Leander', now in Barry scrapyard

Tables

Maps

Foreword

Name plate on LMSR locomotive no. 5428, now at Tyseley

Sir Gerald Nabarro's book *Steam Nostalgia* is a comprehensive survey of railway and steam locomotive preservation in England, Wales, Scotland and the Isle of Man.

The age of steam on public, passenger carrying railways in Britain lasted for 138 years, from the rain-drenched opening of the Liverpool & Manchester Railway in September 1830 to the last scheduled, steam-hauled operations from Carnforth, Lostock Hall and Rose Grove in the summer of 1968 and the famous last run on 11 August that year. Since then, apart from such welcome excursions as that by 'King George V' in the autumn of 1971, all working standard gauge steam locomotives have been confined either to the light railway conditions of the privately owned and operated lines or to the almost stationary settings of the excellent 'live' museums. Nostalgia for the steam era has been made all the more keen by the suddenness of its passing. The splendid series of British Railways Standard locomotives, designed by Mr R. A. Riddles and his colleagues in the austere conditions of the years immediately after nationalisation, to be built in vast numbers and with a life expectancy of thirty years and more, were withdrawn when barely middle-aged as a result of a drastic modernisation plan begun in 1955 and quickly carried out. Thus one of the earliest, no. 70000, 'Britannia', was only fifteen years old when withdrawn in 1966 and the last steam locomotive built at Swindon, no. 92220, 'Evening Star', had served a mere five years when withdrawn in 1965.

While the collection of railway relics has gone on for many years, with the formation of the Railway Museum at York as long ago as 1928, the last decade has been a period of intense and growing activity. It is the fruit of this activity that Sir Gerald surveys here. He begins with the traditional museums, housing magnificent collections of railwayana and historic locomotives such as 'City of Truro', 'Hardwicke' and 'Mallard', not to mention antiques liks 'Sans Pareil' and 'Rocket'. Such engines are beautifully preserved and many of the more recent among them are in good working order but, of course, they are never actually steamed. The next sort of preservation described is the 'live' museums, such as Carnforth, Dinting, Tyseley and the several depots of the Great Western Society which also house historic locomotives like 'Pendennis Castle' at Didcot but which specialise in restoring engines, often from an advanced stage of decay, to working order and displaying them as often as possible in steam.

But the heart of the book lies in the descriptions of the privately owned and steam operated railways, standard and narrow gauge. Some, like the Bluebell Railway, are well-established; others are still in the throes of buying and preparing a line for operation. Between them they provide a marvellous panorama of British railway history including, for example, the Middleton Railway which follows the course of an eighteenth-century wagon way and was the site of a railway worked by a Blenkinsop rack rail locomotive built by Matthew Murray as early as 1812. At the other extreme is the Vale of Rheidol Railway, which represents British Railways' only remaining interest in steam traction, managed by the London Midland Region but which was nearly lost to steam as early as 1899 when the promoters sought powers to work the line by electricity.

Few people are as well qualified to write this book as Sir Gerald, who is not only a railway historian but is actively involved in working the Severn Valley Railway, one of the largest and most important of the lines within the scope of this survey. As a fellow railway enthusiast and writer I am delighted that Sir Gerald undertook the preparation of this book and I welcome its publication. That I am president of the Keighley & Worth Valley Railway adds to my pleasure in being associated with Sir Gerald in this excellent book.

Bishop's Lodge, Eric Treacy
Wakefield,
Yorkshire

Preface

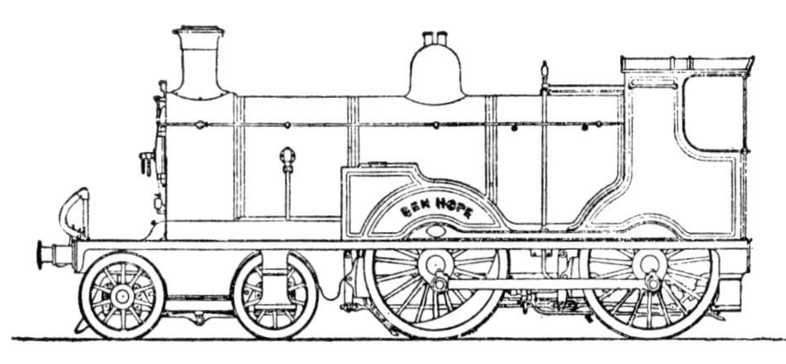

Highland Railway locomotive 'Ben Hope' 4-4-0

The proliferation of steam locomotives preserved in Britain today is the living testimony to a proud era of progress and dynamic expansion in British industrial and transportation history. The age of the steam railway engine was nearly one and a half centuries, 143 years to be exact, bridging the Crimean War, the Boer War and two World Wars. It all began with 'Locomotion' of the Stockton & Darlington Railway, opened in 1825, and ended with a 2-10-0 freight locomotive no. 92220, 'Evening Star', which emerged from Swindon in 1960. The end of steam traction, excepting the narrow gauge Vale of Rheidol Railway, came in 1968 when the last regular steam-hauled train ran on British Railways. Electric and diesel traction had totally ousted steam and approximately nineteen thousand steam locomotives were destined for the breakers' yards.

Then began the era of the steam locomotive preservationists. The number of steam engine lovers in Britain may be counted by the million. So widespread are the preservation bodies, museums, societies, companies and local enthusiasts' clubs that a representative organisation called the Association of Railway Preservation Societies has come into being to help and advise on every branch of preservation of steam engines, rolling stock and railway equipment; also the professional and legal aspects of Light Railway Orders essential to the working of steam-hauled trains on numerous branch lines, many of which are evolving fascinating techniques to capitalise their enterprises as necessary, and furnish facilities to restore and preserve the maximum number of steam locomotives. Interest is enormous and is still growing. Truly, it is a classless movement embracing men and women from every calling, every avocation and every profession. They are of all ages, from schoolboys and girls to the venerable, who can talk with pride and real affection of the halcyon days of steam at the turn of the century, the Edwardian era of unprecedented growth in the weight of passenger trains and their evocative speeding: the Race to the North and the locomotive Exchanges; the great locomotive engineers who vied for supremacy and growing efficiency, of Stirling, Gresley and Ivatt, of Churchward and Collett, of Johnson and Stanier, of Maunsell and Bulleid, each of whom is remembered today by association with preserved steam locomotives of the classes their genius begat. A 'Castle' is a Collett creation, an A4 a Gresley creation, a 'Princess' is a Stanier creation, a 'West Country' or a 'Battle of Britain' Pacific immortalises Bulleid, and Ivatt and Riddles in post-nationalisation days built hundreds of British Railways Standard types, from the 70XXX 'Britannia' class of Pacific locomotive to the mammoth 92XXX freight engines in the twilight years of steam.

Preservation has been largely haphazard as to types but in the event extraordinarily representative. Scottish preservation alone is conspicuously poor, with only seven steam engines preserved out of the 3,001 at work north of the border in 1923 when the Grouping eliminated the old company names: less than one quarter of one per cent preserved in Scotland which is infinitely sad because so many famous types, such as the Caledonian Railway 4-4-0 'Dunalastairs' or the great 4-4-2 Atlantics, with their huge boilers, built for the east coast expresses of the North British Railway, have not a single preserved survivor today. In England and Wales preservation is relatively more numerous and representative, including most of the famous types: the Gresley Pacifics, the Great Western 4-6-0 'Castles' and 'Kings', 'Halls' and 'Manors', the 2-6-2T Prairie and 0-6-0T pannier tanks, the Stanier beasts of burden, the 4-6-0 'Black 5s', his 2-8-08F class and quite a wide range of Southern Railway types, from both pre- and post-Grouping, are well preserved.

All this contributes to a galaxy of steam engine lore and reminiscence, performance and practical achievement.

Thus I was prompted to set to work and endeavour to produce within the covers of a single volume a reliable and ready reference book of the background and history of every steam locomotive preserved in Britain today and also those potential preservations which lie as hulks in breakers' yards, forlorn and cannibalised, awaiting rescue. I hope that many may yet be snatched back to be kept for posterity.

Steam Nostalgia is a big book and on pages 253–55 I express my thanks to the host of willing and generous collaborators, colleagues and advisers who helped me with its compilation.

There are others I would like to mention especially here.

The list of locomotives extant in England, Scotland, Wales and the Isle of Man forms an invaluable Appendix to the book for which I wish to thank Mr R. N. Pritchard, Honorary Publications Officer of the Worcester Locomotive Society. Mr Columb Howell also provided exhaustive information about locomotives in Woodham Brothers' yard at Barry, Glamorgan.

Then there are the photographers (whom I thank individually at the end of the book) for providing material and allowing their work to be reproduced. I thank them all most warmly. If you admire the uniformly peerless quality of the photography, some of which was specially processed and restored, than it is to Mr and Mrs John Beckerley of Hanley Swan, Worcestershire, that you should award the accolade of craftsmanship. For the vignettes, especially those showing three-quarter views of locomotives, I would like to thank Mr Edward J. Lane.

Also I thank Mr C. R. Clinker for his meticulous correction of the book and, as with *Severn Valley Steam*, I pay a tribute to the publishers, Routledge & Kegan Paul of London and Boston, who have displayed great skill and efficiency, and equally important, punctuality.

Finally, I would like to thank the Bishop of Wakefield for providing the Foreword.

I hope you enjoy this book, railway lovers everywhere, as much as I have enjoyed writing it for your edification and pleasure.

House of Commons Gerald Nabarro
13 September 1972

Part One

Locomotive Preservation

1 Museums

Paddington engine house *c.* 1845

The distinction between 'live' and 'static' locomotive museums is in some respects a false one. Many 'static' exhibits are in perfect working order and a comparable proportion of those kept at steam centres and, indeed, in the care of operating railway preservation societies, are not and never will be. With engines such as 'King George V', 'Sir Nigel Gresley' and 'Bahamas' regularly in steam and in most cases with some prospect of working under more realistic conditions over ever-expanding territory, even the recent museum monopoly of the heaviest locomotives no longer exists. In these circumstances the role of the traditional museums in what is now an entirely respectable branch of industrial archaeology could usefully change. Of course, there are many items in the present museums which by reason of their age, gauge and so on can never be exhibited at work. Others must be kept inactive for the reason that their importance as exact specimens of the engineering of their time would be lost by repair and renewal. These, together with the limitless arcana of centuries of transport history, are proper objects for conventional museums. Much of the rest of the job can profitably be left to the enthusiasm and finance of private individuals, companies, societies and trusts, even if their principal aim is to 'play trains'. The two hazards of relying to this extent on private organisations are first, that the available resources will be uselessly strained by the over-preservation of certain classes—the present maintenance of no less than eleven

Stanier 'Black 5s' is possibly an example—and second, that the long-term future of privately preserved engines could be threatened by fluctuations in the current steam 'mania'. The second problem should solve the first in due course and as the following chapters will show, some at least of the organisations concerned are so constituted that the future of their locomotive collections is assured.

Locomotive preservation began very early in the main period of steam traction. Many of the earliest machines, clothed in novelty, were saved from destruction and, like 'Wylam Dilly', 'Puffing Billy' and others, went to museums, by gift or acquisition, immediately after being withdrawn from service. More, like the Canterbury & Whitstable Railway's 0-4-0 'Invicta' of 1830, which has been on one pedestal or another in Canterbury ever since it was withdrawn in 1839, have also survived. The systematic collection of locomotives did not, however, begin for a hundred years and even since then it has seldom been pursued with the thoroughness shown in building up a collection like Henry Ford's Museum of Mechanical Engineering in Detroit, for which Robert Stephenson & Co. built a full size working replica of 'Rocket' in 1929. At the time of the Grouping in 1923 there were some twenty-six locomotives and a century of accumulated bric-à-brac in the care of the railway companies. On the whole the railways showed very little piety towards their past, particularly the Great Western Railway, and this accounts for the present shortage of broad gauge locomotives. In 1928 the London & North Eastern Railway, in most respects the least antiquarian-minded of companies, established the Railway Museum at York and this soon became a repository for engines from outside the LNER system which did not find a permanent home in the Science Museum. York soon became known as the main railway museum in the country and when the Clapham museum was founded in 1961 it was as a transport museum, with interests far beyond steam and rail alone. The recent proposals for a national railway museum at York may give some further reality to the reputation which it has long held, although for reasons outside the scope of this book it is impossible to say when this will be. The present York, Swindon, Clapham and South Kensington collections must, therefore, be considered separately, along with the Glasgow and Edinburgh museums.

The Science Museum

Founded in 1853 as part of the South Kensington Museum, the Science Museum was opened in 1857. Its locomotive collection began in 1862 with William Hedley's second 5ft gauge engine for Wylam colliery, the 0-4-0 'Puffing Billy', built in 1814. This engine is almost the same, though slightly heavier than 'Wylam Dilly' which is now in the Royal Scottish Museum at Edinburgh. The Science Museum's most cele-

Hackworth's 'Sans Pareil', one of the Rainhill competitors

brated locomotive possessions, however, are the two Rainhill contestants, 'Rocket' and 'Sans Pareil', and the replica of a third, 'Novelty'. Robert Stephenson's 0-2-2 'Rocket' which won the Rainhill Trials in 1829 later worked on the Liverpool & Manchester Railway until 1836 when it was acquired by the Brampton Railway in Cumberland and remained there until the end of its working life in 1862. Originally the cylinders on 'Rocket' were inclined at an angle of about 45° on the sides of the boiler, which caused her to sway when at speed. As a result, soon after the engine had entered service on the Liverpool & Manchester Railway they were altered to be almost horizontal. The Science Museum's engine is the converted machine. The two replicas are of the original. One of them, as already mentioned, is in Henry Ford's museum in Detroit and the other, built for the LMS centenary exhibition at Liverpool in 1930, was formerly in the Science Museum with the original but now guards the entrance to the Museum of British Transport in Clapham High Street. Timothy Hackworth's 0-4-0 'Sans Pareil' was disqualified from winning the £500 Rainhill prize because it weighed very slightly more than the maximum permitted. She later worked on the Liverpool & Manchester and Bolton & Leigh railways but came to an undignified end as a stationary boiler at Coppull colliery, Chorley, from 1844 to 1863. 'Novelty' is perforce a replica, the original having blown up at Rainhill.

The Museum's 0-4-0ST 'Bauxite' built by Black, Hawthorn & Co. at Gateshead in 1874 was donated in 1953 to represent industrial locomotive practice of the nineteenth century. She had previously worked at the Hebburn chemical works of the Industrial Aluminium

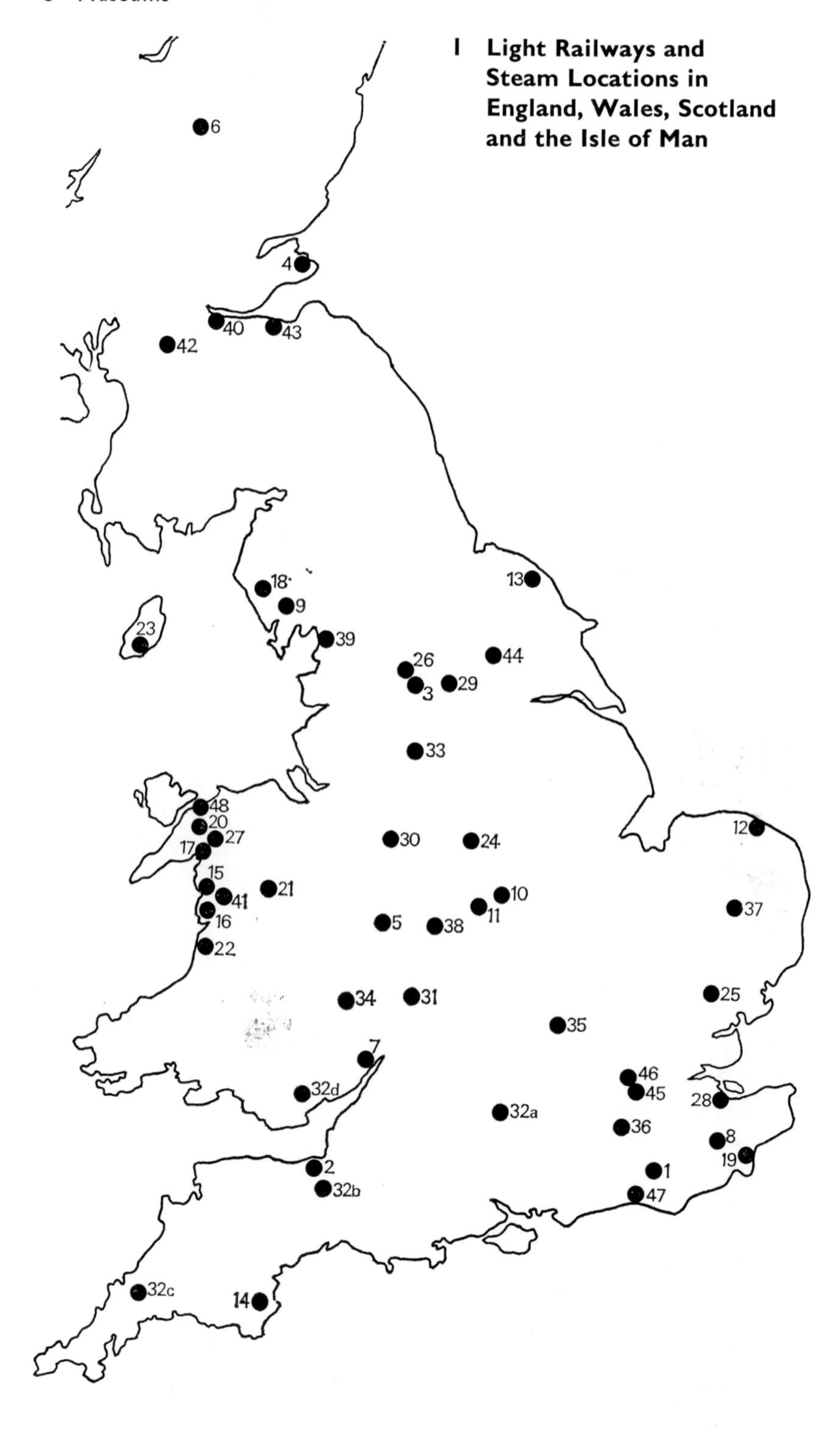

1 Light Railways and Steam Locations in England, Wales, Scotland and the Isle of Man

1 Bluebell Railway
2 West Somerset Railway
3 Keighley & Worth Valley Railway
4 Lochty Private Railway
5 Severn Valley Railway
6 Strathspey Railway
7 Dean Forest Railway
8 Kent & East Sussex Railway
9 Lakeside & Haverthwaite Railway
10 Main Line Steam Trust
11 Midland Railway Society
12 North Norfolk Railway
13 North Yorkshire Moors Railway
14 Dart Valley Railway
15 Fairbourne Railway
16 Talyllyn Railway
17 Festiniog Railway
18 Ravenglass & Eskdale Railway
19 Romney, Hythe & Dymchurch Railway
20 Snowdon Mountain Railway & Llanberis Lake Railway
21 Welshpool & Llanfair Railway
22 Vale of Rheidol Railway
23 Isle of Man Victorian Steam Railway
24 Midland Railway Project
25 Stour Valley Railway
26 Yorkshire Dales Railway
27 Welsh Highland Railway
28 Sittingbourne & Kemsley Railway
29 Middleton Railway
30 Foxfield Railway
31 Dowty Railway Preservation Society
32a Great Western Society—Didcot
b Great Western Society—Taunton
c Great Western Society—Bodmin
d Great Western Society—Caerphilly
33 Dinting Railway Centre
34 Bulmer's Private Railway
35 Quainton Railway Preservation Society
36 Brockham Museum
37 Bressingham Live Steam Museum
38 Standard Gauge Steam Trust, Tyseley
39 Steamtown, Carnforth
40 Scottish Railway Preservation Society, Falkirk
41 Corris Railway
42 Glasgow Museum of Transport
43 Royal Scottish Museum, Edinburgh
44 Railway Museum, York
45 Museum of British Transport, Clapham
46 Science Museum, London
47 British Railways National Relics Store, Brighton
48 Penrhyn Castle Museum, Bangor

Co. until 1947 when she was presented to the North East Historical & Industrial Locomotive Society.

The most recent and striking locomotive exhibit at the Science Museum, ex-GWR no. 4073, 'Caerphilly Castle', is described in chapter 4.

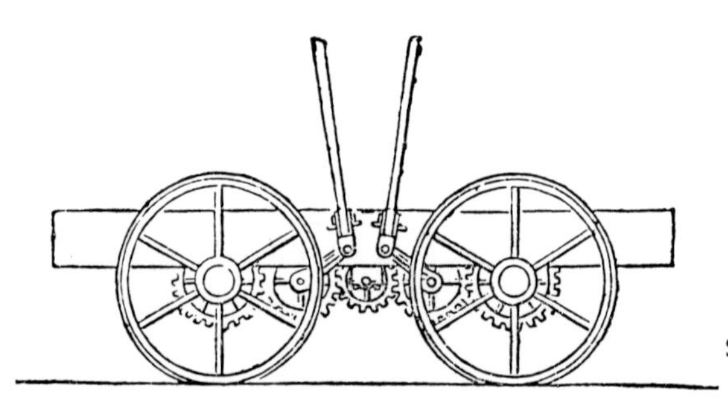

Stephenson's initial driving gear for locomotives

The Railway Museum, York

The oldest locomotive on show at York is also an ex-Durham colliery machine, built in 1822 by George Stephenson and Nicholas Wood for use on the eight miles of line between the Hetton pits and the coal staithes on the River Wear. At less than ten tons inclusive of tender, she was two tons lighter than either of the Wylam locomotives and owes her rather modern appearance to rebuilding in 1857 and 1882. The Hetton colliery locomotive led the procession of engines at the Darlington centenary exhibition in 1925 which was designed to demonstrate the need for a railway museum in the north east of England, and encouraged the LNER's initiative at York. Originally Darlington seemed the natural location but the railway capital of the region prevailed and part of York's historic station was converted for the purpose. It has since been moved a short distance to Queen Street, to a site and building which was once the motive power department. Darlington, as a consolation prize, has two ex-Stockton & Darlington Railway locomotives displayed at Bank Top station: the legendary no. 1, 'Locomotion', built for the opening of the railway in 1825, and the Hackworth 0-6-0 of 1845, 'Derwent'. The latter was one of several similar engines built by W. & A. Kitching between 1845 and 1848, passed much of its working life on the private lines of Messrs Pease of Darlington and was presented by them to the North Eastern Railway in 1898.

Of the non-locomotive exhibits at York which are of particular interest in the context of this book the most important is the specimen of John Blenkinsop's rack rail of 1812, as used on the Middleton Colliery Railway, before the adhesive qualities of smooth rails and wheels were fully appreciated.

Next to the Hetton colliery engine the oldest locomotive at York is

0-4-0 'Agenoria' on loan from the Science Museum. Built in 1829 by Foster Rastrick & Co. of Stourbridge, 'Agenoria' spent the whole of its working life on the Earl of Dudley's Shutt End colliery railway in Staffordshire. An almost identical Rastrick locomotive, 'Stourbridge Lion', built a year earlier, was exported to America and was the first locomotive there to run on rails.

The Grand Junction Railway's locomotive works at Crewe started production in 1845 with Alexander Allan's 2-2-2 no. 49, 'Columbine'. This exceptionally handsome engine worked for fifty-seven years until 1902 although the ugly cab, added in LNWR days, obscures the steam dome which should be the crowning feature of its appearance. 'Columbine' is one of only two engines at York to originate outside the area eventually operated by the LNER. The other interloper is the London, Brighton & South Coast Railway's 0-4-2 tender engine, no. 214, 'Gladstone', built at Brighton in 1882. It was the first of Stroudley's front-coupled express engines and the first locomotive to be preserved privately, on the initiative of the Stephenson Locomotive Society, after it was withdrawn in 1927.

All the other locomotives at York originated on either the North Eastern or Great Northern railways. The NER is represented by five, beginning with the Kitson, Thompson & Hewitson 2-2-4T no. 66, 'Aerolite', of 1851. This engine has been much altered since it emerged from the Airedale foundry at Leeds, including conversion to a 2-cylinder compound on the Worsdell & von Borries system, of which she is now the only surviving example. The NER absorbed the Stockton & Darlington Railway in 1863 but the new company's locomotive superintendent, Edward Fletcher, continued to allow the Stockton & Darlington's locomotive superintendent, William Bouch, almost complete autonomy. Bouch's 0-6-0 tender engine no. 1275, built by Dübs & Co. of Glasgow in 1874, is an example of the continuing Darlington tradition and clearly shows its descent from the long-boilered locomotives of the Stephensons. No. 1275 participated in the 1925 Darlington centenary exhibition which marked the end of its working life and retirement as one of the original York Museum engines. At Gateshead, Edward Fletcher evolved a class of 2-4-0 express locomotives for work on the NER's east coast main line. Fifty-five of them were built, including no. 910 in 1875, when she took part in the Newark brake trials. Like Bouch's no. 1275, no. 910 survived the Grouping but was withdrawn for preservation in 1925. Fletcher's retirement in 1882 was followed first by eighteen tempestuous months under Alexander McDonnell and then an interregnum until the appointment of T. W. Worsdell in 1885. During this time engine design and building was carried on in the Fletcher tradition by the general manager, Henry Tennant. A product of his management is 2-4-0 no. 1463, which worked until 1927, when it was withdrawn for preservation at York. The last NER locomotive is a

Worsdell 4-4-0 no. 1621, which was built in 1893 and remained in service until after World War II. She was the second engine of a class nicknamed 'Rail Crushers' because of their weight which, at 50 tons 2 cwt, was well above anything that had yet been built, although they were closely followed in this respect by their contemporaries, the London & South Western Railway's Adams 4-4-0s. No. 1621 and her sister no. 1620 distinguished themselves in the 1895 Race to the North. No. 1621 ran the 80½ miles from York to Newcastle in 79 minutes and no. 1620 averaged 66mph on the 124½ miles on to Edinburgh with a 100-ton train. Class M, as the 'Rail Crushers' were officially designated, had 7ft 1in driving wheels and Wilson Worsdell produced two engines of the same class with even larger ones in anticipation of more racing.

Of the three former Great Northern Railway engines at York the Stirling 8-foot single driver is unquestionably the star and the class as a whole is one of the biggest landmarks in the history of British locomotive design. The York engine, no. 1, was the first of them, built at Doncaster in 1870 and though the design evolved throughout the twenty-five years of building until 1895, the first examples were hardly surpassed in excellence. Indeed, some of the later locomotives, with their single driving axles overloaded, caused some trouble through derailment at speed. In the 1880s they ran the fastest express trains in the world and with their long, domeless boilers and huge sweep of running plate over the driving wheels, matched speed with elegance. No. 1, which was withdrawn from service in 1907, has the distinction of having been featured on a postage stamp. She was one of the original LNER exhibits at York in 1928 and ten years later returned to east coast main line metals working specials, including the first ever private rail tour, organised by the Railway Correspondence & Travel Society.

The supremacy of Patrick Stirling's 8-footers barely outlasted the reign of their designer at Doncaster. H. A. Ivatt, who succeeded him in 1895, was a Crewe-trained engineer who, at the time of his appointment by the GNR, was locomotive engineer of the Great Southern & Western Railway in Ireland. His first Atlantic (4-4-2) locomotives, nicknamed 'Klondykes' because they appeared in the year of the Gold Rush, 1898, immediately showed power and speed well above that of any existing engine. The locomotive at York, no. 990, was the first of the class and named 'Henry Oakley' in honour of the then general manager of the Great Northern. For nearly twenty-five years, until the appearance of the pioneer Gresley Pacific no. 1470, 'Great Northern', on the eve of the Grouping, no. 990 was unique in being the company's only named locomotive. Under the LNER she was renumbered no. 3990 and was fitted with a superheater and extended smokebox. Although Ivatt's first Atlantics were superseded by his own enlarged and improved design in 1902, 'Henry Oakley' lasted well into the age of Super Pacifics and P2s and was not withdrawn until 1937 when it was restored to GNR livery and installed at York.

'Henry Oakley' was joined in the Museum in 1947 by one of Ivatt's enlarged Atlantics, no. 251. Even this very sturdy class was not perfected until after many more years of evolution and change and then not by its originator but by his successor, Sir Nigel Gresley. The initial differences between the first and the 1902 enlarged Ivatt Atlantics lay in the boiler and firebox and a consequential difference in weight of 60 tons and 69 tons 12 cwt. From the start, Ivatt's Atlantics performed magnificently, demonstrating their great power in sparkling performances on the very heaviest trains and this was much enhanced when Gresley superheated them and enlarged their piston valves and cylinders. Such locomotives were more than equal to their prescribed task of hauling 500-ton trains at high average speeds on the east coast main line.

'North Star'

The Great Western Railway Museum

When the Museum of British Transport at Clapham was founded it was intended that the regional emphasis of institutions such as the York museum should be retained and developed. The only other regional museum to flourish has been the Great Western Railway Museum at Swindon which enjoyed municipal support from the start. Swindon is possibly an even more evocative locomotive location than York, and the five engines at present displayed there are naturally of Great Western origin, although one of them is largely a replica.

The lack of broad gauge locomotives preserved has already been noted. One of the engines which Churchward broke up at Swindon in 1906 in order to make more space was a 2-2-2, 'North Star', built by

Robert Stephenson & Co. at Darlington in 1837. It is ironic that less than twenty years after this brazen act of destruction, attitudes and prospects should have changed so much that the surviving fragments of the engine should have been gathered together and, with such new parts as were needed, that a replica was put together for the Wembley Exhibition of 1925. It is this that is displayed at Swindon today. The original locomotive came into GWR hands by chance and rescued the company from the eccentricities of the rag-bag of engines by which it was then served (1837). 'North Star' had been built for the 5ft 6in. gauge New Orleans Railway and was actually shipped to America. Business difficulties at that end of the operation caused the engine to be returned to England, named and adapted for service on the Great Western's 7ft gauge where she remained at work until 1871. 'North Star', as well as giving excellent service in her own right, had a good influence on the later development of GWR locomotives, most obviously on Gooch's 2-2-2 Firefly class, of which sixty-two were built between 1840 and 1842. These engines completely transformed the reputation of GWR locomotives and one of them, 'Actaeon', averaged 41½mph over the 194 miles from Exeter to London via Bristol on the inaugural return run in 1844.

The other four locomotives at Swindon are originals, although far less venerable than 'North Star'. The oldest, built in 1897, is 0-6-0 no. 2516, one of the very last of 280 Dean 'Goods' engines, double and single framed and all with inside cylinders, turned out of the Swindon works between 1883 and 1898. The first of the class were Great Western novelties in having only inside frames. The earlier engines also had domeless boilers, although bright brass domes reappeared later. The class was ubiquitous on goods and branch passenger work and travelled notably widely in both wars. No. 2516 was superheated in 1935 and remained in service until 1956.

The youngest locomotive in the Swindon collection is almost an interloper in so far as it was only just built under GWR auspices. No. 9400 was the first of a batch of ten 0-6-0 pannier tanks which emerged from Swindon on the eve of nationalisation. The 0-6-0PT was one of the types to be perpetuated under BR and a further two hundred engines of the 94XX class, although not superheated, were built after 1947. No. 9400 was withdrawn, comparatively early, in 1959.

'City of Truro' and 'Lode Star' stand in the foremost rank of historic railway relics. William Dean's 4-4-0 City class of 1901 was the first to incorporate what became the characteristic Great Western tapered boiler. Otherwise, the class retained the cylinders with slide valves and outside frames from existing Swindon practice. No. 3440, 'City of Truro', was built in 1903. On 4 July that year no. 3433, 'City of Bath', hauling a special train, covered the 193⅝ miles from Paddington to Exeter at an average speed of 67mph and continued over the fifty-two miles to Plymouth North Road at an average of 51mph. This performance inflamed an issue for racing between the GWR and the LSWR in competition for the up mail traffic from Plymouth. At 230½ miles Joseph Locke's London & South Western route via Templecombe was shorter, but more severely graded than the Great Western's 246½-mile route via Bristol which, although equally exacting at the western end, had a mean gradient on the Bristol–Paddington section—known as Brunel's billiard table—of 1 in 1,380. On 3 April 1904 two Drummond locomotives brought an LSWR train up in 243 minutes. The Great Western responded with a series of time-clipping runs with special mail trains beginning on 9 April and culminating in the legendary performance by 'City of Truro' and 'Duke of Connaught' on 9 May. The details are set out in Table 1, reproduced from the *Great Western Railway Magazine* for June 1904. 'City of Truro' left Millbay Crossing, Plymouth, at 9.23 a.m. with a five-coach train of 148 tons gross. She had a heavier train and the more exacting part of the road than 'Duke of Connaught' but nevertheless averaged more than 70mph from Exeter to Bristol, including a stretch at more than 100mph down Wellington Bank. Whatever the precise speed it was certainly higher than had ever been achieved before and was unequalled until the twenties when 'Flying Scotsman' reached 100mph with a test train soon after she was built. In the 1930s stretches of 100mph running by Gresley's evolving Pacifics became almost commonplace, leading on to the historic performances by 'Mallard', 'Silver Fox' and 'Silver Link' described in chapter 3. 'City of Truro' arrived at Pylle Hill, Bristol, at 11.30 a.m. where one van was detached and the renowned single-driver no. 3065, 'Duke of Connaught', took the train on to Paddington in similar style. The 246½-mile journey was accomplished in 226½ minutes, an average speed of 65·49mph or, excluding the stop at Pylle Hill, 66·39mph. Such exercises as these had their influence on day-to-day services. In the same summer of 1904 the 'Cornish Riviera' non-stop Paddington–Plymouth run was introduced and when the scheduled time crept down to 267 minutes it was 'City of Truro' and other locomotives of her class which were used initially to work this famous train. No. 3440 was renumbered 3717 and superheated in 1911. On withdrawal she was sent to York Railway Museum but was brought out again in 1957, restored to no. 3440 and worked on scheduled and excursion trains, the latter throughout the country including Scotland, until 1963 when she was put on display in the Swindon Museum and again renumbered as no. 3717.

Churchward's 4-6-0 Star class were more numerous than his predecessor's Cities and seventy-two of them were built between 1907 and 1922. The first, no. 4000, was originally built as an Atlantic (4-4-2) and later converted to 4-6-0. The present Swindon engine, no. 4003, 'Lode Star', was one of the earliest, built in 1907 and one of the last to leave service forty-four years later. There is no Castle at Swindon and thus

Table I Working of special mail trains between Plymouth and London

Distance m	Distance chs	Stations	American Line S.S. *St. Louis* April 9th Arrive	Depart	Time occupied h	Time occupied m	Speed per hour miles	North German Lloyd S.S. *Kaiser Wilhelm II* April 18th Arrive	Depart	Time occupied h	Time occupied m	Speed per hour miles
		Plymouth—Millbay Crossing		a.m. 4.59		·	—	—	p.m. 4.21			
23	79	Totnes ...	5	33	·	34	42·69	4	55	·	34	42·32
8	55	Newton Abbot	5	46	·	13	40·09	5	6	·	11	47·49
20	15	Exeter ...	6.11	6.15	·	25	49·35	5	29	·	23	52·66
30	63	Taunton ...	6	43	·	28	65·97	5	58	·	29	63·69
11	45	Bridgwater ...	6	52	·	9	77·07	6	8	·	10	69·37
32	69	Bristol {Pylle Hill	—	—	·	·	—	—	—	·	·	—
33	19	Bristol {Temple Meads	7.21	7.29	·	29	68·76	6.39½	6.45	·	31½	63·27
34	57	W'ton Bas't {via Badminton	8	7	·	38	54·81	7	19	·	34	61·25
35	36	W'ton Bas't {via Box	—	—	·	·	—	—	—	·	·	—
5	48	Swindon ...	8	13	·	6	56·00	7	25	·	6	56·00
24	13	Didcot ...	8	33	·	20	72·49	7	45	·	20	72·49
17	9	Reading ...	8	46	·	13	78·91	8	2	·	17	60·39
36	0	Paddington ...	9.17		·	31	69·67	8.34	—	·	32	67·50

Stations	American Line S.S. *St. Paul* April 23rd Arrive	Depart	Time occupied h	Time occupied m	Speed per hour miles	American Line S.S. *Philadelphia* April 30th Arrive	Depart	Time occupied h	Time occupied m	Speed per hour miles
Plymouth—Millbay Crossing		p.m. 3.55					p.m. 6.1			—
Totnes ...	4	25½	·	30½	47·19	6	29	·	28	51·40
Newton Abbot	4	36	·	10½	49·64	6	38	·	9	57·91
Exeter ...	5	1	·	25	49·35	7.1	7.5	·	23	52·65
Taunton ...	5	31	·	30	61·57	7	36	·	31	59·58
Bridgwater ...	5	41½	·	10	66·07	7	46	·	10	69·37
Bristol {Pylle Hill	—	—	·	·	—	8.13	8.16	·	27	73·86
Bristol {Temple Meads	6.11	6.15	·	29½	67·60	—	—	·	·	—
W'ton Bas't {via Badminton	6	51	·	36	57·85	—	—	·	·	—
W'ton Bas't {via Box	—	—	·	·	—	8	50	·	34	62·55
Swindon ...	6	56½	·	5½	61·09	8	55	·	5	67·20
Didcot ...	7	18	·	21½	67·43	9	13½	·	18½	78·36
Reading ...	7	33	·	15	68·45	9	27	·	13½	76·06
Paddington ...	8.7	—	·	34	63·53	9.55	—	·	28	77·14

Stations	North German Lloyd S.S. *Kaiser Wilhelm der Grosse*, May 2nd Arrive	Depart	Time occupied h	Time occupied m	Speed per hour miles	American Line S.S. *St. Louis* May 7th Arrive	Depart	Time occupied h	Time occupied m	Speed per hour miles
Plymouth—Millbay Crossing	—	p.m. 12.21			—	—	a.m. 8.27			—
Totnes ...	12	49	·	28	51·40	8	57	·	30	47·97
Newton Abbot	12	58	·	9	57·91	9	7	·	10	52·13
Exeter ...	1	19	·	21	57·66	9	28	·	21	57·68
Taunton ...	1	49	·	30	61·55	9	57	·	29	63·70
Bridgwater ...	2	0	·	11	63·06	10	7	·	10	69·38
Bristol {Pylle Hill	2.29	2.31	·	29	68·76	10.35	10.37½	·	28	71·22
Bristol {Temple Meads	—	—	·	·	—	—	—	·	·	—
W'ton Bas't {via Badminton	—	—	·	·	—	—	—	·	·	—
W'ton Bas't {via Box	3	5	·	34	62·55	11	13½	·	36	59·07
Swindon ...	3	10	·	5	67·20	11	19	·	5½	61·09
Didcot ...	3	31	·	21	69·03	11	41	·	22	65·89
Reading ...	3	45½	·	14½	70·81	11	55	·	14	73·34
Paddington ...	4.17	—	·	31½	68·57	12.28	—	·	33	65·45

* Distance Pylle Hill to East Depot 1m 35chs
† Distance East Depot to Bath 10m 9chs
‡ Distance Bath to Swindon 29m 48chs

Stations	North German Lloyd S.S. *Kronprinz Wilhelm* May 9th Arrive h.m.s.	Depart h.m.s.	Time occupied m	Time occupied s	Speed per hour miles
Plymouth—Millbay Crossing	a.m. —	a.m. 9.23.10	·	·	—
Totnes ...	—	9.50.49	27	39	52·05
Newton Abbot	—	9.59.52	9	3	57·59
Exeter ...	—	10.22.12	22	20	54·23
Taunton ...	—	10.50.1	27	49	66·41
Bridgwater ...	—	10.59.24	9	23	73·94
Bristol {Pylle Hill	11.26.29	11.30.12	27	5	72·80
Bristol {Temple Meads	*Bristol East Dpt	11.33.51	3	39	23·63
W'ton Bas't {via Badminton					
W'ton Bas't {via Box	†Bath	11.43.50	9	59	60·78
Swindon ...	‡	p.m. 12.9.49	25	59	68·35
Didcot ...	—	12.29.20	19	31	74·28
Reading ...	—	12.42.21	13	1	78·88
Paddington ...	Platform	1.9.38	27	17	79.17
	Dead Stop	1.9.58	From Reading 27	37	

	American Line S.S. *St. Louis* April 9th	North German Lloyd S.S. *Kaiser Wilhelm II* April 18th	American Line S.S. *St. Paul* April 23rd	American Line S.S. *Philadelphia* April 30th	North German Lloyd S.S. *Kaiser Wilhelm der Grosse*, May 2nd	American Line S.S. *St. Louis* May 7th	North German Lloyd S.S. *Kronprinz Wilhelm* May 9th
Total time occupied	4h 18min	4h 13min	4h 12min	3h 54min	3h 56min	4h 1min	h.m.s. Paddington platform 3.46.28 dead stop 3.46.48
Speed per hour throughout, including stops	57·21 miles	58·39 miles	58·58 miles	63·27 miles	62·73 miles	60·86 miles	65·49 miles
Speed per hour throughout, excluding stops	60·01 miles	59·69 miles	59·52 miles	65·52 miles	63·27 miles	62·03 miles	66·39 miles
Load of 8-wheeled Vans from Plymouth	5	5	5	4	5	5	5
Load of 8-wheeled Vans from Bristol	3	3	3	2	3	3	4
Engines and Drivers	Plymouth to Exeter No. 3452, Driver Uren Exeter to Bristol, No. 3442, Driver Warren Bristol to Paddington No. 3066, Driver Edwards	Plymouth to Bristol No. 3442, Driver Warren Bristol to Paddington No. 3396, Driver Lee	Plymouth to Bristol No. 3442, Driver Clements Bristol to Padddington No. 3056, Driver T. Burt	Plymouth to Exeter No. 3442 Driver Warren Exeter to Pylle Hill No. 3052 Driver Killock Pylle to Paddington No. 3005, Driver Underhill	Plymouth to Paddington No. 3437, Driver Millard	Plymouth to Paddington No. 3442, Driver J. Warren	Plymouth to Bristol, No. 3440, 'City of Truro', Driver Clements Bristol to Paddington No. 3065 'Duke of Connaught', Driver Underhill

the next link in the GWR 4-6-0 pedigree is not represented although, with 'Defiant', 'Nunney Castle', 'Thornbury Castle' and 'Earl of Mount Edgcumbe' still in Barry scrapyard, this need not always be so. Of the third generation 4-6-0s—the Kings—the engine selected for preservation, no. 6000 'King George V', was originally kept at Swindon but she is now exemplifying most of the advantages of working preservation in the care of H. P. Bulmer Ltd, at Hereford.

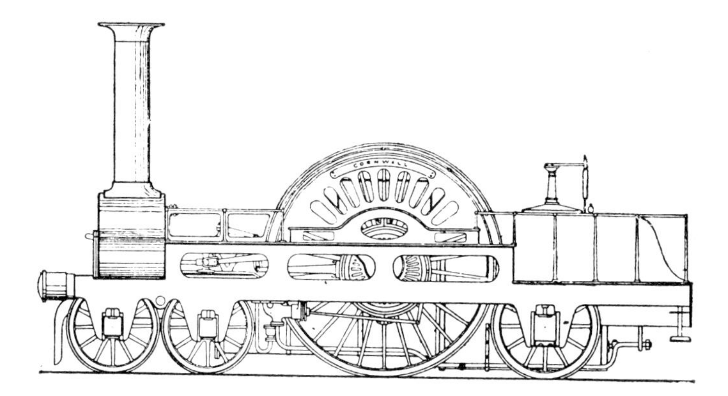

Trevithick's 'Cornwall'

The Museum of British Transport

The present museum is housed in a converted bus garage off Clapham High Street. As the name indicates, it was formed with responsibilities far beyond railways and locomotives alone and even though some of them have been shed—the canal exhibits, for example, have been moved to Stoke Bruerne, Northamptonshire—it remains a transport rather than a railway museum. However, the locomotive exhibits at Clapham, which include such eye-catchers as 'Mallard', form the largest and most comprehensive collection so far achieved.

The smallest and only narrow gauge engine on show at Clapham is 1ft 6in. 0-4-0T 'Wren', built by Beyer Peacock in 1887 for the domestic tramway at the Lancashire & Yorkshire Railway's Horwich works. In its heyday this system employed eight similar locomotives of which 'Wren' was one of the earliest and longest lived. She was withdrawn in 1962, painted in BR livery and immediately installed at Clapham.

Two other Clapham engines were connected with the Brill branch of the Metropolitan & Great Central Joint Railway, formerly the Oxford & Aylesbury Tramroad. An Aveling & Porter 0-4-0WT of 1872 was retired from the Tramway to the Blisworth and Stowe Brick & Tile Co. at Nether Heyford in Northamptonshire and was abandoned there when the works closed down in 1940. It was London Transport who originally rescued and restored her ready to represent tramroad traction at Clapham. The ex-Metropolitan Railway 4-4-0T was one of sixty-six similar engines built by Beyer Peacock from 1864 onwards. Few survived the electrification of the Inner Circle line in 1905 but no. 23 was put to work on the Brill branch. She was retained by London Transport in 1934 and continued in service until after the war when the LTPB kept her at Neasden for many years until the Clapham museum opened.

Eleven locomotives at Clapham originated from nine different companies: the Great Central, LNER, the Midland, South Eastern & Chatham, London Brighton & South Coast, the Furness Railway, LSWR, and two each from the London & North Western and Great Eastern railways. The ex-LNER locomotive is the Gresley A4 Pacific no. 4468 (BR no. 60022) 'Mallard' built at Doncaster in 1938, which is described in chapter 3. The Great Eastern and Great Central engines were, of course, operated by the LNER after the Grouping. Of these three, the GCR's 4-4-0 no. 506, 'Butler Henderson', was one of the second batch of Director class locomotives built at the company's Gorton works in 1920. The first batch of ten locomotives had been built in 1913 to a design specifically developed for work on through London–Manchester expresses. The Atlantics, which they partly superseded, had usually needed a change of locomotive during the 190-mile run. The Director class was so successful that variants were developed for other specialised purposes, particularly in Scotland.

The ex-GER locomotives are a Holden 2-4-0 no. 490 (BR no. 62785) built at Stratford in 1894 and the same engineer's 0-6-0T no. 87 (BR no. 68633) of 1904. James Holden's mixed traffic 2-4-0s first appeared in 1891 and a hundred of them were built over the next five years. No. 490 survived both the Grouping and nationalisation and was not withdrawn until 1959. Holden's 0-6-0Ts were designed mainly for shunting and local goods work but they also flourished on suburban and branch passenger lines. No. 87 also survived until 1959.

The Clapham Museum's ex-London & North Western Railway engines are a 2-2-2 no. 3020, 'Cornwall', of 1847 and a Webb 2-4-0 Precedent class no. 790, 'Hardwicke', both, of course, built at Crewe. 'Cornwall' was designed by Francis Trevithick with the boiler beneath the axle of the 8ft 6in. driving wheels in order to give the engine a low centre of gravity. When fairly new she was converted to a 4-2-2 but recovered her original and present wheel arrangement when rebuilt by John Ramsbottom in 1858. Although withdrawn from service in 1902 she returned to work in 1907, hauling a saloon used by the LNWR directors, and continued to perform this and similar functions until permanent retirement in 1927. 'Hardwicke' is one of Francis Webb's celebrated Precedent class of 2-4-0s which, mainly because of their short, direct steam flow, achieved outstanding power and speed for their size and became the leading class among LNWR express passenger locomotives. 'Hardwicke' was in service from 1873 until 1932 when the LMS restored her to London & North Western livery and kept her in the paint shop at Crewe. 'Hardwicke' provided one of the highlights of the 1895 Race to the North, with a run from Crewe to Carlisle at an average speed of 67·2mph. As late as the twenties 'Jumbos', as the class were nicknamed, continued to double-head Claughton 4-6-0s on heavy west coast expresses from Euston.

0-4-0 no. 3, 'Coppernob', is one of Edward Bury's bar-framed tender engines built by Bury, Curtis & Kennedy for the Furness Railway in 1846 when she was distinguished, as now, by the company's iron-ore red livery and highly polished dome-shaped copper fire box from which the nickname derives. Fairbairn & Son continued to make slightly enlarged locomotives on this model up to 1861. No. 3 worked until 1900 when she was the oldest locomotive in service and was then preserved on a pedestal and in a glass case outside Barrow-in-Furness station. 'Coppernob' remained thus monumentalised, apart from a visit to the 1925 Wembley Exhibition, until Barrow station was destroyed by bombing during the war. The engine escaped destruction, although a few dents are still visible, and was never reinstated at Barrow. The years between the bombing and being installed at Clapham were passed at Horwich works.

Three of the Clapham locomotives were built for companies which became part of the Southern Railway after the Grouping, like the London, Brighton & South Coast Railway's 0-6-0T no. 82, 'Boxhill', built in 1880. The other two are 4-4-0s: ex-LSWR no. 563 and ex-South Eastern & Chatham Railway no. 737. No. 563 is the only surviving example of William Adams's last express engine design of which sixty were built in the 1890s. The preserved locomotive which, but for the war, would have been broken up in 1939 was built in 1893 and remained at work until 1945. After three years of dereliction at Eastleigh she was fully restored at Nine Elms in 1948 and was stored and displayed in various locations before being given a permanent home by the British Railways Board at Clapham. The ex-SE&CR 4-4-0 is one of Wainwright's D class built in 1901, and is slightly heavier and larger in other respects than the Adams but is basically very similar. No. 737 was withdrawn in 1956 and stored at Ashford, where it had been built, and later at Tweedmouth before being fully restored for exhibition in 1960.

The Midland Railway's 4-4-0 no. 1000 was the first of Samuel Johnson's 3-cylinder compounds. She was built at Derby in 1902. Like others of her class no. 1000 was very substantially altered by Henry Fowler in 1914. Although withdrawn in 1951 she was put back to work on specials between 1959 and 1962.

There are some locomotives in the care of the British Railways Board's Curator of Historical Relics which are not on show, mainly because of lack of space in existing museums and it will be part of the function of the National Railway Museum to accommodate them all. Meanwhile these engines are classed as 'stored' and they rest in various places, notably Brighton but also, for example, in Leicester where a 2-6-2 Gresley V2 no. 4771, 'Green Arrow', could be conveniently placed for a working preservation on the Main Line Steam Trust's Leicester–Loughborough line. Four locomotives—Lancashire & Yorkshire Railway 2-4-2T no. 1008; LSWR 4-4-0 no. 120; Southern Railway 4-6-0 no. 777, 'Sir Lamiel'; and SR 4-4-0 no. 925, 'Cheltenham' (see chapter 2)—have been transferred on a long-term loan basis from Brighton to the Standard Gauge Steam Trust at Tyseley and are thus on display. Among the remaining engines at Brighton one most deserving of permanent exhibition is the last steam locomotive ever built at Swindon, in 1960, BR class 9F 2-10-0, 'Evening Star'. Another of this class, no. 92203, 'Black Prince', kept at Eastleigh by David Shepherd, is one of twenty-three locomotives at present eligible to run on BR. The ex-Southern Railway 4-6-0 no. 850 (BR. no. 30850), 'Lord Nelson', is the solitary survivor of R.E.L. Maunsell's heaviest express locomotive class designed after the closest scrutiny of its older contemporaries, the Gresley Pacifics and GWR Castles, and built at Eastleigh in 1926.

Caledonian Railway 4-4-0, 'Dunalastair'

The Glasgow Museum of Transport

The largest and most representative collection of steam locomotives in Scotland is that preserved under the auspices of British Railways and now in the Glasgow Museum of Transport. Six of the seven engines there represent the five pre-Grouping companies: the Highland, Caledonian (two), North British, Great North of Scotland, and Glasgow & South Western railways. By comparison with English companies and locomotive classes, few Scottish engines have survived and indeed, one of the saddest gaps in the whole catalogue of preservation is left by Reid's North British Railway Atlantics, which were among the most powerful of their sort ever built. The work which they had to do suggested a six-coupled locomotive and indeed it was LNER Pacifics which largely displaced them, particularly on the Edinburgh–Aberdeen run, in the 1930s. In 1906, however, the problems of negotiating the curves which characterised much of the Scottish railway system caused W. P. Reid to decide in favour of the 4-4-2 wheel arrangement. In the late thirties, the LNER did set one of these huge locomotives aside for preservation but unfortunately restoration was delayed by the outbreak of war and very soon the engine was consumed in the drive for scrap metal. The LMS had also set aside for preservation just before the war various engines of Scottish interest. Many of these were lost also but two of the most historic survived and are in the Glasgow Museum today.

The older of the two is the ex-Caledonian Railway 4-2-2 no. 123 which was built by Neilson & Co. in 1886 for the Edinburgh Exhibition held in that year. It is unique in being the only 4-2-2 ever to run on a Scottish railway and as the only engine of its class. She soon proved her worth both in ordinary service and in the 1888 Race to the North. The Caledonian used her for the Carlisle–Edinburgh section on the west coast race train, a section which includes an eight-mile stretch where the gradient varies between 1 in 75 and 1 in 88. Her daily average over the $100\frac{3}{4}$-mile run was $107\frac{3}{4}$-minutes and the high spot, a record journey time of $102\frac{1}{2}$ minutes hauling a four-coach (80 ton) train. Although soon superseded by more powerful machines no. 123 survived the Grouping, renumbered no. 14010 by the LMS who used her as the regular power for the Northern Division directors' saloon until early in the 1930s. After a brief return to revenue earning service on Perth–Dundee local trains, no. 123 was withdrawn in 1935 at which time she was the last single wheeled express engine running. For more than twenty years no. 123 was kept impeccably restored to Caledonian livery at St Rollox works making rare appearances on static display at exhibitions. In 1957, inspired by the success of 'City of Truro', then recently exhumed from the York Railway Museum, the Scottish Region of BR decided that she could be steamed again. This was an expensive operation although in the days when steam was still the mainstay of the railway system a perfectly practicable one and no. 123 reappeared hauling a special train from Perth to Edinburgh. Thereafter she worked extensively on rail tours and enthusiasts' specials, reaching as far south as the Bluebell Railway and taking a prominent part in events such as the Scottish Industries Exhibition at Glasgow in September 1959, before being put back on ice in the Glasgow Museum of Transport.

The other LMS preservation is the ex-Highland Railway Jones 'Goods' no. 103 built by Sharp Stewart & Co. in 1894. David Jones's 4-6-0 design was the first example of this wheel arrangement on a British railway. Like many other classes of Scottish locomotive she was required for the heaviest duties over the most taxing terrain. Fifteen of them were built, distinguished by louvred chimneys and the absence of flanges on the centre driving wheels which was a way of reconciling a

4-6-0 to the severe curvature encountered on parts of the Highland Railway system. No. 103 was restored to working order, following the success of no. 123, for the Scottish Industries Exhibition in 1959 although her appearance there in Stroudley's 'improved engine green' rather than Highland Railway green aroused a certain amount of controversy.

Two further locomotives now in the Glasgow Museum were also restored to pre-Grouping livery by BR in 1959 but as they had then only recently left regular service it was a relatively easy job to get them back in working order. The ex-North British Railway 4-4-0 no. 256, 'Glen Douglas', was one of thirty-four designed and built by W. P. Reid at Cowlairs between 1913 and 1920. The Glen class was a development of the Scott class which they supplemented. They proved very successful on the heavily graded West Highland line. 'Glen Douglas' survived well into BR days, renumbered no. 62469. It was not withdrawn until the year of the Scottish Industries Exhibition and continued to work specials for several years thereafter. The fourth Glasgow exhibit in operational condition originated from the Great North of Scotland Railway. 4-4-0 no. 49, 'Gordon Highlander', was one of six class F engines built to Thomas Heywood's design by the North British Locomotive Co. in 1920. Two further examples of class F were built at Inverurie works. Most of them had been withdrawn by the mid-1950s but 'Gordon Highlander', by then BR no. 62277, survived at work on the Speyside line. As the last genuine GNSR locomotive it had strong claims to preservation although there was a gap of two years between withdrawal in 1957 and repainting in its old company's apple green livery. (No. 49 had in fact originally been turned out in black.) After several years working specials 'Gordon Highlander' was presented to the Glasgow Museum in 1966.

The two non-operational exhibits at Glasgow are an 0-6-0 tender engine and an 0-6-0T. The ex-Caledonian Railway no. 828 is one of J. F. McIntosh's seventy-nine 0-6-0s which succeeded the Drummond engines with the same wheel arrangement on Caledonian freight services. No. 828 was among the first batch of twenty-nine engines turned out of the company's St Rollox works in 1899. She was withdrawn from service in 1963 and was acquired by the Scottish Locomotive Preservation Fund from which it is on loan to the museum. When the Glasgow & South Western Railway became part of the LMS in 1923 the G&SWR engines, like those of many of the smaller companies, were systematically withdrawn in the interests of uniformity. 0-6-0T no. 9, built by the North British Locomotive Co. in 1917, survived to represent the company's steam traction in the Museum by way of Llay Main Collieries in Denbighshire to which it was sold in 1934 and from which it was acquired for preservation in 1965.

Like the Clapham Museum the Glasgow collection ranges far beyond railways and locomotives. Indeed, when the museum opened in 1964 using a former tram depot in Albert Drive, all the available space was given over to road transport. The railway section had to await the conversion of the adjacent building to a locomotive gallery, which was ready by 1967. Although somewhat confined this is probably the best display space at present available in any municipal museum.

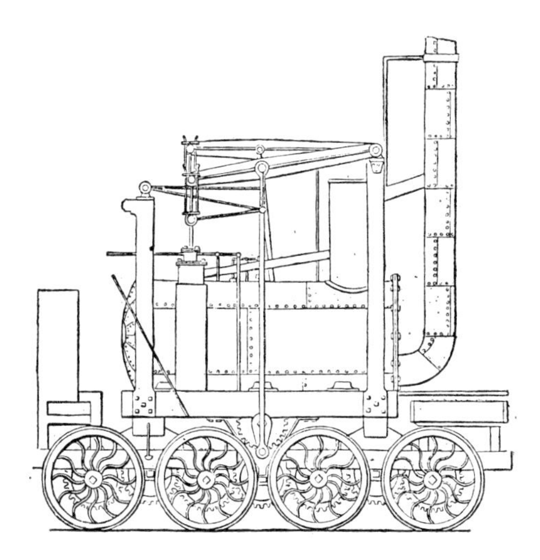

Hedley's second Wylam Colliery locomotive

The Royal Scottish Museum

This museum in Edinburgh has plans to alter its internal layout to accommodate more locomotive relics but at present it has space to exhibit only one of its engines.

Ex-LNER Gresley Shire class 4-4-0 no. 246, 'Morayshire', is at present kept in store at the Royal Elizabeth Admiralty Yard at Dalmeny, West Lothian, and will be displayed in the Royal Scottish Museum as soon as this is possible. 'Morayshire' was built at Darlington in 1927 under LNER auspices and intended for main line service in Scotland.

The Royal Scottish Museum's locomotive, which is actually on show, makes a very appropriate ending for a survey of this degree of preservation for it is the oldest in existence. 'Wylam Dilly' was built in 1813 by William Hedley, probably in association with Timothy Hackworth, to haul the coal wagons or 'dillies' over the 5ft gauge railway from Wylam colliery to the staithes at Lexington-on-Tyne five miles away. This engine, together with its younger companion at Wylam, 'Puffing Billy', was built partly to exemplify Hedley's belief in the practicability of smooth wheel adhesion on metal rails and, indeed, its superiority over chain-and-wheel and toothed rack devices. 'Wylam Dilly' was briefly converted into a tug boat during the Tyneside keelmen's strike of 1822 when it was taken off its wheels, erected on a paddle-fitted keel and used for towing. After reconversion she worked at Wylam until the colliery closed in 1862 and then moved to Craghead for similar mining work. On withdrawal in about 1867 she was bought by the Hedley family and presented to the Royal Scottish Museum in 1882.

2 Live Museums

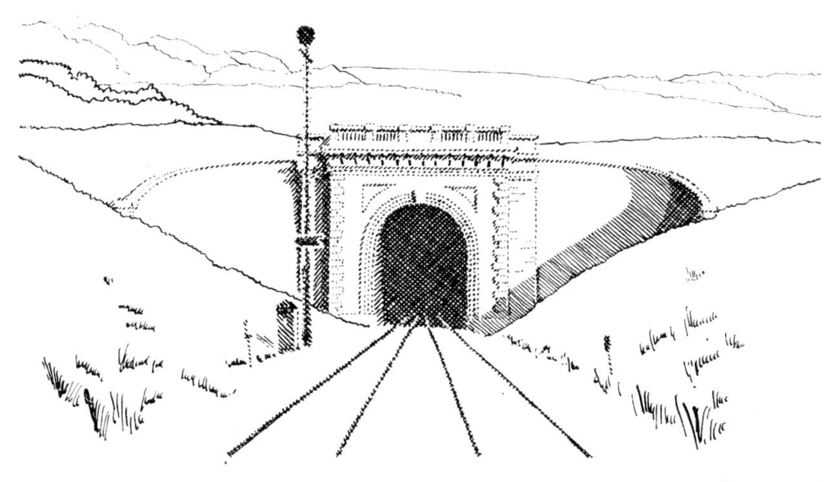

Box tunnel

The last static exhibit described in chapter 1, the Royal Scottish Museum's 'Wylam Dilly', was built to exemplify the adhesive qualities of smooth iron wheels on smooth metal rails, relegating such antiques as the rack rail to a level where anything more sophisticated than animal or human muscle was largely undreamed of. In pursuit of the locomotive and railway preserver's ideal the live museums and steam centres represent a comparable advance on the conventional museums and though even these may fall far short of the ideal of a full size operating railway they are doing some permanently valuable work in the service of 'steam nostalgia'.

The main problem of looking after a collection of steam locomotives is maintenance and probably also restoring the engines in the first place. Even when this has been overcome there is the problem of where to keep them. Most privately operated lines, quite apart from being light railways in law, are branch lines, wholly unsuited to accepting locomotives of the heavier classes. Thus 'Britannia' is incarcerated at Bridgnorth and, although being restored to impeccable order, can never run on the present Severn Valley Railway, although once the Hampton Loade–Foley Park halt section of the line is fully operational she should be seen at work on the two miles south from Bewdley. Meanwhile, she is a monument to both the splendours and the frustrations of railway and locomotive preservation.

The role of the organisations described in this chapter was enlarged by the announcement in April 1972 that BR would permit as an experiment limited running by steam-hauled trains over five lightly used, main line routes, totalling 300 miles of track:

Birmingham (Moor Street)–Didcot	77 miles
York–Scarborough	42 miles
Newcastle–Carlisle	60 miles
Shrewsbury–Newport	94 miles
Carnforth–Barrow	28 miles

This followed the review of the British Railways Board's policy towards steam traction promised by its chairman, Mr Richard Marsh, after the highly successful experimental outing of 'King George V' from Hereford in the autumn of 1971. Under the rules which are to govern the operations, twenty-three locomotives have been named as eligible to be considered for main line running. All are in the care of organisations falling within the scope of this chapter. The locomotives are: ex-BR 2-10-0 class 9F no. 92203 'Black Prince', and 4-6-0 class 4 no. 75029 'The Green Knight'; ex-GWR and BR 4-6-0s nos 6000 'King George V', 4079 'Pendennis Castle', 7029 'Clun Castle' and no. 6998 'Burton Agnes Hall', 2-6-0 no. 5322, 2-6-2T no. 6106, 0-6-2T no. 6697, 0-6-0PTs nos 7752 and 7760, and 0-4-2T no. 1466; ex-LMS and BR Jubilee class 4-6-0s nos 5593 'Kolhapur' and 5596 'Bahamas', and Stanier Black 5s nos 4871, 4932, 5231, 5407 and 5428 'Eric Treacy'; ex-LNER and BR A2 Pacific no. 532 'Blue Peter' and A4 Pacifics nos 4498 'Sir Nigel Gresley' and 60019 'Bittern'; and ex-SR and BR Merchant Navy class 4-6-2 no. 35028 'Clan Line'.

Bressingham Steam Museum

This is a many-sided venture. In addition to a splendid selection of working standard gauge exhibits, Mr Alan Bloom has developed narrow gauge and miniature railways which serve a double purpose: displaying historic locomotives and providing the motive power for trains which carry visitors around the estate at Bressingham Hall. Other forms of steam traction are, of course, well represented there and the scope of the collection attracted the interest of the Transport Trust. The Trust has played a leading part in creating the present climate for preservation in this country and has, in particular, emphasised the advantages of restoring machines to their original condition and, where possible, to working order. It was thus a particularly happy development when the Trust took over responsibility for the administration of the museum in June 1971.

The 1½ mile narrow gauge Nursery Railway at Bressingham provides an excellent setting for three Hunslet 0-4-0STs from the Dinorwic and Penrhyn quarries in North Wales—'Maid Marion', 'George Sholto'

Royal Scot class 4-6-0 no. 6100

and 'Gwynedd'—to work in retirement. A Hudswell Clarke 0-6-0WT, 'Bronwllyd', was bought with 'George Sholto' from Penrhyn as a scrap chassis but in the event a new boiler was fitted and so she, too, is now working on the line. The Hunslet 0-4-0STs from the slate quarries of Snowdonia have been preserved in some quantity and the class is more fully discussed in chapter 29 on the Llanberis Lake Railway, where several more of them are still at work, closer to home.

The principal interest of Bressingham in the context of this book is the standard gauge museum and the way in which Mr Bloom has brought together the items in it. The two most conspicuous locomotives are no. 70013, 'Oliver Cromwell', and no. 6233, 'Duchess of Sutherland', the latter on loan from Butlin's holiday camp at Ayr. The survival of BR class 7 no. 70013, 'Oliver Cromwell', in addition to no. 70000, 'Britannia', now on the Severn Valley Railway at Bridgnorth, is a bonus for which credit must go to Mr Bloom's personal initiative. In accordance with BRB practice, 'Britannia' was chosen for preservation as the first of the fifty-five locomotives of her class. She was put into store after being withdrawn on 28 May 1966. However, she was partly cannibalised before being moved to Brighton. At the time that Mr Bloom was considering possible locomotives from Bressingham 'Oliver Cromwell' was still in service. It was, moreover, to be the last engine overhauled for BR at Crewe and to remain in service until the very end of steam operations, hauling the last passenger train on 11 August 1968. In the event, the preservation order on no. 70000 was transferred to no. 70013, which went straight to Bressingham on withdrawal. She has been steamed there regularly throughout retirement. For a while after the transfer of the preservation order it seemed that 'Britannia' would be scrapped. She was saved by a group of enthusiasts who formed the East Anglian Locomotive Preservation Society and was eventually bought by the Steam

Locomotive Preservation Co. in 1970. 'Britannia' was delivered to Bridgnorth in April 1971.

As might be expected of a locomotive design founded upon 125 years of experience and development, the Britannia Pacifics were superb engines. R. A. Biddles, first CME of the British Transport Commission, was required to design a new series of standard engines in the light of what had been revealed by the Interchange trials of 1948. These designs incorporated all the best and most compatible features of existing locomotive classes and at the time of their introduction it was assumed that they would serve for thirty years or more and be built in huge numbers. Class 7 was, of course, intended mainly for express passenger work and these engines were active in this role on continental expresses on the Southern Region, and in East Anglia and on the Western Region for some years after their introduction in 1951. However, the decision gradually to abandon steam in favour of diesel and electric traction was taken as early as 1955 and soon after the Britannias were relegated to a class of work rather below that for which they had been intended. In speed, economy and power they performed excellently as long as their utility lasted and when they were withdrawn, subject to normal maintenance and overhaul, most had years of working life left in them.

The same is probably true of the ex-LMS Stanier Pacific no. 6233, 'Duchess of Sutherland', which is at Bressingham for restoration to working order. Thirty-eight of these engines were built between 1937 and nationalisation. No. 6233 (BR no. 46233) was one of fourteen (nos. 6230–6234 and 6249–6257) built without the streamlined casing which added nearly three tons to the weight of a class which was already the heaviest ever in regular service on a British railway. Sir William Stanier's second Pacific design followed the Princess Royal class of 1933 which were particularly distinguished for high-speed non-stop running over long distances. The later Pacifics emulated them in all respects and one, 'Duchess of Gloucester', recorded the highest power output of any British steam locomotive.

Apart from 'Duchess of Sutherland' two other locomotives originally kept at Butlin's camps are also at Bressingham for restoration or on loan. One of these is an 0-6-0T built in 1875 for the London, Brighton & South Coast Railway and named 'Martello'. The Stroudley Terriers are one of the most preserved classes and an astonishing number, ten, out of the fifty constructed, have survived the hundred years since they were introduced. This survival rate is matched by their longevity in revenue-earning service, for several of them remained at work under BR management until the early 1960s. The Butlin organisation has been a good friend to the Terriers and of those that remain no. 40, 'Brighton', and no. 78, 'Knowle', are on their premises at Pwllheli and Minehead respectively.

No. 46100, 'Royal Scot', is yet another Butlin's preservation and is at Bressingham for extensive restoration while on loan from their Skegness holiday camp. This class is also represented at Dinting by no. 46115, 'Scots Guardsman', and is described in the section on the Dinting Railway Centre.

The 4-4-2T no. 80, 'Thundersley', was built by Stephenson & Co. in 1909 for the London, Tilbury & Southend Railway and is an excellent example of an express tank engine. Under Midland Railway ownership, that is to say from 1912 onwards, 'Thundersley' lost both her name and her LT&SR livery and for fifty-five years was regaled in crimson lake. She was restored specially for the London, Tilbury & Southend's centenary in 1956 and worked a special train from Southend to Liverpool Street in celebration of the event on 3 March that year before being withdrawn. 'Thundersley' arrived, motion dismantled, with 'Oliver Cromwell' at Diss on 16 August 1968 for transport by road to Bressingham.

Dinting Railway Centre

This Centre occupies the former Great Central Railway steam locomotive depot at Dinting, two miles on the Manchester side of Glossop in Derbyshire. The site was acquired by the Bahamas Locomotive Society as a home for their Jubilee 4-6-0 no. 5596, 'Bahamas', which is still the principal attraction there. The ten-acre site at the foot of the Pennines is leased from British Railways and was completely derelict when the Society moved in during August 1968. It has now been cleared and covered accommodation provided for the exhibits. The Centre is registered as a charity for educational purposes and is affiliated to the Transport Trust, the Association of Railway Preservation Societies and the Manchester Museum of Science & Technology. The Centre has a number of trams and industrial locomotives as well as an Austerity 0-6-0ST WD150, 'Warrington', built by Robert Stephenson & Hawthorns in 1944 but the principal engines are ex-LMS express passenger locomotives, 'Bahamas' and 'Scots Guardsman'.

4-6-0 Royal Scot class no. 6115 (BR no. 46115), 'Scots Guardsman', was built for the LMS by the North British Locomotive Co. at Glasgow in 1927. In the late 1920s Sir Henry Fowler, Chief Mechanical Engineer of the LMS, was required to produce a new range of express locomotives. By the time the Royal Scots appeared the need had become urgent and fifty were built within a matter of months. Fowler had been planning a Pacific in emulation of the locomotives of his east coast rival Sir Nigel Gresley but the GWR/LNER Exchanges of 1925, followed by the performance of a Castle class locomotive on tests between Euston and Carlisle the following year, caused these designs to be reconsidered. The engine which emerged was as successful as the contemporary

4-6-0s of other companies which, in addition to the Castles, included R. E. L. Maunsell's Lord Nelson class introduced on the Southern Railway in 1926.

They all lasted well but unlike the Castles which were built in batches over a period of more than thirty years, most of the Royal Scots were built in the year of their introduction and by the late thirties were in some need of rejuvenation. The result was Sir William Stanier's progressive 'rebuild' of the class whereby all seventy locomotives underwent substantial modification. This related mainly to valves and cylinders but most visibly to the addition of distinctive tapered boilers which had long been characteristic of comparable classes of Swindon locomotive and which had appeared on LMS designs like the Jubilees and Black 5s since 1927. 'Scots Guardsman' was rebuilt at Crewe in 1947 and was the last of the class to remain at work, that is, until December 1965. She is owned by Mr R. A. Bill of Birmingham and was kept at first on the Keighley & Worth Valley Railway in Yorkshire. In May 1969 she was moved to Dinting, where she was restored exactly to the 1946 black livery and overhauled mechanically.

When he took over as CME of the London, Midland & Scottish Railway, Sir William Stanier, FRS, was required to provide some new classes of standard locomotive. The 4-6-0 Jubilee class of 1934 was the express passenger equivalent of the mixed traffic Black 5 introduced the same year. By the late thirties Stanier's LMS had an integrated and balanced locomotive stud, led by his three varieties of Pacific. The Princess Royal class Pacifics of 1933 were specially developed for high-speed, non-stop runing on the west coast main line. One of the two surviving 'Lizzies', no. 6201, 'Princess Elizabeth', preserved by the Princess Elizabeth Locomotive Society on the Dowty Railway Preservation Society's premises at Ashchurch near Tewkesbury, ran the 401¼ miles from Glasgow to Euston in November 1936 with a 260-ton train at an average speed of 70mph.

Two working Jubilees survive, 'Kolhapur' at Tyseley and the Dinting engine, no. 5596, 'Bahamas'. Until no. 5552, 'Silver Jubilee', was named in 1935 to mark the twenty-fifth anniversary of the accession of King George V, engines of the class were not named but thereafter many of the 190 examples were given the names of places in the Commonwealth. 'Bahamas', which was turned out by North British Locomotive Co. in January 1935, bore a name almost from the start. In capacity the Jubilees were roughly the equivalent of the 'Baby Scots' of the previous LMS locomotive generation and they succeeded them in their express passenger work. At the time of its withdrawal in 1966, 'Bahamas' was shedded at Edgeley MPD, Stockport. The 'Bahamas' Locomotive Society which preserved, restored and installed it at Dinting was originally a group of local, Stockport, enthusiasts. They financed a major overhaul of the engine by the Hunslet Engine Co. in the autumn of 1967. Since her arrival at Dinting on 15 November 1968, 'Bahamas' has been impeccably restored externally to 'Derby red' livery.

'Hinderton Hall'

Great Western Society

The Great Western Railway retained its personality long after all its rivals of the proud and individualistic years of British railway history had been submerged by successive acts of rationalisation. The name 'Great Western Railway' was the only one to survive the Grouping and the goodwill and affection which the company's standards of service created were to survive even nationalisation. Nostalgia for the Great Western has already lasted over twenty-five years and has nurtured one of the best locomotive preservation societies. The Great Western Society, which now has nearly 3,000 members, has its main base at Didcot but parts of its locomotive, rolling stock and small relics collection are located elsewhere on the former GWR system, at Bodmin, Taunton, Caerphilly and Swindon.

The Society has unrivalled basic material: a railway built by Brunel; a company administered by men such as Charles Russell and Sir Felix Pole; and a locomotive tradition founded by Gooch, developed by Armstrong and Dean and crowned by Churchward and Collett. It began, however, as a group of adolescents planning to acquire a solitary engine (a 14XX 0-4-2T) and trailer coach. Although its objective was achieved, this pioneer society did not last long. Soon after its foundation in 1961 the aims of the 48XX Preservation Society were clarified and enlarged to justify the name Great Western Society. Being early in the field at perhaps the one fleeting period when the supply of realistic locomotive preservations was slightly ahead of the demand, the Society rapidly built up a good Great Western collection by gift, loan and purchase. These were dispersed at various locations throughout the

Western Region and for a few years the Society's sole unifying feature was its magazine, *Great Western Echo*, which first appeared properly printed in 1965 and has since developed in quality and editorial excellence to be one of the finest amateur publications in its field. In 1967 the structure of the Society was altered to meet its by then very substantial responsibilities and two companies were formed: a holding company for the preserved items (Great Western Preservations Limited), and a guarantee company to administer the Society (Great Western Society Limited). In the same year BR ceased to use the locomotive depot at Didcot and offered it to the Society. It has proved an ideal centre, with workshop facilities which the more active members had not previously enjoyed and covered accommodation for most of the stock.

The Society's locomotives are at present located as shown in Table 2. The obvious star of this collection is the victor of the 1925 Exchanges, no. 4079, 'Pendennis Castle', but this, together with no. 5051, 'Earl

Table 2 Steam locomotives at Great Western Society depots

Type	Number	Name	Where built	Year
Didcot motive power depot				
0-4-0ST	1	'Bonnie Prince Charlie'	Robert Stephenson & Hawthorns	1951
0-4-0WT	5	'Shannon'/'Jane'	George England	1857
0-4-0ST	1340	'Trojan'	Avonside	1897
0-4-2T	1466		Swindon	1936
4-6-0	4079	'Pendennis Castle'	Swindon	1924
4-6-0	5051	'Earl Bathurst'	Swindon	1936
4-6-0	5900	'Hinderton Hall'	Swindon	1931
4-6-0	6998	'Burton Agnes Hall'	Swindon	1949
4-6-0	7808	'Cookham Manor'	Swindon	1938
2-6-2T	6106		Swindon	1931
0-6-2T	6697		Armstrong, Whitworth	1928
4-6-2	532	'Blue Peter'	Doncaster	1948
Bodmin motive power depot				
0-4-0ST	19		Bagnall	1951
0-6-0ST	1363		Swindon	1910
Taunton motive power depot				
0-6-0ST	2	'Pontyberem'	Avonside	1900
2-6-2T	5572		Swindon	1927
Caerphilly motive power depot				
0-6-0PT	3650		Swindon	1940
2-6-0	5322		Swindon	1917

Bathurst', is described in chapter 4. Didcot has three other 4-6-0s, the first of which to arrive was no. 6998, 'Burton Agnes Hall'. This engine, like many of F. W. Hawksworth's seventy-one Modified Halls of 1944–50, was named after a house far outside the Great Western system because the 259 locomotives built to Collett's original design had already immortalised all estates of substance within it. Although designed for mixed traffic work the Halls were as versatile as they were numerous and when called upon in emergencies individual engines consistently showed themselves to be capable of the highest class of express running. 'Burton Agnes Hall', named after the celebrated sixteenth-century mansion in Yorkshire, was the Society's first large locomotive and the purchase price of £2,500 was handed over before she was actually withdrawn in January 1966. At the time when the range of possible purchases was being considered many members favoured a Hall built to Collett's 1928 design. Three years later several redeemable examples still lay in Barry scrapyard and through the generosity of one of the members, the best of them, no. 5900, 'Hinderton Hall', was acquired for the Society in 1970 and has now been completely restored.

Another possible purchase in 1965–6, and one which again was favoured by a significant minority of members, was an example of the smaller 4-6-0s, such as a Grange or Manor. In the event the Society was very fortunate to acquire no. 7808, 'Cookham Manor', in addition to the two Halls already described. The Manors were evolved for service over lines with tight weight restrictions hitherto limited to 4-4-0s and 2-6-0s at the heaviest, and introduced in 1938. They were a versatile and vivacious class and indeed no. 7808 in the early days of retirement reached nearly 80mph on a special from Birmingham to Taplow, where much of the Society's stock was then kept. 'Cookham Manor' was later fully restored on the Dowty Railway Preservation Society's premises at Ashchurch, near Tewkesbury, and I was lucky enough to be able to drive her there during the later stages of the work.

Churchward 2-6-0 no. 5322, at present located at the Society's depot in Caerphilly, is a veteran of World War I and entered service with the Railway Operating Division of the Royal Engineers direct from Swindon in 1917. The 43XXs were a typically ubiquitous GWR mixed traffic class and 342 were built between 1911 and 1932. No. 5322 served for forty-six years and ran for 1,355,622 miles before being withdrawn in 1963. After five years in Barry scrapyard she was close to being irredeemable but eighteen months of dedicated work by volunteers made steaming possible in January 1971 and she is now fully operational.

The oldest locomotive in the Great Western Society's collection is an 0-4-0WT, 'Shannon', built by George England in 1857 for Captain William Peel's Sandy & Potton line in Bedfordshire and named after one of the ships which he had previously commanded. When the Sandy & Potton line was absorbed by the LNWR, 'Shannon' became a shunter at Crewe until 1878 when she was sold to the Wantage Tramway, which ran between the town and the GWR station, Wantage Road. She worked there, called 'Jane', until the tramway closed in 1945. GWR restored her original name and they, and later BR, kept her on Wantage Road station until that too closed. 'Shannon' is on loan from the Museum of British Transport and is kept at Didcot in working order.

No. 6106 was one of seventy locomotives built to Collett's 2-6-2T design of 1931 especially for use on suburban services and to replace the earlier 22XX County class of tank engines over the level main line out of Paddington. On this road and over limited distances they were equally effective at speed or on stopping trains with the brickest schedules. No. 6106 was withdrawn for preservation in 1966, not long after her last major overhaul, and has been as reliable under the Great Western Society as she and the rest of her class were in revenue-earning service. For similar work in the provinces, on branch lines and on less exacting schedules the GWR built seventy-five of Churchward's 45XX class 2-6-2T of 1906. No. 5572, now being restored at the Society's Taunton depot, was one of a slightly modified 55XX design of 1927: a further hundred were built at Swindon. An example of Collett's 0-6-2T 56XX class, no. 6697, built by Armstrong, Whitworth in 1928, completes the Society's collection of heavy tank engines. This class was specially developed in 1924 for the heavily graded lines in South Wales, like the Taff Vale Railway, which the GWR had recently absorbed. The severe axle loading and adhesive weight limited their route availability to 'Red' lines. No. 6697 was acquired by the Bristol Group of the Society in 1966 and restored at Ashchurch, before moving to Didcot in 1970.

At its Bodmin depot the Society has the oldest genuine Great Western locomotive still in working order. This is an 0-6-0 saddle tank, no. 1363, built at Swindon in 1910. Until Churchward introduced the square-topped Belpaire fireboxes, leading to the 'pannier' tanks slung on either side of the boiler, most GWR tank engines carried their water in the saddle-shaped tanks built over their round fireboxes. No. 1363 is the only survivor of the hundreds of saddle tanks built at Swindon and belongs to a special class of five (nos. 1361–1365), built for work over very sharp curves in Cornwall and shedded at St Blazey.

Once the pannier tank form of construction had been developed its application spread very quickly. Many old saddle tanks were converted to panniers when they were reboilered. In 1929, the 0-6-0PT 57XX class appeared and, with 863 examples, soon became the most numerous in Britain. No. 3640 was built at Swindon in 1940 and was sold for industrial use twenty-three years later. She was acquired for preservation in 1969 and is now at Caerphilly.

There are four saddle tanks around the Society's depots which are not of GWR origin. 'Trojan' and 'Pontyberem' were built by the Avonside Engine Co. of Bristol in 1897 and 1900 respectively. 'Ponty-

1 Canterbury & Whitstable Railway Invicta 0-4-0, built in 1830. Here the engine is shown outside the city wall at Canterbury. Road improvements have since caused it to be moved within the city wall into Dane John Gardens

Railway Museums, York, plate 2

2 (above) Stroudley 0-4-2, no. 214, 'Gladstone', built for the LB&SCR in 1882 and the first locomotive to be preserved privately, by the Stephenson Locomotive Society

Museum of British Transport, Clapham, plates 3–6

3 (below) Johnson 3-cylinder compound 4-4-0, no. 1000, built at Derby in 1902 for the Midland Railway and service on top link main line expresses

4 (opposite above) Adams 4-4-0, no. 583, built at Nine Elms for the London & South Western Railway in 1893. She is identical with the preserved example of her class, no. 563

5 (opposite centre) Holden 2-4-0, no. 490, built for the Great Eastern Railway at Stratford in 1891. Here seen at Stratford in 1960 shortly after she had been withdrawn and restored

6 (opposite below) The last steam locomotive built for BR left Swindon works in 1960: class 9F 2-10-0, no. 92220, appropriately named 'Evening Star'. She is at present in store awaiting display by the BRB in the National Railway Museum

L S W R
690
EVENING STAR
92220

3440
CITY OF TRURO

S·L·S
SPECIAL
25
2516

Great Western Railway Museum, Swindon, plates 7–9

7 (opposite above) Dean 4-4-0, no. 3440, 'City of Truro' (later no. 3517), built at Swindon in 1903. On 9 May 1904 she became the first steam locomotive to reach 100mph, down Wellington Bank, Somerset, on route from Plymouth with the Ocean Mails

8 (opposite below) Dean Goods 0-6-0, no. 2516, built in 1897, seen at Oldbury in May 1955. Her GWR Oswestry shed symbol, 'OSW', can be discerned on the front frame

9 (above) Churchward's 4-6-0 Star class, no. 4003, 'Lode Star', built at Swindon in 1906, seen at Newport, Monmouthshire, in July 1938

Royal Scottish Museum, Edinburgh, plates 10, 11

10 William Hedley's 5ft gauge 0-4-0, 'Wylam Dilly'. Built in 1813 and now Britain's most venerable locomotive

11 Ex-LNER 4-4-0, no. 246 (BR no. 62712), 'Morayshire', built at Darlington in 1928, here seen at Stonehaven in January 1965

Museum of Transport, Glasgow, plates 12–16

12 Ex-Caledonian Railway 4-2-2, no. 123, built by Neilson & Co. in 1899, seen at Perth, *c.* 1932, double heading 'Glen Douglas', ex-NBR 4-4-0

13 (centre) No. 123 at Kipps in 1966

14 (below) Ex-GNSR 4-4-0, no. 49, 'Gordon Highlander', built by the North British Locomotive Co. in 1920. Seen resting at Macduff, during a railtour in 1960

15 Ex-Highland Railway 4-6-0, no. 103, leaving Inverness for Forres with a special Highland Railway centenary train in 1965

16 Ex-NBR 4-4-0, no. 256 (BR no. 62469), 'Glen Douglas', built at Cowlairs in 1913, seen at Kipps in 1966

STEAM MUSEUM
70013
ALAN BLOOM

MACHINE SHOP
70013
OLIVER CROMWELL

Bressingham Steam Museum, plates 17–20

17 (opposite above) A general view of the 'Live' museum

18 (opposite below) The last steam locomotive to be overhauled for BR, 'Oliver Cromwell', on the traverser at Crewe works, 2 February 1967

19 (below) Ex-LMS 4-6-0, no. 6100 (BR no. 46100), 'Royal Scot', the first of her eponymous class

20 Ex-London, Tilbury & Southend Railway 4-4-2T, no. 80 (BR no. 41966), 'Thundersley'

Dinting Railway Centre, plates 21, 22

21 Ex-LMS 4-6-0 Jubilee class, no. 5596, 'Bahamas', acquired for preservation in 1967 by the Bahamas Locomotive Society

22 Dinting at night. *Left to right:* 'Bahamas'; ex-LMS 4-6-0 rebuilt Royal Scot class no. 6115 'Scots Guardsman'; and WD 0-6-0ST, no. 150, 'Warrington'

berem' worked on the Burry Port & Gwendraeth Valley Railway until 1914 and thereafter for various industrial users, including the NCB. 'Trojan' began life on the Alexandra Docks Railway, also absorbed by the Great Western in 1923, but the engine was disposed of in 1934 to the Victoria Colliery at Wellington. She ended her working life in industrial service at Tamworth and returned to Great Western metals for preservation at Didcot in 1968. Neither of these locomotives was in working order when the Society took them over and several years of expenditure and voluntary labour have been needed to restore them to operational condition. The other two saddle tanks, 'Bonnie Prince Charlie' at Didcot and Bagnall no. 19 at Bodmin, were newer (1951) and in better order when the Society acquired them in 1969. Both have since been in steam.

The first locomotive preserved by the Society, in 1964, was an 0-4-2T of the 48XX class (renumbered 14XX in 1946), no. 1466, built at Swindon in 1936. Like the rest of her class she was very extensively used for auto-train working and has been employed to work the Society's auto-trailer no. 231 on the Cholsey & Moulsford–Wallingford branch during operating days on that line.

The Great Western Society, and its Didcot centre in particular, is maintaining, in their own words, 'an authentic fragment of the old GWR'. This is a reasonable claim, for the Didcot MPD stands alongside Brunel's main line and the buildings and equipment on it are representative of standard Great Western designs and, performing their original functions, are as powerful in evoking the railway's past as the locomotives and rolling stock kept there. The facilities at Didcot include a four-road engine shed 200 feet long, lifting shop, ash shed and 75,000-gallon water tower. The Society has installed at least some of the heavy machinery necessary for the restoration and long-term maintenance of locomotives and has been able to take in large engines from Barry, like 'Hinderton Hall' and 'Earl Bathurst', in a decayed and cannibalised condition, with a realistic chance of restoring them to working order.

At present, no plans for purchasing and operating a stretch of line, even for demonstration purposes, are being actively pursued but such an extension of activities might be considered if a suitable piece of line presented itself. The Cholsey & Moulsford–Wallingford branch, some five miles up the line, is perhaps a natural candidate for this purpose and the Society has used it on operating days in the past. Meanwhile, the Society is concentrating all its resources on building up a large and representative collection of ex-GWR locomotives and rolling stock for preservation in its live museums. Furthermore, Didcot is the southern terminus of the seventy-seven mile route from Birmingham, Moor Street, which may now be used for steam traction. With six Didcot locomotives eligible for main line running, it is clear that this will be a big enough role in itself.

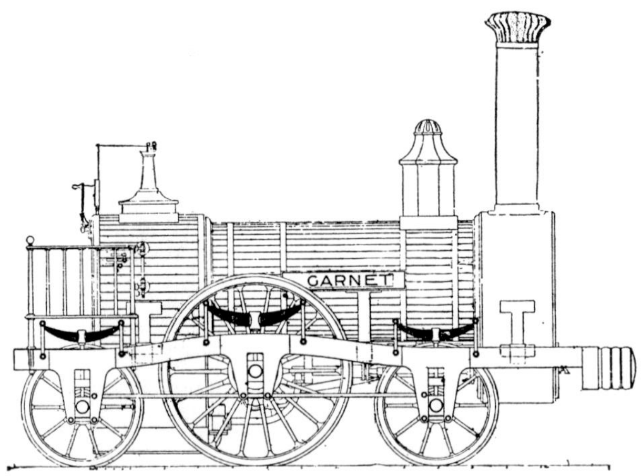

One of the first London and Southampton Railway locomotives

Quainton Railway Society

This Society, which has its headquarters at Quainton Road station on the former Metropolitan & Great Central Joint Railway a few miles north of Aylesbury, is one of the older locomotive preservation bodies and originated in the late 1950s. One of the groups from which the present Society grew, the London Railway Preservation Society, was a founder member of the Association of Railway Preservation Societies.

The possibility of acquiring a stretch of line, including those from Hatfield to St Albans, and Audley End to Bartlow, has been considered in the past. This idea has not, however, been pursued and all effort has been concentrated on the formation of the second largest locomotive collection in the country and the setting up of a live museum, though the possibility of working farther afield remains for the future. Various sites have been occupied in the Society's development, including space obtained from the Ministry of Works at Luton and Bishops Stortford but since 1969 activities have been consolidated at Quainton, where regular well-attended open days are held.

At Quainton Road the Society owns the land and track on the down (Brill) side of the station, with planning permission for the erection of buildings for locomotive restoration on the site of the present yard. Outline planning permission has also been granted for a running shed. In addition to what is already owned, the Society rents the station building on the up side and is negotiating towards ownership of the whole site. This could not be achieved for financial reasons when the Society first became interested in the complex. However, the number of engines at Quainton has grown very considerably since the Society moved there and the need for more space is now urgent.

The only narrow gauge locomotive in the Society's collection is the

1ft 10¾in. gauge 0-4-0ST, 'Holy War', which is one of the Hunslet Engine Co's Dinorwic slate quarry engines. Many of these eccentrically named quarry locomotives have survived in various parts of the world, a good proportion of them in working order, including 'Holy War' which has been at Quainton Road since March 1970.

All the other steam locomotives in the depot are standard gauge, the majority of industrial origin but with a significant number which served on main lines. The ex-London & South Western Railway 2-4-0WT no. 30585, for example, built by Beyer Peacock in 1874, was one of eighty-five Beattie well tanks which worked on the Railway's suburban services from the 1870s until they were replaced by the larger Adams 4-4-2Ts. The Beatties were transferred to country depots in 1886 where they continued to do excellent work. By 1899 only three examples remained and these were sent to the Wenford Bridge mineral railway in Cornwall. Their 12ft 6in. wheelbases made them uniquely suitable for so tortuous a line. The Quainton engine (LSWR no. 314) was rebuilt in 1899 and survived a mammoth eighty-nine years of service until 1963. She was bought by the Society in 1964 and after painstaking renewal and repair was ready to steam again in the spring of 1970 and later to work trains on the Quainton sidings during open days.

The present Quainton Road station dates from 1896 although the Aylesbury & Buckingham Railway which its predecessor a few yards down the road had been built to serve, was opened in 1868. This line linked Quainton with the Metropolitan Railway, when it reached Aylesbury in 1892. It is thus most appropriate that one of the locomotives at Quainton today is a T. F. Clark class E 0-4-4T built at Neasden in 1898. She was one of seven locomotives built for working the heaviest Metropolitan trains and which continued to do so until after World War I. L44 was originally numbered no. 1, replacing the Railway's previous engine of that number which had been damaged in an accident at Baker Street in September 1897. Under London Transport management L44 was used on engineering and general service trains and as a pilot engine at Rickmansworth in the 1940s, where she also occasionally hauled passenger trains. In July 1960, she headed the last steam train to run on the Chesham branch and survived to be one of the two last ex-Metropolitan locomotives in service. When the Society bought her in 1964 she was fit to be delivered to their premises at Luton in steam and took part in celebrations held at Bedford in 1968 to mark the centenary of the Midland Railway's London extension.

The last steam engine ran on London Transport metals on 6 June 1971 having outlasted main line steam by nearly three years. The Society, in common with the Standard Gauge Steam Trust and the Severn Valley Railway, has benefited from this and is now the owner of an 0-6-0PT no. L99, ex-GWR no. 7715. Between 1928 and 1950, 863 pannier tanks of the 5700 class were built and no. 7715 was one of a batch of twenty-five turned out by Kerr Stuart at Stoke-on-Trent in 1930. She spent the whole of her main line career in the Newton Abbot division until being transferred by BR to London Transport in June 1963. Like no. L44, L99 spent her last years on service and engineering trains and also on shunting duties around Lillie Bridge and Neasden. She was withdrawn, in good working order, in December 1970.

No. 41298 is a 2-6-2 side tank built under BR auspices (class 2P/2FA) at Crewe in 1951 to a design introduced on the LMS by H. A. Ivatt. The class was so successful in the two years before nationalisation that many more examples were built for work on all regions. The Quainton engine was one of thirty specially built for the Southern Region and worked throughout the system including parts of the withered arm of the old LSWR west of Exeter. She was shedded at Nine Elms when bought for preservation by the Ivatt Trust in 1967 and kept at Longmoor until the end of 1970 when she was transferred to Quainton Road.

The Society's plans for the immediate future centre round the purchase of the Quainton Road station yard on the up side to relieve overcrowding on the existing site and to provide accommodation for further large locomotives and rolling stock. Thereafter, the erection of buildings in which to carry out maintenance and restoration will be imperative, as will the installation of an efficient signalling system to control movements on the site. The Society's signals and telegraph section hopes to combine the latter with the establishment of a display of vintage signals. Still longer-term plans must depend on the continuing success of Society open days to produce an adequate revenue and also on the plans of BR for the future of the line into Aylesbury. At present the Society's lines are not connected to those of BR but clearly there would be some prospect of being able to steam trains into Aylesbury, should the Board's policy towards steam traction change. Similarly, if the line into Aylesbury were to be closed—for which there are no plans at present—the Society would be encouraged to consider ways and means of working trains over it.

Scottish Railway Preservation Society

This is the only major locomotive preservation group in Scotland. It was formed in 1961 following the successful preservation of an 0-4-0WT, 'Ellesmere', built in 1861, which is the only surviving Hawthorn of Leith locomotive in Britain. When withdrawn from service in 1957 she was the oldest locomotive still at work in the country. It was nearly ten years before the engine, which was constructed under Davidson's patent, with the watertanks mounted between the frames and with Stephenson outside valve gear, was housed under cover at the SRPS headquarters in Grahamston Depot, Falkirk. When the Royal Scottish Museum's new nineteenth-century power gallery is opened in a year or so, 'Ellesmere', which was built at Leith even though she spent most of her working life at Howe Bridge colliery at Leigh in Lancashire, will be exhibited there to represent the locomotive-building industry of the Edinburgh area.

The preservation of 'Ellesmere' was well in advance of the new railway 'mania'. This was further anticipated when the Society organised the 'Scottish Railways 1722–1963' exhibition held at the Royal Scottish Museum, which was opened by Mr C. Hamilton Ellis. At about the same time the SRPS acquired its first base at Murrayfield station on the former Caledonian Railway's Edinburgh, Princes Street to Leith North suburban line, which had been closed to passengers in 1962. The station served as the Society's headquarters and housed a small relics museum until the end of the 1969 season, when activities were consolidated at Falkirk.

As steam operations on BR ended the preservation of older classes of locomotive, including those of pre-Grouping companies, became urgent. The Society's 0-4-4T ex-Caledonian no. 419 (BR no. 55189) is an example of a Scottish pre-Grouping class which survived until well into the 1960s, all over Scotland from Carlisle to Kyle of Lochalsh. She was one of ninety-two, built to the design of J. F. McIntosh between the turn of the century and 1925, and descended from Dugald Drummond's CR 0-4-4Ts of 1884. They were intended for suburban and branch line duties throughout the Caledonian system and later the Scottish areas of the LMS and BR. In their last years they were much used as station pilots, as was no. 55189 at the time she was withdrawn after fifty-five years' service in 1962. Her restoration to CR Prussian blue livery was carried out at Cowlairs works, once the locomotive works of the Caledonian's great rival the North British Railway. It was not originally planned to restore the engine to working order but this has followed slowly and she was steamed publicly in September 1971.

With no. 419 undergoing extensive and costly restoration, the problem of finding suitable accommodation for this and the Society's other possessions grew. The goods transit shed at Springfield Yard by Grahamston Depot, Falkirk, had been vacated by BR following a fire there which had damaged part of the roof although leaving the structure sound. BR decided not to make good the damage because of freight traffic rationalisation in the area and so the Society was able to lease the 200ft long two-track shed at a reasonable rent. The Society took over the Falkirk depot early in 1965 and no. 419 arrived there on 20 August that year.

By this time the SRPS had acquired its only narrow gauge locomotive, the 'Fair Maid of Foyers'. This was a 3ft gauge Andrew Barclay 0-4-0T of 1899, which is believed to have worked on reservoir construction in Wales, and latterly at Foyers Aluminium Works on Loch Ness, which closed in the early 1960s. The British Aluminium Co. put her in store at Grangemouth before presenting her to the Society in 1964.

By 1966 the Society's position was becoming much stronger and the first public open day was held at Falkirk during the year. At the end of 1966 the Society purchased, with the help of the Association of Railway Preservation Societies, the ex-North British Railway 0-6-0 tender locomotive, 'Maude', built at Cowlairs in 1891. 'Maude' was one of a fairly numerous class built from 1888 to a design of Matthew Holmes intended mainly for freight but also for passenger service. She was rebuilt just before World War I and posted abroad in 1917 for service on the supply line to the Western Front. Twenty-five of this class served abroad during the war and on their return to this country the NBR named them after military figures or places. No. 673 was named after Lt-Gen. Sir Stanley Maude when she returned to Scotland in the summer of 1919. Thereafter most of her career was passed in central Scotland and at the time of her withdrawal in July 1966 she was shedded at Bathgate, outliving, with several other engines of her class, many more modern machines. 'Maude' is now at Falkirk undergoing restoration to working order.

The Society's principal benefactor in 1968 was the National Coal Board in Scotland which donated two interesting locomotives of Scottish origin. The first to arrive was a Neilson 0-4-0ST built in 1876. She was typical of many 'Pugs' built by this maker in the seventies and eighties and the design was followed by the North British Railway for a series of 0-4-0STs which later became the LNER Y9 class, one of which is preserved in the Lytham Motive Power Museum in Lancashire. The Falkirk engine was delivered to William Baird's Iron Founders at Gartsherrie and was there named 'Kelton Fell'. She later worked at Gartshore colliery, adjacent to the Edinburgh–Glasgow main line and became redundant when the colliery closed in 1966. In the same year the NCB donated a larger engine, Neilson Reid 0-6-0T no. 1, built in 1902. Neilson Reid were the successors to Neilsons but the name lasted only from 1898 to 1902, when the North British Locomotive Co. was formed. No. 1 was built for the Coltness Iron Co. and worked at Newmains until sold to the NCB in 1955. Its last base was at Bedlay colliery; it was withdrawn with a broken crosshead in 1968.

Yet another locomotive presented to the Society in 1968 was 'Dailuaine', an Andrew Barclay 0-4-0ST built in 1939. She was sent new to the Dailuaine Distillery on Speyside and was made redundant when the branch line from Aberlour to Boat of Garten and Aviemore was closed in November 1967. It is stored at present at Aviemore, along with some wagons also from the distillery, and is to become the property of the Strathspey Railway Co. in due course.

Although the Society does not as yet run its own railway, it has run excursions, using its own coaches, to places as far afield as Oban and

Mallaig. It also defied, in a small way, the BR steam ban when two further locomotives were delivered to Falkirk under their own steam in 1970. In January an Andrew Barclay 0-4-0ST arrived. This was donated by the South of Scotland Electricity Board. In October, ex-Wemyss Private Railway 0-6-0T no. 20, a Barclay of 1939, was steamed from Fife. Since 1961 the Society has acquired thirteen locomotives, twelve carriages and twenty-two wagons and thus has more than adequate basic equipment to run a line of its own. Several possible stretches of line have been considered, including Crieff–Comrie, Doune–Callander and, most promisingly so far, Aviemore–Boat of Garten.

During 1971 the original Aviemore–Boat of Garten scheme fell though but, as is described in chapter 22, it has been kept alive by a consortium of businessmen, many of whom are still connected with the SRPS. They have floated a limited company which has negotiated with BR and other interested bodies. It seems likely that some of the Society's locomotives and rolling stock may be used on the Strathspey line and collaboration will clearly be mutually beneficial. In the meantime the SRPS is fully occupied at Falkirk restoring stock and locomotives to working order and, where possible, original condition. There are three tracks available to the Society, two of which run into the former transit shed, and there is also a locomotive siding with ash pit.

The problems are that the life span of the shed is limited and there is growing urgency to find an alternative site. The Society's present collection is, in any case, rapidly outgrowing the facilities at Falkirk.

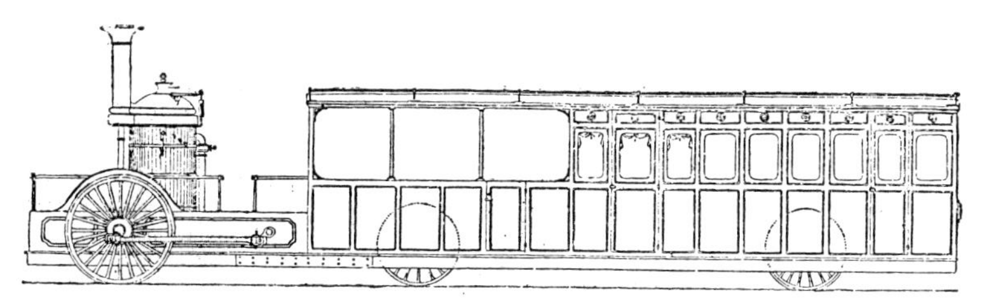

The 'Fairfield': Bristol and Exeter Railway, combined locomotive and coach

The Standard Gauge Steam Trust

Steam locomotives at the end of their working lives have often been sold for nothing more than their value as scrap and it is from breakers' yards that many have been rescued for preservation. Between a few thousand pounds' worth of metal and the reincarnation of a pulsating leviathan a chasm yawns which can be bridged only by expert and dedicated work, and money. The same applies to keeping a locomotive in good working order, an order dictated not only by pride of possession but by properly exacting safety and insurance requirements. The problems of maintenance are increased by the growing obsolescence of the engineering facilities required for the job, yet these facilities are as important a part of industrial archaeology as the machines they serve. In addition to providing a home for a growing and distinguished collection of locomotives the Standard Gauge Steam Trust's depot at Tyseley in Birmingham (TYS in Great Western days) has a unique role in locomotive preservation through the provision of them.

The Tyseley collection began with the acquisition of no. 7029, 'Clun Castle', in 1966. In the last years of steam on British Railways she worked many well-publicised 'specials' and the resulting wear and tear illustrated the need for regular maintenance, as did the arrival in October 1966 of the much older LMS no. 5593, 'Kolhapur', which was in immediate need of major repairs. These early experiences crystallised the objectives of the Trust under the leadership of its present chairman, Mr P. B. Whitehouse, OBE, and under the direction of the chief engineer, Mr A. J. Kent, which in addition to the general aim of setting up a working museum predominantly of large main line locomotives, are:

1. To set up proper workshops with adequate machinery to restore locomotives to first-class operating condition and to see that the exhibits remain in constantly good running order; in addition, to ensure the continuity of human skills required, and the acquisition of all necessary records.

2. To ensure that these workshops represent a cross-section of the specialised machinery used in the manufacture and repair of steam locomotives.

3. To enable the workshops to carry out work for existing privately-owned railways which have only minor repair facilities, and for the Trust to maintain and operate an advisory and consultancy service for them.

The site occupied by the Trust consists of the coaling and ash-dropping roads of the depot at Tyseley originally built by the GWR. At the time it was taken over it was full of rubbish associated with those functions. The track, furthermore, was dilapidated, involving substantial renovations, including relaying one of the roads. This operation was put out to the BR Permanent Way gang because the imminent arrival of locomotives necessitated the completion of work much sooner than would have been possible had it been left to the voluntary labour available. General repairs followed, such as the restoration of two water columns, in order to make the depot serviceable for steam engines. During 1968, as steam operations ended on BR, there was a final opportunity to acquire tools and spare parts from such stocks as remained. At the same time the conversion of the old coaling stage at Tyseley into a two-road shed with an inspection pit on one side and large enough to hold 'Clun Castle' and 'Kolhapur' was completed. Much of the machinery collected then and since had to be completely taken apart, cleaned and rebuilt. Some of the heavier items are even now not installed, neither are all the locomotives under cover, but the Trust has assembled the basic elements of a complete steam museum and engineering works. It can rely on the dedication and expertise of its supporters for much that remains to be done but around £100,000 will also be needed to bring the scheme to fruition.

On the engineering side, the tool room at Tyseley is almost complete and contains a 7½in. centre Triumph lathe, a 6½in. Edge-Wick centre lathe, a 30in. Richmond universal milling machine with vertical head and slotting head, a Browne & Sharpe 30in. horizontal milling machine with universal dividing head, a jig borer, a Browne & Sharpe universal grinder with internal head, a Norton tool and cutter grinder, and a Wolfe off-hand pedestal grinder. Equipment for the heavy machine shop has also been assembled and most of it reconditioned and installed. It comprises a 6ft 6in. stroke double head planing machine, special purpose railway running shed combination machine (lathe, drilling machine and shaper), an 8in. centre by 6in. between centres Lang centre lathe, an 8in. centre short bed Deane, Smith & Grace centre lathe, a Hendy Norton 7in. centre lathe with taper turning attachment, a no. 4 Herbert capstan lathe with a wide range of tooling, a Cincinnati no. 2 vertical milling machine, a Herbert drilling machine, a Lumsden 4-wheel carbide tipped tool grinding machine, and a straightening press.

One essential item of heavy equipment was a wheel drop. Most of those available either required prohibitive repairs or were hydraulically operated, which would need yet more equipment to work. The electrically operated one eventually bought for Tyseley had been built just before the war for the LNER by Ransome & Rapier of Ipswich. At the time of purchase from BR it was under vast quantities of dirt at Ipswich running shed. After cleaning, each part was numbered and photographed prior to dismantling, removal and re-erection at Tyseley where the necessary pit had been constructed of reinforced concrete. This wheel drop is now operative.

Another machine needing substantial foundations and creating formidable removal and installation problems was a wheel lathe. A running shed axle and wheel lathe was chosen as most suitable and a machine built in 1947 by Noble & Lund of Gateshead was eventually located at the former LNWR running sheds at Bescot. No lifting facilities were available there, not that the lathe would have been accessible if they had been, and hardly any of the parts could be removed by hand. Every movement required jacks and block and tackle. This too is now in working order.

There are one or two pieces of equipment which it was impossible to get hold of in any condition, such as an overhead crane capable of lifting a boiler from the frames. Nothing suitable could be found and so the engineering team designed their own. The base was prepared and the lifting carriages are due for delivery in 1972.

The restoration of locomotives at Tyseley had begun long before the depot had become so well equipped. 'Clun Castle' arrived in January 1966. In November she was stripped and restored to Great Western livery ready for service on 'specials' during the following year. A heavy programme was planned both on familiar Western metals and in the Eastern Region in the autumn. During the return journey from Birkenhead on 5 March 1967 it became evident that something was amiss and detailed examination back at the depot revealed the trouble to be that the left-hand inside valve spindle had stripped its thread and come adrift. Further investigation showed that the entire valve gear was excessively worn and in view of the heavy commitments outstanding, it was decided to renew the whole of the valve gear and motion. These and other repairs were carried out, often working from scratch with the aid of drawings from Swindon, where the locomotive was built in 1950. Since this major restoration she has been maintained, in accordance with the aims of the Trust, in first class operating condition.

Tyseley's second locomotive was one of Sir William Stanier's Jubilee class, no. 5593, 'Kolhapur', built in 1934 for the LMS by the North British Locomotive Co. at Glasgow. There was some urgency in the decision to take her on because at the time few of her class remained in service and none with so good a boiler as no. 5593. In most other respects she was in a bad way. Much of the smoke box, cab roof, tender footplate and boiler fittings had to be substantially replaced and all the cylinders, which were loose to the frames and with the holes elongated, refitted.

Though a true Castle, 'Clun' was built three years after nationalisation, under BR and not Great Western auspices. A real GWR tender engine was wanted and by the time she was chosen no. 4983, 'Albert Hall', had been in Woodham Brothers' yard at Barry for some time. Various parts had been reclaimed for scrap, including all the brass and copper fittings. Basic repairs were necessary before she could even be towed to Tyseley for restoration. As with no. 7029 much use has been made of drawings from Swindon in preparing new parts. The cross-section of Swindon locomotives has been completed by the arrival of two 0-6-0 pannier tanks, nos. 7752 and 7760.

These and the other Tyseley locomotives illustrate admirably the last fifty years in the evolution of steam traction. The present collection is as shown in Table 3.

The Castle, Hall, Jubilee and Black 5 classes (the last-named represented by no. 5428 which was named 'Eric Treacy' in May 1969 in honour of the Bishop of Wakefield, of which there are several survivors, are discussed elsewhere. Others demand consideration here, not least because in some instances the Tyseley engine is the last operational survivor of its class.

No. 1008, for example, was the first of 330 2-4-2Ts to emerge from

Table 3 Steam locomotives at Tyseley

Type	Number and name	Where built	Year	Origin
4-6-0	7029 'Clun Castle'	Swindon	1950	BR
4-6-0	5593 'Kolhapur'	North British	1934	LMS
4-6-0	5428 'Eric Treacy'	Armstrong, Whitworth	1937	LMS
4-6-0	777 'Sir Lamiel'	North British	1925	SR
4-4-0	925 'Cheltenham'	Eastleigh	1934	SR
4-4-0	120	Nine Elms	1899	LSWR
2-4-2T	1008	Horwich	1899	LYR
0-6-0ST	1247	Sharp, Stewart	1899	GNR
4-6-0	4983 'Albert Hall'	Swindon	1931	GWR
0-4-0ST	No. 1	Peckett	1941	GEC Swinton
0-6-0T	7752	North British	1930	GWR
0-6-0T	7760	North British	1930	GWR

Horwich between 1889 and 1911 in a design originating under Sir John Aspinall for the Lancashire and Yorkshire Railway. They were ubiquitous on that varied and cruelly graded railway system where their work was surely more arduous than any ever demanded of a British tank engine elsewhere.

Tyseley has an example of every LSWR/SR express locomotive in service between the wars with the exception of a Lord Nelson, the solitary survivor of that class being the eponymous no. 30850 in the British Rail National Relics Store at Brighton. Dugald Drummond's 4-4-0 T9s of which sixty-six were built between 1899 and 1901 were nicknamed 'Greyhounds'. Soon after their introduction the competition between the LSWR and the GWR for the Plymouth boat train traffic reached its height. They performed brilliantly though they failed to equal the performance of 'City of Truro'. Such contests were, in any case, inimical to Drummond's philosophy of economical and reliable running. The T9 was his masterpiece and his later 4-6-0 designs never equalled them in grace or relative performance. It was not until R. E. L. Maunsell took over, assisted by two former members of Churchward's staff at Swindon, that a really first class locomotive of this wheel arrangement emerged from the SR works at Eastleigh. When it did, in the shape of the King Arthur class, it established itself almost as the peer of the GWR Castle and quite without equal on the exacting road from Salisbury to Exeter. The very engine preserved at Tyseley, no. 777, 'Sir Lamiel', took a 345-ton train over the 84 miles from Salisbury to Waterloo in 73 minutes during the autumn of 1934. A later Maunsell design, the Schools, introduced in 1929, were the most powerful 4-4-0s in Europe, specially developed for the Tonbridge–Hastings section of the former South Eastern and Chatham Railway with its heavy gradients, difficult curves and clearance restrictions in the tunnels south of Tunbridge Wells. No. 925, 'Cheltenham', is not the only working survivor, as no. 928, 'Stowe', is preserved in Lord Montagu's Motor Museum at Beaulieu Abbey.

In 1950 there were 114 locomotives allocated to Tyseley. In 1971 the depot held twelve but in all respects except numbers its stature in what remains of the steam locomotive world has grown.

Thompson B1 4-6-0 no. 61306, 'Mayflower'

Steamtown

Steamtown Locomotive Depot and Works occupies the former BR Motive Power Depot at Carnforth in Lancashire. It is open daily throughout the year and on special days the locomotives are in steam. The collection was founded by a group under the leadership of Dr P. L. Beet, whose original intention was to purchase the former LMS branch from Plumpton Junction to Lakeside (Windermere). In the event the branch was severed from the main line and only the isolated stretch from Haverthwaite to Lakeside was available for preservation. A majority of the supporters of the original venture decided to concentrate their efforts on building a locomotive collection and steam centre at Carnforth. Others pressed on with the Lakeside–Haverthwaite line and founded the Lakeside & Haverthwaite Railway Co., Ltd, supported by the Lakeside Railway Society, which is described elsewhere.

Carnforth Motive Power Depot (10A in the British Railways shed classification) was one of the last in the country to retain steam locomotives. After the final withdrawal of steam traction in 1968, a private company promoted by some steam enthusiasts leased the depot in order to house various locomotives which had been bought for preservation. The area leased covers nearly 20 acres and in addition to the running shed, offices and workshops contains a coaling tower, ash disposal plant, water columns, a 70ft turntable and a carriage and wagon shop. From end to end the site is about a mile long and has about five miles of track. The southern end lies on the west side of the main line from London to Glasgow, now being electrified. A rail connection at the northern end allows access to and from the Furness line of British Railways. The company's intention is to create a live steam museum which will be one of the foremost in the country, preserving as far as possible the authentic atmosphere of a main line depot.

Steamtown employs a small permanent staff and enjoys the support of a considerable force of volunteers of all ages and both sexes. Locomotives are steamed regularly, providing the opportunity for footplate rides. The scope of the engineering work which the depot is equipped to undertake is considerable and the machinery now installed there includes a 7ft wheel lathe. Some of the locomotives at the depot at any one time have been sent there by individuals and preservation societies for overhaul and repair and will eventually be removed to provide the motive power on fully operational light railways. A notable feature of Steamtown's work in this field is the overhaul of current working industrial steam locomotives. The Welsh Highland Railway's 2-6-2T 'Russell' has been a recent visitor for overhaul.

This activity complements and assists Steamtown's other main function which is the collection, preservation and steaming of locomotives. The present standard gauge British engines there are shown in Table 4.

The Stanier Black 5, it has already been noted, is the most preserved main line locomotive class and of the eleven that survive, five are at Steamtown. Two of them have particular claims to fame and strong nostalgic associations with the north-west of England where steam traction lingered to the very end on British Railways. No. 45407, which was one of the Black 5s built by Armstrong Whitworth at Scotswood-on-Tyne, was the last steam engine to haul a BR freight train; and no. 44871 was one of those used to haul BR's special 'Last Steam Hauled Train' on 11 August 1968.

Thompson BI 4-6-0 no. 61306, 'Mayflower', on the other hand, while having its own nostalgic niche as the last steam locomotive to haul the 'Yorkshire Pullman', is more important as the sole working survivor of

Table 4 Steam locomotives at Steamtown

Class	Type	Number	Where built	Year	Origin
Stanier 5MT	4-6-0	44767	Crewe	1947	LMS & BR
	4-6-0	44871	Crewe	1945	LMS & BR
	4-6-0	44932	Horwich	1945	LMS & BR
	4-6-0	45231	Armstrong Whitworth	1936	LMS & BR
	4-6-0	45407	Armstrong Whitworth	1937	LMS & BR
Ivatt 2MT	2-6-0	46441	Crewe	1950	BR
Thompson BI	4-6-0	61306	North British	1948	BR

its once numerous class. When Edward Thompson took over as CME of the LNER after the death of Sir Nigel Gresley in 1941, he was required to produce a new general-purpose locomotive to supplement and succeed the company's generally ageing mixed traffic locomotive stock, much of which had been inherited from the pre-Grouping companies. Many of the skills and resources on which Thompson could normally have drawn for the design, development and manufacture of a new locomotive class were totally committed to war-time priorities and so he drew extensively and ingeniously on existing patterns. Nevertheless, the BI class which resulted was a very good engine indeed and one of them performed brilliantly on Great Western metals during the post-nationalisation interchange trials of 1948. No. 61306, which was built under BR auspices by the North British Locomotive Company at Glasgow in 1948, was the last to be withdrawn in 1967. Apart from the first forty-one engines of the class—the 'Antelopes'—they were not named and the Steamtown locomotive was not given its present name, 'Mayflower', until May 1971.

Steamtown is at present the home of two European locomotives. The former East German Railways 0-8-0 no. 993462 was built in 1934 by Orenstein & Koppel of Berlin for the Mecklenburgische Pommersche Schmalspurbahn. This 60cm (1ft 11½in.) gauge locomotive is owned by Mr J. B. Snell of London and may eventually work on the Vale of Rheidol Railway.

A more spectacular Carnforth acquisition is the ex-SNCF Pacific no. 231K22 built at Lille by S. F. Cail et Cie in 1914 and rebuilt there in 1937. Many of these magnificent, long-serving locomotives survive, derelict, at various locations in France and the present French railway authorities fully recognise the value and attraction of steam-hauled specials over the main line network. The last 4-6-2s were withdrawn in January 1969 but two have been restored to working order, one of them, no. 231K8, from the same series as the Steamtown engine, and over the last two years both have worked enthusiasts' trains on 200-mile round trips which have included stretches of 70mph running. Of all the locomotives at Steamtown, no. 231K22 had the most difficult journey to Carnforth. Locomotive and tender travelled on separate road low-loaders by way of Le Havre and Southampton and the English end of the journey took seven days. At 95 tons K22 is almost one-third as heavy again as either the Black 5s or the B1 and this, together with her other generous dimensions, initially caused some housing problems in the depot. However, K22 has now been installed in the running shed where she is soon to be joined by a German main line locomotive.

No. 6023, 'King Edward II', one of three surviving 'Kings'

Worcester Locomotive Society & Bulmer's Private Railway

The Worcester Locomotive Society has grown over the last ten years from a small, local group of trainspotters and teenage rail fans into a formidable part of the locomotive preservation movement with more than a thousand supporters.

The Society was formed at the end of 1960 when the Worcester branch of a Gloucester-based society became too large for running coach trips to steam depots. Many of the fifty or so founding members were still at school but their dedicated support for the Society carried it through the formative years and into maturity. So great was this enthusiasm that the magazine *The Big Four*, consisting of a duplicated sheet or sheets, was delivered by hand in order to save money on postal costs. It also carried the Society's reputation farther afield and by 1964 it had established a membership in Birmingham and its suburbs and soon afterwards in the north and east Midlands and in London, where area organisations have since been formed. Organising visits to nationalised and industrial rail installations remains one of the Worcester

Locomotive Society's principal functions even though these have necessarily broadened, and in some opinions been corrupted, to include diesel and electric depots. It is probably due to the fact that the Society has been willing to cater for more general railway interests that has enabled it to flourish at a time when many Midland societies of a basically similar character have had to close down. This prosperity has enabled the committee to expand activities yet further and organise tours abroad, to Germany, France, Italy, Spain, Portugal and Austria, and to make a valuable contribution to the bibliography of preservation in the shape of their *Pannier Parade* and R. N. Pritchard's *Preserved Locomotive Checklist*, apart from the quarterly magazine, *The Big Four*.

Given the character and purpose of the Worcester Locomotive Society it was hardly surprising that it should have become interested in preserving a locomotive of its own. A fund for this purpose was launched early in 1967 with no specific locomotive in view but within two years had nevertheless reached £2,000. When the prospect of making a purchase became real a majority of members favoured an ex-GWR 0-6-0 pannier tank but in view of the Society's complete lack of engineering facilities the criterion was that the engine acquired should be in full working order.

However, the first locomotive came from the stock of Stewarts & Lloyds at Corby, where the company was withdrawing its steam locomotives and the purchase of a Kitson 0-6-0 saddle tank in excellent condition was completed for £330. Because of the moderate price a large number of spare parts could be acquired with the engine, thus considerably enhancing the value and long term practicability of the investment.

The locomotive, no. 5474, had been in industrial service since it was built at the Airedale foundry of the Kitson Locomotive Co. in 1934. Though in excellent condition, some restoration was necessary after it had been installed on the private railway of H. P. Bulmer, Ltd off Whitecross Road in Hereford, before I named the engine 'Carnarvon' on 19 September 1971 in my capacity as president of the Society. The locomotive is unique in so far as it is the only Kitson saddle tank preserved and regularly steamed in Britain.

The purchase of the Society's first locomotive did not long delay the search for a GWR pannier tank. This ended in August 1969 with the completion of negotiations with London Transport for L92 (ex-GWR no. 5786). This cost £1,100 which again left the Society with funds to stock up with spares from various sources, including Woodham Brothers of Barry, and to carry out a full restoration to Great Western livery.

The Society's two locomotives are in distinguished company on the private railway of H. P. Bulmer, Ltd whose managing director, Mr Peter Prior, is a vice-president, for the company's 'Cider Train' is headed by 'King George V' which represents the culmination of GWR locomotive design. The King class, developed by C. B. Collett from Churchward's four-cylinder 4-6-0 engines, was the equal of the heavier and larger Pacific locomotives built for other railways. No. 6000, built in 1927, was the first of thirty which operated on the heaviest passenger traffic up to 1962, and began its working life in the United States at the centenary celebrations of the Baltimore and Ohio Railroad. At the time that she was withdrawn for preservation the engine had covered some two million miles of very high speed working.

For five years after being withdrawn from service, no. 6000 was stored in a Swindon stockshed until, in 1968, the Bulmer company reached an agreement with Swindon Corporation whereby it undertook to restore her provided she could then be exhibited at Hereford for at least two years. The company had little doubt that she would be an enormous attraction, not only for steam enthusiasts but also for the 8,000 or so visitors to the cider factory each year. The engine left Swindon in August 1968 for restoration at Newport and arrived at Hereford in November, where a special exhibition shed has been built. The colour specification to which 'King George V' was restored was that of BR in 1959, the year of its final modification. The five Pullman coaches which form the 'Cider Train' have been dressed out in Bulmer's red, green and white livery with the Royal Arms, the company being a Royal Warrant Holder, alongside those of the city of Hereford on their sides. Four of them were formerly in normal Pullman service on the Southern Region and have since been named after the wives of directors of Bulmer's, but the fifth, 'Aquila', was built in 1951 specially for the use of the Royal Family and visiting heads of state. The second category has included dignitaries as various as the President of Liberia and Mr Kosygin. The coaches were acquired at the same time as the locomotive, and the train has been on tour several times since then. At other times 'King George V' is frequently in steam at Hereford with the Worcester Locomotive Society's engines.

Officially described as 'a marketing tool unique in British industry today', the 'Cider Train' and the working preservation of 'King George V' is a brilliantly successful example of the variety of interests that can be harnessed in the service of the history of steam locomotion. The longest of the routes on which BR now allows the running of steam trains is the ninety-four miles from Shrewsbury to Newport. Hereford lies roughly half way along this route and is thus ideally placed to continue to play a prominent part in the working preservation of steam locomotives.

3 The Gresley Pacifics

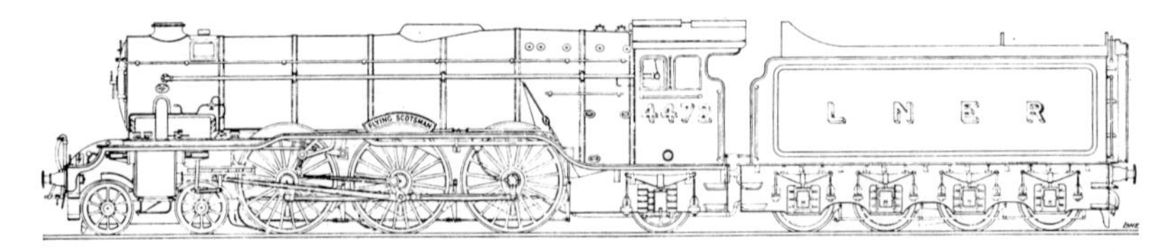

Gresley AI, no. 4472, 'Flying Scotsman'

Sir Nigel Gresley left his post as Assistant Carriage and Wagon Superintendent of the Lancashire & Yorkshire Railway in 1905 to serve the Great Northern Railway under H. A. Ivatt. Ivatt was already famous for his Atlantics working the east coast expresses north from King's Cross on the Peterborough–Grantham–Doncaster route, and for numerous other sturdy steam locomotives. Both Ivatt and Gresley were Crewe-trained as steam locomotive engineers and until 1911, when Gresley took over as Locomotive Engineer to the Great Northern Railway, they ran harmoniously in harness. It was in these six years, 1905 to 1911, that Gresley designed the first of the bow-ended coaches with elliptical roofs, which were to become standard express stock for the Great Northern Railway and later the LNER until British Railways' standardisation ended the characteristic teak coaches of the pre-nationalisation group. In 1911 Gresley became the Locomotive Engineer of the Great Northern Railway at the age of thirty-seven and in 1923, Chief Mechanical Engineer of the London & North Eastern Railway, a post which he occupied until he died in 1941.

On Grouping in 1923, he inherited a remarkable miscellany of locomotives from the Great Northern Railway, the Great Eastern, the Great Central, the North Eastern, the North British and several smaller lines. Throughout the years of World War I Gresley had been champing at the bit, at Doncaster, stultified and frustrated by priority requirements of war, deferring the fruition of plans for faster, heavier east coast trains and his dream of a non-stop express, in eight hours covering the 392 miles from King's Cross to Waverley. The first Gresley Pacific matured at Doncaster between 1919 and 1921. Further north, Sir Vincent Raven at his Darlington works of the North Eastern Railway was creating a mighty Pacific as well. They were born almost simultaneously, the first two Gresleys, nos. 1470, 'Great Northern', and 1471, 'Sir Frederick Banbury'. Their superiority over the larger Atlantics for increasingly heavy east coast expresses was comparable to the superiority of the first Ivatt Atlantics over Stirling's wonderful 8ft singles, at the turn of the century. Shortly after the two Gresley Pacifics emerged, the Great Northern Railway ended its illustrious and romantic history and was absorbed into the London and North Eastern Railway. These Gresley Pacifics were the Great Northern Railway's locomotive swan-song.

The working pressure of the A1 no. 1470, 'Great Northern', was 180lb per sq. in., the grate area 41¼sq. ft, total heating surface 3,455sq. ft and the engine had three cylinders 20in. × 26in. stroke. The coupled wheels were 6ft 8in. and with 5,000 gallons of water on board and eight tons of coal, the whole machine weighed 148¾ tons. Of course, the corridor tender and other refinements for long-distance, non-stop working came later. Very quickly after Grouping, the huge Pacifics designed at Darlington by Sir Vincent Raven were cast down by the manifestly superior design of Gresley's locomotives and all five of Raven's engines, nos 2400–2404 inclusive, beginning with no. 2400, 'City of Newcastle', were scrapped. Gresley marched on, and scores of his Pacifics were built, replete with operational improvements. These came about through many factors, notably the increasing weight and speed demands of main-line passenger traffic; the locomotive exchanges of 1925 with the Great Western Castles (which had appeared in 1923); the intense competition between the new railway groups, the Big Four as they were called; but especially through the boundless ambition of Gresley himself, bent on producing the fastest and most economical locomotives of his era. Gresley, an outstandingly versatile engineer, profited from the illuminating data of the locomotive exchanges in 1925 between the Great Western and London and North Eastern railways. No. 4074, 'Caldicott Castle', positively scintillated on the west country run and twice brought the 'Cornish Riviera Limited' into North Road station, Plymouth, some fifteen minutes early on her 225 miles non-stop journey, while the Gresley Pacific performed rather less well. The Great Western engine no. 4079, 'Pendennis Castle', on the run out of King's Cross to Doncaster, certainly had the edge on her opponent Gresley A1 Pacific no. 2545, later named 'Diamond Jubilee'. Gresley moved with alacrity in making numerous technical changes to his engines, notably to valves, and by 1928 the great improvement in working economy led to the inauguration on May Day of that year of the historic non-stop run by no. 4472, 'Flying Scotsman', and no. 4476, 'Royal Lancer', between

King's Cross and Waverley. Five hundred tons behind the tender were regular loads for these trains and average speeds inter-city were well over 60mph, often climbing to speeds of 100mph even in the early nineteen-thirties.

Evolution in heavy passenger locomotive design and the tireless energy and enthusiasm of Nigel Gresley quickly led on to experiments for even more powerful and speedy locomotives than the A1 Pacifics. In 1927, no. 4480, 'Enterprise', was reboilered for 220lb per sq. in., to replace her original 180lb, the super-heating was enlarged and tractive effort raised from 29,835lb to 36,465lb, thus greatly surpassing the Great Western Castles' 31,600lb. Of course, the long lap-valves were included and more amendments still were introduced to the specification of no. 2544, 'Lemberg', another of the earlier A1 Pacifics. The results were gratifying and were followed quickly by the A3 Super Pacific led by no. 2743, 'Felstead', first of a batch of ten A3s. More conversions from the A1 followed and then the final batch of Gresley A3 Super Pacifics, built specifically as such, comprising nine locomotives, left their Doncaster works in 1934–5. Every one was a racer. Nearly twenty-five years of Gresley's assiduity and faultless application to the operational needs of the east coast route had achieved truly sensational results: Super Pacific A3 no. 2750, 'Papyrus', running from Newcastle to London, 268 miles in 227½ minutes net, or well below four hours, at more than 70mph; then no. 2595, 'Trigo', in 225 minutes at 71¾mph average, and no. 2507, 'Singapore', in 227½ minutes again at more than 70mph. The train loads were light by recent standards, though it is on record that no. 2744, 'Grand Parade', hauled a 500-ton train start to stop on the 76-mile run to Peterborough in 74 minutes at nearly 62mph. All this was indeed the curtain-raiser for the A4 streamlined Super Pacifics, the acme of Nigel Gresley's locomotive design and performance, and probably the greatest steam locomotives of our time.

From 180lb per sq. in. of the A1 to the 220lb pressure of the A3 Gresley now advanced his three-cylinder design to a working pressure of 250lb per sq. in. and a higher degree of super-heat for the A4. The cylinders were reduced to 18½in. from 19in. on the A3 Pacifics. The streamlining of the A4 led in practice, on the road, to a power saving of about ten per cent.

On 27 September 1935 the first streamlined Gresley A4 Pacific, no. 2509, 'Silver Link', made her debut on the new Silver Jubilee Express. She twice reached 112mph between King's Cross and Newcastle according to the contemporary *Railway Magazine*, and ran at more than 100mph for 43 miles with an average of 108·7mph over the 10·6 miles from Biggleswade to St Neots. Gresley was knighted: a fitting tribute in coronation year to his engineering genius.

More and better was to come, as the A4s took over the still faster and heavier express trains on the east coast route. 'Mallard', herself an A4

Pacific, fitted with Kylchap blastpipe and double chimney, one of four A4 Pacifics so equipped at the time, was put to work on a test train including a dynamometer car to establish absolute authenticity. On 3 July 1938, 'Mallard' won for Britain the accolade of the world record by steam, 126mph down Stoke Bank.

Seven months earlier, the one-hundredth Gresley Pacific, an A4, had emerged from Doncaster. With 'Mallard', no. 4468 in the LNER numerology, and no. 4472, 'Flying Scotsman', this one-hundredth locomotive was destined to match the fame of her sisters. She was works number 1863, LNER no. 4498, and on 26 November 1937 the nameplates on her forward boiler casing were unveiled at Marylebone station by the chairman of the Railway, Sir William Whitelaw. She was accorded the supreme dignity and named 'Sir Nigel Gresley'.

As recorded later, these three incomparable Gresley Pacifics are preserved and with us still, two of them in perfect operational order. All bear their original nomenclature. All have run more than 1½ million miles. All are preserved and in good hands. All are priceless.

The best narrative about no. 4498, 'Sir Nigel Gresley', was contributed to the Journal, *Main Line*, in the autumn of 1970 by J. A. Evans, Chairman of the London and North Eastern Railway Society:

> When new, 4498 differed from other members of the same class, in that she had silver instead of the usual gold blocking to the transferred letters and numerals. Otherwise she carried that standard A4 livery of Garter blue with black smoke-box door and red wheel centres. In December 1938 she went into Doncaster Works ('Plant') for general repairs and emerged with new stainless steel, Gill Sans letters and numerals as fitted to sister engines 4488–92/5/6.* Photographs in the collection of the author show 4498 in this condition, at the head of the famous 'Flying Scotsman' express train, in March 1939. At this time she was shedded at King's Cross and was regarded as one of the most capabable locomotives in the class.
>
> During the war, side valances were removed to ease maintenance and in common with many other locomotives, 4498 was repainted in the drab wartime black. To avoid possible confusion with air-raid sirens, her chime whistle was removed and in August 1943 she exchanged tenders with 4485, presenting the odd spectacle of black painted metal numbers on the cabside and 'N.E.' in transfers on the tender. 'Sir Nigel Gresley' moved from King's Cross to Grantham in 1944 and in March 1947 was restored to her pre-war livery of Garter blue with stainless letters and numerals, except that the latter had been changed to 7 in accordance with the Thompson 1946 renumbering scheme. At nationalisation 60,000

* No. 4496 appears in this form Plate 48.

was added to all former LNER locomotive numbers and 'Sir Nigel Gresley' became BR no. 60007.

In 1950 she returned to King's Cross shed, repainted in the early BR livery of dark blue with black and white lining. The stainless steel letters and numerals were replaced by transfers and the BR 'Cycling Lion' emblem was carried on the tender sides. This was followed in April 1952, by the standard British Railways (GWR) dark green livery with orange and black lining, which remained unchanged, apart from repositioning the Lion in 1956, until withdrawal from service in 1966.

In December of 1957, 'Sir Nigel Gresley' was fitted with a Kylchap double blast pipe, similar to that fitted to the record-breaking 'Mallard' of the same class. At this time she became associated with that famous top-link speed merchant Bill Hoole, and on an up Tees-Tyne Pullman she is believed to have achieved a speed of 117mph descending Stoke Bank. There are no officially recorded times to substantiate this, but it is known that Driver Hoole was in serious trouble with British Railways officials over a witnessed speedometer observation and Hallade record.

On 23 May 1959, on a train of 295 tons gross, some very fast running was achieved on the 'Stephenson Locomotive Society's Jubilee Special' from King's Cross to Doncaster and back. Highlights of the run were 101mph northbound through three counties, 80mph average up Stoke Bank, 112mph on the southbound descent of Stoke Bank, near Essendine, followed by yet another 'ton' on level track at Tempsford.

There could have been no finer 'swan song' to mark Bill Hoole's retirement shortly afterwards. Bill has since said, 'but for a speed restriction in operation at the time, enforced by the presence of an Inspector on the footplate, "Mallard's" 126mph descent of Stoke Bank in 1938 might well have been exceeded that day in 1959!'

In the closing days of the steam era on British Railways, the A4s found little work on the east coast main line and in the early 1960s they were often found working freight and parcels traffic. The high rate of diesel failures at this time often led to an A4 deputising, on the improved timings, without loss of time. In 1963 'Sir Nigel Gresley' headed an Enthusiasts' Special from Kings Cross to York and back. As if to prove she could still do it, 103mph was reached on the southbound descent of Stoke Bank, with a load of 400 tons gross. Later in the same year she finally left King's Cross shed and after a brief stay at New England, she moved north to Scotland.

'Sir Nigel Gresley' was finally withdrawn from British Railways service on 1 February 1966. She had spent her last years working from Aberdeen Ferryhill shed and was immediately purchased for active preservation by the A4 Preservation Society. After a major overhaul at Crewe, costing the Society £15,000, she hauled an inaugural rail-tour in April 1967. This was followed by a total of ten rail-tours over British Railways metals, eventually curtailed by the steam ban announced in October 1967. She remained at Crewe South shed until closure in 1968 and then moved to her present home at the National Coal Board Depot at Philadelphia, Co. Durham. She is still steamed at regular intervals and has an annual boiler inspection and general maintenance. A second tender was purchased in 1967 to allow long-distance running should the British Railways steam ban be lifted.

'Sir Nigel Gresley' is the finest preserved steam locomotive in this country today, her future is secure and she is maintained in first-class running order. Today, she carries her original running number, 4498, and Garter blue livery. She has retained her double chimney and improved motion which made her so lively in the hands of Bill Hoole and is still without the side valences removed during the War.

Table 5 Principal dimensions of 'Sir Nigel Gresley'

Cylinders	18½″ dia. × 26″ stroke
Driving wheels	6ft 8in. dia.
Heating surface	2,576 sq. ft
Superheater surface	750sq. ft
Firegrate area	41¼sq. ft
Boiler pressure	260lb per sq. in.
Tractive effort	35,455lb
Adhesion weight	66 tons
Total weight	168 tons
Maximum speed	126mph plus
Maximum drawbar	2,500hp plus

As the LNER, capturing public and romantic sentiment alike, had demonstrated by the inauguration of the 'Silver Jubilee Express' in 1935, so in 1937 the Coronation of King George VI was celebrated by the second streamlined express, 'The Coronation', which ran over the 392 miles from London to Edinburgh in six hours. For all the acclaimed prowess of diesel-electric traction the journey thirty-five years later, in the nineteen-seventies, takes the same time. The A4-hauled 'Coronation' in 1937 was scheduled, start to stop, King's Cross to York, at 71·9mph, which matched for speed the 77 miles from Swindon to Paddington in 65 minutes of the Great Western 'Cheltenham Flyer', or about 71mph, though the latter is less than one-half the distance from King's Cross to York. On 'The Coronation' the last coach was a streamlined observation car shaped to form a tailpiece to this completely streamlined train, known as the beaver tail. This observation carriage is preserved today along with an A4 Pacific, 'Union of South Africa' (see Plate 111).

The prowess, performance and reliability of Gresley's Pacifics are legendary. Scores of examples are available of their remarkable resilience, economy and infinite capacity to tackle with distinction every kind of operational requirement, north and south of the Border, with loads up to 700 tons and achieving over long periods and distances sustained high speeds. Their most impressive qualities were sheer beauty and symmetry. They looked like patricians and behaved like the nobility they were. Nobody who has experienced the sensation of an A4 Pacific lifting a 500-ton train out of King's Cross through Finsbury Park in six minutes, or a 600-ton train in 7½ minutes, listening to the muffled roar of the engine, could fail to accord to Nigel Gresley the utmost admiration for his magnificent creations of power and speed.

Happily, eight of the LNER Pacific breed are preserved (including a Peppercorn), well cared for and in most cases available for steam operations when circumstances and conditions allow (see Table 6).

No. 4472, 'Flying Scotsman', is the most famous steam engine in the world today. The third of the A1 Pacifics, she was originally commissioned by the Great Northern Railway at Doncaster Works, emerged as no. 1472 (directly after no. 1470, 'Great Northern', and no. 1471, 'Sir Frederick Banbury') very soon to become LNER no. 4472 and then no. 103, and in due course after nationalisation, BR no. 60103.

Mr Alan Pegler bought her in 1963. She tours in the United States of America, complete with bell and cowcatcher, painted proudly in her apple-green LNER livery. She hauled the first non-stop express from King's Cross to Waverley on May Day 1928, and repeated the performance forty years later through the enterprise of Alan Pegler and the co-operation of British Railways. She was the first British express locomotive to be equipped with a corridor tender for changing engine crews on long runs and today has a double tender to avoid the problems of watering on the road, where troughs and tanks and towers for servicing steam engines have nearly disappeared in this day and age of diesel and electric locomotive traction.

The romance of 'Flying Scotsman' is indelibly bound up with the origins in 1862 of the expresses, both starting at ten o'clock in the morning, north bound from King's Cross to Waverley and south bound from Waverley, Edinburgh to King's Cross. Though it is reputed that the starting time of the southbound train varied a little until 1876, since then simultaneous ten o'clock departure from northern and London terminals has remained unchanged. The original 10½ hours for the journey came down to six hours with Gresley's A4 Pacifics shortly before World War II, and is now slightly less, but only very slightly, diesel hauled.

No. 4472 had her share of racing in the thirties. In 1934 'Flying Scots-

Table 6 The eight remaining LNER Pacifics

BR no.	LNER no.	Doncaster Works no. and year	Name	Present location	Owner
60103	4472	1564:1923	A1 'Flying Scotsman'	USA	Alan Pegler
60007	4498	1863:1937	A4 'Sir Nigel Gresley'	National Coal Board, Philadelphia, Co. Durham	A4 Locomotive Society
60009	4488	1853:1937	A4 'Union of South Africa'	Lochty Private Railway, Fife	John Cameron
60019	4464	1866:1937	A4 'Bittern'	BR Neville Hill, Motive Power Depot, Leeds	Geoffrey Drury
60022	4468	1870:1938	A4 'Mallard'	Museum of British Transport	British Railways
60532	532 (BR)	2017:1948 (Peppercorn)	A2 'Blue Peter'	Great Western Society, Didcot	Geoffrey Drury
60008	4496	1861:1937	A4 'Dwight D. Eisenhower' (formerly 'Golden Shuttle')	National Railroad Museum, Green Bay, Wisconsin, USA	National Railroad Museum, Wisconsin
60010	4489	1854:1937	A4 'Dominion of Canada' (formerly 'Buzzard' then 'Woodcock')	Canadian Railroad Museum, Delson Montreal, Canada	Canadian Railroad Museum

man' headed a test train out of King's Cross. Her load was four coaches. In 152 minutes she drew to a halt in Leeds, 185½ miles away. She had run, start to stop, at over 73mph. Coming back later the same day with six coaches she did the journey in 157½ minutes, slightly slower, certainly, but including a race down Stoke Bank at 97½–100mph recorded faithfully in the dynamometer car behind her. The trail was blazed for 'Papyrus', an A3 Super Pacific, to reach 108mph on Stoke Bank in March 1935 and then, of course, in 1938, the A4 record by 'Mallard' at 126mph. 'Flying Scotsman' was the first of the Gresley Pacific 100mph performances.

Of the eight Pacifics preserved, and described in this chapter, the former LNER no. 532 is a post-war A2 by A. H. Peppercorn. Of the remaining seven Pacifics, one only—'Flying Scotsman'—is an A1. The six others are A4 Pacifics. They are ageless, and because of their historical importance to say nothing of sentiment and nostalgia, they are truly priceless.

Table 7 Gresley A1 and A3 Pacifics (with LNER numbers)

No.	Name	No.	Name	No.	Name
2500	'Windsor Lad'	2561	'Minoru'	2599	'Book Law'
2501	'Colombo'	2562	'Isinglass'	2743	'Felstead'
2502	'Hyperion'	2563	'William Whitelaw'	2744	'Grand Parade'
2503	'Firdaussi'		(renamed 'Tagalie',	2745	'Captain Cuttle'
2504	'Sandwich'		August 1941)	2746	'Fairway'
2505	'Cameronian'	2564	'Knight of the	2747	'Coronach'
2506	'Salmon Trout'		Thistle'	2748	'Colorado'
2507	'Singapore'	2565	'Merry Hampton'	2749	'Flamingo'
2508	'Brown Jack'	2566	'Ladas'	2750	'Papyrus'
2543	'Melton'	2567	'Sir Visto'	2751	'Humorist'
2544	'Lemberg'	2568	'Sceptre'	2752	'Spion Kop'
2545	'Diamond Jubilee'	2569	'Gladiateur'	2795	'Call Boy'
2546	'Donovan'	2570	'Tranquil'	2796	'Spearmint'
2547	'Doncaster'	2571	'Sunstar'	2797	'Cicero'
2548	'Galtee More'	2572	'St Gatien'	4470	'Great Northern'
2549	'Persimmon'	2573	'Harvester'	4471	'Sir Frederick Ban-
2550	'Blink Bonny'	2574	'St Frusquin'		bury'
2551	'Prince Palatine'	2575	'Galopin'	4472	'Flying Scotsman'
2552	'Sansovino'	2576	'The White Knight'	4473	'Solario'
2553	'Manna'	2577	'Night Hawk'	4474	'Victor Wild'
	(renamed 'Prince of	2578	'Bayardo'	4475	'Flying Fox'
	Wales', Nov. 1926)	2579	'Dick Turpin'	4476	'Royal Lancer'
2554	'Woolwinder'	2580	'Shotover'	4477	'Gay Crusader'
2555	'Centenary'	2581	'Neil Gow'	4478	'Hermit'
2556	'Ormonde'	2582	'Sir Hugo'	4479	'Robert the Devil'
2557	'Blair Athol'	2595	'Trigo'	4480	'Enterprise'
2558	'Tracery'	2596	'Manna'	4481	'St Simon'
2559	'The Tetrarch'	2597	'Gainsborough'		
2560	'Pretty Polly'	2598	'Blenheim'		

Table 8 Gresley A4 Pacifics (with LNER numbers)

No.	Name	Renamed	Date renamed
4500	'Gargeney'	'Sir Ronald Matthews'	Mar. 1939
4499	'Pochard'	'Sir Murrough Wilson'	April 1939
4494	'Osprey'	'Andrew K. McCosh'	Oct. 1942
4462	'Great Snipe'	'William Whitelaw'	July 1941
4901	'Capercaillie'	'Charles H. Newton'	Oct. 1942
4466	'Herring Gull'	'Sir Ralph Wedgwood'	Jan. 1944
4498	'Sir Nigel Gresley'		
4496	'Golden Shuttle'	'Dwight D. Eisenhower'	Sept. 1945
4488	'Union of South Africa'		
4489	'Woodcock'	'Dominion of Canada'	June 1937
4490	'Empire of India'		
4491	'Commonwealth of Australia'		
4492	'Dominion of New Zealand'		
2509	'Silver Link'		
2510	'Quicksilver'		
2511	'Silver King'		
2512	'Silver Fox'		
4463	'Sparrow Hawk'		
4464	'Bittern'		
4465	'Guillemot'		
4467	'Wild Swan'		
4468	'Mallard'		
4469	'Gadwall'	'Sir Ralph Wedgwood'	Mar. 1939
4482	'Golden Eagle'		
4483	'Kingfisher'		
4484	'Falcon'		
4485	'Kestrel'	'Miles Beevor'	Nov. 1947
4486	'Merlin'		
4487	'Sea Eagle'	'Walter K. Whigham'	Oct. 1947
4493	'Woodcock'		
4495	'Great Snipe'	'Golden Fleece'	Sept. 1937
4497	'Golden Plover'		
4900	'Gannet'		
4902	'Seagull'		
4903	'Peregrine'	'Lord Faringdon'	Mar. 1948

4 Castles and Kings of the Great Western Railway

No. 7037, 'Swindon', built August 1950, the last of her class

The Great Western Railway was the only one to keep its name unchanged after the Grouping of 1923. C. B. Collett, the Chief Mechanical Engineer at Swindon, commanded, on Grouping, 1,486 tender locomotives, 2,415 tank locomotives and 63 railcars, a total of almost 4,000 steam motive power units. He inherited the glorious tradition of Brunel and Gooch, Armstrong and Dean, Churchward, his immediate predecessor, and all the romance and lore of Britain's proudest and most renowned railway.

Collett maintained and enhanced this Great Western tradition during the years until he retired in 1941 and was replaced by Hawksworth. The golden years of Collett at Swindon produced a complete generation of highly individualistic six coupled locomotives, the Castles (1923), the Kings (1927), the Halls (1928), the Granges (1936) and the Manors (1938). All these 4-6-0s had outside cylinders and outside steam pipes—some curved, some straight and some elbow—and in consonance with long-established Great Western practice all the five classes were named. Only one more class of Great Western 4-6-0s was to come, namely the two-cylinder Hawksworth Counties after the War.

There were 171 Castles and 30 Kings, a total of 201. Only eleven survive: eight Castles and three Kings and of these several are still in the breaker's yard awaiting rescue.

The era of the Castles was the forty-two years from 1923 to 1965. The first, no. 4073, 'Caerphilly Castle', which emerged from Swindon in

August 1923, was withdrawn from service in May 1960, and the last, no. 7037, came out of the Swindon shops in August 1950, and was later named 'Swindon' by the then Princess Elizabeth, now the Queen, and ran only thirteen years before her withdrawal in 1963. The last Castle to leave service was no. 7029, 'Clun Castle', which officially departed from British Railways in December 1965. 'Caerphilly Castle', of course, is preserved in the Science Museum at South Kensington and the Standard Gauge Steam Trust has preserved 'Clun Castle' at Tyseley. For the latter credit must go to Mr Patrick Whitehouse, OBE, who deserves the gratitude of all locomotive and railway enthusiasts for his enterprise and leadership in creating the Trust, financing developments, and acquiring additional locomotives and stock.

Of the Kings only three survive. One is no. 6000, 'King George V', the first and most renowned of her class, now restored by H. P. Bulmer, the cider makers of Hereford. The other two Kings lie derelict, cannibalised, rusting and forlorn in the breaker's yard. They are no. 6023, 'King Edward II', and no. 6024, 'King Edward I', both built in 1930 costing £7,182 and £7,175 respectively, both in the second lot of Kings (nos. 6020–6029), both batch no. 267. They ran respectively 1,554,201 and 1,570,015 miles. Both were fitted with double chimneys in 1957 and they were condemned on the same day, 19 June 1962. Identical twins, indeed.

But back to the Castles which, along with the Gresley A1 Pacifics, captured the public imagination in 1923, the first full year of their main line operations: no. 4073, 'Caerphilly Castle', and no. 4074, 'Caldicott Castle' (the Caldecot later spelt thus) on the Great Western main lines, and nos. 1470, 'Great Northern', 1471, 'Sir Frederick Banbury', and 1472, 'Flying Scotsman', on the London & North Eastern main lines. The Great Western Castles, based on their tractive effort of 31,625lb (compared with the Gresley A1 Pacific's 29,835lb) were proclaimed by Paddington propagandists as the most powerful express engines of their day, worthy successors to the Saints and the Stars which had handled with such verve and efficiency the growing loads and speed requirements of the Western main lines. The Stars had been built continuously from 1906 to 1914, when construction halted for World War I, and resumed in 1922. There were sixty-one pre-war Stars and twelve post-war, and they worked alongside their immediate predecessors the Saints, on all the fastest main-line services up to 500 tons. But there was no dramatic advance in Great Western express engine design between the first Star, no. 4000, 'North Star', which appeared in 1906, and the first of the Castles seventeen years later in 1923. The evolution from Saints to Kings during the quarter of a century, 1902–27, is shown in Table 9.

The Castles were, to a large extent, fattened up and improved Stars, but they rapidly became the first locomotives of their age. Fast, economical and sturdy, lacking perhaps the grace and symmetry of the Gresley

Table 9 The evolution from Saints to Kings, 1902–27

First built	Type	Class	Tractive effort (lb)	Cylinders and stroke	Working pressure per sq. in. (lb)	Total weight of engine and tender full (tons)	Progenitor and no. of the class, all Swindon built
1902	4-6-0	Saint	24,395	2·18½ × 30″	225	112·10	2900, 'William Dean' (76 in use)
1906	4-6-0	Star	27,800	4·15 × 26″	225	115·12	4000, 'North Star' (73 in use)
1923	4-6-0	Castle	31,625	4·16 × 26″	225	119·17	4073, 'Caerphilly Castle' (171 in use)
1927	4-6-0	King	40,300	4·16½ × 28″	250	135·14	6000, 'King George V' (30 in use)
							Total 350 locomotives

A1 Pacific, the Castles nevertheless were not slow to prove their absolute mastery of the road, with 500 tons behind the tender. They knocked spots off the competing Gresley Pacifics in the locomotive trials and exchanges of 1925, whether playing at home between Paddington and Plymouth, or between King's Cross and Doncaster, playing away. Of course, dispute and controversy ensued, and tremendous publicity, but at a distance of nearly fifty years a true appraisal and assessment of relative merit can be established. On grounds of speed, reliability, economy in fuel and general efficiency, even allowing for bad luck breakdowns by the Gresley Pacifics, there can be little doubt that Great Western engine no. 4079, 'Pendennis Castle', newly built and out of Swindon in February 1924, won easily on the North Eastern road, over the 156 miles from King's Cross to Doncaster. Similarly, the Gresley Pacific no. 1475, 'Flying Fox', fared little better against the Great Western locomotive no. 4074, 'Caldicott Castle', the second of her class, new from Swindon shops in December 1923. She twice covered the distance between London and Plymouth non-stop in 3¾ hours fifteen minutes ahead of schedule for the 225 miles run and comparable only to today's dieselised timing for the 'Cornish Riviera Limited' of 3½ hours, including the stop at Exeter (St David's): forty-seven years' progress has clipped one quarter of an hour off the schedule, say a seven per cent speed-up in nearly half a century.

So the Great Western Castles were ahead of their time, as Churchward's Saints and Stars had been ahead of their time. And, in 1926, no. 5000, 'Launceston Castle', new from the Swindon shops in September of that year was at it again, this time over the London Midland & Scottish main line, 299 miles from Euston to Carlisle including the formidable climb over Shap summit. Again, the Castle showed her superiority over the existing LMSR engines, the six-coupled Claughtons, Princes and Precedents built in earlier North Western days. Jealous eyes were upon Swindon's Castles. There followed Gresley's Super Pacifics, the A3s, the Southern Railway's Lord Nelson class, 4-6-0s, and in the autumn of 1927 the LMS Royal Scot class. Swindon was indeed setting a spanking pace. The original twenty Castles, nos. 4073 to 4092, were built there between 1923 and 1925. Another six were converted, five from Stars and one the rebuilt Pacific no. 111, 'The Great Bear', and another ten new Castles were built in 1926 and again in 1927. Then there was a lull for five years (1927–32) while the thirty Kings, nos. 6000–6029, were built and put into service—though the Kings were actually on to the road by August 1930.

In 1932 ten more Castles came out, then after a gap of twenty months, another ten in 1934, a further ten in 1935, fifteen in 1936, thirteen in 1937, twelve in 1938 and a further fifteen by 1940. So, broadly speaking, pre-war construction, including a few engines in the early days of the war, comprised 131 Castle class locomotives. The last pre-war machine was no. 5097, 'Sarum Castle'. After the war, with adaptations and improvements, another forty were added, making 171 in all, ten in 1946, ten in 1948, ten in 1949 and ten in 1950.

As the list of Castles shows the majority of these splendid engines carried titles of castles, all on the Great Western system and all calculated to romanticise the line. In addition, the great names of the GWR were immortalised, such as 'Isambard Kingdom Brunel' (no. 5069), 'Sir Daniel Gooch' (no. 5070), 'G. J. Churchward' (no. 7017), 'Viscount Portal' (no. 7000), 'Sir Felix Pole' (no. 5066), 'Great Western' (no. 7007) and 'Swindon' (no. 7037). Substantial renaming occurred, as for example in 1937 when the names of Earls were used, some transplanted from the earlier Duke 4-4-0, 3252 class, such as former no. 3270, 'Earl of Devon', later Castle class, no. 5048, or the former Bulldog 4-4-0, 3300 class, no. 3411, 'Stanley Baldwin', which prompted the re-naming of the Castles nos. 5043 to 5063 inclusive in 1937. That was the year of Mr Stanley Baldwin's ennoblement as Earl Baldwin of Bewdley, three times Prime Minister of England, and a former Director of the Great Western Railway, as his father Mr Alfred Baldwin had been before him. He was 'upgraded' from Bulldog class, no. 3411, to Castle class, no. 5063: twenty-one Castle names were thereby lost, but some came back on post-war Castles, as for example 'Drysllwyn Castle' (no. 5051 to no. 7018), 'Thornbury Castle' (no. 5063 to no. 7027), and pre-war 'Barbury Castle' (no. 5043 to no. 5095). Table 10 shows the twenty-one Earls which replaced the original Castle names in the five months, July to

Table 10 The newly named Earls, July–November 1937

No.	New name	No.	New name
5043	'Earl of Mount Edgecumbe'	5053	'Earl Cairns'
		5054	'Earl of Ducie'
5044	'Earl of Dunraven'	5055	'Earl of Eldon'
5045	'Earl of Dudley'	5056	'Earl of Powis'
5046	'Earl Cawdor'	5057	'Earl Waldegrave'
5047	'Earl of Dartmouth'	5058	'Earl of Clancarty'
5048	'Earl of Devon'	5059	'Earl St Aldwyn'
5049	'Earl of Plymouth'	5060	'Earl of Berkeley'
5050	'Earl of St Germans'	5061	'Earl of Birkenhead'
5051	'Earl Bathurst'	5062	'Earl of Shaftesbury'
5052	'Earl of Radnor'	5063	'Earl Baldwin'

November 1937. Two of the withdrawn Castle names reappeared shortly as 'Bishops Castle' (no. 5064) and 'Newport Castle' (no. 5065).

Again, in 1940, immortalising the aircraft, fighters and bombers which were flown in the Battle of Britain, the twelve Castle class locomotives built shortly before the war were renamed (see Table 11).

Table 11 Castle class locomotives re-named in 1940

No.	New Name	No.	New Name
5071	'Spitfire'	5078	'Beaufort'
5072	'Hurricane'	5079	'Lysander'
5073	'Blenheim'	5080	'Defiant'
5074	'Wellington'	5081	'Lockheed Hudson'
5076	'Gladiator	5082	'Swordfish'
5077	'Fairey Battle'		

Other special re-names were no. 4009, 'Shooting Star', re-christened in 1936 as 'A1 Lloyds' and no. 4016, 'Knight of the Golden Fleece', re-named 'The Somerset Light Infantry (Prince Albert's Own)', with regimental crest. No. 5017, 'St Donat's Castle', became 'The Gloucestershire Regiment', with regimental arms, to commemorate their gallantry in the Korean War. Table 12 lists the Castles with their dates.

There are now eight Castles left, three in splendid condition and five derelict, awaiting reconditioning and restoration. These eight locomotives are listed in Table 13.

The preservation aspect of the Kings is even more dismal than that of the Castles. There are eight of the latter, but only three Kings left, of which no. 6000, 'King George V', is in perfect operational condition at Bulmers, at Hereford. Details of the thirty Kings, all built at Swindon, are given in Table 14.

'King George V' and the other two survivors of her class, which lie in Woodham's yard at Barry, Glamorgan, rusting, derelict and grotesquely cannibalised, are all that now remain of the thirty proud Kings (see Table 15.)

Thus, preservation may save eleven locomotives, comprising eight Castles and three Kings, but only if funds are available to buy, rebuild and restore six of them from the breaker's yard at Barry.

Eleven is the maximum that can now survive out of the total of 201 Castles and Kings, surely the world's finest steam locomotives. A sad end indeed.

Table 12 Castle class locomotives

No.	Original name	Built	Withdrawn
4073	'Caerphilly Castle'	8.23	5.60
4074	'Caldicott Castle'	12.23	5.63
4075	'Cardiff Castle'	1.24	11.61
4076	'Carmarthen Castle'	2.24	2.63
4077	'Chepstow Castle'	2.24	8.62
4078	'Pembroke Castle'	2.24	7.62
4079	'Pendennis Castle'	2.24	5.64
4080	'Powderham Castle'	3.24	8.64
4081	'Warwick Castle'	3.24	1.63
4082	'Windsor Castle'	4.24	9.64
4083	'Abbotsbury Castle'	5.25	12.61
4084	'Aberystwyth Castle'	5.25	10.60
4085	'Berkeley Castle'	5.25	5.62
4086	'Builth Castle'	6.25	4.62
4087	'Cardigan Castle'	6.25	10.63
4088	'Dartmouth Castle'	7.25	5.64
4089	'Donnington Castle'	7.25	9.64
4090	'Dorchester Castle'	7.25	6.63
4091	'Dudley Castle'	7.25	1.59
4092	'Dunraven Castle'	8.25	12.61
4093	'Dunster Castle'	5.26	9.64
4094	'Dynevor Castle'	5.26	3.62
4095	'Harlech Castle'	6.26	12.62
4096	'Highclere Castle'	6.26	1.63
4097	'Kenilworth Castle'	6.26	5.60
4098	'Kidwelly Castle'	7.26	12.63
4099	'Kilgerran Castle'	8.26	9.62
5000	'Launceston Castle'	9.26	10.64
5001	'Llandovery Castle'	9.26	2.63
5002	'Ludlow Castle'	9.26	9.64
5003	'Lulworth Castle'	5.27	8.62
5004	'Llanstephan Castle'	6.27	4.62
5005	'Manorbier Castle'	6.27	2.60
5006	'Tregenna Castle'	6.27	4.62
5007	'Rougemont Castle'	6.27	9.62
5008	'Raglan Castle'	6.27	9.62
5009	'Shrewsbury Castle'	6.27	10.60
5010	'Restormel Castle'	7.27	10.59
5011	'Tintagel Castle'	7.27	9.62
5012	'Berry Pomeroy Castle'	7.27	4.62
5013	'Abergavenny Castle'	6.32	7.62
5014	'Goodrich Castle'	6.32	2.65
5015	'Kingswear Castle'	7.32	4.63

Table 12 Castle Class locomotives—*cont.*

No.	Original name	Built	Withdrawn
5016	'Montgomery Castle'	7.32	9.62
5017	'St Donats Castle'	7.32	9.62
5018	'St Mawes Castle'	7.32	3.64
5019	'Treago Castle'	7.32	9.62
5020	'Trematon Castle'	7.32	11.62
5021	'Whittington Castle'	8.32	9.62
5022	'Wigmore Castle'	8.32	6.63
5023	'Brecon Castle'	4.34	2.63
5024	'Carew Castle'	4.34	5.62
5025	'Chirk Castle'	4.34	11.63
5026	'Criccieth Castle'	4.34	11.64
5027	'Farleigh Castle'	4.34	11.62
5028	'Llantilio Castle'	5.34	5.60
5029	'Nunney Castle'	5.34	12.63
5030	'Shirburn Castle'	5.34	9.62
5031	'Totnes Castle'	5.34	10.63
5032	'Usk Castle'	5.34	9.62
5033	'Broughton Castle'	5.35	9.62
5034	'Corfe Castle'	5.35	9.62
5035	'Coity Castle'	5.35	5.62
5036	'Lyonshall Castle'	5.35	9.62
5037	'Monmouth Castle'	5.35	3.64
5038	'Morlais Castle'	6.35	9.63
5039	'Rhuddian Castle'	6.35	6.64
5040	'Stokesay Castle'	6.35	10.63
5041	'Tiverton Castle'	7.35	12.63
5042	'Winchester Castle'	7.35	6.65
5043	'Barbury Castle'	3.36	12.63
5044	'Beverston Castle'	3.36	4.62
5045	'Bridgwater Castle'	3.36	9.62
5046	'Clifford Castle'	4.36	9.62
5047	'Compton Castle'	4.36	9.62
5048	'Cranbrook Castle'	4.36	8.62
5049	'Denbigh Castle'	4.36	3.63
5050	'Devizes Castle'	5.36	8.63
5051	'Drysllwyn Castle'	5.36	5.63
5052	'Eastnor Castle'	5.36	9.62
5053	'Bishop's Castle'	5.36	7.62
5054	'Lamphey Castle'	6.36	11.64
5055	'Lydford Castle'	6.36	10.64
5056	'Ogmore Castle'	6.36	11.64
5057	'Penrice Castle'	6.36	3.64
5058	'Newport Castle'	5.37	3.63
5059	'Powis Castle'	5.37	6.62
5060	'Sarum Castle'	6.37	4.63
5061	'Sudeley Castle'	6.37	9.62
5062	'Tenby Castle'	6.37	8.62
5063	'Thornbury Castle'	6.37	2.65
5064	'Tretower Castle'	6.37	9.62
5065	'Upton Castle'	7.37	1.63
5066	'Wardour Castle'	7.37	9.62
5067	'St Fagans Castle'	7.37	7.62
5068	'Beverston Castle'	6.38	9.62
5069	'Isambard Kingdom Brunel'	6.38	2.62

No.	Original name	Built	Withdrawn
5070	'Sir Daniel Gooch'	6.38	3.64
5071	'Clifford Castle'	6.38	10.63
5072	'Compton Castle'	6.38	10.62
5073	'Cranbrook Castle'	7.38	3.64
5074	'Denbigh Castle'	7.38	5.64
5075	'Devizes Castle'	8.38	9.62
5076	'Drysllwyn Castle'	8.38	9.64
5077	'Eastnor Castle'	8.38	7.62
5078	'Lamphey Castle'	5.39	11.62
5079	'Lydford Castle'	5.39	5.60
5080	'Ogmore Castle'	5.39	4.63
5081	'Penrice Castle'	5.39	10.63
5082	'Powis Castle'	6.39	7.62
5083	'Bath Abbey'	6.37	1.59
5084	'Reading Abbey'	4.37	7.62
5085	'Evesham Abbey'	7.39	2.64
5086	'Viscount Horne'	12.37	11.58
5087	'Tintern Abbey'	11.40	8.63
5088	'Llanthony Abbey'	2.39	9.62
5089	'Westminster Abbey'	10.39	11.64
5090	'Neath Abbey'	4.39	5.62
5091	'Cleeve Abbey'	12.38	10.64
5092	'Tresco Abbey'	4.38	7.63
5093	'Upton Castle'	6.39	9.63
5094	'Tretower Castle'	6.39	9.62
5095	'Barbury Castle'	6.39	8.62
5096	'Bridgwater Castle'	6.39	6.64
5097	'Sarum Castle'	7.39	3.63
5098	'Clifford Castle'	5.46	6.64
5099	'Compton Castle'	5.46	2.63
7000	'Viscount Portal'	5.46	12.63
7001	'Denbigh Castle'	5.46	9.63
7002	'Devizes Castle'	6.46	3.64
7003	'Elmley Castle'	6.46	8.64
7004	'Eastnor Castle'	6.46	1.64
7005	'Lamphey Castle'	6.46	9.64
7006	'Lydford Castle'	6.46	12.63
7007	'Ogmore Castle'	7.46	2.63
7008	'Swansea Castle'	5.48	9.64
7009	'Athelney Castle'	5.48	3.63
7010	'Avondale Castle'	6.48	3.64
7011	'Banbury Castle'	6.48	2.65
7012	'Barry Castle'	6.48	11.64
7013	'Bristol Castle'	7.48	2.65
7014	'Caerhays Castle'	7.48	2.65
7015	'Carn Brea Castle'	7.48	4.63
7016	'Chester Castle'	8.48	11.62
7017	'G. J. Churchward'	8.48	2.63
7018	'Drysllwyn Castle'	5.49	9.63
7019	'Fowey Castle'	5.49	9.64
7020	'Gloucester Castle'	5.49	9.63
7021	'Haverfordwest Castle'	6.49	9.63
7022	'Hereford Castle'	6.49	6.65
7023	'Penrice Castle'	6.49	2.65
7024	'Powis Castle'	6.49	2.65
7025	'Sudeley Castle'	8.49	9.64

Table 12 Castle class locomotives—*cont.*

No.	Original name	Built	Withdrawn
7026	'Tenby Castle'	8.49	10.64
7027	'Thornbury Castle'	8.49	12.63
7028	'Cadbury Castle'	5.50	12.63
7029	'Clun Castle'	5.50	12.65
7030	'Cranbrook Castle'	6.50	2.63
7031	'Cromwell's Castle'	6.50	7.63
7032	'Denbigh Castle'	6.50	9.64
7033	'Hartlebury Castle'	7.50	1.63
7034	'Ince Castle'	8.50	6.65
7035	'Ogmore Castle'	8.50	8.64
7036	'Taunton Castle'	8.50	9.63
7037	'Swindon'	8.50	3.63
Conversions			
111	'Viscount Churchill'	9.24	7.53
4000	'North Star'	11.29	5.57
4009	'Shooting Star'	4.25	3.50
4016	'Knight of the Golden Fleece'	10.25	9.51
4032	'Queen Alexandra'	4.26	9.51
4037	'Queen Philippa'	6.26	9.62

Summary

Pre-war Castles	125
Post-war Castles	40
Conversions	6
Total	171

Table 13 The eight remaining Castle class locomotives

Number and name	Built	Cost £	Batch Lot no.	Total mileage	Withdrawn	Location
4073 'Caerphilly Castle'	8.23	6,841	1st lot 224	1,910,730	May 1960	Science Museum
4079 'Pendennis Castle'	2.24	6,841	1st lot 224	1,758,398	May 1964	GWS, Didcot
7029 'Clun Castle'	5.50	11,640	12th lot 375	618,073	Dec. 1965	Standard Gauge Steam Trust, Tyseley, Birmingham
5051 'Earl Bathurst' (being restored)	1936	5,800	6th lot 303	1,316,659	March 1963	GWS, Didcot
5029 'Nunney Castle'	5.34	5,971	5th lot 295	1,523,415	Dec. 1963	Barry S. Wales
5080 'Defiant'	5.39	6,344	7th lot 310	1,117,030	April 1963	Barry S. Wales
5043 'Earl of Mount Edgcumbe'	3.36	5,801	6th lot 303	1,400,817	Dec. 1963	Barry, S. Wales
7027 'Thornbury Castle'	8.49	10,793	11th lot 367	728,843	Dec. 1963	Barry, S. Wales

Summary

Museums	1
Operational	2
Restorations	5
Total	8

Table 14 The thirty King class locomotives

No.	Original name	Built	Withdrawn
6000	'King George V'	6.27	12.62
6001	'King Edward VII'	7.27	9.62
6002	'King William IV'	7.27	9.62
6003	'King George IV'	7.27	6.62
6004	'King George III'	7.27	6.62
6005	'King George II'	7.27	11.62
6006	'King George I'	2.28	2.62
6007	'King William III'	3.28	9.62 *
6008	'King James II'	3.28	6.62
6009	'King Charles II'	3.28	9.62
6010	'King Charles I'	4.28	6.62
6011	'King James I'	4.28	12.62
6012	'King Edward VI'	4.28	9.62
6013	'King Henry VIII'	5.28	6.62
6014	'King Henry VII'	5.28	9.62
6015	'King Richard III'	6.28	9.62
6016	'King Edward V'	6.28	9.62
6017	'King Edward IV'	6.28	7.62
6018	'King Henry VI'	6.28	12.62
6019	'King Henry V'	7.28	9.62
6020	'King Henry IV'	5.30	7.62
6021	'King Richard II'	6.30	9.62
6022	'King Edward III'	6.30	9.62
6023	'King Edward II'	6.30	6.62
6024	'King Edward I'	6.30	6.62
6025	'King Henry III'	7.30	12.62
6026	'King John'	7.30	9.62
6027	'King Richard I'	7.30	9.62
6028	'King Henry II' * *	7.30	11.62
6029	'King Stephen'†	8.30	7.62

* Nominally withdrawn on 5.3.36 and renewed on 24.3.36.
* * Renamed 'King George VI' in January 1937.
† Renamed 'King Edward VIII' in May 1936.

Table 15 The three remaining Kings

No.	Name	Year built	Cost £	Batch Lot no.	Mileage	Condemned
6000	'King George V'	June 1927	7,546	1st lot 234	1,910,424	Dec. 1962
6023	'King Edward II'	June 1930	7,182	2nd lot 267	1,554,201	June 1962
6024	'King Edward I'	June 1930	7,175	2nd lot 267	1,570.015	June 1962

Part Two

Railway Preservation

5 Dart Valley Railway

South Devon Railway saddle tank 'Ovid'

In the autumn of 1971 the Dart Valley Railway was hit by one of the constant hazards of railway preservation in being severed and lifted in part to make way for road improvements. The road was the A38 Exeter–Plymouth route and its diversion involved the $2\frac{3}{4}$ miles of line from Buckfastleigh to Ashburton. Quite apart from the loss of this stretch of line which reduced the length of the railway to seven miles, the engine shed at Ashburton was lost, together with workshops there and siding accommodation at Buckfastleigh. Far from allowing this blow to cripple their future, however, the management and membership of the Dart Valley Railway and its Association courageously placed a deposit on another stretch of line a little further down the Dart Valley from Kingswear to Paignton on Torbay. Thus the Dart Valley Railway may eventually operate two lines but if it is decided to cease working the present section then there will be an alternative line on which to consolidate activities. The Paignton–Kingswear line has most of the attractions of the Dart Valley and possibly a few advantages of its own. At present, however, this may be no more than a footnote in the Railway's history.

The Dart Valley Railway is a branch line running from the main line at Totnes for nine meandering miles northwards beside or close to the River Dart to Ashburton. It was the northern terminus which dominated the branch's origins. From the middle ages until the middle of the nineteenth century Ashburton had an importance, founded on the wool industry and tin mining on Dartmoor, of which the town shows little trace today. It was, indeed, like other towns prominent in this book—Bewdley, Pickering or Tenterden, for example—which, having been by-passed by the first wave of railway building, were largely passed by in the ensuing revolution. Thus the South Devon Railway reached Plymouth from Newton Abbot by way of Totnes in 1849 and Ashburton retained enough importance and inherited self-confidence to plan a connection with it immediately. Newton Abbot, seven miles east of Ashburton, had had a railway since 1846 and the earliest plans were thus aimed, over very difficult country, in this direction. An Act for building such a link, 10½ miles long, was passed in 1846 and the line's engineer, Brunel, estimated, as always optimistically, that it would cost £103,500 to build. But this company was a true child of the 'mania' and financial and managerial crises led it inexorably towards dissolution in 1851.

Remarkably enough, the next scheme proposed did not in the first place include Ashburton. The Buckfastleigh, Totnes & South Devon Railway was an altogether less ambitious project than its predecessor and was planned to meet the main line at Totnes, by way of the valley of the River Dart, which would present few engineering or construction problems. The company was incorporated in July 1864, the provisions specifically prohibiting the use of atmospheric propulsion which Brunel had tried with disastrous consequences on the South Devon line in 1847–8, and with a short branch to the 'Plains', the town quay at Totnes, and the head of the River Dart navigation. The extension of the line north to Ashburton was authorised in 1865 and building of the broad gauge line began in August that year. The Totnes–Buckfastleigh section was finished within three years but the opening awaited the completion of the whole and did not take place until 1 May 1872.

The new branch was worked by the South Devon Railway until it amalgamated with the Great Western in 1897. Neither company pampered passengers to Staverton, Buckfastleigh or Ashburton with the quality of their rolling stock and locomotives, at any rate until the conversion of gauge on 21–23 May 1892. Thereafter much of the stock, for obvious reasons, was new. 0-4-2Ts of the 517 class were the mainstay of the motive power and both rail motor cars and trailer coaches were tried on the line early on. The latter were ideally suited to the passenger requirements of the line and so the railway entered the hazardous post-war years with stock that was new in both make and design. The 517 class remained at work throughout the twenties until their planned successors, the 14XX (originally 48XX) class, began to take over. Freight traffic was always based on the traditional local industries, wool and agriculture. Mining no longer played any part at all. Had it done so, the railway's place as a carrier of freight might have been less rapidly superseded by road transport. As it was, passenger services were withdrawn from 3 November 1958 and freight from 10 September 1962.

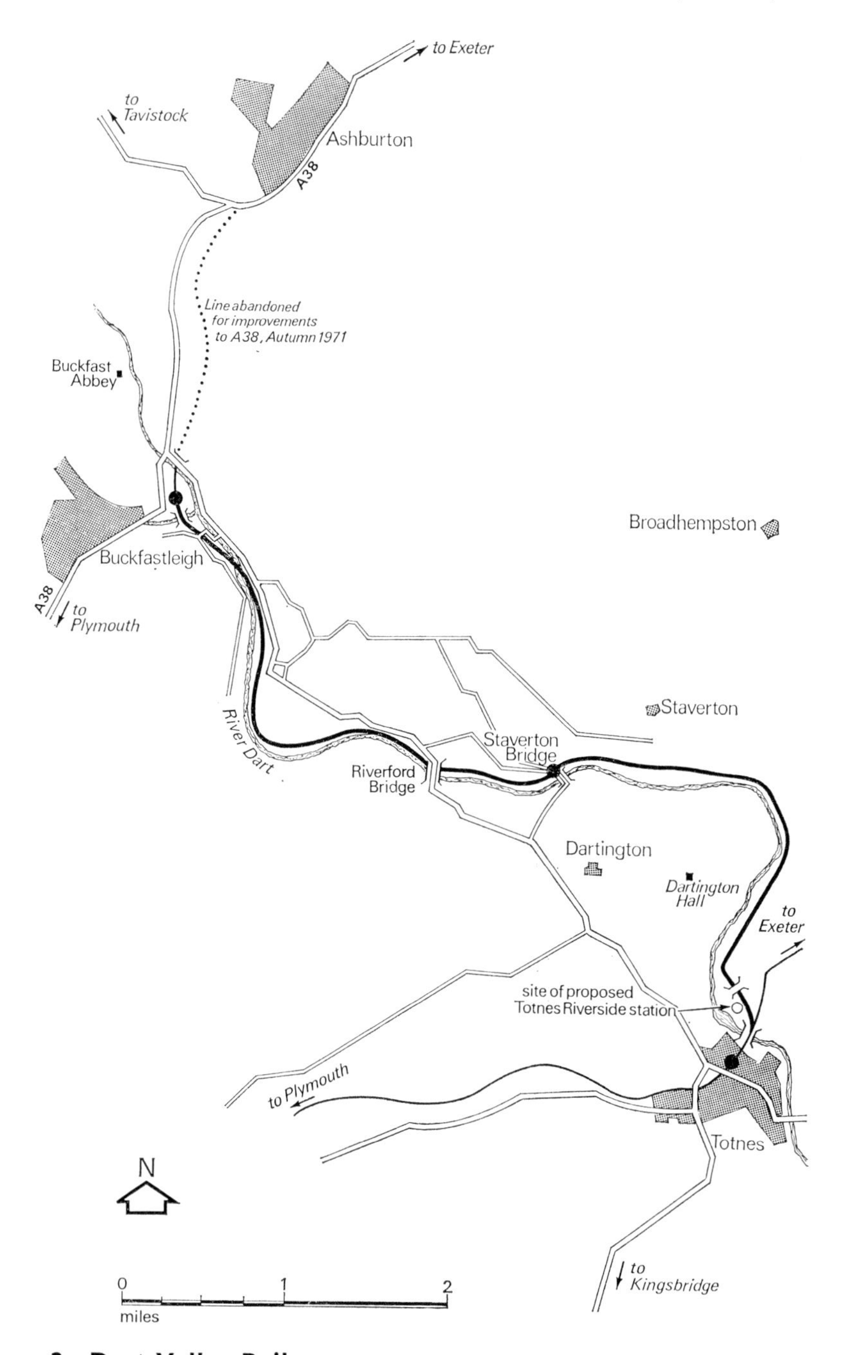

2 Dart Valley Railway

Plans to reopen the line had been made before the final closure. The preservation body, the Dart Valley Light Railway Ltd, was a commercial venture from the start, although always enjoying active volunteer support. This was just as well because it was to be seven years before the line was fully operational again and it is unlikely that a commercial venture alone, even one with a board composed of distinguished and expert enthusiasts, would have sustained an inoperable railway and a station yard full of what looked like scrap for so long. The line suffered from the usual vandalism and like others closed by stages for passengers and freight, it had no signalling system, which was to be cumbersome and difficult to replace. Two other problems are more peculiar to the Dart Valley line. As a South Devon Railway, Great Western and BR branch, the line was never provided with a bay in Totnes station. Since BR ceased to work the line it has been officially severed but trains could obviously not be allowed to negotiate the main line in any case. The preservers have responded with characteristic enterprise and plan to build their own platform and loop at the beginning of the branch in Totnes just north of the River Dart and Ashburton junction. The other long-term problem which the preservation body has had to face from the start was the development of the A38 road already mentioned and services have never been run on the Buckfastleigh–Ashburton section.

The line was ready for opening to the public on a limited scale in 1967 and its excellent prospects immediately became apparent. 14,000 visitors were recorded in 1967 and 35,000 the following year, both before the grant of the second Light Railway Order and the inauguration of a full public service in 1969. This began at Easter that year followed by a ceremonial reopening by Lord Beeching on 21 May. For motive power, the company has made excellent use of the traditional 'push and pull' trains which have been indispensable with neither loop nor turn-round facilities available at Totnes. Careful attention has been given throughout the collection of locomotives to their suitability for work on the line. Curiosity value and other considerations have been secondary and the result is a most satisfying and authentic re-creation of a GWR branch line. With the exception of the Peckett 0-4-0ST from Exeter Gas Works, all the locomotives are Swindon-built and with two exceptions all were turned out under GWR auspices.

One of the BR engines is the most recent arrival on the line, 4-6-0 no. 7827, 'Lydham Manor', built in 1950 and originally painted in the nationalised authority's mixed traffic black, but painted in lined green half way through her sixteen-year career in revenue-earning service. 'Lydham Manor' was allocated successively to Oswestry, Machynlleth and Shrewsbury until being withdrawn in June 1966. She was at Barry for four years, part of the time undergoing preliminary restoration, prior to removal to the Dart Valley in the summer of 1970. The other BR engine on the line is a Hawksworth 0-6-0PT no. 1638, built in 1951, although like the 'Manor' this is, of course, a pure Great Western design. No. 1638 was acquired for preservation from Croes Newydd in good working order, repainted at Tyseley and travelled to Buckfastleigh in steam in November 1967.

There are four other 0-6-0 pannier tanks on the line, all designed by Collett and built in the thirties. No. 1369 was built in 1934, one of a class of six designed with a short wheelbase especially for work at Weymouth Docks. No. 1369 also worked at Swindon and Reading, and was withdrawn from Wadebridge in 1964, when she was the last steam locomotive at work for BR in Cornwall. The other three panniers, nos. 6412, 6430 and 6435, belong to a class which was specially adapted for auto-train working. They are thus ideally suited for their duties on the Dart Valley line and have often been worked between two pairs of auto-coaches. The volume of traffic also ensures that there is plenty of work for the Railway's two most powerful working engines. These are 2-6-2 prairie tanks nos. 4555 and 4588. The former is an old Dart Valley locomotive, which worked on the line in the last days of BR's freight service, including the very last train in November 1962. The very agreeable 14XX (originally 48XX) class 0-4-2Ts nos. 1420 and 1450 also have long Dart Valley connections. It was this class, much criticised for its antique appearance when it was first put into service in 1932, in spite of the modern mechanical excellence within, which succeeded the 517 class which had been the mainstay of passenger work on the branch from the days of the conversion of gauge. Both these engines, built in 1933 and 1935 respectively, worked throughout the Great Western system. For auto-train work their limit was normally two trailers, so they have been hard pressed to meet peak summer requirements on the Dart Valley line.

The present Dart Valley Railway is one of the most prosperous of its kind. It has an excellent collection of rolling stock and locomotives and

Table 16 Steam locomotives on the Dart Valley Railway

Type	Number/name	Where built	Year	Origin
0-4-0ST	—	Peckett	1942	Exeter Gas Works
0-6-0PT	1369	Swindon (Collett)	1934	GWR
0-4-2T	1420	Swindon (Collett)	1933	GWR
0-4-2T	1450	Swindon (Collett)	1935	GWR
0-6-0PT	1638	Swindon (Hawksworth)	1951	BR
2-6-2T	4555	Swindon (Churchward)	1924	GWR
2-6-2T	4588	Swindon (Churchward)	1924	GWR
0-6-0PT	6412	Swindon (Collett)	1934	GWR
0-6-0PT	6430	Swindon (Collett)	1937	GWR
0-6-0PT	6435	Swindon (Collett)	1937	GWR
4-6-0	7827 'Lydham Manor'	Swindon (Collett-class)	1950	BR

enjoys all the benefits of being in one of the leading tourist areas in the country. The last point is equally true of the nearby Paignton–Kingswear line. Unlike the Totnes–Ashburton branch, this will be run as a service to the community as well as an attraction for tourists and steam enthuiasts. For these reasons, although the line received no subsidy in BR days, it may eventually be supported by the Devonshire County Council. The 6½-mile line is in excellent condition, having been inherited direct from BR but there is much to be done on it in connection with the maintenance and refurbishment of stations, signalling and other facilities and equipment. Finally, the line has an advantage which is becoming ever more substantial among steam operated lines in being able to accept the heaviest locomotives. Unlike the Totnes–Ashburton branch it could be in a position to accept some of the growing number of large GWR locomotives restored to working order, beautifully maintained but imprisoned by circumstances on no more than a few yards of siding.

Whether or not the Dart Valley Railway expands to become the first preservation body to operate two separate lines or whether activities are consolidated on one or other of them, it is a unique venture and by example has done much to set the high standards emulated by other railways.

6 West Somerset Railway

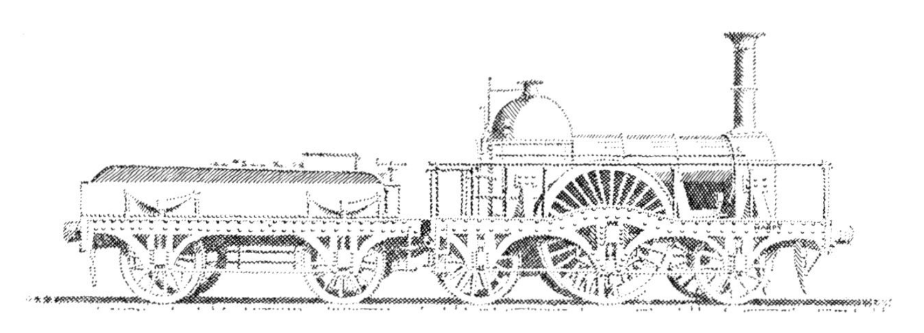

Gooch broad gauge Firefly class locomotive 'Harpy'

Of all the private standard gauge railway ventures in Britain the Taunton–Minehead line of the West Somerset Railway is the only one which is specifically and primarily a passenger-carrying public-service venture. At twenty-five miles, it will also be the longest.

The first West Somerset Railway was opened in 1862, initially between Taunton and Watchet harbour. By post-'mania' branch-line standards the railway was built quickly. The West Somerset Railway Co., incorporated in 1857, was promoted by local landowners under the chairmanship of Sir Peregrine Acland. The authorised capital of £160,000 was not readily available and the first sod was not cut until 10 April 1859. Brunel had been engaged as engineer in 1857 but was personally able to accomplish very little of the work, which was mostly done by R. P. Brereton, his assistant of many years' standing. On completion in March 1862, the 14½ miles of broad gauge single track was leased in perpetuity to the Bristol & Exeter Railway. Passenger traffic began on 31 March that year but goods services were delayed until August because the necessary facilities had not been finished on time. The journey from Taunton to Watchet took fifty minutes and the intermediate stations at Bishop's Lydeard, Crowcombe (known as Heathfield station until 1889), Stogumber and Williton were served by four trains a day in each direction. A further station, at Norton Fitzwarren, two miles from Taunton where the railway branched north-west from the Bristol & Exeter main line, was opened in 1873.

In the early years traffic on the line grew and it became evident that this growth would be encouraged and sustained if the line was extended west along the coast to Minehead. Business would be gained not only from the area in between but the line would establish a sound link with places like Lynton (not, of course, served at this date by its celebrated narrow gauge line to Barnstaple) and Porlock which were isolated by Exmoor on the one hand and the precipitous Somerset coast on the other. The first move for a railway to Minehead was made by the West Somerset Mineral Railway whose Act of 1857 authorised the construction of a $6\frac{3}{4}$-mile line from near their Washford station to Minehead Harbour, it being envisaged that the harbour at Watchet would soon become too small to handle all the ore traffic. In the event, Watchet Harbour was enlarged and the Minehead branch dropped. The following year (1871) the company was reconstituted under the same name by Act of Parliament and this time work got under way, albeit slowly, and the line was ready for traffic in July 1874. The Bristol & Exeter took a lease on it at a rent of half the net receipts and a guaranteed minimum of £2,000.

Although the Minehead Railway Co. did not finally lose its identity until 1897, the operating company, the Bristol & Exeter, amalgamated with the GWR in 1876, two years after the new branch was opened. In February that year Minehead was visited by a delegation of Great Western dignitaries, including the chairman, Sir Daniel Gooch, who, according to the *West Somerset Free Press*, was impressed by the railway, the town and the surrounding country. The West Somerset Railway Co. retained its independence until 1921.

By branch line standards the West Somerset Railway as a whole was a great commercial success. Nevertheless, there were loud and successful local protests when the GWR attempted to economise in any respect on operations, particularly on the Minehead extension. The local gentry pointed out that the line had been built largely on their money and that they were entitled to more than minimal services in return. Two individuals, Sir Alexander Hood and Sir Peregrine Acland, the chairman of the 1857 company, had between them put up £70,000 for the Minehead branch as a service to the community. Such sums, equivalent perhaps to £350,000 in current money values, would solve most problems of railway preservation and must make all who have had any experience of promoting a light railway, from Totnes to Boat of Garten, regret the decline of private wealth.

The Minehead extension ran parallel to the West Somerset Mineral Railway from Watchet to Washford. The Mineral Railway was always an entirely separate enterprise and the two companies maintained competing stations in the two places which they both served. At Washford, the two lines turned sharply north and south respectively and the Mineral line ran down to Roadwater and Combe Row in the Brendon

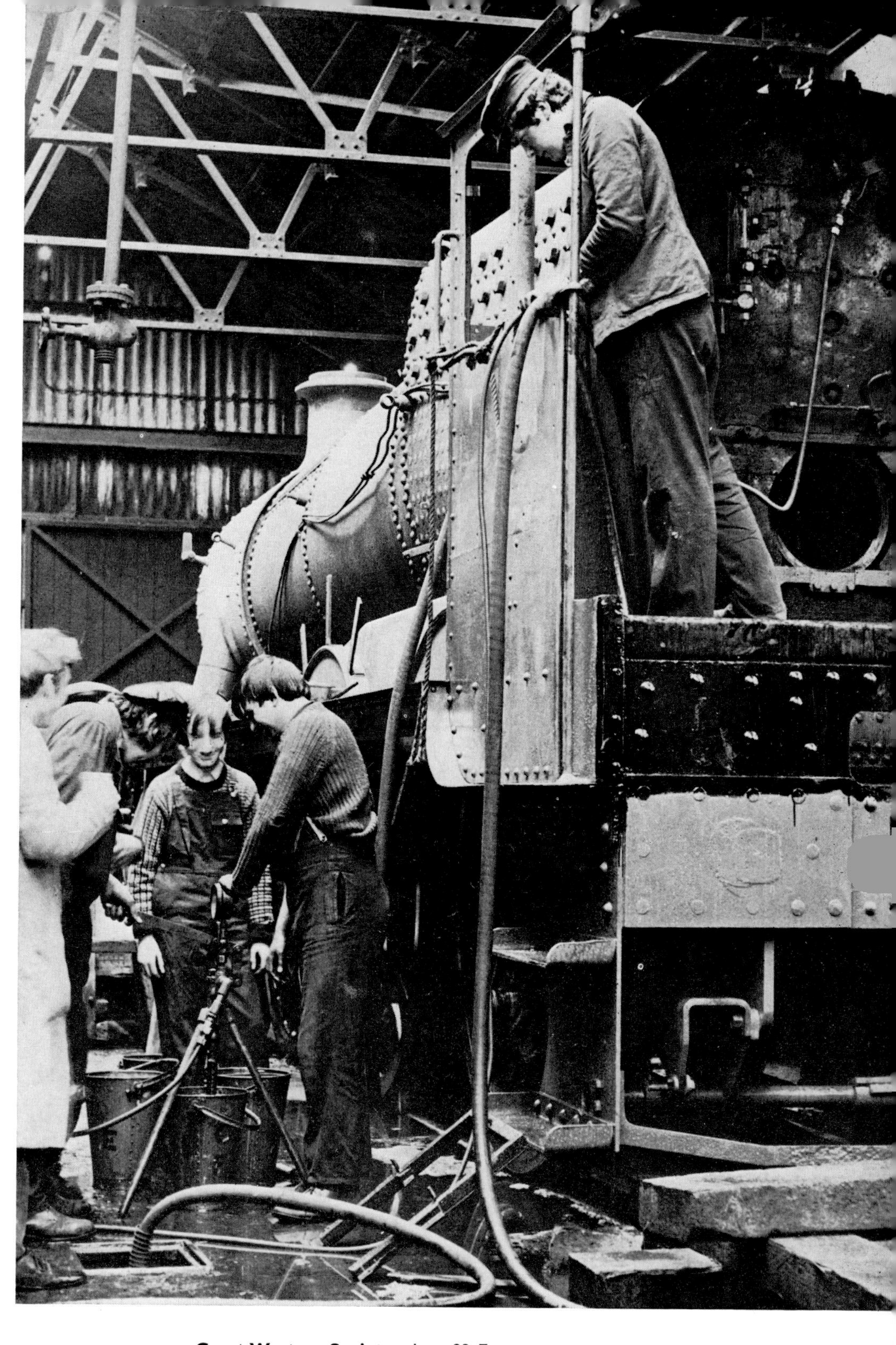

Great Western Society, plates 23–7

23 No. 6998, 'Burton Agnes Hall', undergoing a hydraulic test at Didcot

24 (above) Line-up at Didcot, Septemper 1971, *left to right*: no. 7808, 'Cookham Manor'; 0-4-2T, no. 1466; 2-6-2T, no. 6106; and 0-6-2T, no. 6697

25 (below) 0-6-0ST, no. 1363, at Bodmin. Built at Swindon in 1910 no. 1363 is one of a special class of saddle tanks (nos 1361–5) for work over very sharp curves in Cornish china clay pits. They were all shedded at St Blazey

26 0-4-2T, no. 1466, at Abingdon Open Day, May 1970

27 (above) Victor of the 1925 locomotive exchanges, no. 4079, 'Pendennis Castle'

Quainton Railway Society, plates 28–30

28 (below) Three of the five locomotives which were in steam at Quainton on Open Days in August 1971. *Left to right:* ex-GWR and London Transport 0-6-0PT, no. 7715/L99, ex-LSWR 2-4-0WT, no. 314 (BR no. 30585), and Cunarder Hunslet 0-6-OST, no. 1690

29 (opposite above) No. 30585 after a trip along the siding

30 (opposite below) Hudswell Clarke 0-6-0T, 'Sir Thomas', in steam

30585

No 1
SIR THOMAS

4983

5428

Standard Gauge Steam Trust, plates 31–7

31 (opposite above) No. 4983, 'Albert Hall', at Swindon after an overhaul for BR in October 1956

32 (opposite below) Self portrait: Stanier 'Black 5', no. 5428, 'Eric Treacy', photographed by the Bishop of Wakefield

33 (above) Jubilee class no. 5593, 'Kolhapur', being fitted with a new top half to her smoke box in the winter of 1967–8 by a team directed by the Trust's chief engineer, Mr A. J. Kent

34 (below) LSWR T9 class, 4-4-0, no. 120, built Nine Elms 1899, with Pullman cars Ibis, Ione and no. 54. Note the eight-wheeled tender and characteristic Eastleigh smokestack

35 A throng of enthusiasts at Barbican station to see the last train to run on London Transport metals, 6 June 1971. No. 544's sister engine, L95, is now on the Severn Valley Railway

36 (above) GNR saddle tank, no. 1247, built in 1899, restored to her original condition and livery

37 (below) Maunsell's Southern Railway 4-4-0 Schools class, no. 925, 'Cheltenham'. No. 928, 'Stowe', is preserved at the Montague Motor Museum, Beaulieu Abbey, Hampshire

Steamtown, Carnforth, plates 38–41

38 (above) Ivatt 2 MT 2-6-0, no. 6441 (BR no. 46441), now restored to LMS maroon livery, was Steamtown's first acquisition

39 (below) Ex-LNER 4-6-0, no. 1306, 'Mayflower', built by the North British Locomotive Co. in 1948, owned by the BI Locomotive Society, after the naming ceremony at Steamtown in May 1971. The locomotive bears the 'Yorkshire Pullman' headboard. In the background visitors can be seen taking rides on no. 44871. Over her dome can be seen signs announcing electrification of the west coast main line to Glasgow

40 (above) Stanier class 5 4-6-0, no. 44871, was one of the locomotives used to haul BR's last steam-hauled train on 11 August 1968. Sir William Stanier, FRS, built 842 'Black 5s' of which eleven have been preserved

41 (below) Steamtown's 70ft turntable can only just accommodate ex-SNCF Pacific no. 231 K22

Worcester Locomotive Society and Bulmer's Private Railway, plates 42–4

42 (above) Ex-GWR 0-6-0T, no. 5786, the finest of her class

43 (opposite above) The author, President of the Worcester Locomotive Society, naming Kitson 0-6-0ST, 'Carnarvon', at an Open Day on 19 September 1971 attended by more than two thousand people. On the footplate are Mr David Wood (left), Chairman of the Society, and Mr Howard Griffiths, driver

44 (opposite below) The Society's two locomotives, no. 5786 (left) and 'Carnarvon' (centre), with 'King George V' on Bulmer's Private Railway

5786
6000

1470
G N R

Nº 4498

Gresley Pacifics, plates 45–50

45 (opposite above) The first of Sir Nigel Gresley's Pacifics: GNR no. 1470 (LNER no. 4470), 'Great Northern', as illustrated in the *Railway Magazine* in 1922, later rebuilt to Thompson class AI/I

46 (opposite centre) Unnamed AI no. 4474 (later 'Victor Wild') leaving Paddington during the 1925 locomotive exchanges

47 (opposite below) 'Sir Nigel Gresley' rescued and restored to LNER no. 4498

48 (above) A4 no. 4496, 'Golden Shuttle', at Potters Bar with the up 'West Riding Limited'. This locomotive was renamed 'Dwight D. Eisenhower' in September 1945 and withdrawn in July 1963 for preservation at the USA National Railroad Museum, Green Bay, Wisconsin

49 (below) 'Dwight D. Eisenhower' on route to her American home

50 Peppercorn A2 BR no. 60532, 'Blue Peter', as preserved by Geoffrey Drury at Neville Hill MPD, Leeds.
Now located at the Great Western Society, Didcot

Hills. It had been completed in 1859 to carry iron ore mined in the Brendon Hills to Watchet Harbour for shipment to South Wales. Passenger traffic was entirely secondary and did not begin at all until 1865. The line's prosperity, being wholly dependent on the demand for ore, was spasmodic and led to its closure in 1898. A revival, for industrial use only, in 1907, lasted less than three years and thereafter the line was used only for some automatic brake trials in 1911 before being lifted. However, the Mineral Railway has two distinctive claims to fame. The first is the 1 in 4 cable-operated Brendon Hill incline and the second is the fact that one of the very few head-on collisions ever to occur on a British railway took place on the line. It was near Washford and happened while the railway was being completed in August 1857. Head-on collisions were uncommon in this country largely because of the Board of Trade's vigilance over operating rules on single track railways. The cause of the Washford accident was no more complicated than the refusal of the engineer in charge of construction to observe a direction to wait.

The Taunton–Minehead line was in no way a natural victim for BR rationalisation but by the middle 1960s the grant required to maintain it was such that the situation was reappraised. The total annual cost of the line, it emerged, was £183,000, less £42,000 in earnings, leaving a grant required of £141,000. This British Railways decided was too much and the closure procedure began. The South Western Area Transport Users Consultative Committee set to work to prepare a reply and after digesting written representations and oral evidence at a public hearing at Minehead on 28 November 1968, reported that the closure of the branch would cause unreasonable hardship and would create difficulties with which alternative methods of transport were quite unequipped to cope. It was argued in particular that the flow of holidaymakers to the west Somerset coast would be impeded and that the line was very heavily used by such visitors travelling to and from the Butlin's Holiday Camp at Minehead. Such tourist traffic boosted the weekly average of 4,850 passengers on the line to as much as 5,000 per day in peak summer periods. Butlin's have been good allies of the West Somerset preservationists, as indeed they are of locomotive and railway enthusiasts in general, with several large exhibits on their premises throughout the country. They have donated £10,000 to the Taunton–Minehead line venture.

Further representations were conveyed to the Ministry, including a petition containing 5,000 signatures, presented by Mr Tom King, then newly-elected MP for Bridgwater, in March 1970. The official reaction, preceding consent to the closure of the branch, accepted the 'hardship' arguments as far as summer traffic was concerned but asserted that the railway was not irreplaceable in that role and was in any case rapidly being superseded. There was no justification for the £141,000 grant required to maintain the line and closure should go ahead. Actual closure did not, however, follow immediately. The additional bus services which the Ministry had stipulated as the prerequisite of closure took time to arrange but after a year's delay the last BR train ran on 2 January 1971.

The West Somerset Railway runs through an area of great and fully recognised natural beauty, first between the Quantocks and the Brendon Hills and then along, or near, the west Somerset coast. The line begins in the county town and runs out of Taunton parallel to the Western Region main line for about two miles to Norton Fitzwarren where it branches north-west towards the large village of Bishop's Lydeard. Thereafter the railway meanders through the beguiling countryside to Combe Florey and Crowcombe, where it joins the course of the little river Doniford and proceeds through Stogumber, Bicknoller, and Sampford Brett to Williton. A little beyond Williton, it emerges on to the cliff top and runs on into Watchet, which is the only real centre of industry on the line apart from Taunton itself and is still a busy port, serving the nearby paper mills with Scandinavian timber. To Washford the line runs alongside what remains of the West Somerset Mineral Railway which was closed and lifted sixty years ago. At Washford it turns sharply north into the very popular tourist area around Blue Anchor, Dunster and Minehead.

It is unlikely that any commercial company could run the railway only on tourist and local passenger traffic any more than BR could. It is equally improbable that so long a line could be run solely as an enthusiasts' light railway. The bright prospects for the West Somerset Railway lie in the exceptional possibilities for combining the two: serving a real, if seasonal, transport requirement with the intrinsic attractions of steam locomotion. The closure of the line, as has already been noted, aroused strong feeling locally, so strong, indeed, that it was the Somerset County Council which took the initiative in organising a public meeting for the expression and formulation of opinion on the matter. This took place in the Shire Hall at Taunton in February 1971 and set up a working party to consider the possibility of reopening and operating the line privately.

The problems fall into two categories: financial and operational. Among the latter is the fact that the viability of the scheme will depend on BR's willingness to allow trains to be run into Taunton station and whether the difficulties which such an arrangement will create can be permanently overcome. Another problem arises from the basic nature of the West Somerset Railway project. The line is much longer than any that other railways have attempted to work and twice the length of any that has so far been operated successfully. At the same time, the project cannot depend on a group of active supporters for practical help to quite the extent that other organisations are able to do which began as nothing more than groups of train spotters wishing to play trains. Here again it will be interesting to see whether the West Somerset Railway's unique composition can meet the challenge.

On the financial side, the early experiencecs of the railway have been encouraging. The £25,000 deposit on the line required before serious negotiations could begin was raised comparatively easily, although with a certain amount of large-scale support such as the contribution from Butlin's already mentioned. BR have asked £276,000 for the line. Such a figure may seem high when, commercially, it is no more than the first stage in the arduous process of sweating an income out of the line from passenger-carrying services. But the longer the line, the greater the incidental assets accruing from it will be. Such assets, most notably the surplus land which is a feature of the railway system as a whole and of branch lines in particular, transform the complexion of all comparable investments. In contemporary circumstances, property companies are very popular.

By reason of its size alone the West Somerset Railway faces every hazard known to railway preservationists but if it succeeds the rewards will be correspondingly great. With its dedicated and expert leadership the Railway should prosper and by doing so it will be an example to all other privately owned lines and will add a new and more grandiose aspect to the industry.

7 Kent & East Sussex Railway

Stroudley 'Terrier'

By the last quarter of the nineteenth century the South Eastern Railway's lines to the coast of England at Hastings, Folkestone and Dover were among some of the most prosperous in the country. The ever-tighter labyrinth of branch routes between these main lines was equally well established. Yet the South Eastern, dividing at Tonbridge, left much of the Weald untouched and with it such established and prosperous towns as Tenterden. Even the Light Railways Act 1896 framed specifically to stimulate and assist the construction of railways in commercially implausible areas produced no attempt by a major company to penetrate further south across country than the Tonbridge–Ashford line.

The Rother Valley (Light) Railway, which sprang up soon after the passage of the Act, was a predominantly local body. Under the new, streamlined procedure, application was made to the Board of Trade to construct a light railway from the South Eastern & Chatham (as it was about to become) main line at Robertsbridge, to the foot of Tenterden Hill, twelve miles east along the Rother Valley. The system as projected at this stage was to be quite extensive, with far-flung branches to Rye from Northiam, to Cranbrook from Tenterden and eventually by way of Headcorn, up the Sutton Valence escarpment to Maidstone. The first accomplished extension, three years after the opening in April 1900, was more modest and carried the railway one and a half miles beyond its first eastern terminus (the present Rolvenden station) to Tenterden Town station. In 1905 a far bigger step took the line north to Headcorn on the Tonbridge–Ashford main line, within striking distance of Maidstone, and the name of the enterprise was enlarged to the Kent & East Sussex (Light) Railway.

The engineer of the line had been Lt.-Col. Holman F. Stephens who nursed and nurtured it as general manager, and subsequently managing director, until his death in 1931. Like many of the other branches and light railways which he controlled, the Kent & East Sussex became wholly dependent upon his genius and guidance as much for money as for technical and managerial leadership. Colonel Stephens was very enthusiastic about the Maidstone extension and even ordered a locomotive specially for the gradient which would be involved on any completed line. 'Hecate', as the Hawthorn Leslie 0-8-0T was called, was quite unsuitable, and untypical of the locomotive stock as a whole and performed very little useful service beyond a weekly run from the railway's shed at Rolvenden (it was completely unusable further west) and Headcorn during the twenty-eight years before it passed into Southern Railway hands. After Stephens's death the line fell into the grip of the Depression but was fortunate in finding a new saviour in the Official Receiver, W. H. Austen, who sustained its independence for some years although the SR had to be asked to help out with locomotives later in the thirties.

During World War II the geographical location of the line gave it great strategic importance. Much of the equipment connected with Operation PLUTO was siphoned down it on route for Littlestone-on-Sea (see chapter 35). As an agricultural area also the line acquired a completely new stature and the Ministry of Food established a depot right beside Tenterden Town station. After the war, however, the line relapsed. Its basic character as an unprofitable branch line shone through and BR withdrew passenger services throughout in January 1954. This early closure put the long-term future of the freight services in doubt as well and the end of these came in June 1961.

The formation of the Kent & East Sussex Railway Preservation Society accompanied the withdrawal of freight traffic and Tenterden Town station was rented from BR as its headquarters almost immediately. The Society was quick to think in terms of working part of the line but by this time (1962) BR had already formulated their policy towards such redundant but preservable lines and the prospect of leasing the line had to be abandoned for the formidable problems of outright purchase. For a while this and other difficulties seemed to kill all hope of reviving the line but they have been reconciled over the years and the present section of operational line between Rolvenden and Tenterden Town seems likely to be successfully extended to Bodiam in due course.

The railway has a good collection of serviceable and characteristic locomotives, most of which are kept at Rolvenden (see Table 17).

Table 17 Steam locomotives on the Kent & East Sussex Railway

Type	Number/Name	Where built	Year	Origin
0-6-0T	3 'Bodiam'	Brighton	1872	LB&SCR, K&ESR, & BR (no. 32670)
0-6-0T	50 'Sutton'	Brighton	1876	LB&SCR, & BR (no. 32650)
0-4-0TVB	10 'Gervase'	Manning Wardle	1900	Standard Brick Co., Surrey
4wTGVB	11 'Dom'	Sentinel	1927	Eastern Railway, Jersey
0-4-0T	12 'Marcia'	Peckett	1923	Hardman & Holden, Manchester
0-6-0ST	14 'Charwelton'	Manning Wardle	1955	Sproxton Quarry, Leicestershire.
0-6-0ST	15 'Hastings'	Hunslet	1888	Sproxton Quarry, Leicestershire
0-6-0ST	17 'Arthur'	Manning Wardle	1903	Portland Cement, Stone, Staffs.
0-6-0T	21 'Wainwright'	Vulcan, Wilkes Barre, USA	1943	US Army, SR & BR (no. 30070)
0-6-0T	22 'Maunsell'	Vulcan, Wilkes Barre, USA	1943	US Army, SR & BR (no. 30065)
0-6-0ST	'Minnie'	Fox Walker	1878	Skinningrove Iron Co. Yorkshire
0-6-0ST	'Met'	Hawthorn Leslie	1909	CEGB Bow, London
0-6-0T	'Pride of Sussex'	Ashford	1909	SE&CR, & BR (no. 31556)
0-6-0ST	5 'Westminster'	Peckett	1914	Portland Cement, Shipton-on-Cherwell
0-6-0ST	196 'Errol Lonsdale'	Hunslet	1953	Longmoor Military Railway
0-6-0ST	91	Hunslet	1953	Longmoor Military Railway
0-6-0ST	95	Hunslet	1953	Longmoor Military Railway
2-6-0	376	Nydquist & Holm, Norway	1919	Norwegian State Railways

'Bodiam' and 'Sutton' are Stroudly Terriers like those bought from the London, Brighton & South Coast Railway in 1901 and 1905. 'Bodiam', indeed, is one of these very engines and was no. 70, 'Poplar', in LB&SCR days.

The Kent & East Sussex line was typical of many light railways in that its stations tended to be remote from anywhere, let alone the settlements after which they were named. Thus the original terminus at Rolvenden was in fact rather nearer to Tenterden, though not very near to either, and the railway management was well ahead of its time in seeing the need to supplement the trains by 'bus services. Right from the start, in 1900, a horse bus carried passengers from the station at the foot of Tenterden Hill up to the town centre. This bus is now in the Museum of British Transport at Clapham. Part of the reason why the line stopped short of Tenterden was the gradient that was involved in getting any nearer and until the arrival of the LB&SCR 'Terriers', the railway had no locomotive which would have been capable of negotiating it. This, of course, was part of the paradox of the theory of light railways in so far as they were often built with curves and gradients which required far heavier locomotives than limitations on the line would allow. 'Hecate' was a working monument to this fact for many years on the K&ESR. The Terriers filled the gap very successfully and the K&ESR's second acquisition from the LB&SCR, no. 697, 'Wapping', was bought to work the Tenterden–Headcorn extension in 1905.

Why should the Kent & East Sussex Railway, or part of it, be preserved? There are limits to which this is now possible at both ends of the line. The track from just north of Tenterden has been lifted and in part built on and at the other end, the railway cannot run into Robertsbridge BR station, its old terminus, because this would involve manning level crossings on main roads. What remains, and in particular the Tenterden–Bodiam section of the line, is both highly suitable for preservation and will open up in a quite unobtrusive and traditional way an idyllic tract of country of the sort which roads and motor cars usually manage first to ravage and then to by-pass. From the historical point of view the line should be preserved as an example of a light railway built under the 1896 Act and as the last of the many once owned by Colonel Stephens.

8 Bluebell Railway

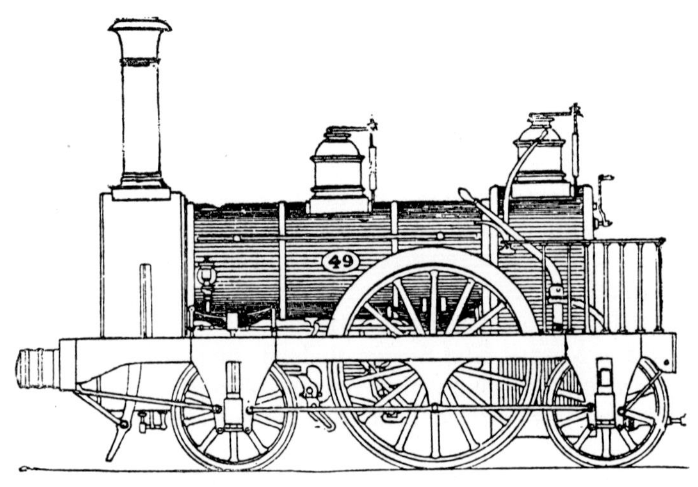

London and Brighton Railway: Gray's prototype of 'Jenny Lind'

In the period of consolidation which followed the 'mania' the London, Brighton & South Coast and the South Eastern railways were locked in conflict over exploiting the great traffic potential of mid-Sussex between their established main lines to Brighton and Eastbourne respectively. A crop of locally promoted schemes came and went, sown in the heat of speculation by the major companies and frosted by local apathy and lack of money. Such was almost the fate of the Lewes, East Grinstead & London Railway Co., which was planned and supported by a group of local landowners under the chairmanship of the Earl of Sheffield to run north and south of East Grinstead to the LB&SCR main line at Copyhold Farm, just north of Haywards Heath. The LB&SCR, by adopting the proposed line in 1877, seized this scheme as an opportunity to push the SER's territory firmly to the east. Thereafter, all plans and applications in respect of the northern section of the line were encouraged to lapse and the railway took shape as a feeder for the LB&SCR.

Building was soon under way, making full use of the ground work and planning already done for the Lewes, East Grinstead & London Railway, under the supervision of J. Wolfe-Barry and the contractor, Joseph Firbank. There was the usual branch line indecision about whether to build a single or double track, resolved by the equally normal compromise, south of Horsted Keynes, of laying a single line on works substantial enough to take a second should one ever be necessitated by the volume of traffic. Although built less than twenty years before the Light

Railway Act, the construction of the line in no way anticipated it and the Board of Trade inspector, Colonel Yolland, was impressed with all that he saw when the line was inspected prior to opening. The LB&SCR was always generous with its stations and the new limb of the system was to be no exception, reflecting not only the tastes of the age at their best and most substantial but also the standing of many of the passengers using them, and even more that it was mainly their money which had paid for them. Provision for goods traffic, which it was anticipated would be the principal revenue earner, was also first class. These two factors, together with the fragmented character of most of the villages and other settlements in the area, meant that many of the stations on the line, although built near a road, were otherwise isolated. The headquarters of the present Bluebell Railway Preservation Society at Sheffield Park station is a surviving example.

The line opened on 1 August 1882 when the Lewes & East Grinstead Railway Co., though not legally dissolved until 1884, surrendered all control to the LB&SCR. The opening of the link with the main line at Copyhold Junction followed on 3 September 1883. From the first the railway prospered. At the time of the opening the service from Brighton to East Grinstead ran via Lewes, with five trains a day in each direction and three on Sundays during the summer. Once the Ardingly branch was open a service ran via Copyhold junction and Haywards Heath in addition to the trains through Lewes. The timetables continued unco-ordinated until 1884 when the Lewes line lost some of its prestige as a through route to London, although it continued to be worked by up to six trains a day in each direction until the turn of the century. In 1909 the LB&SCR introduced motor trains, consisting of a Terrier and a Marsh Balloon coach, on the line with very satisfactory results. Indeed, the Lewes–Sheffield Park line was ideal for such trains and after the grouping the Southern Railway used them extensively.

Locomotives on the line in these early years included Stroudley's D class 0-4-2Ts, introduced in 1873 and used throughout the LB&SCR for light passenger work, and also Stroudley's 0-4-2 Gladstone engines with their 6ft 6in. driving wheels, which had entered service the year the line opened, 1882. The older Craven 2-2-2s were also used on goods trains. Goods traffic on the line, apart from general commodities, consisted mainly of timber, cattle and milk. Milk traffic at Sheffield Park was so heavy that the Mid-Sussex Dairy Co. built its own 2ft 6in. gauge line for moving milk trolleys to the platform. However, rationalisation began in the twenties, in spite of a continuing good level of passenger and freight traffic and Barcombe, Newick and Sheffield Park were placed in the care of one stationmaster. Electrification, carried out on the Ardingly line in 1935, was postponed on the Lewes–East Grinstead section by the war and was never finished afterwards. Thus the line was worked by steam traction until the very end of operations. From 1943, when the existing restriction on the weight of locomotives was lifted, heavier classes began to appear on the line, including Maunsell 2-6-0s, Brighton Atlantics, West Country Pacifics and WD 2-8-0s.

After nationalisation, the Horsted Keynes–Lewes line was an early victim of the austerities imposed by economic conditions and the British Transport Commission. In the event it was the whole line, including the double track section from Horsted Keynes to East Grinstead, that fell and was closed in the middle of a national rail strike on 13 June 1955. The last scheduled train ran on 28 May, followed by a valedictory special on 14 August. A year later the requirement, embodied in the Act transferring the operation of the line from the Lewes & East Grinstead, to the London, Brighton & South Coast Railway, and through the Southern Railway to the BTC, to provide a service of four trains a day in each direction, was resurrected and enforced. A service was duly organised and the trains left Lewes at 9.30 a.m. and 11.30 a.m. and at 1.30 p.m. and 3.30 p.m., returning from East Grinstead at 10.28 a.m., 12.28 p.m., and 2.28 p.m. and 4.28 p.m. At first most of these trains ran through from Brighton but later they were terminated at Lewes and were worked by one coach and two locomotives, one for the morning and the other for the afternoon trains. The terms of the requirement were followed slavishly and thus these trains stopped neither at Barcombe, formerly the busiest station on the line, nor at Kingscote, because they were not named in the Act. In these circumstances the viability of the line was not enhanced and in 1958, after a three-day hearing at Lewes, the Ministry of Transport was advised to authorise its closure. This took place on 16 March that year and the line south of Sheffield Park was lifted in 1959–60. One platform at Horsted Keynes remained to serve the electric shuttle service on the Ardingly branch to Haywards Heath, one track of which was used during this period for storing new stock ready for the completion of electrification on the Kent Coast line. They were succeeded by obsolete steam stock from the same division, in quantities of up to two hundred vehicles ,which were gradually removed for breaking up at Newhaven.

North of Horsted Keynes the track was left in place for emergency use but soon began to deteriorate through lack of maintenance. Passenger services on the Ardingly branch came to an end in October 1963 but the line was partly kept up to serve a newly built roadstone plant in the goods yard at Ardingly, with a link with the main line at Copyhold junction. The tracks from Ardingly to Horsted Keynes and from there north to East Grinstead were then to be lifted and work began at the western end on 15 July 1964. By this date, of course, the Bluebell Railway was in operation and when the demolition contractor's diesel locomotive proved inadequate to the task of hauling three single bolster wagons loaded with lifted track up a 1 in 75 gradient, the preservationists' 0-6-0T was hired, complete with crew, to work these trains. She was

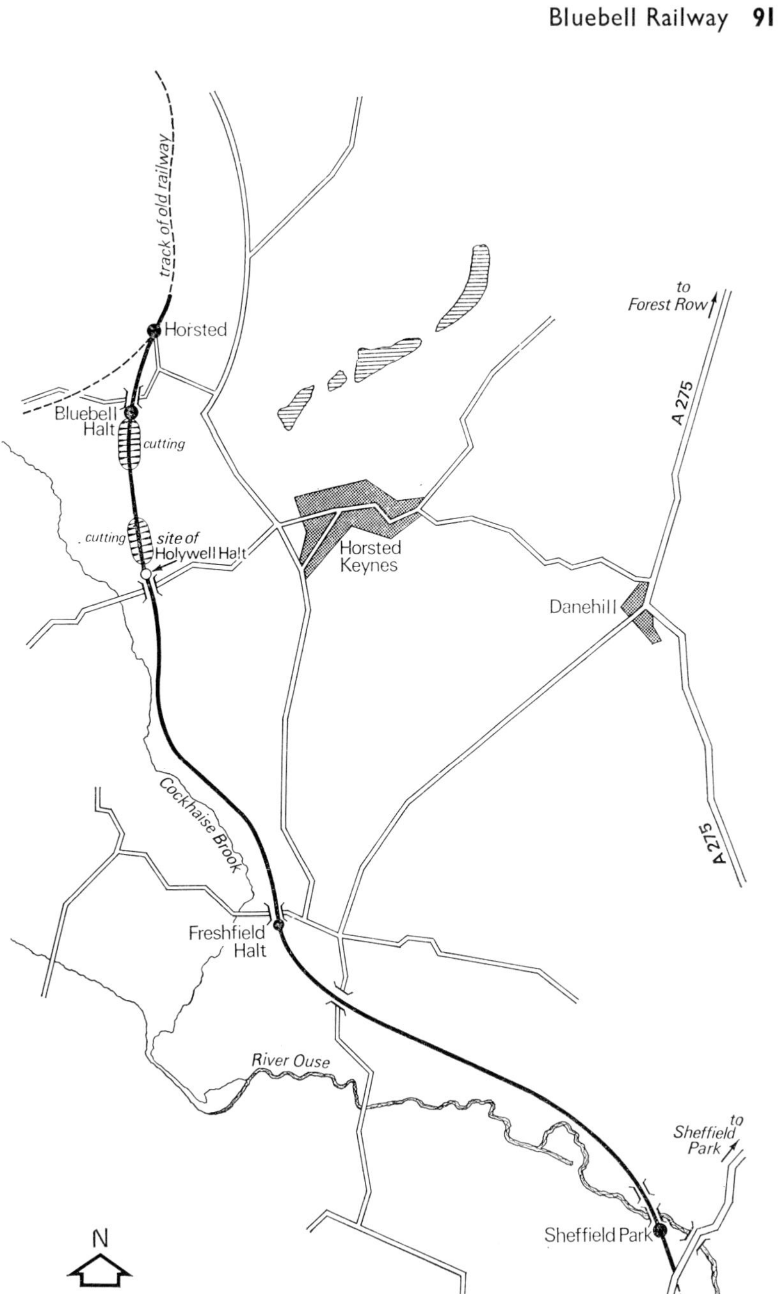

3 Bluebell Railway

replaced during maintenance work by no. 473, 'Birch Grove'. Work began north of Horsted Keynes in September 1965 and by March the following year was completed, leaving the Bluebell line isolated.

Following the second closure of the Lewes–East Grinstead line in March 1958, the line and buildings began to decay. However, the reprieve and temporary reopening of the line had attracted national attention and the possibility of doing so permanently on a private basis developed. The preservers had encouraging precedents in the Welsh narrow gauge lines and the days of the standard gauge steam locomotive were clearly numbered. This last point was emphasised at about the same time by the destruction, in the face of widespread protest, of the last Atlantic type locomotive in the country (no. 32424, 'Beachy Head', built at Brighton in 1911). A public meeting at Hayward's Heath on 16 March 1959, the first anniversary of the line's closure, marked the formation of the Lewes & East Grinstead Railway Preservation Society.

At this time, of course, considerable parts of the line were still intact but the Society decided at an early date that a realistic stretch should be chosen before negotiations began with BR. The Sheffield Park–Horsted Keynes section recommended itself because it presents comparatively few engineering, maintenance and operating problems in the form of bridges, tunnels, cuttings, level crossings and so on, while offering certain basic amenities and advantages such as accessibility, space and abundant water supplies from the River Ouse at Sheffield Park. The Trustees of the new Society therefore approached BR for a lease—still at this date countenanced by the authorities—and option to buy this part of the line. BR named a figure of £55,000 for the land, stations, track and fittings, which was reduced by negotiation to £34,000. The Sheffield Park booking office had already been let to the Society for 5*s*. a week when the Society was reconstituted as the Bluebell Railway Preservation Society, ready to begin the battle to raise the purchase price within the three-month time limit imposed by BR. Negotiations were resumed with a view to leasing the line only but BR replied that they could neither lease nor recommend the Ministry of Transport to grant a Light Railway Order to an unincorporated body. The Bluebell Railway Ltd was thus formed, with the Trustees of the Society as directors, and notification that BR would be willing to lease the line with an option to buy and to recommend the grant of a Light Railway Order had arrived by the end of 1959.

Details of the collection of locomotive and carriage stock can be seen in Table 18. In addition to these locomotives the Bluebell Railway has been the home of the Bulleid Pacific Preservation Society's no. 34023, 'Blackmore Vale', since it was displaced from the Longmoor Military Railway in the autumn of 1971.

The line was reopened on 7 August 1960 and since then the preservation company has prospered, not only in its efforts to restore and operate

Table 18 Steam locomotives on the Bluebell Railway

Type	Number/name	Where built	Year	Origin
0-6-0T	473 'Birch Grove'	Brighton	1898	LB&SCR & BR (no. 32473)
0-6-0T	72 'Fenchurch'	Brighton	1872	LB&SCR & BR (no. 32636)
0-6-0T	55 'Stepney'	Brighton	1875	LB&SCR & BR (no. 32655)
4-4-0	3217 'Earl of Berkeley'	Swindon	1938	GWR & BR (no. 9017)
4-4-2T	488	Neilson	1885	LSWR & BR (no. 30583)
0-6-0T	323 'Bluebell'	Ashford	1910	SE&CR & BR (no. 31323)
0-6-0T	27 'Primrose'	Ashford	1910	SE&CR & BR (no. 31027)
0-6-0T	'Pioneer II'	Ashford	1910	SE&CR & BR (no. 31178)
0-6-0	592	Longhedge	1901	SE&CR & BR (no. 31592)
0-6-0T	2650	Bow	1880	North London Railway LNWR & BR (no. 58850)
4-6-0	75027	Swindon	1954	BR
0-6-0ST	'Stamford'	Avonside	1927	Stewarts & Lloyds, Pilton
0-4-0T	'Baxter'	Fletcher Jennings	1877	Dorking Greystone Lime Co.
2-2-0WT	'The Blue Circle'	Aveling & Porter	1926	Portland Cement Holborough

a standard gauge line but also in re-creating a line with a strongly Victorian atmosphere and style. Certainly the volume of passenger traffic would have satisfied, indeed amazed, any nineteenth-century investor, with 15,000 people carried in the first three months of operations and corresponding returns ever since. In the early days this was just as well, for the annual rent of the line was £2,250 and by 1964 BR's policy towards privately operated lines had hardened to the point where only outright ownership was acceptable. Accordingly the infant preservation line was required to find a purchase price of £43,000 in the autumn of 1967, but after several years of successful operation it was able to put down a deposit of £23,500, with the balance payable in twenty quarterly instalments of £1,000. So the railway was saved.

The Bluebell line is well past the first perilous steps and now faces the more rewarding, if even more exacting, process of development and consolidation. As time goes by the complex and heavy repairs to both line and locomotives must be undertaken and the construction of a locomotive works at Sheffield Park is now in hand. The track has so far needed no more than basic maintenance but it and some of the bridges will need further attention during the next five years. The Bluebell Railway now has the heart and resources to face all these problems and to develop its foremost position among British preservation railways.

9 Stour Valley Railway

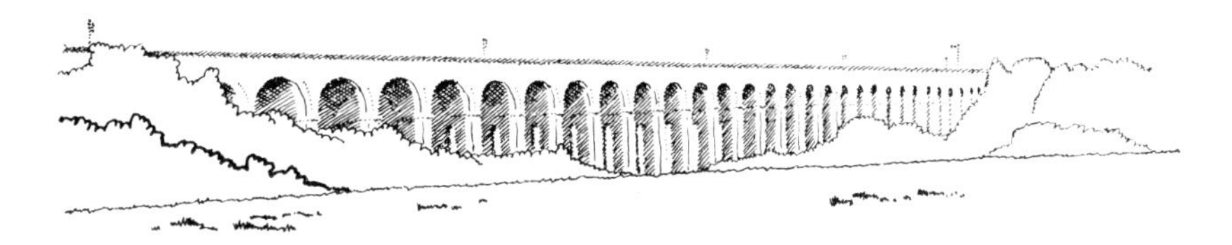

Chappel viaduct

The Eastern Counties Railway opened to Colchester in 1843. It was later to go on north to Ipswich, Norwich and Great Yarmouth, while the other main line of what became the Great Eastern Railway in 1862 ran further west to Bishops Stortford, Cambridge, Ely and King's Lynn. Between these two lay the prosperous agricultural area drained by the River Stour and the River Colne along the borders of Suffolk, Essex and Cambridgeshire and centred round elegant and established country towns like Sudbury and Halstead. With the main line as close as the regional capital at Colchester (eleven miles from Sudbury) plans for a railway link with it were quickly drawn up and the grandiloquently named Colchester, Stour Valley, Sudbury & Halstead Railway was incorporated in 1846. Even allowing for the fact that those plans included a branch from the Eastern Union Railway at Colchester to the riverside port of Hythe, the authorised capital of £250,000 was generous. Powers for various extensions and branches followed. The line was leased to the Eastern Union Railway for 999 years from November 1848, although this was soon superseded by the Great Eastern Railway which did not amalgamate with the Stour Valley line until many years later.

The Sudbury branch left, and leaves, the main line at Marks Tey, between Witham and Colchester. It was built as a single track, with works wide enough to allow a second to be built if it should be necessary at a later date. The principal engineering feature is the viaduct over the

River Colne at Chappel, with its thirty-two arches spanning 1,066 feet and rising to seventy-five feet in the middle of the valley. Otherwise the line is undramatic, though the landscape is classically East Anglian, and includes some surprisingly stiff gradients.

The line was opened from Marks Tey to Sudbury on 2 July 1849. The service of four trains a day in each direction on weekdays and none at all on Sundays was typical of a line of this class; and the fares, 3*d.*, 2*d.* and 1*d.* per mile for first second and third class fares respectively, were at the rates fixed by Parliament in 1846. However, within a few years of the opening there were loud and organised complaints about the standards and cost of the service provided by the Company. The timetable, it was alleged, was quite unrealistic, unrelated to the needs of the community, and in any event bore little relation to the way the trains were actually run. The prices charged for the carriage of certain classes of goods appeared to be completely arbitrary. The waiting room at Marks Tey was described as an 'enclosure . . . unfitted for all classes, into which no person ventures excepting under the direst necessity'. There is no evidence that conditions on the line were really as bad as the volume of complaint would suggest. It certainly made a profit in these early years and branches and extensions, building up an ever tighter network of railways—to Halstead, Bury St Edmunds and Shelford, on the London–Cambridge main line—were proposed, planned and constructed long before the Colchester, Stour Valley, Sudbury & Halstead Railway was absorbed by the Great Eastern in 1898.

The GER took the branch through the golden age of the railways in the decade and a half leading up to World War I. Traffic of all sorts was not hard to win and the service expanded up to seven trains a day in each direction on weekdays and a Sunday service of up to two trains a day in each direction. Motive power in these years was based on James Holden's 2-4-0 passenger locomotive, introduced in 1891. These were a modified version of the express 2-4-0 'T19' class which had appeared five years earlier, and had been specially developed from them for branch line work. They were ably supported by Holden's 0-6-0 side tank engines introduced in 1890 and built in large numbers with modifications, principally an increase in boiler pressure, up to 1912. Many of the class survived to work under British Railways. At the end of this era Chappel station, now the headquarters of the Stour Valley Railway Preservation Society and of the Branch Line Preservation Co. Ltd, was changed to Chappel & Wakes Colne and has been known by this name ever since. After the war and the Grouping, when the line came under the LNER, it continued to be comparatively prosperous and traffic figures showed that the service was standing up well to the attractions and advantages of road transport. Through carriages to Sudbury and Bury St Edmunds from London were not reintroduced after 1918 but a slip coach for Bury St Edmunds, detached at Marks Tey, continued to run on an afternoon train from Liverpool Street to Clacton until 1939 by which time it was the last slip carriage in use on the LNER.

After World War II, the general railway recession and the ever-growing attractions of road transport began to make a real impression on the line's prosperity. Untypically, it was the freight traffic which first began to look uneconomic. One innovation was the appearance of diesel multiple units in the late fifties working through passenger stopping trains over the Stour Valley line over fairly long distances, Ipswich to Norwich for example. But the contraction of services was well under way before the Beeching age. By 1965, BR had applied to the East Anglian Transport Users' Consultative Committee for permission to close the line from Marks Tey to Cambridge and for the Cambridge–Sudbury section closure was duly sanctioned and carried out early in 1967. The track was lifted soon afterwards.

The Sudbury–Marks Tey section had been reprieved on the grounds that growth and prospects for the further growth of the population of the area and Sudbury in particular demanded the maintenance of a railway connection. It did not, however, qualify for a grant on the grounds of being a social necessity to the area (the sum required would have been £90,000 p.a.) and within a year the Board had announced further plans to close the remains of the branch. Well over one thousand objections were lodged before the public inquiry at Sudbury in July 1969 but the Minister's decision has not yet been announced.

The Stour Valley Railway Preservation Society, with its headquarters at Chappel & Wakes Colne station, is now active at this end of the line, although it had been formed in September 1968 with the initial objective of reopening the whole of the newly closed Sudbury–Shelford section. By the time it had been decided to concentrate on the shorter stretch from Sudbury to Long Melford the track had been lifted. To manage later initiatives and to organise fund raising the Branch Line Preservation Co. Ltd was formed in February 1970 to look after these aspects of the Society's interests. It has since become the Society's policy to be financially and administratively prepared to take over a section of line immediately a suitable piece has been closed and for this the shorter remaining part of the Stour Valley branch from Marks Tey to Sudbury is ideally suited.

Two objectives have thus been pursued: to obtain a lease on the goods yard at Chappel & Wakes Colne station as a headquarters for the Society and its collection of locomotives and rolling stock, and to be ready financially to buy part at least of the Marks Tey–Sudbury line. The first of these objectives has been largely accomplished and the Society took up residence at Chappel & Wakes Colne in December 1970. Little more than three months later, a third of a mile of track had been relaid and was being used to steam the first engine to arrive, 'Gunby' (see Table 19). In due course, a public service will be operated, initially on a short section between Marks Tey and Chappel & Wakes Colne, later probably as far as Bures and possibly even to Sudbury.

Table 19 Steam locomotives at Chappel & Wakes Colne

Type	Name	Where built	Year	Origin
0-6-0ST	'Gunby'	Hunslet	1941	WD, LNER & BR
0-6-0ST	'Jupiter'	Robert Stephenson & Hawthorn	1950	Stewarts & Lloyds, Corby
0-6-0ST	'Castle Hedingham'	Hunslet	1952	WD Long Marston, & Shoeburyness

10 Dean Forest Railway

Forest of Dean Railway 0-6-0PT of the 2021 class

The Dean Forest Railway Preservation Society exists to create a working example of the once extensive railway system in the Forest of Dean. The section chosen is the last remaining part of the Severn & Wye Railway beginning at Lydney Town and winding northwards for $3\frac{1}{2}$ miles through an attractive wooded valley, past the village of Whitecroft and into the Royal Forest of Dean National Park. Parkend is the present headquarters and northern terminus of the line.

A tramway has been in existence since the beginning of the nineteenth century and was originally known as the Lidney [*sic*] and Lidbrook Railway and later the Severn & Wye Railway and Canal Co. The tram-road, built on a gauge variously estimated at 3ft 6in. and 3ft 8in., was built of rails three feet in length. A broad gauge railway was built, for the most part alongside the tramway, in the 1860s and opened in 1869. It was an early victim of the drive for standardisation and was converted to standard gauge in 1872. The first public passenger train left Lydney junction for Lydney Town on 23 September 1875 and was hauled by an 0-6-0 tank engine named 'Robin Hood'. Passenger services north of Lydney Town did not last very long and the last regular one ran in July 1929.

This last development was unusual in the circumstances. The line had an established and soundly based role as a freight carrier and the conditions in the surrounding country and the inadequacy of the roads made the railway the solitary means of passenger communication, apart, of course, from travel by horse or on foot, which had dominated the sequestered life of the Forest of Dean until the largely unwanted intrusion of the railway. However, the withdrawal of the new facility caused quite an upheaval and the end of passenger services was vigorously challenged. Proposals to restore them, however, led nowhere and the only passenger trains in latter years have been the summer seaside excursions and railway enthusiasts' specials. The allure of the railway system of the area has attracted enthusiasts of all sorts, steam and railway alike, and while the last steam-hauled passenger excursion ran in 1961, a diesel multiple unit full of railway enthusiasts reached Parkend as recently as May 1971.

The Society's only steam locomotive at present is a Peckett 0-4-0ST, no. 2147, 'Uskmouth 1', built in 1952 for the Central Electricity Generating Board. The engine spent most of her life at Newport (Mon.) and was acquired for preservation by the Forest Peckett Fund.

11 Severn Valley Railway

Victoria bridge

The Severn Valley Railway was conceived in 1847 and this historic and romantic line is now firmly established as one of the premier preservation steam railways in Britain. During a century and a quarter, 1847 to 1972, it has suffered every kind of vicissitude and may proudly proclaim that since the opening of the original line in 1862, steam-hauled trains have operated over all or part of the line continuously, without interruption. The changing fortunes of the Severn Valley Railway are fascinating and may graphically be traced by the following chronology over a period of 125 years:

1847 The Severn Valley Railway conceived, approximately 40 miles long, Hartlebury to Shrewsbury.
1852 Bill deposited in parliament to build the Severn Valley Railway.
1853 The Severn Valley Railway Company incorporated.
1862 The Severn Valley Railway line opened to passenger and freight traffic from Hartlebury to Shrewsbury (Salop), the enterprise to be operated by the West Midland Railway.
1863 Statutory dissolution of the West Midland Railway, and the Great Western Railway to accept all obligations and rights.
1872 Great Western Railway Act absorbs the Severn Valley Railway Company by exchange of stock.
1878 Kidderminster Loop opened, thus creating network Shrewsbury, Bridgnorth, Bewdley to Hartlebury and to Kidderminster, the two

last named on the G.W. Worcester–Stourbridge Junction–Wolverhampton main line.

1923 Grouping of railways into the 'Big Four', the Severn Valley Railway remaining on the Great Western system, as during the preceding half-century.

1947 Nationalisation and creation of British Railways.

1963 The final passenger train ran on 9 September and the final freight train ran on 30 November, though the line remained open for colliery and power station mineral trains, the former for the Highley coalmine of the N.C.B., and the latter for electricity power stations at Buildwas and Stourport-on-Severn.

1965 The Severn Valley Railway Society formed by Kidderminster steam locomotive enthusiasts, to save the Severn Valley line.

1966 Decision to buy for preservation in a sum of £25,000 the 4½ miles of line from Bridgnorth to Eardington and Hampton Loade and deposit paid, £2,500, in February 1967.

1967 Arrival of Collett 0-6-0 no. 3205 and four ex-G.W.R. coaches at Bridgnorth for preservation.

1968 Shrewsbury Planning enquiry held for operation of the 4½ miles of line from Bridgnorth to Hampton Loade; won for the Railway by the advocacy of Mr Richard Dunn.

1969 Ministerial consent given for the operation of the line, subject to Light Railway Orders (2), granted respectively in 1969 and 1970. The Society formed in 1965 was dissolved in December 1969, and a guarantee company (i.e. a company without shares) formed in 1967 in anticipation of the granting of the Light Railway Orders, called The Severn Valley Railway Company Limited, took over the membership and assets of the society.

1970 Last BR passenger services withdrawn from Bewdley to Kidderminster and Bewdley to Stourport-on-Severn and Hartlebury.

1970 On 23 May, the Severn Valley Railway is re-born at Bridgnorth, with steam-operated scheduled services by volunteer unpaid preservationists. 65,000 passenger journeys operated in seven months at a trading profit of £3,093 for the fifteen months to 31 December.

1971 Annual General Meeting decides by overwhelming majority to buy from British Railways for approximately £75,000 the line ten miles southward from Alveley, thus completing an overall length almost to Kidderminster (for link-up later with BR) of sixteen miles, the longest steam-operated railway line in Britain; and to create a public company to finance the operation, the new public company to be called Severn Valley Railway (Holdings) Ltd and later (after dissolution of the guarantee company) to be renamed the Severn Valley Railway Company Limited. The new public liability company was duly incorporated on 15 March 1972.

1972 The Severn Valley Railway successfully capitalised in a sum of £150,000 (150,000 shares of £1 each) and preparations made for full scheduled passenger and freight traffic, Bridgnorth via Bewdley to Kidderminster, with supplemental school-trains, railway shopping services, and excursion traffic, all to be fully operational by 1975, and with ancillary catering and bookstall services, and special rail facilities for the proposed wild life park at Spring Grove, Bewdley. The future of the railway is bright indeed.

Perhaps historians will recall that the frustrations, obstacles and troubles of the preservationists in the twentieth century were less than those of the original promoters and builders of the Severn Valley Railway in the nineteenth century. There is a certain similarity between their problems and certainly not least of these, for both promoters and preservationists alike, was the acute shortage of funds. At times, when troubles on that account were greatest, the men in control had little to sustain them other than their enthusiasm for a concept and vision of a steam railway threading its way through the gorgeous unspoiled countryside of the Severn Valley. In the nineteenth century it was in pursuit of profit and reward in the literal Victorian sense. In the twentieth century the revivalists and preservationists use commercial methods to sustain their enterprise as a leisure industry, appealing to men and women alike, from all over Britain and overseas, and especially the seven million people of the Midland conurbation, so many of whom among the rising generation have never seen a great steam engine in action, or experienced its unique aroma. There are now eighteen engines, ranging in size from a fussy little tank engine, 0-6-0 wheel arrangements, such as no. 2047, 'Warwickshire', by Manning Wardle, built in 1927, and another 0-6-0ST, no. 813, built by Hudswell Clark in 1901, weighing respectively 30 tons and 44 tons, 'Thomas The Tank Engine', for all the world to see, up to the giant Britannia 4-6-2 Pacific locomotive no. 70000, weight 143 tons, and WD 600, 2-10-0, 'Gordon', owned by the Ministry of Defence and weighing 134 tons. All are there, and more to come.

The original promoters of the Severn Valley Railway Company saw the forty-mile link from Hartlebury in the south, on the main line of the Oxford, Worcester & Wolverhampton Railway, affectionately called the 'Old Worse and Worse', to Shrewsbury in the north, as the fastest and shortest available route through the Midlands. Thus, the promoters argued, the congested industrial zone already established in the middle years of the last century, the densely packed Black Country towns, bounded by Birmingham in the South and Wolverhampton in the north, could be by-passed or circumvented. Certainly, the Severn Valley route was more direct than the London, Oxford, Banbury, Birmingham to Wolverhampton route and on to Shrewsbury: Hartlebury to Shrewsbury

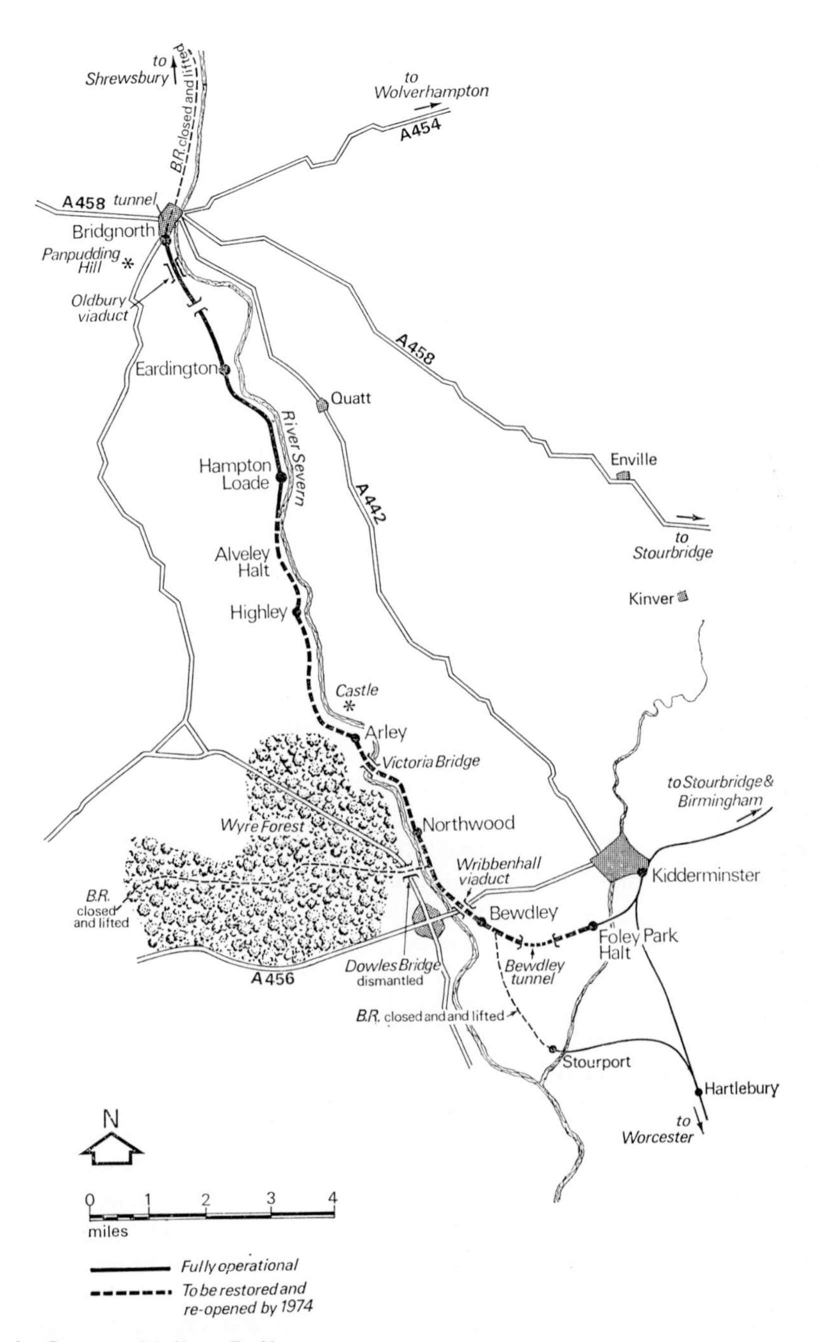

4 Severn Valley Railway

could be a cut-off. Yet, it was never realised as a major route, this Severn Valley concept, mostly because of the inordinate delays and financial difficulties from the beginning, and problems of terrain and topography which, between them, lengthened the period of gestation to fifteen years from 1847 to 1862 and time and again it all nearly foundered. Three Acts of Parliament were needed to keep it afloat, and innumerable crises of finance, in management and operations, occurred in this decade and a half. Even the Parliamentary Committee on the first Bill, in spite of years of lobbying, sat for nineteen days in Committee, from 9 May to 27 June 1853; the cost to the new company was £5,600 and ninety-seven witnesses were examined. Many averred that the River Severn was adequate for all inland transport, whereas others, more progressive, inveighed that trade and commerce would suffer without a railway, unknown at that time in the Severn Valley. The land owners were vehemently opposed, many for characteristic and retrogressive reasons, not excluding the frightening of their cattle by the locomotives. The promoters eventually won, but expensively and tediously. The first Severn Valley Railway Act was passed without division and received the Royal Assent on 20 August 1853. Section XIX defined the route as follows:

> 1 Commencing by a junction with the main line of the Oxford, Worcester and Wolverhampton railway in the Parish of Hartlebury in the County of Worcester at or near a point five and a half furlongs or thereabouts southwards of the Hartlebury station on that main line, and terminating at or near a certain road situate in the Parish of Holy Cross and St Giles, within the Borough of Shrewsbury and the County of Salop.
> 2 A Branch railway or tramway commencing and diverging from and out of the intended railway at or near certain limekilns or limeworks situate at or near Benthall Edge in the Parish of Benthall in the County of Salop, occupied by John Patten, and terminating at or near a certain inclosure situate in the Parish of Madeley in that County.

Within two months of its incorporation, the Company was looking for economies. A deviation suggested in the Report of the Parliamentary Committee on the Bill had proposed that the new railway could join the Shrewsbury & Hereford line at Sutton Bridge junction, south of the proposed terminus, and that the two companies should share a station in Shrewsbury. Negotiations towards this end were accordingly begun, though the Shrewsbury & Hereford was uncooperative in the early stages. The issue was causing some concern by the time of the General Meeting in February 1854—one of the two General Meetings between 1853 and December 1857 which did not have to be adjourned for want of a quorum. At the same meeting, Thorp (the Chairman) announced that 'the expenditure of the Company will be confined within the narrowest possible limits'.

Stringent economies were indeed made in the ensuing two years, but the Company was heavily under-subscribed financially, even allowing for borrowing powers, and a further Bill, as an amending measure, was laid before parliament in March 1854. It was withdrawn later after much controversy and a new Bill reached the Statute Book in 1855. It was the Second Severn Valley Railway Act and twice the length of the first. It ran to 102 sections, or about 2½ sections of the Act per mile of railway track, over the total 40 miles route. This new Act effected many economies in cost by eliminating several river crossings on the meandering Severn, and fixed the capital of the Company at a more realistic level. Yet, by 1857, the Special General Meeting of the Company was authorising the Directors to apply for a 'Bill of abandonment', and curiously gave them authority for preceding with a Bill to extend the time for completion of the works. In the event, an Act of 1856 gave an extension of one year to the time of five years delineated in the 1853 Act, for completion of the line and associated works by August 1858. Eventually all was done and the great masterpiece of the Victoria Bridge at Arley (designed by Sir John Fowler, the builder of the Forth Rail Bridge) to cross the River Severn north of Bewdley was duly begun on 24 November 1859, and a commemorative parchment placed beneath the foundation stone where it reposes to this day, inscribed with this memorial to a splendid railway engineering achievement:

> The Foundation Stone of this Bridge was laid by Henry Orlando Bridgman, Esq., C.E., Resident Engineer, on the 24th Day of November, in the Year of Our Lord One Thousand, Eight Hundred and Fifty-Nine, and in the Twenty-Third Year of the Reign of Her Majesty, Queen Victoria. The arch of the Bridge is to be constructed principally of cast-iron—200 feet span—and, up to the present time, will be the largest cast-iron arch constructed in these Kingdoms. John Fowler, Esq., Engineer-in-Chief, London: Messrs. Brassey, Peto, and Betts, Contractors, also of London. The railway works were commenced in the Autumn of 1858, and are expected to be completed and the line opened to the Public in the Spring of 1861. This railway commences at Shrewsbury, and terminates at the Hartlebury station of the Oxford, Worcester and Wolverhampton Railway, a distance of 40 miles.

In 1860 many landslips took place on the line. It could have received railway traffic by 1861, but Sir John Fowler advised time for 'essential consolidation' in order 'to obtain a permanently substantial formation for the permanent way'. Thus it was 1862 before the Severn Valley Railway was officially opened, thereby justifying the three years' extension applied for by the Directors on grounds of constructional difficulties, after expiration of the one year extension included in the Act of 1856. Even after the Victoria Bridge at Arley had been officially opened in 1859, more landslips had maddeningly taken place at Arley and Bridgnorth. In retrospect, it is quite remarkable that the first train, with accompanying pageantry and jollification, ran on Friday 31 January 1862. This first official train left Worcester (Shrub Hill) at about 11.30 a.m. with twenty-two carriages, carrying a hundred people, including two MPs, namely Sir Thomas Winnington (Con. Bewdley) and Rt. Hon. George Cecil Weld Forester (Con. Wenlock). Also on board were Lord Shelburne, Chairman of the Great Western Railway, John Fowler, Engineer of the line, and A. C. Sherriff, General Manager of the West Midland Railway. The hundred people on board initially had been joined by nearly four hundred more, almost filling the twenty-two coaches by the time the train reached Bridgnorth, half way up the line: there, alighting from the train outside the station, the same station used today by the Severn Valley Railway Company, the band of the local yeomanry unit, The Bridgnorth Rifles, rendered appropriately 'See the Conquering Hero Comes'. It was all a notable piece of railway saturnalia, reminiscent of the arrival of the 'Old Worse and Worse' at Evesham in 1852, when the Burgesses received this manifestation of transportation progress by ringing church bells, firing ceremonial cannon, decorating the line and station with flags and triumphal arches of evergreens and flowers, and a public dinner in the High Street where banners and streamers bade 'success to the Ox. Wor. and Wol. Railway' and 'Eat, Drink and be Merry'. So, at Bridgnorth, and after refreshment, the train proceeded easily to Shrewsbury, arriving at that confluence of railway routes at two o'clock in the afternoon. Here joined the Shrewsbury to Hereford line (later GWR/LNWR Joint), the Shrewsbury to Crewe line of the LNWR into Welshpool and Montgomeryshire on the Cambrian route, to Wolverhampton on the Great Western and northwards to Chester and Birkenhead on the Mersey, the final link in the long-sought London to Merseyside route of the Great Western Railway. Thus the Severn Valley terminal at its northern end was at one of the most fascinating and diverse of all railway junctions of Victorian times.

On the evening of 31 January, a great celebration took place at Bridgnorth for all who had bought return tickets for the Opening Day's train and then on 4 February 1862, at the rival borough of Bewdley, a similar event occurred, packed to capacity, to hear the local Member of Parliament, Sir Thomas Winnington, speak eloquently of 'the quickening influence of the new power placed within our reach'. Today, with a lively recognition of both tradition and nostalgia, the Board of Directors hold their monthly meetings and luncheons following, at the same George Hotel, Bewdley, more venerable by 110 years but indelibly associated with the Severn Valley Railway and all its works and fortunes.

Nabarro is the lineal descendant of Weld Forester, MP, and Winnington, MP, and emulates, in his time, their love of the railway.

But the Severn Valley Railway missed the crest of nineteenth-century railway demand. It was too late to capture the Midlands 'through' traffic. It declined in one hundred years to a tourist line mainly, a third-rate branch railway, attracting little freight and few passengers, though the need to transport the coal from the prosperous pit at Highley, and the later needs of great electricity generating stations at Buildwas a few miles north of Bridgnorth, and the mighty power stations at Stourport-on-Severn (the 'A' station opened in 1927, and the 'B' Station in 1952), brought much-needed revenue to the line. Similarly, reprieve was granted by both the first and second World Wars, when the Severn Valley Railway route provided good alternative access from the midlands to the north, avoiding the packed and therefore highly vulnerable main line routes through the industrial midlands by the Great Western and London Midland and Scottish Railways. Particularly in World War II, the coal traffic was very important and the Severn Valley connection to the Bewdley to Tenbury Wells branch of the Great Western Railway, to reach the admiralty base at Ditton Priors, Shropshire, in the Clee Hills, gave a new importance to the line and the traffic on it.

But, in the peace-time economy and especially during the great Depression of the inter-war years, when draconian economies were inescapable, the role of the Severn Valley Railway became increasingly touristic in nature and part of the 'holiday haunts' aura which was Great Western legend. Here was the 'Land of the Lords Marchers' through which flowed the upper waters of England's greatest river, the Severn, and on the banks of which were the many castles standing in that Border country, castles built to dominate and govern the unruly Welsh. The names of these great medieval strongholds found their way, as part of the lore and romanticism of the Great Western Railway on to the finest of the Swindon-built steam engines, all the names on them designed in measure to popularise rail tourism in the Severn Valley in inter-war years. There was 'Shrewsbury Castle' (No. 5009), 'Ludlow Castle' (No. 5002), 'Montgomery Castle' (No. 5016), 'Gloucester Castle' (No. 7020), 'Hartlebury Castle' (No. 7033), 'Evesham Abbey' (No. 5085), but sadly 'Bridgnorth Castle' was forgotten: and the 'Halls' and the 'Courts' of the Saint (2900) Class, and the Bulldogs such as 'Stanley Baldwin' (No. 3411) and earlier the Dukes such as 'Severn' (No. 3290), 'Cotswold' (No. 3280), and the Counties, such as 'County of Salop' (No. 3819) and 'County of Worcester' (No. 3820). All contributed to the Great Western Railway stimulus to tourism in the twenties and thirties, which replaced on many of the Western lines the lack of freight and passenger traffic. The Severn Valley was an ideal subject for this initiative and demand was widespread for such publications as the 'Handy Aids' series of the Paddington promoters, who announced on No. 7

Booklet, *The Severn Valley, 'through the Land of the Lords Marchers from Shrewsbury to Worcester'*.

The growth of road transport for holidays was inexorable and after World War II, in the later forties and fifties, branch line traffic was too small to sustain economic viability. Their closure was inevitable and had it not been Dr Richard Beeching (later Lord Beeching) it would have been another executive by a different name. Such romantic lines as the Severn Valley Railway were doomed and duly closed by the nationalised authority, British Railways. The days of measured and gradual closure, related in the chronology of events on the Severn Valley Railway from 1847–1972, shows the actual closure by British Railways of the Severn Valley line from 1963 to 1970, a closure span of seven years.

Fortunately, the era of the preservationists had then begun and, by 1970, these dedicated enthusiasts were firmly and securely in command, insistent upon perpetuating the Severn Valley Railway for a second century. The railway was then 110 years old and, in 1972, had celebrated a one hundredth anniversary since becoming part of the Great Western system in 1872.

The transition from a guarantee company, that is a company without shares (which had taken over from the Severn Valley Railway Society in 1969) was delicate and complex: delicate because the members of the railway, all of whom had worked selflessly and without payment since 1965, were justifiably apprehensive that conversion of the enterprise to a public limited liability company would endanger the voluntary endeavour and spirit on which the growth of the undertaking had been based. The Chairman of the guarantee company, Mr A. B. Marsden-Smedley, therefore addressed a letter to each of the two-and-a-half thousand members of the railway, explaining the essential need to convert the company to a limited liability company if the southern section of the line was to be purchased from British Railways for £75,000, failing which it would go the same way as the Bridgnorth to Shrewsbury section which had been lifted years earlier and the land sold. The chance of reconstructing the Severn Valley Railway from Bridgnorth to Kidderminster would then be lost for ever. The Chairman wrote to members as follows:

> Accompanying this letter is a formal notice of the adjourned Annual General Meeting on 6th August, 1971, and you will see that you will be asked to pass a resolution altering the structure of your Company so that it will be legally possible to raise money by the issue of shares to buy the southern portion of the line from Hampton Loade to Foley Park.
>
> When I spoke to you on the subject of this purchase at Kidderminster Town Hall on the 23rd October, 1970, and received

your overwhelming support to proceed with this enterprise, I promised to keep you informed of developments and I am therefore writing to explain why I would like you to approve the Resolution.

Those of you who were at that meeting will probably remember that I said that I thought it was imperative that the Company should acquire the southern section of the line because, if it did not, and if the proposed Bridgnorth by-pass were constructed, then the Company's terminus would be severed from the rest of the property unless the Company could find a sum of money variously estimated at between £10,000 and £80,000 to build a new rail bridge. Since that date, our information is that the Bridgnorth by-pass will definitely be built at some date between now and 1975 and that it will follow the route referred to in our Agreement with the Shropshire County Council of 25th February, 1970, so that the severance of our existing line is virtually certain within the next two to four years.

The lowest estimate for replacing the bridge at about £10,000 assumes that we shall be able to acquire bridging materials comparatively cheaply through our good relations with British Railways and to make some use of our own resources in the erection of the structure. It now seems unlikely that such a course will be possible. The Bridgnorth by-pass runs through lovely country and the aesthetic appearance of the bridge and its ability to blend into the landscape will be uppermost in the minds of the planners. The bridge will have to be built to the very highest standards, not only as regards its structure to carry our heavier locomotives, but also as regards materials, finish and workmanship and it seems likely that the cost may well be nearer the higher figure suggested. If this is so, the existing company has very little chance of finding the resources to preserve the railway in its present form, because its route would be curtailed to a section of under one mile.

It is for this reason that for some months now your Directors have been looking at possible ways of raising enough money to buy the southern half of the line. Once we own the whole line, and even if thereafter the bridge is built, there are still two courses of action open to us.

The new line with termini at both Bridgnorth and Bewdley will earn more revenue. In addition our borrowing powers would be increased since we would have larger assets against which to borrow. There would therefore be a reasonable chance of raising money for the bridge but even if this failed it would not be a total disaster because we could move our operation to the southern end of the line and continue to work out of Bewdley, and possibly even Kidderminster and thus retain the all-important link with British Railways.

When I spoke to you in the Town Hall, I said that I hoped that we might be able to form some kind of charitable trust, but I have since been advised that this would not be a satisfactory solution partly because of the severe restrictions it would impose on our operation as a railway and partly because of the difficulty in raising such a substantial sum of money through charitable sources.

Your Board's attention then turned to the possibility of raising money by forming a Holding Company and selling shares to the public. Although this course of action would have produced the money, the cost of such an issue through normal channels would be prohibitive and its success would entail the transfer of the assets of your company to the new company, and your Board felt that this weakened the position of existing members. On the other hand, if this step were to fail, it could well be disastrous.

It has been decided therefore that the only practical solution at this time would be to raise money by an issue of shares in your company for cash. At the same time the position of existing members would be preserved by a free issue of shares in the company.

Your company in its present form is limited by guarantee and cannot therefore issue shares. It will, therefore, be necessary to wind up this company and simultaneously to re-form it as a company limited by share capital and with the same name. The existing members will become the existing shareholders and shares will be issued to them immediately. The current arrangements for members including subscriptions would be retained. The authorised capital of the new company will be £150,000 in £1 shares. Of this £40,000 will be allocated, free of cost, to existing members and the balance of £110,000 will be offered at par for cash at £1 each by private subscription. The money so raised will be allocated as to £75,000 to buy the line and £35,000 for working capital to enable the company to increase the scope of its operations.

An essential part of the issue of shares will be to use the good offices of Sir Gerald Nabarro, M.P., who has agreed to prepare a personal letter to potential subscribers and to arrange for substantial publicity for the issue so that it may be assured of success.

To facilitate this operation, I have agreed to retire as Chairman after the A.G.M. on 6th August, 1971, provided these proposals are approved by the members, and then at its next meeting your Board will move the election of Sir Gerald in my place. I want you to know that this action is entirely in accordance with my personal wishes and at my suggestion. Some of you may know that I asked to be relieved of my duties at the end of 1970, but I eventually agreed to stay on to assist with the changeover of the Company from its present form to the form needed to operate the longer line. Pressure from my other commitments has made it difficult for me to give the time to your company that I would wish and on the appointment of Sir Gerald, I shall retire from your Board just as I had intended to do at the end of last year.

Your Board has given some thought to the fairest way of distributing the 40,000 £1 shares among the members. Clearly there must be regard to the period of membership and also work done on the line and any donations made. It is suggested that the proper way to handle this matter would be for the members to appoint a small body of Trustees whose responsibility would be to hold the 40,000 shares until such time as they had prepared a fair scheme for the distribution of the shares to members and this scheme had the approval of a General Meeting of the Members.

Apart from these matters, however, the one most important single factor facing the Board at this moment is that if we wish to purchase the southern section of the line to Foley Park, then contracts must be exchanged without delay otherwise we shall lose this opportunity to buy it at a reasonable price, or at all, and may even jeopardise the whole venture.

I hope I have made it clear not only how it is proposed to develop your company, but also how to save Bridgnorth station and the line we have already purchased and operated for over a year now, with conspicuous success. May I please, therefore, have your overwhelming support for the Resolution at the Extraordinary General Meeting on August 6th, 1971, to ensure the continuation of Severn Valley steam.

(Signed) A. B. Marsden-Smedley,
Chairman.

Kidderminster,
Worcestershire.
2nd July, 1971.

On 6 August 1971, at Bridgnorth, railway history in the preservation era was made. Almost seven hundred members of the Severn Valley Railway thronged the hall, packed like sardines, and standing three and four deep along the sides and at the back: not too bad an attendance when it is considered that Britain's biggest public companies rarely attract more than one hundred members to their Annual Meetings. Three hours of animated debate ensued between Directors and members. No member could be found to move rejection of the Chairman's proposals embodied in his letter of 2 July and the proposition was put to endorse the scheme, exactly as related in the Chairman's letter: the result was not quite 'nem con', but almost: say 670 votes for the Resolution and only 4 against. The line was saved and expansion could go ahead. A few months later the Prospectus and Invitation to Subscribe for capital, nearly £60,000, in the form of Equity Shares of £1 each, was successfully launched and the new Severn Valley Railway Association representing the members of the former guarantee company, appointed their Trustees to hold for them the 40,000 shares of £1 each issued to them in exchange for the assets of the northern section of the line, Bridgnorth to Hampton Loade and on to Milepost 144½, a distance of 5 miles and 34 chains, with all the fixtures and fittings thereon, also any other assets, fixed or moveable, of the former guarantee company.

Of course, success is still subject to Light Railway Orders from the Secretary of State for the Environment for the southern section of the line. Scheduled passenger and freight services, Bridgnorth to Kidderminster, should begin by 1974–5, subject to granting of these Light Railway Orders. Most of the Severn Valley Railway's magnificent collection of locomotives (see Table 20) will work on the extended line.

Table 20 Steam locomotives on the Severn Valley Railway

Type	Number and name	Where built	Year	Origin
0-6-0	3205	Swindon	1946	GWR & BR
2-6-0	46443	Crewe	1950	BR
0-6-0ST	2047 'Warwickshire'	Manning Wardle	1926	Portland Cement, Rugby
0-6-0ST	813	Hudswell Clarke	1901	Beckworth Collieries
0-6-0T	47383	Vulcan	1926	LMS & BR
0-4-0ST	1738	Peckett	1928	Hams Hall Power Station, Coleshill
2-6-0	43106	Darlington	1951	BR
2-8-0	8233	North British	1940	LMS, WD & BR
0-6-0T	686 'The Lady Armaghdale'	Hunslet	1898	Manchester Ship Canal, & ICI
4-6-0	45110 'RAF Biggin Hill'	Vulcan	1935	LMS & BR
2-6-2T	4566	Swindon	1924	GWR & BR
0-6-0PT	1501	Swindon	1949	BR & NCB
2-6-0	46521	Swindon	1953	BR
4-6-2	70000 'Britannia'	Crewe	1951	BR
2-6-4T	80079	Brighton	1954	BR
0-6-0PT	L95	Swindon	1929	GWR & LTPB
0-6-0ST	WD193	Hunslet	1953	WD
2-10-0	WD 600 'Gordon'	North British	1943	WD
2-6-0	3442 'The Great Marquess'	Darlington	1937	LNER & BR (no. 61994)

Sir William Stanier's 8Fs, introduced in 1935, became one of the most numerous and popular classes. Over 850 2-8-0s were built by the 'Big Four' railway companies and by private builders as well. They survived to the very last days of steam operations on British Railways, often performing exceptionally arduous duties, such as hauling 1,000-ton limestone hopper trains from the Peak District.

No. 8233 was built by the North British Locomotive Co. in August 1940 at their Hyde Park works in Glasgow, destined for war service, but after the fall of France was delivered instead to the LMS. In 1941, like many others of her class, she was requisitioned for war service again and sent to Persia. After three years on the Trans-Iranian Railway, she was moved to the Suez Canal Zone and worked by the Egyptian State Railways until 1952 when the War Department brought her back to this country. After an overhaul at Derby, she was used on the Longmoor military railway.

On return to British Railways, renumbered 48773, the engine was allocated to Polmadie Depot, Glasgow, until withdrawn from service in 1962. In the following year she was reinstated after an overhaul and transferred to Carlisle, withdrawn again, but returned to spend her last years at Stockport (Edgeley) and Rose Grove depots. She had received a heavy intermediate overhaul at Crewe in 1966, including the fitting of a newly-overhauled boiler and was selected as the 8F in a condition most suitable for preservation. Eventually she was acquired by the Stanier 8F Locomotive Society and arrived at Bridgnorth on 4 January 1969, only 36,000 miles after the last overhaul. Since then she has been restored as LMS no. 8233, and joined the exclusive ranks of preserved locomotives permitted to travel to BR open days.

No. 46443 is one of 128 class 2MT 2-6-0 tender locomotives built to the design of H. G. Ivatt, last chief mechanical engineer of the LMS. Twenty of them were completed under LMS auspices in 1946 and a further 108 by BR between 1948 and 1953, when the design was superseded by the very similar BR 78XXX class of 2-6-0s. The engines operated on all regions of British Railways except the Southern.

This example was built at Crewe and commissioned in February 1950. For over ten years she was shedded at Derby and worked on passenger trains, mainly to Burton, Nottingham and Birmingham until being moved to Saltley in 1961. Her last overhaul followed a collison with a diesel engine. In April 1967 she was purchased by Richard Wilcox, a member of the then Severn Valley Railway Society, and was taken to Bridgnorth later that month.

Like no. 46443, the 2-6-0, no. 43106, was one of a class designed by Ivatt for the LMS which was continued in the early years of BR. They were built at Doncaster and Darlington between 1947 and 1952. No. 43106 was completed at Darlington in April 1951.

The engine was shedded first at South Lynn on the Eastern region and subsequently at Woodford Halse, Saltley and Kingmoor (Carlisle). During her last two years at Preston, she was slightly damaged in a derailment at Colne in April 1968, after which she was withdrawn and purchased by eighteen members of the Severn Valley Railway Society and installed at Bridgnorth in August 1968.

Another Ivatt 2 MT tender locomotive, 2-6-0, no. 46521, although one of a slightly modified batch built after nationalisation at Swindon for service on the Western region, was finished in February 1953.

She was shedded first at Oswestry and then for over six years at Brecon, at one time the centre for a number of lines, in central Wales, and worked on passenger and freight services to Llanidloes, Hereford, Newport and Merthyr Tydfil. In October 1959 she was transferred to Oswestry and did similar duties to Welshpool, Ellesmere and Whitchurch, and in April 1963 moved to Machynlleth depot for service on the Pwllheli, Aberystwyth, Barmouth and Dolgellau lines. She was withdrawn in November 1966 and sent to Barry whence she was recovered by two members of the Severn Valley Railway for restoration to the Swindon green livery and to work on the line.

The Stanier class 5 4-6-0, known as the Black 5, was introduced in 1935 and over the following twenty years 842 examples were built. They were the backbone of the London Midland Region until the end of steam in 1968. No. 45110 was one of the third batch to be constructed and was completed at the Vulcan Foundry, Newton-le-Willows, in June 1935.

For twenty-nine years she was shedded at Holyhead and worked on express passenger and freight trains to Chester, Birmingham, London, Manchester and Liverpool. In March 1964 she was moved to Stafford and used on freight services in the west Midlands. Steam operations ended at Stafford the following year when the engine was moved first to Bolton and later to Lostock Hall, Preston, from where she participated in the last scheduled steam operations on British Railways.

No. 45110 was purchased by a fund set up on the initiative of David Porter of the Flairavia Flying Club at Biggin Hill civil airport. She was moved to Ashford in Kent early in 1969, to be kept in the former BR shed there with three ex-Southern locomotives. Mr Porter later decided that her preservation days should be spent more actively and she was towed in goods trains from Ashford to Bridgnorth in August 1970. Now fully restored, she was named 'R.A.F. Biggin Hill', with LMS pattern nameplates, on 12 September 1971.

No. 80079 was one of 155 2-6-4Ts built to a standard design under the direction of R. A. Riddles, chief mechanical engineer of BR at Derby, Doncaster and Brighton between 1951 and 1956, and derived from the Fowler, Stanier and Fairbairn 2-6-4 tanks first constructed under LMS auspices in 1930.

The Severn Valley engine was built at Brighton in March 1954 and shedded at Tilbury for service on the London, Tilbury and Southend line. On 30 January 1958 she was involved in the Dagenham East accident, colliding with a preceding train at 25mph in thick fog, though she was not seriously damaged. On the electrification of the Fenchurch Street–Shoeburyness line in 1962, the engine was transferred to the Western region at Croes Newydd depot, Wrexham. In common with other Wrexham locomotives, she worked on the Severn Valley line during the last year of scheduled BR passenger services in 1962–3.

In July 1965 no. 80079 was sold to Woodham Bros of Barry and was bought by a large group of Severn Valley members in 1970 for complete restoration and service on the line.

The 120 locomotives of Collet's 2251 0-6-0 class were used all over the GWR system after their introduction in 1930. No. 3205 was completed at Swindon in October 1946 and shedded at Gloucester for nine years for use on local passenger and freight workings to Ross, Hereford, Ledbury, Cheltenham and Swindon. For four years from 1956, the engine was shedded at Worcester and employed on banking duties between Honeybourne and Campden before her allocation to Shrewsbury for a year which included work on the Severn Valley line.

Her last years before withdrawal in June 1965 were spent on the SR line between Templecombe and Exeter, after which she was bought by the 2251 Preservation Fund and restored at Buckfastleigh in 1965–6 by a small team led by Tony Goss. The custodian of the engine, David Rouse, was responsible for the decision to link the locomotive with the Severn Valley line and she was towed by diesel to Stourbridge in February 1967 whence she travelled under steam with four coaches to Bridgnorth on 25 March. No. 3205 was chosen to head the first public passenger train on the Severn Valley line on 23 May 1970.

No. 1501 was the second of a batch of ten new 0-6-0 PTs with outside cylinders completed at Swindon during the summer of 1949. The design originated under F. W. Hawskworth to a GWR order but no examples were built until after nationalisation. They were mainly designed for heavy shunting, but in practice they were principally used for moving empty passenger stock. With several others of her class no. 1501 began work in this capacity between Old Oak Common and Paddington before being transferred to Southall in December 1950 where she remained on normal depot duties for ten years.

The advent of 350hp diesel shunters rendered the 15XXs redundant unusually early and at the beginning of 1961 no. 1501, together with no. 1502 from Didcot and no. 1509 from Newport, was assembled at Swindon and sold to the National Coal Board for service at the Keresley colliery, Coventry. No. 1501 survived both its stablemates at Keresley and remained active there until September 1969. All three had been reserved for preservation by the Severn Valley and by the Warwickshire Railway Society. The other two were plundered for spare parts before being surrendered for scrap, while no. 1501 arrived at Bridgnorth in November 1970 for full restoration, which is now in hand.

The small Prairie 2-6-2T, no. 4566, was built at Swindon and entered service in October 1924. It was one of 175 engines constructed to G. J. Churchward's design in two batches, first at Wolverhampton in 1906–8 and then at Swindon from 1909 until 1929. They were very successful and became great favourites of the GWR for branch line work, including the Severn Valley line.

No. 4566 served mainly in the south-west from Bristol and Penzance and has the distinction of being the last steam engine to be repaired at the Newton Abbot works in July 1959. After storage at Plymouth she was withdrawn in April 1962 and sold to Woodham Bros of Barry for breaking up. The engine lay there for seven years but in 1969 David Rouse and Bob Sim examined all the Prairies at Barry with a view to selecting one for possible purchase and use on the Severn Valley line. Apart from a number of missing fittings no. 4566 was found to be in surprisingly good condition and was consequently bought through a preservation appeal. She was towed to Bewdley in a succession of freight trains in August 1970, where full restoration, which is expected to take two or three years, is now in progress.

The 'Jinty' 0-6-0T, no. 47383, was constructed for the LMS by the Vulcan Foundry, Newton-le-Willows, and entered service in October 1926. Her shunting and transfer trip work over a period of forty years was done from a number of sheds including Devons Road in East London, Chester, Carlisle, Burnley and Newton Heath, Manchester. She was first withdrawn at the end of 1966 but was returned to work at Williamsthorpe colliery, Chesterfield, for another year.

The initiative to purchase the 'Jinty' came from F. G. Cronin and B. H. Crick of Manchester, and the Manchester Rail Travel Society was formed to raise funds for the purchase of the engine in collaboration with the Severn Valley Railway. In the event she was bought as part of an Association of Railway Preservation Societies package deal and was moved to Bridgnorth by road in May 1967.

0-6-0T, no. 686, 'The Lady Armaghdale', was built by the Hunslet Engine Co. of Leeds in 1898 for service on the Manchester Ship Canal Railway. The engine was specially designed for work on that line which had many short radius curves. Originally named 'St John', she worked continually on the MSCR, apart from overhauls at Leeds in 1938 and 1958, until withdrawn as surplus to requirements in 1963. However, she was immediately bought by ICI for use at their Dyestuffs Division works at Blackley, close to the engine's former depot, where she was renamed 'The Lady Armaghdale' and worked transferring coal from the electrified Manchester–Bury line to the boiler house within the works.

In 1968, for reasons of economy, rail operations at the works were abandoned and the engine was offered for preservation. She arrived at

Bridgnorth in July 1969 where, after minor repairs, she has been used for shunting and similar duties, normally alternating with the Manning Wardle, no. 2047, described below.

No. 813 is a typical example of the small fleet of 0-6-0STs owned by the Port Talbot Railway Co, and used for shunting and coal traffic on their system in South Wales. She was built by Messrs Hudswell, Clarke of Leeds in 1901 and allocated to Duffryn Yard depot, which was absorbed by the GWR in 1908. Early in 1934 she was bought by Beckworth Collieries Ltd of Northumberland where she worked until 1967.

The fund to save her was launched by P. H. Goss and the purchase completed in August 1967 ready for delivery to Bridgnorth by road in November.

0-6-0ST, no. 2047, was the last locomotive to be built by the Leeds firm of Manning Wardle, which went into voluntary liquidation in 1927 after sixty-eight years of engine building. She was ordered by the Rugby Portland Cement Co. in April 1926 and delivered to their New Bilton works in August that year.

Initially the engine worked hauling special wooden-framed tippler wagons of cement ore on the very steep line between the quarry and the crushing plant and for this reason was fitted with 'dumb buffers'. Apart from a short period at the Southam works in 1943 she remained at New Bilton until superseded by a conveyor system at the quarry in the early 1950s. Thereafter she worked on the dwindling coal traffic from the main line into the works until the end of 1966.

The cement company, wishing to see the locomotive preserved, offered her for sale at the very modest price of £150, which was enthusiastically accepted. The engine was transported by road to Bridgnorth in October 1967. Since then, she has been completely overhauled and named 'Warwickshire' to commemorate forty years' work in the county.

The 0-4-0ST, no. 1738, was built in 1928 by Peckett & Sons at the Atlas Locomotive Works, Bristol, and delivered later that year to Hams Hall power station at Coleshill. Pecketts built very little other than small saddle tanks for industrial use and no. 1738 is a typical example of their W6 class of which over forty were constructed between 1926 and 1940. Her work, together with that of an identical engine at Hams Hall, consisted of the transfer of coal wagons from the exchange sidings of the then LMS at Coleshill to the power station boilers. Later the two Pecketts were relegated to feeding the older 'A' station which in its later years was only used in winter and thus the engines spent a part of each year in store.

In 1968 the 'A' station was closed altogether and the fleet of steam engines displaced by diesels. No. 1738 was bought by a regular driver at Bridgnorth, J. McNally, and delivered for immediate operation in July 1968.

4-6-2, no. 70000, 'Britannia', is the largest locomotive at Bridgnorth.

She was built at Crewe at the end of 1950 and named at Marylebone in January 1951. R. A. Riddles's class 7MT Pacifics, of which 'Britannia' was the first engine built, was the first pure BR locomotive design. As such, she was tested at length between Crewe and Carlisle before being allocated to Stratford for service on the Eastern Region. This included working very fast trains from Liverpool Street to Norwich and other main centres on the Region and also exceptional tasks such as hauling King George VI's funeral train from Sandringham to London, on the first stage of its journey to Windsor in February 1952.

No. 70000 was transferred to Crewe in 1963 in advance of dieselisation on the Eastern Region, for general duties. In 1965 she went to Newton Heath, Manchester, from where she was withdrawn for preservation by BR the following year. In the event, as related on page 25, the preservation order was transferred to no. 70013, 'Oliver Cromwell', and for a while no. 70000's future seemed to be imperilled, but she was salvaged by the East Anglian Preservation Society and arrived at Bridgnorth in April 1971.

The 57XX 0-6-0PTs were designed by C. B. Collett and introduced in 1929. They were very successful and 863 examples were built, both at Swindon and by outside contractors, until 1950. No. 5764 was one of the first, built in 1929, and allocated to Old Oak Common, where she remained until withdrawn from British Railway service in May 1960. London Transport, who acquired no. 5764 along with several similar engines, renumbered her L95 and worked her throughout their system, though principally from Lillie Bridge (Kensington) and Neasden. With her sister engine, L94, now at Tyseley, L95 was withdrawn from London Transport service in June 1971. A fund had previously been set up by Kidderminster supporters of the Severn Valley Railway to buy her and she was duly transported by road from Neasden to Bridgnorth on 19 June 1971, and put to work immediately, still in London Transport maroon livery, though she is to be restored to Swindon green.

The Ministry of Supply had 377 0-6-0STs built for them to a standard design of the Hunslett Engine Co. between 1942 and 1946. Seventy-five of them were acquired after the war by the LNER and classified J94. Production continued for many years and with its combination of great power and ability to work over tight curves, the class was very popular with the National Coal Board. The army continued to use them and no. WD193 was in fact ordered for military use when built in 1953. She worked on the Shropshire and Montgomeryshire Light Railway, being shedded at Kinnerley, and thus strayed occasionally almost on to Severn Valley Railway metals at Shrewsbury.

No. WD193 was in store at Long Marston Camp, Stratford-upon-Avon, for most of the 1960s until she was acquired for the Severn Valley Railway in June 1971, repainted and transported to Bridgnorth by road in August that year.

During World War II R. A. Riddles introduced a 2-10-0 locomotive for running on lightly laid track and over tight curves, while retaining enormous power. The North British Locomotive Co. built 150 examples at Glasgow, of which no. WD600, 'Gordon', was the second in December 1943. She was sent immediately to the Longmoor military railway and remained there throughout her official working life for instructional purposes. Only twenty-five engines of the class were taken into British Railways service after the war, mostly for work in Scotland, and the only occasion when 'Gordon' was seen on the main line was moving to and from Eastleigh works for repair. She was to have been one of the major items in the Longmoor Trust's locomotive stud, but when the project was given up the army asked the Transport Trust to find the engine a home, and in due course the Severn Valley Railway was chosen.

She is leased on terms which would facilitate her return to Ministry of Defence service in the event of national emergency. 'Gordon' has worn several liveries in its time—khaki, army green and blue—but is in first class condition and will be preserved in its present army livery.

LNER class K4 2-6-0, no. 3442, 'The Great Marquess', is representative of a small and specialised class consisting of six engines designed by Sir Nigel Gresley to cope with the difficult operating conditions on the West Highland line, from Glasgow to Fort William and Mallaig. By 1935 it had become apparent that the K2s then in service on this line would have to be replaced by a more powerful locomotive to eliminate the amount of double heading demanded by the ever-increasing weight of the trains. The severe curvature and gradients, coupled with problems arising from weight restrictions gave the designer a difficult task. However, when the first K4 emerged from Darlington, by the use of high boiler pressure, small driving wheels and the standard three cylinder arrangement, a locomotive had been created with a tractive effort of almost 37,000lb which could tackle this formidable route with trains of 300 tons unassisted. This was a great improvement on the 220-ton limit of the K2. No. 3442 was built at Darlington in 1937. With the exception of the original K4, all six locomotives of the class were named after a clan or family connected with the territory served by the West Highland line, 'The Great Marquess' being Montrose, who campaigned in tremendous style over that country. The K4s were eventually superseded on the West Highland route by diesels and finished their days in freight service. After withdrawal, 'The Great Marquis' was brought down to Yorkshire and thence to Bridgnorth by Lord Garnock and is now preserved in LNER livery and in working order.

12 Foxfield Railway

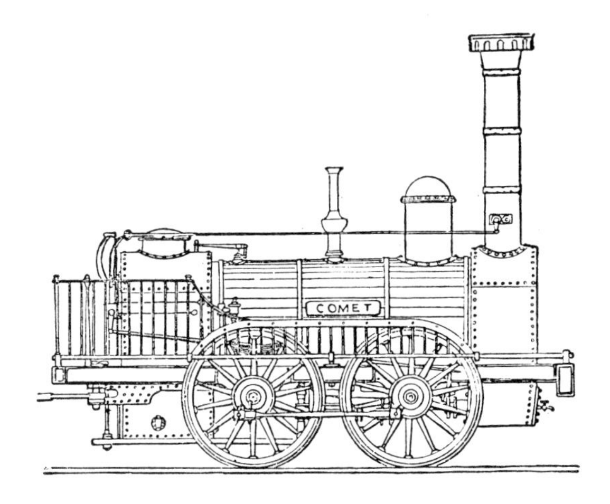

Hawthorn's 'Comet',
Newcastle and Carlisle
Railway, 1835

The Foxfield Light Railway Society which, since January 1972, has been a company limited by guarantee, was formed in 1967 to preserve and operate the Foxfield line of nearly four miles between Dilhorne and Blythe Bridge, five miles south-east of Stoke-on-Trent.

The standard gauge railway was originally built during the eighteen-nineties to link Foxfield colliery, at Dilhorne, with the North Staffordshire Railway's main line at Blythe Bridge. The colliery closed in August 1965 and the land and some of the buildings were bought the following year by Tean Minerals Ltd. The new owners had no use for the line, which rapidly fell into disrepair. However, it was a natural choice for a preservation society, being a good length, on private land and unencumbered with engineering features and hazards. The Society has been fortunate in enjoying the use of the works locomotive shed, stores shed and other facilities as well as the line itself under the present owners.

Although a former mineral line, the railway runs through beautiful country throughout its length to Blythe Bridge, where the link with the main line has now been cut. Woodlands give way to open pastures, with cuttings, embankments and severe gradients, such as the 1 in 22 stretch just outside Foxfield Works, which are ideal for showing the beauty of steam at its best. From the climb out of Foxfield, heading south-west, the line curves through Foxfield Wood and Pearcroft Wood, where there are two turnouts of an earlier branch and a train assembly siding.

Passing the summit of the line (about 750ft), the track passes through Dilhorne Wood and is then straight, heading south past Stansmore Hall to circle the foot of Blakely Bank Wood and cross the Caverswall–Dilhorne road by a gated level crossing. Continuing downhill there is a further straight section and deep cutting, with the bridge carrying the Caverswall–Blythe Bridge road over the line, and a little further on there is a view of Caverswall Castle. The line terminates in a fan of sidings at Blythe Bridge, near the 550ft contour.

The terminus and only access point at the present time is at Foxfield Works, where the nine steam locomotives which work on the line are shedded. These consist of five 0-6-0s and four 0-4-0s, all saddle tanks. 0-6-0ST no. 35 is the oldest locomotive at Foxfield and was delivered new to Birmingham Corporation Waterworks from Manning Wardle in 1895. It was transferred to Lloyds Ironstone Co. at Corby in 1912 and remained there until removed to Foxfield for preservation in October 1969. No. 35 is privately owned, as is the next oldest of the 0-6-0STs, 'Cranford', built by the Avonside Engine Co. in 1924 for the Staveley Iron Co. at Devonshire Ironworks, Derbyshire. It worked in ironstone quarries there and at Byfield and Cranford until withdrawn and acquired for preservation in 1971. 'Lewisham', built by Bagnall in 1927, arrived at Foxfield on permanent loan from the British Sugar Corporation in November 1970. 0-6-0ST, 'Robert', built by Avonside in 1933 worked at Lamport Ironstone Quarries throughout its life until preserved privately in 1969. 'Robert' was originally kept at Quainton Road but was transferred to Foxfield in October 1971. The newest of the 0-6-0STs, no. 39, built by Robert Stephenson & Hawthorns, was latterly in NCB service at Gedling Colliery, Nottinghamshire.

The 0-4-0STs are also all of industrial origin. 'Henry Cort', built by Peckett in 1903, is the property of the Society and was the first locomotive to arrive at Foxfield in 1967. The others are another Peckett, no. 11, built in 1947 for the West Midlands Gas Board; 'J. T. Daly', built by Bagnall in 1931 for Thomas Piggott & Horsley Bridge structural engineers of Tipton; and 'Marston Thompson & Evershed No. 3', built by Hawthorn Leslie for the firm after which the engine is named, in 1924. All are privately owned.

The Foxfield Light Railway Society is mainly concerned with operating the locomotives on it, nearly all of which are privately owned. Members of the public may ride on the trains through the device of day membership on the second Sunday of each month between April and October, when there are normally four trips in each direction.

13 Midland Railway Society

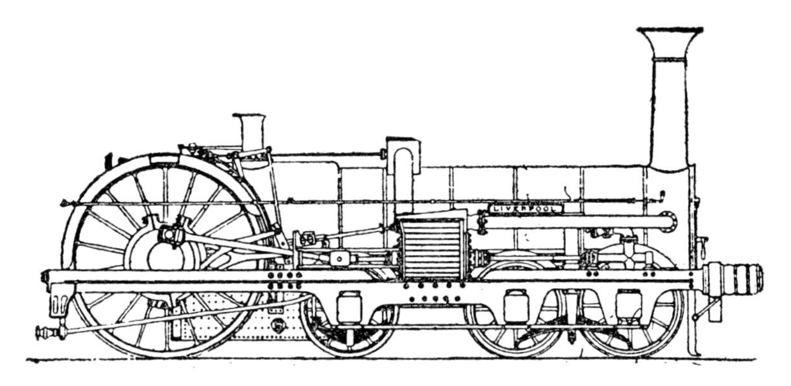

Crampton's 'Liverpool'

The Midland Railway Society was formed to create a working steam museum and this has expanded into plans to acquire and work a 2¾-mile stretch of line between Shackerstone, where it is already in possession of a section of track, and Market Bosworth.

The Society's headquarters are at Shackerstone station on the former Ashby & Nuneaton Joint Railway. This line, opened in 1873, was twenty-nine miles long, ran from Moira West to Nuneaton Abbey and junctions and was jointly operated by the London & North Western and Midland railways. The other part of the joint line was a branch from Shackerstone to Coalville. All of it became part of the LMS at the time of the Grouping. Passenger services ended in 1931 but the line continued to carry excursion traffic until the early 1960s when the Coalville branch was closed altogether. The Nuneaton line remained open to freight traffic until the beginning of 1970, since when the line has been used only for the storage of wagons.

The history of the line was uneventful, apart from a private visit by King Edward VII to his friend, Lord Howe, at Gopsal Hall in 1906, when the platform at Shackerstone was specially raised. Several thousand people from the area gathered to catch a glimpse of the King but when the door of the train fouled the platform his emergence was less dignified than had been planned and he left immediately and without ceremony in a closed carriage.

A large 'Midland' signal box controlled the junction at Shackerstone and immediately after the Grouping there were five through trains in each direction between Nuneaton and Ashby and another between Nuneaton and Burton-on-Trent. From 1890 onwards there had been a through coach from Ashbourne to Euston, worked for a while by a North Stafford locomotive as far as Rugby. The Shackerstone–Coalville branch was worked principally by an LNWR motor train. After the withdrawal of passenger services most of the freight and mixed traffic classes, including the heaviest, worked over the line.

The stations on the line follow a fairly standard MR pattern but Shackerstone is notable for its setting. The approach from the village is by a long drive which climbs gently through an avenue of trees. It is flanked on the right by the Ashby canal and on the left by the railway embankment which declines into a deep cutting immediately beyond the station, so deep, indeed, that it was afterwards agreed that it should really have been a tunnel. At the station end the cutting is wide enough to embrace the goods yard which is now the home of the Society's rolling stock.

The Society was formed in the summer of 1969, initially with the aim of preserving the Jubilee class no. 5690, 'Leander', which was, and still is, in Woodham's yard at Barry. This plan came to nothing but it left the nucleus of a locally based preservation society for the East Midlands, and plans to preserve a local line followed. No obvious stretch of line presented itself but the Society's need for a permanent location became urgent in the autumn of 1969 with the acquisition of a Borrows well tank, 'The King'. This engine was temporarily kept at Market Bosworth station which, with the closure of the Ashby–Nuneaton line in sight, had already been leased to a garage proprietor. Shortly after this Mr Alan Tingay, the well-known traction engine enthusiast, purchased Shackerstone station and offered the Society the use of part of the station and yard. The Market Bosworth–Shackerstone section of the line thus emerged as the Society's area of action. Once this is in operation it is intended to extend southwards by a further 1½ miles to Shenton station, close to the site of the battle of Bosworth Field, making the whole line a little more than four miles long.

A considerable amount of restoration, especially on the station buildings, has already been carried out. Quite apart from the inevitable deterioration of an empty building, the station at Shackerstone has suffered from the usual attention of vandals. At one time it had neither a waterproof roof nor windows left but most of this has been repaired, not only to make the building a serviceable headquarters for the Society but also with an eye for re-creating an authentic Midland Railway station. Unfortunately, in 1964, following the closure of the Coalville branch, all the sidings were lifted, the line to Market Bosworth was singled and the signal box demolished. Most of this has now been redeemed and a long siding relaid. The new signal box, which will eventually regulate the operation of the line, will be used in part as a much-needed extension to the small relics museum which has been set up in the main station building.

In August 1970 'The King' locomotive was hauled by diesel from Market Bosworth to Shackerstone and then lifted by crane from BR track to the Society's siding. The two other locomotives in the present collection, NCB no. 11 from Pye Hill, Nottinghamshire, and British Gypsum's Peckett, 0-4-0ST, 'Lady Angela', arrived in May 1971, making the locomotive stock as shown in Table 21. 'The King' was delivered

Table 21 Steam locomotives at Shackerstone

Type	Name/number	Builder	Year
0-4-0WT	'The King'	Borrows	1906
0-4-0ST	11	Hunslet	1925
0-4-0ST	'Lady Angela'	Peckett	1926

new to the United Glass bottle manufacturing works at St Helens in Lancashire and later served at the same company's London works from 1923 to 1967, when it was acquired by the Industrial Locomotive Preservation Group and taken to Robertsbridge. It was bought by Mr A. Hunt of Hinckley, a few miles south of Market Bosworth, and placed on permanent loan to the Society. At the time it arrived it was not in working order but it is now being restored. The ex-NCB Hunslet 0-4-0ST, no. 11, worked throughout its life at Jacksdale and Pye Hill collieries. The engine has cut-down boiler mountings and no cap, just front and rear spectacle plates, and was one of several 'cut-down' locomotives used at Pye Hill because of a very low bridge which carried the BR (ex-GNR) Pinxton branch over the sidings. Since the closure of this line the bridge has been removed and the individualistic steam traction of Pye Hill was superseded by normal sized diesel engines. The third locomotive, a Peckett 0-4-0ST of 1926, 'Lady Angela', was supplied new to British Gypsum at Kingston-on-Soar and worked all its life between the mine and the sidings at Kegworth on the LMS main line. Like no. 11 she worked as a spare engine for a few years after replacement by diesels until she was purchased by the Society.

This collection attracted 3,000 people to the Midland Railway Society's first open day in August 1971 and a further 5,000 to the second open day in October. BR finally abandoned the line in November 1971 when serious negotiations for acquisition of the line began.

14 Main Line Steam Trust

Gresley V2 class, 2-6-2, no. 4471, 'Green Arrow'

The long-term future of large locomotives in steam and working at speed may depend on the attitude of British Railways and the steam ban. If it does not prove practicable to work steam-hauled trains to any worthwhile extent on main line BR metals then the Main Line Steam Trust may come closer than any other preservation body to providing an alternative. Whether or not circumstances make the Trust unique in this respect, it has an outstanding contribution to make to railway preservation. The Trust exists to buy, restore and work a ten-mile stretch of the former Great Central Railway from Thurcaston Road in Leicester to Loughborough Central station, traversing some splendid country, including the Swithland Reservoir and part of Charnwood Forest.

The Great Central Railway, developed out of the Manchester, Sheffield & Lincolnshire Railway, opened in 1847. This in its turn had been formed by the amalgamation of the Sheffield, Ashton-under-Lyme & Manchester, Sheffield & Lincolnshire Junction and Great Grimsby & Sheffield Junction railways. The name, Great Central Railway, was adopted in 1897 in preparation for the opening, two years later, of the railway's extension from Annesley, Nottinghamshire, south to London (Marylebone), making a fourth trunk route between London and the midlands and north of England. Until this line was opened the MS&LR relied for its London connection on a fifty-year agreement dating from 1857 with the Great Northern Railway, under which services ran from

Manchester (London Road) to King's Cross via East Retford. Sir Edward Watkin, chairman of the MS&LR from 1864, had extensive railway interests in the south, including the chairmanship of the Metropolitan Railway. He advocated the building of a London extension from quite early on, including a scheme which was planned in collaboration with the Midland Railway. Watkin's Metropolitan connections dictated the route of the line to London when planning reached that stage and thus it was built south from Annesley, near Mansfield, by way of Nottingham, Leicester and Rugby to Quainton Road, from where the GCR ran over Metropolitan metals to Canfield Place, Finchley and thence over a new line to the specially built terminus at Marylebone.

Building did not begin until after Watkin had retired. It was to be the last main line and its progress was a microcosm of seventy years of railway planning and construction. The cost of land, particularly at the London end, amazed even the most experienced and cynical old investors of the dormant market of railway speculation. Costs were enormous, though not prohibitive, thanks largely to the ingenuity and perseverance of Alexander Henderson, a financier, who had been on the board throughout the years of building and became chairman shortly after the line was opened in 1899. By 1902 Henderson had built up a team which included (Sir) Sam Fay as general manager and John Robinson as chief mechanical engineer, but far from breaking into a new class of profitability after the opening of the London extension the enterprise faltered and the Great Central never again paid a dividend, even on its preference stock. Nevertheless, investment in the future continued. The Company's locomotives and rolling stock were always first class and the system absorbed several smaller railways in the Midlands, continuing to grow right up to 1914. It was an enterprising company in other respects also and was a party to the attempt, in anticipation of the Grouping, to form a working union with the Great Northern and Great Eastern railways.

Most of the GCR locomotives were designed by John Robinson, with others inherited from the MS&LR. The latter railway system included some severe gradients and spectacular engineering features, including Woodhead Tunnel. For it Charles Sacré designed one of the outstanding locomotives of the age in the form of his 423 class 4-4-0s of 1878. One of these engines, no. 434, was the locomotive involved in the notorious Penistone accident of July 1884 when twenty-four people were killed. The circumstances of the accident are well-known and the cause was an unfortunate combination of mechanical failures none of which was specifically attributable to any defect in the design or construction of Sacré's engine. The rest of the class gave excellent service for many years. So also did his other MS&LR locomotives, such as the 2-2-2 single of 1882 and a heavy goods engine design of 1880 for the mineral traffic which was the backbone of the system. Unfortunately, Sacré was an advocate of the Smith vacuum brake which contributed both to the Penistone accident and to another even more serious crash on the MS&LR system at Hexthorpe platform near Doncaster in 1887. A third disaster involved the failure of a similar brake at Armagh in 1889. Although, of course, this was quite remote from any responsibility of Sacré's, it appears to have contributed to his suicide very shortly afterwards.

John Robinson's Great Central locomotives are justly celebrated. They included the handsome 'Jersey Lily' Atlantics of 1904 (the nickname derived from a legendary barmaid in Gorton in the purlieus of the GCR locomotive works), of which twenty-seven were built. They were enormous engines, with power far in excess of anything required at the time of their introduction and so they survived to work with distinction on the LNER up to 1939. Other Robinson engines were the 4-4-0 Director class of 1913 and the 2-8-0 heavy goods engines introduced in 1911. Before World War I 130 were built for normal service on the GCR's heavy mineral traffic, followed by no less than 521 after the outbreak of war for service with the Railway Operating Division. Of these, 273 survived to work under the LNER after the Grouping. One of this numerous and very successful class is still in existence, and until recently was stored at Leicester awaiting restoration and display. This engine (no. 102) was withdrawn in 1963 and is well suited to the Main Line Steam Trust's philosophy and aims.

The only other surviving GCR locomotive (4-4-0 no. 506, 'Butler Henderson') is now, of course, in the Clapham Museum but the locomotives of the LNER are at least as much a part of the tradition which the MLST exists to preserve. Thus it is fortunate that another locomotive until recently stored in Leicester, but not on display, is a Gresley V2 class 2-6-2 no. 4771, 'Green Arrow', built in 1936 and withdrawn in 1962. In his days with the Great Northern Railway Sir Nigel Gresley became very familar with the requirements of a locomotive designed for heavy, high-speed, non-stop goods trains and he had plenty of scope to develop and advance such designs for the LNER. Initially work of this sort was done by the K3s and the V2s were designed to work even heavier trains. At ninety-three tons 'Green Arrow' is in the same weight classification as, for example, 'Britannia' and is far too heavy to work at all on most light railways, let alone to do so at speed, but she would be an ideal subject for working preservation on the MLST's line.

These engines immediately suggest themselves for work on the line because of their weight, the fact that they are stored in Leicester and because of their GCR/LNER associations. On the last count another possibility is the A4 no. 4498, 'Sir Nigel Gresley', which is beautifully restored and maintained but nevertheless incarcerated at Philadelphia in County Durham as long as the steam ban endures. She is certainly

Bulleid Pacific Preservation Society, plate 51

51 Bulleid Pacific, no. 34023, 'Blackmore Vale', in steam at Longmoor, June 1968

WORCESTER LOCOMOTIVE
SOCIETY SPECIAL
6000

Castles and Kings, plates 52–6

52 (opposite above) 'Clun Castle', with valve gear and motion renewed, resumed her heavy programme of specials in the autumn of 1967 and is here seen gathering speed at Wortley junction on route from Leeds to Carlisle on 30 September

53 (opposite below) 'King George V' on Bulmer's Private Railway, Hereford, during the Worcester Locomotive Society's Open Day on 19 September 1971

54 (above) 'King Edward I' passing Dauntsey box at 100mph in May 1957

55 (below) 'King Edward I', derelict and cannibalised in Barry scrapyard, November 1971

56 (above) No. 4073, 'Caerphilly Castle', the first of her class, on the Teignmouth sea wall with an up Plymouth–Paddington express in 1932

Dart Valley Railway, plates 57–61

57 (opposite above) Ex-GWR 2-6-2T, small prairie tank, no. 4555, in Buckfastleigh yard. Her sister, no. 4588, is also on the railway. Two other engines of the same class are being restored: no. 4566 at Bewdley for the Severn Valley Railway, and no. 5572 at Barry, by Taunton members of the Great Western Society

58 (opposite below) Ex-GWR branch line and auto-train engine 0-4-2T, no. 1420, at Buckfastleigh. She is restored to Great Western Railway livery but with the monogram 'GWR' on her tanks in contrast to the words 'Great Western' borne by her sister, no. 1466, preserved by the Great Western Society at Didcot

GREAT WESTERN
LA

1420
LA

GREAT WESTERN

BUCKFASTLEIGH SIGNAL BOX

59 (opposite above) Ex-GWR 0-6-0PT, no. 1369, with outside cylinders, built at Swindon in 1934, one of only ten of this unusual type. Here seen with immaculate GWR stock being prepared for Ashburton carnival celebrations in 1970

60 (opposite below) Ex-GWR 0-4-2T, no. 1420, passing Buckfastleigh signal box

61 (above) Ex-GWR 0-4-2T, no. 1420

West Somerset Railway, plate 62

62 (above) Minehead station, looking towards the buffers

Kent & East Sussex Railway, plates 63–5

63 (below) Ex-SER Stirling 0-6-0, class 01, no. 1370 (BR no. 31370), at Tenterden Town station

64 Stroudley 0-6-0T, BR no. 32670, entering all that remained of Wittersham Road station in 1959. A similar locomotive, BR no. 32650, 'Sutton', owned by the Greater London borough of that name, is at present kept at Rolvenden

65 End of the line, just north of Tenterden. The track to Headcorn has been lifted

Bluebell Railway, plates 66–70

66 (above) Ex-LB&SCR no. 72, 'Fenchurch', on Freshfield Bank. She has been restored to commemorate her years with the Newhaven Harbour Company

67 (below) Aveling & Porter 2-2-0WT, 'The Blue Circle', with ex-LNWR observation car at Sheffield Park

68 (above) Ex-SE&CR Wainwright 0-6-0Ts, no. 27, 'Primrose', and no. 323, 'Bluebell', with a train at Freshfield summit

69 (below) Ex-LSWR Adams 4-4-2T, no. 488, built by Neilson in 1885, at Horsted Keynes in April 1962. The engine had brought the 'Blue Belle' on its return journey from Sheffield Park

70 (below) Ex-GWR Dukedog 4-4-0, no. 3217, 'Earl of Berkeley', built at Swindon 1938, with a train at Freshfield summit

Stour Valley Railway, plates 71, 72

71 (opposite above) Unloading 'Gunby' from a low-loader

72 (opposite below) Inside the restored signal box at Chappel & Wakes Colne

Dean Forest Railway, plates 73, 74

73 (above) Ex-GWR 0-6-0PT, no. 3643, approaches Tufts junction in June 1964 with a Lydney–Coleford freight

74 (below) Peckett 0-4-0ST, 'Uskmouth'

Severn Valley Railway, plates 75–83

75 (opposite) Oldbury viaduct, just south of Bridgnorth, built in 1859

8233
10

76 (opposite) Stanier 8F, no. 8233, heading southwards over the Cleobury Mortimer road bridge just outside Bridgnorth

77 (above) 0-6-0T, 'Warwickshire', crossing Oldbury viaduct with a works train

78 (below) Ex-LNER K4 class, 2-6-0, no. 3442 (BR no. 61994), 'The Great Marquess', one of six of this class specially designed by Gresley for service on the West Highland line. Now owned by Lord Garnock and preserved in working order and LNER livery

SEVERN VALLEY
SPECIAL
3205

70000
SPL
2

79 (opposite above) Ex-GWR Collett Goods 0-6-0, no. 3205, at Bridgnorth in 1969, shortly before regular passenger services began. Telford's church of 1794 is visible in the background

80 (opposite below) No. 70000, 'Britannia', at Waterloo after arriving with the LCGB 'Vectis Farewell' Railtour on 4 November 1964

81 (above) Ivatt 2MT, no. 46443, at Hampton Loade. Note rebuilding of the GWR signal box

82 (above) Ex-GWR no. 4930, 'Hagley Hall', in the early stages of restoration at Barry by members of the Severn Valley Railway for service on the line. Hagley Hall, near Stourbridge, is the seat of Lord Cobham, President of the Severn Valley Railway Co. One of the engine's name-plates is displayed there

83 (below) 2-10-0 no. WD600, 'Gordon', showing her ability to negotiate sharp curves, on the Longmoor Military Railway in July 1959.
She is now at work on the Severn Valley Railway on loan contract from the Ministry of Defence

Foxfield Railway, plates 84, 85

84 (above) *Left to right:* Manning Wardle 0-6-0ST, Robert Stephenson and Hawthorn's 0-6-0ST and 'J. T. Daly'

85 (below) Bagnall 0-4-0ST, 'J. T. Daly', at the beginning of the 1 in 22 section of the climb from Foxfield works

Midland Railway Society, plates 86–9

86 Shackerstone junction, *c.* 1910, looking from the Loughborough branch towards the station and Nuneaton

87 Shackerstone station today, headquarters of the Society

88 The pumping engine at Shackerstone used for lifting water from the river Sence to feed the water columns

89 0-4-0WT, 'The King', built by Borrows in 1906

Main Line Steam Trust, plates 90, 91

90 (above) Part of the viaduct over Swithland reservoir in Charnwood Forest, Leicestershire

91 (below) Belgrave & Birstall station, looking north

an engine which one might hope to see on the line given suitable conditions. Other locomotives which might seem to recommend themselves are those kept in major steam centres, again in perfect working order, which could usefully be exercised between Leicester and Loughborough. 'Bahamas', for example, kept on former GCR metals at Dinting, or 'Pendennis Castle', 'Clun Castle' and even 'King George V' are all examples of heavy locomotives in perfect working order which have only infrequent opportunities to work either over any real distance or at more than a few miles per hour. For these engines and their owners, the opportunity to work for limited periods over the Trust's line could be mutually rewarding.

The Loughborough to Leicester section of the GCR was part of the London extension. It is thus only just over seventy years old and its construction incorporated years of experience in railway building. Though it has been closed since 1969, the line remains structurally sound. On leaving Loughborough Central station, which is on the south-eastern edge of the town, the line passes along a cutting with housing development on the west side. After about half a mile, the line passes under the A6 Loughborough to Leicester road and then traverses a celebrated tract of hunting country, of rolling, windswept pasture and woodland. Two miles from Loughborough, Quorn and Woodhouse station, situated at the western extremity of Quorn, is passed and the line then skirts the Charnwood Forest hills before crossing Swithland Reservoir by means of two viaducts and a small island. Swithland north viaduct consists of five brick arches each of a 30ft span, carried on piers about 4ft wide, making an overall length of 212ft. Like Swithland south viaduct, it is 26ft wide but the latter is longer (449ft). It crosses the city of Leicester reservoir by nine brick arches and a central plate girder bridge. Immediately south of the reservoir is the site of Swithland sidings where it is proposed to build a new locomotive shed and maintenance facilities.

The next landmark is Rothley station, five miles south of Loughborough and from there to Belgrave and Birstall station the railway traverses undulating farmland by means of alternating cuttings and embankments. Belgrave and Birstall station itself is approached through a deep cutting (43ft at the most), with a golf course on one side and the village of Birstall on the other. Beyond Birstall the line is carried on a high embankment, which commands panoramic views of parts of Leicester, and to Thurcaston Road Bridge, the proposed terminal point of the line, nine miles from Loughborough station.

15 North Norfolk Railway

Midland and Great Northern Joint Railway 4-4-0 no. 55

The North Norfolk Railway Co. operates the Sheringham–Weybourne section of the former Midland & Great Northern Joint Railway, perhaps the most individualistic of the pre-Grouping companies and one which retained its character long after 1922. The basis of the company was a largely unconnected system of branch lines in north Norfolk and Lincolnshire built before the Light Railways Act 1896 but filling what were really light railway requirements. The wider possibilities of a through route in the area were suggested by the development in the 1870s of the seaside resorts of north-east Norfolk at places such as Cromer, Sheringham and Great Yarmouth, and the Eastern & Midlands Railway was formed in 1882 to exploit them. The branch from Melton Constable to Sheringham and Cromer via Holt was built in 1884–7 but the Eastern & Midlands Railway remained viable as a feeder only and by the nineties had run into financial trouble. Fortunately, the Midland and Great Northern railways, jealous of the Great Eastern's ever more profitable holiday traffic, intervened and formed the Midland & Great Northern Joint Railway in 1893. A link with the GNR already existed at Peterborough and a similar junction with the Midland was quickly established at Little Bytham.

From then until 1936 the M&GNJR continued to enjoy considerable independence. As a joint line it was not affected by the Grouping. The offices at King's Lynn and the workshops at Melton Constable serviced a heavily-graded line which, though mostly single track, carried seasonally heavy traffic, including through express trains. In 1936 the Midland (by then, of course, absorbed into the LMS) surrendered its interest and the LNER assumed full control, succeeded by the Eastern Region of British Railways. Under BR the consequences of being a limited cross-country route were again felt and closure began in 1952. Seven years later, when the 146 miles from Peterborough and Little Bytham to Norwich and Cromer were closed, British Railways argued that there was not one town of over 10,000 people served by the lines which was not also served by a main line of GNR or GER origin. The annual saving on closure was a colossal £500,000.

The Cromer–Melton Constable branch remained open until April 1964 but interest in preserving parts of the Midland & Great Northern Joint Railway had been alive for some years. Indeed, the M&GNJR Society had been founded in 1959 with a view to preserving and running public services over the line from North Walsham to Salisbury Road, Yarmouth. By reason of its length and the number of obstacles such as level crossings along it, this project did not advance very far but eventually it became obvious that BR were going to withdraw services between Sheringham and Melton Constable. At Sheringham a halt had recently been built on the Norwich side of a level crossing which any would-be preservationists would otherwise have had to man but as it was, the 2¾ miles west to Weybourne were ideal for private operation.

Track had already been lifted between Melton Constable and Weybourne and British Railways asked for £5,000 per mile for the section towards Sheringham, although it was being offered to scrap dealers for £3,000 per mile. This ridiculous situation was resolved by arranging for scrap dealers to buy the track at that price and to resell it at £3,300 per mile to Central Norfolk Enterprises Ltd, a company which had been formed to take over the railway. At the same time the company bought four Gresley quad coaches while the Midland & Great Northern Joint Railway Society bought two locomotives, an ex-GER J15, built in 1912 and an ex-LNER B12, built in 1928.

The money for all this was raised partly by Society subscriptions, the sale of about 2,000 £1 shares in the company, the sale of books and other fund-raising events. The largest contribution, however, came from a supporter in Berkshire, who made a loan of £5,000. Throughout its history this project has been largely financed and directed from sources outside East Anglia and even today 75 per cent of the finance comes from outside the area. The directors of the private company were a television engineer (David Rees, who had also founded the M&GNJR Society), a schoolmaster, a lecturer and a young surveyor. They realised from the first that much greater amounts of money would be needed and that more professionals would have to be brought in. A member of the Society's committee suggested the formation of an Industrial and Provident Society which could issue shares far more economically than a conventional company. Unfortunately, as so often happens in voluntary bodies, and railway preservation societies are no exception, disagreements arose and the schism was made permanent by the fact that instead of converting the existing company a completely new organisation was set up. The dispute dragged on until July 1968 when Captain Peter Manisty, RN (retd), chairman of the Association of Railway Preservation Societies, intervened and an arbitration committee under him recommended a compromise solution. Since Central Norfolk Enterprises Ltd owned the more important assets of the railway it was decided that this should continue but with the name changed to North Norfolk Railway Co., Ltd. The board of the operating company changed and by the beginning of the following year consisted of John Snell, the author of several books on railway subjects, the owner of two European narrow-gauge locomotives and one of the ARPS arbitrators, together with remaining directors of the private company, supporters of the Provident Society and the company's new secretary, David Morgan.

The company then set about raising the money necessary to reopen the line and with some trepidation issued a prospectus, inviting members of the public to purchase £1 shares. The problem had been to decide what the minimum amount needed for the realisation of the company's operating plans would be and whether there would be a realistic chance of obtaining sufficient applications within forty days in order to comply with the Companies Act 1948. The amount aimed for was £11,700 and obviously the issue had to be done without the costly advertising in the *Financial Times*, *The Times* and the *Daily Telegraph* usually taken by commercial organisations inviting public subscriptions for shares. Fortunately the company managed to get editorial comment in all these papers and others besides, in addition to national and regional television and radio coverage. In the event, with the help of the M&GNJR Society, the issue raised nearly £14,000 in five weeks, the largest amount in the shortest period raised by any comparable enterprise at that time. Instead of forty-two shareholders, the secretary had 500 on his books. During the next two years these bought another 3,000 shares. Contracts for the purchase of the line were exchanged in the summer of 1971 and BR applied for a Light Railway Order on the company's behalf. The lengthy procedure involved should be complete by the beginning of 1973. Thereafter, the purchase, restoration and operation of the line to Holt, part of which has been lifted, will be considered but only if it does not threaten the viability of the shorter route.

In the heyday of the Midland & Great Northern Joint Railway the company's engineer and locomotive superintendent, William Marriott, presided over the workshops at Melton Constable. Most of the locomotives, in the very distinctive M&GNJR mustard-yellow livery, were modified versions of Midland Railway types, although Marriott also designed his own. The mainstays of the through express traffic were somewhat underpowered 4-4-0s from a Midland design of 1894 which at the height of the season were required to struggle over the severe gradients on the line with trains of fifteen or more coaches. Unfortunately, no locomotive of this class has survived and so the North Norfolk Railway has been denied what would have been an essential item in its collection. However, two of the six steam engines kept at Sheringham station do have strong local associations (see Table 22).

Table 22 Steam locomotives at Sheringham

Type	Number/name	Where built	Year	Origin
4-6-0	8572	Beyer Peacock	1928	LNER & BR (no. 61572)
0-6-0	564	Stratford	1912	GER & BR (no. 65462)
0-6-0ST	5 'Dougal'	Peckett	1939	NCB Ashington, Northumberland
0-6-0T	40 'The Shannock'	Robert Stephenson & Hawthorns	1954	NCB Ashington, Northumberland
0-6-0ST	'Ring Haw'	Hunslet	1940	Nassington Barrowden Mining Co., Peterborough
0-6-0T	'Colwyn'	Kitson	1945	ex-Stewarts & Lloyds, Corby

James Holden's 1500 class 4-6-0s (LNER classification B12/3) were introduced in 1912 for heavy passenger work of the sort then handled by his earlier Claud Hamilton 4-4-0s. The first engines of the class were built at the GER works at Stratford in 1912 but the Sheringham locomotive was one of those ordered by the LNER and built by Beyer Peacock in 1928. She worked from Liverpool Street to Norwich and Cromer on some of the heaviest trains in Britain and in later years on the Southend line before it was electrified in the late 1950s. No. 61572 was the last of her class in service and was not withdrawn until 1962. Although earmarked for preservation it was several years before serious work began on her and full restoration is not complete even now.

0-6-0 no. 65462 is a true Great Eastern locomotive. T. W. Worsdell's J15 class first appeared in 1883 and 189 engines were built at Stratford between then and 1913 for general passenger and freight duties. No. 65462 was one of the last, built in 1912. When the last of them were withdrawn in 1962 no less than four were retained with a view to preservation until the Midland & Great Northern Joint Railway Society chose no. 65462. She was last steamed in 1968 and extensive and basic repairs are still being carried out. If the Holden 4-6-0 and no. 564 were painted in Great Eastern livery, even though not strictly appropriate in the case of the former, they would be the only locomotives preserved in this glamorous form.

16 Midland Railway Project

Ambergate station

The Midland Railway Project is an impressive example of private and local authority initiative combined. The dedication and varied expertise of enthusiasts is supplemented by generous financial support from the Derbyshire County Council, in whose area the museum and working length of line are to be situated, and the Derby Corporation, whose project it is. It exists to restore and preserve railway relics of Midland Railway and LMS origin. Local and national interest are thus well combined, for the Midland was one of the largest pre-Grouping companies and had its headquarters at Derby from 1844 onwards. The railway and its associated work were almost entirely responsible for the transformation and growth of the town from a local centre to an industrial metropolis of the first rank. The Derby Museum and Art Gallery has had a working scale-model of the Midland Railway since 1949 but it was twenty years before the same body suggested the formation of a collection of full size exhibits. By that time the MR proper had ceased to exist for nearly half a century, steam had been banished from BR metals and even collectable remnants of the LMS were rapidly disappearing. Nevertheless, the project has been a great success to date and seems likely to develop into an important feature of the railway preservation world.

The Midland Railway was one of the largest in Britain. It was formed in 1844 by the amalgamation of the Birmingham & Derby Junction, Midland Counties and North Midland companies. Like the London,

Midland & Scottish Railway, of which it became a part at the time of the Grouping, it penetrated far outside the territory suggested by the name. The MR was remarkable less because of its own route miles, which by 1914 had reached 1,497, than by the extent of its running rights on other systems which at the same date gave its locomotives a total range of 2,443 miles. Joint lines were another major constituent of this empire and the company was prominent in many of the most ambitious examples of railway development, including the building of the Forth Bridge. Yet the whole complex was always controlled from Derby.

The Midland had a splendid locomotive tradition, built up by engineers like Matthew Kirtley, S. W. Johnson, R. M. Deeley and Sir Henry Fowler. However, perhaps because the LMS system which absorbed them was so vast and demanding or perhaps because of the simple excellence of the locomotives designed by their successors, H. G. Ivatt and Sir William Stanier, very few genuine Midland Railway engines have survived. Indeed, only five still exist and just one of them is in working order.

The scheme approved by Derby Corporation in 1969 to record this immense tract of transport history involved both a working length of line and a static museum. The latter got under way immediately and attracted volunteer helpers from the start. This body of supporters became known as the Midland Railway Project Group in December 1969 and was only just in time to salvage large quantities of MR signalling equipment before the introduction of power signalling at Derby and Trent. Further historic equipment was removed from obsolete boxes at Codnor Park, Clay Cross, Trowell Junction, Westhouses, Blackwell, Alfreton, Radford, Ambergate, Long Eaton, Coates Park, Nottingham, Burton and Leicester. In addition, four complete boxes, at Riddings, Radford Junction, Derby engine sidings no. 1, and New Street, Burton-on-Trent, had been dismantled and removed by the end of 1970.

For a stretch of working line there were nine possibilities, although most, of course, involved going well outside the boundaries of the county borough of Derby. In the end, the line selected was a 5½-mile stretch from Pye Bridge to Ambergate, which had been opened by the Midland Railway in 1875. This choice completed the involvement of the Derbyshire County Council in addition to the City Corporation. The working arrangement is that the County Council will own the site, while the Project Group concentrates on maintenance and operation. Motive power would ideally be of MR origin but the shortage of suitable locomotives has already been noted. The only true Midland engine still in working order is the Fowler 0-6-0 no. 3924, built at Derby in 1920, which is now on the Keighley & Worth Valley Railway. Eventually the Group located twelve ex-LMS locomotives, seven of the same class, 3F 0-6-0Ts, in Barry scrapyard. After detailed examination most turned out to be beyond redemption, but two, nos. 47327 and 47357, were eventually transported to Derby in July 1970. They were soon joined there by a third engine of the same class, no. 47445, straight from service at the British Oak Coal Screens at Crigglestone near Wakefield. All three have now been exhaustively restored and overhauled.

The Group has also acquired two other locomotives of non-LMS or Midland origin: a Markham 0-4-0 and an Andrew Barclay 0-4-0 crane tank locomotive. The Markham was bought from the Stanton and Staveley Group of the British Steel Corporation in excellent condition, having been fitted with a new firebox and copper tubes in 1965. Little more than cleaning and repainting was needed to restore her to working order. The same was almost the case with the crane locomotive, 'Stanton no. 24', built in 1925.

One hundred and fifty items of MR/LMS rolling stock have been located and inspected for possible acquisition. Two outstanding coaches are among those which have thus been added to the collection. Midland Railway Special Saloon, built at Derby in 1912, and an ex-LMS Dynamometer Car, built at Newton Heath in 1913 and kept at Derby for most of its working life between test runs. This vehicle (no. M45050), presented to the Group by British Railways, is a particularly valuable and instructive addition because the instrumentation in it is complete and intact. The Special Saloon is a unique and historic vehicle, on loan to Derby Corporation from Chasewater.

17 Middleton Railway

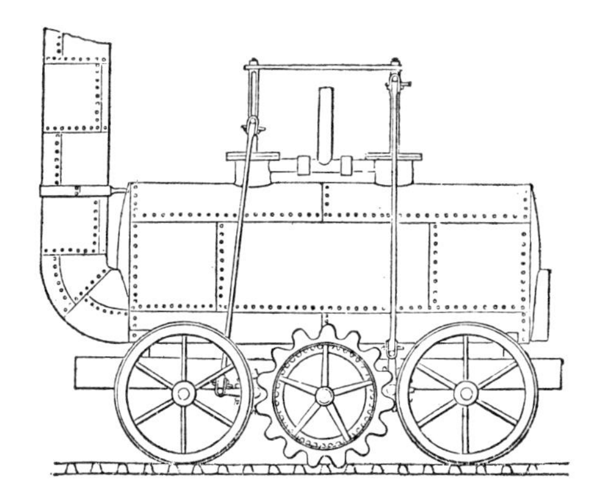

Matthew Murray locomotive on Blenkinsop rack rail

The Middleton Railway at Hunslet, south of Leeds, can claim an impressive succession of 'firsts': running over much the same route as the first railway ever to be authorised by Act of Parliament, in 1758; the first railway to change to steam locomotives, in 1812; and the first standard gauge line to be successfully reopened by amateurs, in June 1960. The line is now a privately operated industrial railway which offers a daily service to firms along it and steam-hauled trips by brake van from Hunslet Moor to Middleton Park Gates on weekend and bank holiday afternoons between March and October.

The first railway in the area was designed to help with the exploitation of the Brandling family's mineral interests. The Brandlings, though a Tyneside family from Felling, had come into the ownership of coal deposits at Hunslet through the marriage in 1697 of the Rev. Ralph Brandling to the heiress and granddaughter of Sir Ferdinand Leigh who fifty years before had sunk one of the first horizontal adits into an outcrop at Middleton. The Brandlings continued to live at Felling but were lucky in their succession of vigorous and far-sighted agents at the Leeds property, among them, from 1754, Richard Humble. Humble arrived at the moment when the competition from other mines in providing the burgeoning city of Leeds was beginning to grow. Leeds was then an unremarkable market town but by 1801 it had become the eighth city of Britain, with a population of 53,000.

The AIRE below is doubly dyed and damned;
The AIR above, with lurid smoke is crammed;
The ONE flows steaming foul as Charon's Styx,
Its poisonous vapours in the other mix.

So declaimed William Osburn before the Leeds Philosophical and Literary Society in 1857, by which time the blessings of material advance were all but outbalanced by the attendant squalor. But by then the great innovating days at Middleton were over, the Brandling estates were in the hands of trustees and steam traction on the colliery railway had temporarily capitulated to the horse.

When Humble took up his position as agent transport by water was still favoured for the heaviest commodities and the Middleton colliery was less accessible to the river Aire than were some of its competitors. In 1755 Brandling obtained leave to construct a wooden wagon-way of 960ft on Woodhouse Hill Lane, the object being to obtain better access to the river Aire. Private agreements then and over the next three years were superseded by a Bill which was passed on 9 June 1758, entitled:

> An Act for Establishing Agreements made between Charles Brandling, Esq., and other Persons, Proprietors of Lands, for laying down a Waggon Way, in order for the better supplying the Town and Neighbourhood of Leeds, in the County of York, with coals.

This was the first Act of Parliament for the construction of a railway. Prior agreements between Brandling and his neighbours were confirmed and provisions for his continuing use of the railway, as long as he supplied not less than 24,000 tons of coal a year at 50·3*d*. a ton, were incorporated in it. The Act refers to a 'waggon-way (such as is used for and about the coal mines in the Counties of Durham and Northumberland)'. This suggests that the rails would have been of oak, with a strip of beech on the top surface which could be renewed when necessary. The wheels of the wagons would have been beech as well, small in diameter and with metal plates attached to the inner faces to serve as flanges. The cross-sleepers at intervals of three feet or so would have been covered in gravel or cinders to protect them from the horses' hoofs.

The wagon-way quickly reversed Brandling's trading disadvantages, reduced the price of his coal and caused the output of the Middleton colliery to double within ten years. In 1779 he sought and obtained a second Act of Parliament whereby he was allowed to ask up to 8*d*. a ton more for his coal and undertook to supply twice as much of it. The price was put up again in 1793 in an Act which referred to the 'very great expense in making fresh winnings in the said coal working, and in making additional waggon-ways therefrom'. Yet another Act, of 1803, further recognised the high costs of mining and fixed the top price at

83·4*d*. a ton. Both these Acts countenanced the supply of coal from other Brandling mines in the area, notably the new workings at Beeston.

When the Middleton colliery was valued in January 1808, there were 4¼ miles of wagon-way, one half of the total made of iron, and six machines for drawing coals. The tradition of far-sighted and innovating management of the mine was more than upheld following the appointment in the same year of John Blenkinsop as agent. Blenkinsop's rack rail method of traction was patented in 1811 and the firm of Fenton, Murray & Wood was shortly afterwards commissioned to design and construct a locomotive on these lines at their Round Foundry at Holbeck, near Leeds. The locomotive which emerged had a cast-iron boiler 9½ft long and oval in section. At the time it was unique in having two cylinders, 8in. in diameter and 24in. stroke. The cost, variously quoted at between £350 and £400, included a £30 royalty to one W. West, as owner of Trevithick patent, 'for the use of the high pressure steam'. Her first practical test was on 24 June 1812 when she demonstrated her ability to do the work of sixteen horses and duly lived up to all expectations. On the level when lightly loaded she could manage 10mph, and 3½mph with a load of over ninety tons. This and another locomotive, topically named 'Prince Regent' and 'Salamanca' respectively, began work at Middleton on 12 August that year. They performed well enough although one of them blew up in 1818 killing the driver who, according to George Stephenson giving evidence about the accident before a Committee of the House of Commons, 'had been in liquor and had put a considerable load on the safety valve, so that upon going forward the engine blew up' and that 'if proper precautions had been used with that boiler, the accident would never have happened'.

Blenkinsop's management, together with the voracious war-time markets of the Napoleonic era, boosted output to an all-time record of just over 100,000 tons in 1814, the year before Waterloo. Conditions changed over the next twenty years. Competition continued to grow but demand levelled out. Not all the agents and managers were the equal of Blenkinsop and the trustees into whose hands the estates passed in 1834 naturally had little of the entrepreneurial zeal of the Brandlings themselves. With the price of coal down by one-third on its war-time peak and production no more than 25,000 tons a year there was little incentive either to expand and invest or even to maintain existing standards. Locomotives were thus abandoned and horse traction took over.

The Brandling estates were sold in 1862 and the new owners, who formed themselves into the Middleton Estate & Colliery Co., took over all the rights and responsibilities connected with the wagon-way. Steam traction, still on the original 4ft 1in. gauge, reappeared in 1866 in the form of a Manning Wardle 0-4-0ST, 'Blenkinsop', followed by a similar one, 'Matthew Murray', in 1869. By the time the line was converted to 4ft 8½in. gauge in 1881, 'Blenkinsop' had been scrapped but

'Matthew Murray' was sent back to the Manning Wardle works nearby for conversion to standard gauge and was returned together with a new 0-6-0ST 'Blenkinsop No. 2'.

The conversion was carried out because the character of the area had changed as a result of further industrial development. This gave the railway a potential role beyond the shipment of coal into Leeds and called for links with the main lines which ran into the city. By 1893 contact with the Midland Railway had been made by way of the Leeds Gas Co. lines and Kidacre Street level crossing and a second link with the Midland was completed at Balm Road in 1895. The Parkside spur to the Great Northern came into operation in 1899. Coal, of course, continued to be the major traffic for many years but it was joined by steel, steel manufactures and scrap as new companies moved in. Many of these newcomers built their own sidings, like Clayton's, to whom the Dartmouth branch was opened in 1920, with extensions to their neighbours, Robinson & Birdsell (scrap) and Kings (steel). Later, under the management of the National Coal Board, the Hunslet locomotive building firm of John Fowler used the line for test purposes and this facility has been extended in part under the preservation group to Hudswell Clarke.

Early in 1958 the NCB announced its plans to close the line. The colliery was losing money and much of the coal was in any case transferred to lorries at Hunslet Moor. Once again the heavy cost of track renewal and general maintenance threatened the line's future. The triumph of road transport was already half complete and it was argued that if the line was abandoned altogether the track-bed could be used for providing streamlined road access. The latter solution was abandoned on grounds of expense. The City Council's support for the case against the NCB led in due course to a compromise whereby a section of the line, from Parkside junction to Broom pit, was retained and restored. The railway thus remained, although with its freight monopoly broken and the percentage of coal carried from the colliery by rail cut by half.

Meanwhile the railway had celebrated its bicentenary in June 1958 with a special passenger train from Moor Road to Broom pit and back. This event naturally aroused great interest in the line and its long history and made the abandoned section of it a natural choice when, in September 1959, the Leeds University Union Railway Society resolved to try to acquire or build a stretch of line on which to keep rail-borne railway relics. The idea was coolly received by some of the University authorities but the enthusiasts, led by Dr R. F. Youell, persevered by founding the Middleton Railway Preservation Society. This differed initially from the University society in name alone and the support and assistance of the University, especially in engineering matters, has continued.

Ownership of the abandoned section of line which the Society proposed to use had been dispersed among many interests, led by the Middleton Fireclay Co., Clayton's, the City Corporation, BR, Robinson & Birdsell, John King & Co., Parkfield Metals and the Acme Engineering Co. The private owners were advised by British Railways that the line would not be workable without complete relaying and experience aboard some of the test trains rather confirmed this view. However, the line was ceremonially reopened with a train, albeit diesel hauled, on 18 June 1960, and with a coach from the recently closed Swansea & Mumbles Railway which, when it opened in 1804, was the first passenger-carrying railway. On 20 June the Society began to run 'free rides at your own risk' between Moor Road level crossing and Parkside bridge.

When the Society was founded there was no intention that the railway should be regularly operated but when this idea did develop it was less with a view to creating a tourist attraction than to restoring the line to its original role as a carrier of goods. Two of the most important firms previously served by the railway, Clayton and Robinson & Birdsell, agreed to patronise the venture, provided there was a regular daily service. This was introduced in September 1960 and has continued ever since, enabling the Middleton Railway to claim to be the only private line at the time of writing to provide a daily service throughout the year. The freight service is hauled mainly by diesel engines but the aim of the

Table 23 Steam locomotives on the Middleton Railway

Type	Number/name	Where built	Year	Origin
0-4-0WT	'Windle'	Borrows	1909	Pilkington Bros.
0-6-0ST	'Swansea'	Avonside	1909	Bynea Steel Ltd & Swansea & Mumbles Rly
0-6-2T	999	Stratford	1924	LNER & BR (no. 69621) last locomotive to be built at Stratford works
0-4-0ST	'Matthew Murray'	Bagnall	1943	Cohens, Stanningley
0-4-0T	1310	Gateshead	1891	NER & NCB, Pelaw
0-6-0ST	21	Avonside	1913	Mersey Docks & Harbour Board; now dismantled for spares
0-4-0ST	'Lord Mayor'	Hudswell	1893	—
0-4-0ST	'Henry de Lacy II'	Hudswell Clarke	1917	Kirkstall Forge
0-4-0ST	'Chairman'	Hudswell Clarke	1940	Yorkshire Tar Distillers, Stourton
0-6-0ST	6	Hawthorn Leslie	1935	Now cannibalised Portland Cement, Swanscombe, Kent

Society as a preservation body has been fully realised. Table 23 shows the present collection of steam locomotives.

Because it is situated in the heavily industrialised outskirts of a great city the Middleton Railway is unusually vulnerable both to vandalism and to the depredations arising from more legitimate works and activities on and near the line. For the same reasons it may appear to be the least glamorous of privately run lines but it is a uniquely faithful example of railway preservation and since 1962 has been protected by the National Trust against demolition or closure.

18 Keighley & Worth Valley Railway

LNER Gresley N7, no. 69715

The Keighley & Worth Valley Railway Co., incorporated in 1862, succeeded where the Manchester, Hebden Bridge & Keighley Junction proposal had failed seventeen years before. It brought the railway to Oxenhope and the Worth Valley, with stations at Haworth, Oakworth, Damems and Ingrow, and established a junction with the Midland Railway which had reached Keighley in 1847. Building the Worth Valley branch began in 1864, took rather longer than the year planned and cost a great deal more than the £36,000 estimated. These delays were caused principally by some difficulty in acquiring land and later by weather which aggravated the already difficult nature of some of the ground, leading to such mishaps as the subsidence at Ingrow Tunnel and consequential damage to the nearby Wesley Place Methodist Chapel. The eventual cost was £105,000 and the line was opened for passengers on 15 April 1867 and for goods traffic on 1 July.

From the beginning the line prospered and justified the expectations of the local promoters and also the Midland Railway which worked it in return for half the receipts, until it absorbed the branch completely in 1881. Although it never justified the construction of a second track the business on which the line depended was stable and grew steadily for most of its working life. Traffic was firmly founded on the worsted mills, supplying them with coal and raw materials, removing their products and transporting the labour force on which they depended. Other industries, like slate and stone quarrying, were stimulated by the railway's arrival. This business reflects the source of most of the financial and managerial impetus for building the line in the first place but the Gradgrinds of the Worth Valley were supported by such genteel investors as the perpetual curate of Haworth, Rev. Patrick Brontë, promoter of the abortive Manchester, Hebden Bridge & Keighley Junction Railway. Even in those days parsons loved railways.

In 1883 a new station was built at Keighley to accommodate the double track Great Northern Railway line from Halifax, which ran parallel with the Worth Valley branch over the last mile into the town. Modest improvements, like the building of passing loops at Oakworth and Haworth in 1900, were made in order to improve the timing and frequency of the services but the replacement of the wooden trestle bridge over Vale Mill Dam in 1892–3 was an expensive and largely gratuitous alteration, although it is true that the wooden structure carried a speed restriction, was somewhat shaky and is said to have caused anxiety among some of the passengers. To replace it a deviation leading, incidentally, to an easing of the gradient on this section of line was required and this in turn needed a substantial embankment, four bridges, a three-arch viaduct and a seventy-five yard tunnel. The cost to the Midland Railway was £25,000.

After World War I, in spite of its exceptional prosperity from opening to 1914, the branch began to sink through the early stages of rationalisation and contraction in the face of growing road competition and the exceptionally hostile conditions of the Depression. After World War II, judged against the ever more exacting profit requirements of the nationalised authority, the line's chances of survival looked increasingly dim, although in the last year of passenger operations, 135,535 passengers were carried and the deficit was an inconsiderable £4,000. In these circumstances it is somewhat surprising that the line was closed so early, for plans for closure were first referred to the Transport Users' Consultative Committee in April 1959. Their decision was deferred several times but following an experimental reprieve, during which an extra sixty-six trains per week were run without the anticipated growth in passenger use of the line, it was decided to close to passengers at the end of 1961. Damems station, allegedly the smallest on the former Midland Railway, had been closed since 1949.

As a newly closed branch a little under five miles long, it was inevitable even as early in the preservation mania as 1961–2, that the Keighley & Worth Valley line should attract the interest of enthusiasts. The Keighley & Worth Valley Railway Preservation Society was formed after a meeting in Temperance Hall, Keighley, in March 1962, three months after the ceremonial valedictory passenger train had been run over the line and three months before the withdrawal of freight services. The Society already had such encouraging precedents as the success of the Bluebell Railway—in many respects a similar venture—to sustain confidence and enthusiasm when they rented Haworth station as a headquarters and centre from which to plan the restoration, reopening and operation of the branch. In the very earliest months of the Society's work the continuing use of the line for freight trains facilitated the running of specials, culminating in a very successful run from Bradford, Forster Square, to Oxenhope and back in June 1962.

The Keighley & Worth Valley Light Railway Ltd was formed in February 1966 to complete the negotiations for the purchase of the line and as a necessary preliminary to the application for Light Railway Orders. The first part of the process was completed early in 1967 when the purchase of the line from Bridge 5 to Oxenhope was completed. The remaining mile or so into Keighley was to be leased but before this arrangement came into effect the Ingrow East goods line, running over the GNR metals parallel to the Worth Valley branch at this point, was closed, and the Company was able to purchase the line as far north as Bridge 1. Platform 4 of Keighley station is held on a twenty-five year lease. A year's hard work, inspection by the Ministry of Transport and the grant of the second Light Railway Order enabled the line to be reopened to the public on 29 June 1968. Since then a regular service has been maintained by the mainly volunteer staff of the Company on Saturdays, Sundays, Bank Holidays and some weekdays in the summer.

The northern terminus of the present railway is at platform 4 of the 1889 Keighley station, the rest of which is still in full BR use. At the end of the platform, having turned sharply right, the gradient, at 1 in 58, is the steepest on the line and is a tough beginning especially on wet days. The whole line lies within the boundaries of the borough of Keighley and the first mile or so runs through the industrial heart of it. About two-thirds of a mile from the start the development on the left is broken by a gap and a space which are the site of the junction with the GNR, closed in 1967 and lifted a year later. Ingrow, which was once served by a GNR station as well as the one on the branch, is soon reached. The station on the Worth Valley line, known as Ingrow West until June 1961, was severely vandalised during the years of closure and little apart from the waiting room remains of the buildings. The line then delves through Ingrow tunnel to emerge 150 yards further on near Clough's Mill, which is one of what were once many mills in the area which the railway was built to serve.

From this point the landscape opens up a little on the way to Damems, two miles from Keighley, where the station is so small that the platform is only long enough to accommodate one coach. Leaving Damems the gradient steepens to 1 in 64 and the line is carried first on an embankment and then through a cutting to Oakworth, where the Preservation Society is restoring the station as exactly as possible to its condition at the end of the last century. From here the line climbs for nearly a mile, including a stretch at 1 in 61, through Mytholmes tunnel (73yds) to

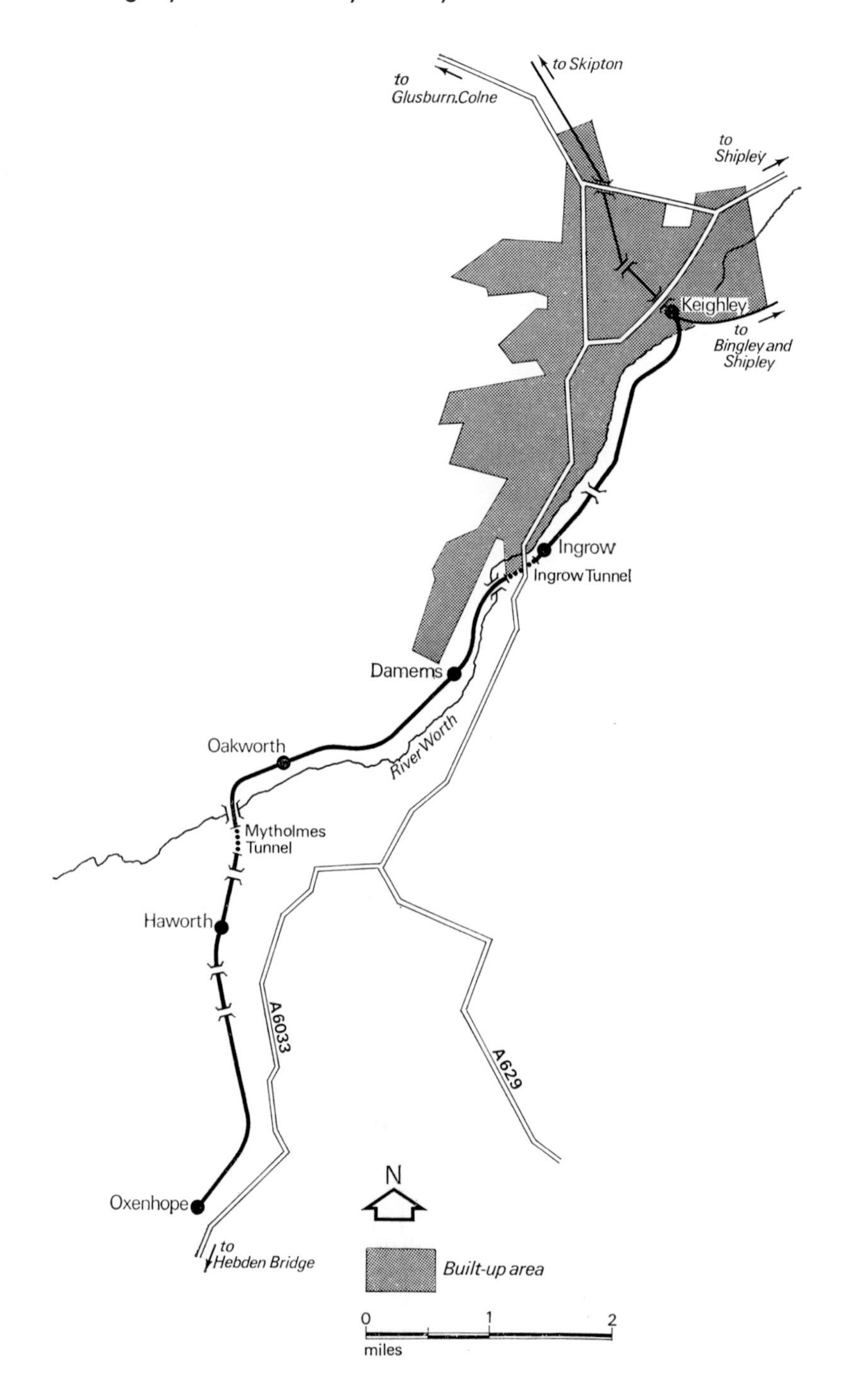

5 Keighley & Worth Valley Railway

Haworth, which is the headquarters of the railway and location of most of its collection of locomotives and rolling stock (see Table 24).

The collection of locomotives at Haworth is the largest at present in

Table 24 Steam locomotives on the Keighley & Worth Valley Railway

Type	Number/name	Where built	Year	Origin
0-6-0WT	'Bellerophon'	Haydock	1874	NCB, Lea Green
0-6-0T	1708	Derby	1880	MR, LMS & BR
0-6-0ST	752	Beyer Peacock	1881	LYR, LMS & NCB
0-6-0	957	Beyer Peacock	1887	LYR, LMS & BR
0-6-0ST	'Sir Berkeley'	Manning Wardle	1891	Cranford Ironstone
0-4-0ST	'Lord Mayor'	Hudswell Clarke	1893	Cohens, Stanningley
0-4-0ST	51218	Horwich	1901	LYR, LMS & BR
0-4-0ST	19	Horwich	1901	LYR, LMS, Mowlem, & United Glass
0-6-0T	31	Hudswell Clarke	1903	Manchester Ship Canal
0-6-0T	67	Hudswell Clarke	1919	Manchester Ship Canal
0-6-0	3924	Derby	1920	MR, LMS & BR
0-6-2T	4744	North British	1921	GNR, LNER & BR
2-6-0	42700	Horwich	1926	LMS & BR
0-6-0PT	5775	Swindon	1929	GWR & LTPB
4-6-0	45212	Armstrong, Whitworth	1935	LMS & BR
0-4-0ST	1999	Peckett	1941	Southport Gas Works
0-6-0T	'Harlaxton'	Andrew Barclay	1941	Stewarts & Lloyds, Harlaxton
0-6-0T	72 'Tornado'	Wilkes Barre	1941	US Army, SR & BR
0-6-0ST	'Fred'	Robert Stephenson & Hawthorns	1945	NCB
0-4-0ST	2226	Andrew Barclay	1946	ICI, Huddersfield
2-6-2T	41241	Crewe	1949	BR
0-6-0ST	57 'Samson'	Robert Stephenson & Hawthorns	1950	Stewarts & Lloyds, Corby
0-6-0ST	62	Robert Stephenson & Hawthorns	1950	Corby
0-6-0ST	63	Robert Stephenson & Hawthorns	1954	Corby
2-6-4T	80002	Derby	1951	BR
0-6-0T	69023 'Joem'	Darlington	1951	BR
4-6-2	34092 'City of Wells'	Brighton	1949	BR
0-6-0ST	68077	Andrew Barclay	1946	NCB & BR
0-6-0ST	'Brussels'	Hudswell Clarke	1945	Longmoor Military railway
4-6-0	5025	Vulcan	1934	LMS & BR

the care of any comparable organisation. It is also varied, ranging from an 1874 well tank such as 'Bellerophon' to a Bulleid Pacific, 'City of Wells'. An impressive proportion of the engines are in full operating order, including such splendid preservations as Mr W. E. C. Watkinson's 'Black 5', no. 5025, which is destined eventually to work on the Strathspey Railway in Scotland. Among the stars of the Railway's own locomotives is the only engine of Midland Railway origin still in working order. This is one of Henry Fowler's 0-6-0 intermediate goods engine class introduced in 1911, of which 197 were built before the Grouping including no. 3924 which emerged from Derby in 1920. The other MR engine at Haworth is not at present in working order, which is a pity, particularly because it is the last survivor of S. W. Johnson's 0-6-0 tank engine design of 1874 of which 240 were built over the ensuing twenty-five years. Engines of this class were much in evidence on the Worth Valley branch in its heyday and between the wars. No. 1708, built at Derby in 1880, has been fully restored externally in LMS livery rather than MR crimson because she was fitted with a new boiler in the twenties.

There are no less than four locomotives on the line which were originally built for the Lancashire & Yorkshire Railway. Two of them, nos. 752 and 957, are closely related. Two hundred and eighty of W. Barton Wright's standard goods engines, the 'Ironclads', were built by various makers for the LYR between 1876 and 1887. When (Sir) John Aspinall took over at the Railway's newly opened Horwich works he began to produce a more powerful goods engine and all but fifty of the 'Ironclads' were rebuilt as saddle tanks for shunting duties. 0-6-0 no. 957, built by Beyer Peacock in 1887, survives in its original Barton Wright form, while no. 752, built at the Beyer Peacock foundry in Gorton six years before, is one of the saddle tank conversions. The other LYR engines are 0-4-0ST 'Pugs'. No. 51218 served for sixty-four years under the LYR, LMS and BR and was the first steam locomotive at Haworth in K&WVRPS days, in January 1965. No. 19, which had been sold into industrial service by the LMS in 1931, arrived at Haworth from the Charlton works of the United Glass Bottle Manufacturers Ltd in November 1967.

The Great Northern Railway is represented at Haworth by one of Gresley's powerful N2 class 0-6-2Ts. These were a superheated development of H. A. Ivatt's N1 class and were designed for use on the GNR's London suburban services. They were specially equipped with condensing apparatus for service on those many-tunnelled lines and this accounts for the conspicuous piping on no. 4744's smokebox and water tanks. No. 4744 was built by the North British Locomotive Co. at Glasgow in 1921 and served for forty-one years on the GNR, LNER and BR. She is now owned by the Gresley Society and is on loan to the Keighley & Worth Valley Railway.

0-6-0T no. 72, 'Tornado', built by the Vulcan Ironworks, Wilkes Barre, Pennsylvania, in 1943 for United States Army service in Europe, was one of fifteen of her class bought by the Southern Railway in 1946. No. 72 saw little active service and spent most of her working life at Southampton, Willesden, Cricklewood and Guildford until she was withdrawn in 1967. Another interloper from the south, though not from abroad, is a Swindon built 0-6-0PT of the 57XX class. No. 5775, built for the Great Western Railway in 1929, was one of several of her class eventually sold to London Transport, becoming L89 in 1963. She was sold to the K&WVRPS in 1970 and like all her class is proving as sturdy and reliable now as she did during forty-one years' service for the GWR, BR and LTPB.

Locomotives of LMS origin are the Society's own Black 5, no. 45212, the second at present on the line, and one of George Hughes's Horwich 'Crabs', no. 42700. The numerous class to which the latter locomotive belongs derived their nickname from the distinctive high running plate and sloping cylinders. Although capable of running for long distances at 75mph or more, the 'Crabs' were at their best with heavy loads at lower speeds on difficult curves and gradients and were thus in demand for work on such notoriously exacting routes as the West Highland line. It is planned to bring Stanier 8F no. 48431 from Barry to Haworth for restoration.

Of the four BR-built locomotives, 'City of Wells' (Bulleid Southern Railway 'West Country' Pacific), no. 41241 (Ivatt LMS Prairie tank) and no. 69023 (Wilson Worsdell North Eastern Railway 0-6-0T) are all designs of pre-nationalisation origin. No. 80002 is one of two survivors of 155 BR standard 2-6-4Ts of a class, descended from LMS tanks of the same wheel arrangement, introduced in 1951 and built at Derby, Doncaster and Brighton. No. 80002, built at Derby, spent most of its working life in Scotland, mainly on suburban services in the Glasgow area.

The environs of the Worth Valley line are varied, ranging from the industrial waste around Keighley to the narrow river valley around Oakworth and the limitless moorland south of Haworth towards Oxenhope. These characteristics, together with the excellence and variety of the locomotives, rolling stock and permanent way, have made the railway much in demand for filming and associated purposes. The line has been used for films such as *The Virgin and the Gypsy*, *The Railway Children* and *The Private Life of Sherlock Holmes* and for documentaries.

The Keighley & Worth Valley Railway is already among the best of preserved railways and more than most other lines could profitably expand beyond its present five miles. Perhaps the Railway will add further lustre to its name by becoming the first preserved line to take advantage of the earthworks built by optimistic Victorian engineers and businessmen wide enough to take a double track and expand as far as possible in this way.

19 Yorkshire Dales Railway

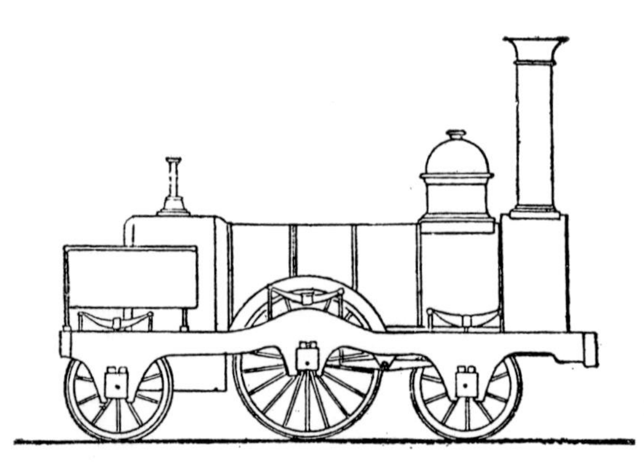

First type of Great Northern Railway passenger locomotive

The Yorkshire Dales Railway is one of the smaller preservation ventures and is situated on the former Skipton–Ilkley line at Embsay, about 1½ miles north-east of Skipton. It was built by the Midland Railway and opened in 1888. The line was closed by British Railways in 1965.

The present railway occupies an eighteen-acre site, which includes the station, goods shed and original signal box, and 4,400 yards of track, including some very interesting point work. Since operations began at Embsay in 1969 a great deal of work has been done, including the conversion of the goods shed into an engine shed and the introduction of electricity to the station. Track relaying and modification has produced the only working metre/standard dual gauge railway in Britain. Plans to relay track over 400 yards east from the present termination are also being considered.

The project began in 1968 when a group of railway enthusiasts in Skipton first had the urge to preserve a steam locomotive and to work it over a realistic stretch of line. The old Yorkshire Dales Railway from Embsay Junction, on the former Skipton–Ilkley line, to Grassington in Wharfedale (a distance of about nine miles) which had been closed by BR three years before, seemed the natural location. The Embsay & Grassington Railway Preservation Society was formed by the nucleus of pioneers, together with further enthusiasts recruited after a public meeting in Skipton Town Hall, in October 1968. The Grassington line at that stage was still partly in use as a mineral line from Swinden

Quarries and British Railways had plans to dispose of it in due course. For the time being the infant society decided to establish its headquarters at Embsay station, adjoining the still vulnerable branch. An income to maintain the site was to be provided by a working steam museum.

In 1969 the name of the society was changed to the Yorkshire Dales Railway Society in order to create more national appeal and interest but it still lacked affluent members who might guarantee its survival, at any rate in the short term. Some £17,000 was needed to buy the site and provide minimum facilities and it was clear that the society's effort would have to be very effectively deployed to have any chance of success. In response, the supporters ceased to think in terms of running a railway but became instead itinerant fund raisers. A very efficient sales organisation was set up and a traffic in every branch of railwayana developed. With careful planning and management the society's resources began to grow until, having begun with no more than could be collected in a hat, the organisation started to look financially plausible.

Even more important, constructive activity began at Embsay. In June 1970 British Railways gave access to the site on a 'care and maintenance basis' and permitted the society to store its first locomotive on it. With an engine, Hudswell Clarke 0-4-0ST 'Nellie', on the site the society leased the station and other buildings and began to establish its headquarters. By the end of that year three open days had been organised with machines from the society's rapidly growing collection in steam. Embsay has become a centre for forms of steam traction other than railway engines and these more versatile and less exacting machines, such as traction engines, have been invaluable during the formative years of the enterprise.

In December 1970 the Yorkshire Dales Railway Co., Ltd was formed to handle the society's business interests and to facilitate the share issue which took place in April 1971. This latter step provided funds for many improvements on the site and the acquisition of seven locomotives. With this additional motive power the new company had the makings of a very fine collection of working exhibits and with provision for wider transport history interests the 1971 open days attracted much attention both locally and from farther afield.

The Yorkshire Dales Railway Society, which is the principal shareholder in the company, provides all the volunteer labour and most of the expertise. Its members supply the engine crews, shed staff, sales staff and station, signal and permanent way staff under all conditions of season and weather. Indeed, the organisation of the railway is in many respects more impressive than that of many other railways which have advanced further as far as operations are concerned. However, despite its undoubted commercial success the demands on the company's income are enormous and additional capital is still required to complete the purchase

Table 25 Steam locomotives at Embsay

Type	Name	Where built	Year	Origin
0-4-0ST	'Nellie'	Hudswell Clarke	1922	Esholt Sewage Works
0-4-0ST	'Pony'	Hawthorn Leslie	1912	Blyth Harbour
0-4-0ST	'Fred'	Avonside	1925	ICI, Tunstead
0-4-0ST	'Chemicals'	Andrew Barclay	1925	Various industrial locations in south Yorkshire
0-6-0ST	'Banshee'	Peckett	1933	Stewarts & Lloyds, Wellingborough
0-4-0VB	'Ann'	Sentinel	1927	British Tar Products, Manchester
0-4-0ST	—	Bagnall	1921	Associated Portland Cement, Shipton-on-Cherwell, Oxon.

of the site and line, and the provision of more covered accommodation for the exhibits. All, of course, are former industrial locomotives. 'Nellie's' presence on the site is something of a heresy in so far as she is oil-fired. Nevertheless she is steam driven. She is on loan from Bradford Corporation for which she worked for forty-five years and will eventually be located in their Museum of Industrial Archaeology.

It is the Peckett 0-4-0 saddle tank, 'Banshee', that makes Embsay unique, for she is built on a gauge of one metre, as opposed to 4ft 8½in. which has been standard in this country since 1892, and the Yorkshire Dales Railway Co. has most enterprisingly re-laid some of the track on a dual gauge so that she can be worked along with their standard gauge engines. At the time of closure in 1966 Stewarts & Lloyds were running three such engines at Wellingborough and all were acquired for preservation. 'Banshee' was originally kept at Bressingham but was subsequently bought by Mr Plunkett of Ilkley and transferred to Embsay in 1971.

20 North Yorkshire Moors Railway

LMS 0-6-2T, no. 27585

Unlike its Yorkshire neighbour the Keighley & Worth Valley Railway, the North Yorkshire Moors Railway, which aims initially to reopen six miles of line south from Grosmont to Goathland and Eller Beck, has room to expand for up to twelve miles further south to Pickering.

It is an historic line, particularly the northern section, and was part of the very early Whitby & Pickering Railway opened in two stages, in 1835 and 1836. The Act of Parliament authorising the building of the line was obtained in 1833 and is remarkable if only because it contained provisions on the one hand permitting, and on the other expressly forbidding, the use of locomotives. Steam locomotion was, of course, well established at this date, with many examples of its more cautious use as well on the Canterbury & Whitstable line where 'Invicta' had been bowling up and down the level middle section for three years, leaving the steeper sections at either end to stationary engines. The Whitby & Pickering Railway was more conservative still in being horse-worked. It remained a horse railway until 1847 when it was absorbed and converted to steam by the Yorks & North Midland Railway. From the start, however, the 1500-yard incline from Grosmont to Beck Hole required something exceptional. Coaches and wagons were hauled up the incline by a rope wound round a horizontal drum and attached at the other end to a water tank wagon. The water wagon discharged its load at the foot of the incline and was duly hauled back to the top by descending Whitby-bound coaches and wagons. Later a stationary steam engine was used but even after the whole line had been converted for locomotives by George Hudson, the Beck Hole incline continued to be worked by a stationary engine. The incline was closed on 1 July 1865 after a four-mile deviation south of Grosmont had been built, including a new station at Goathland.

The country through which the line passes is remote and thinly populated, following Newtondale at the southern end through the heart of the North Yorkshire Moors, but in its heyday it was prosperous enough. It connected Whitby and Pickering which were both local centres of importance and served the industries of the area which, though pursued on a comparatively modest scale, were heavy and included stone quarrying and at one time an ironworks at Grosmont. The line passed to the LNER in 1923 and was closed completely from Grosmont to Pickering on 8 March 1965.

The closure of the line was based on the calculation by British Railways that the line was losing £50,000 p.a. This figure was not universally accepted, particularly in the area which had thus been deprived of the railway. Attempts to achieve a reopening subsidised by the local authorities concerned came to nothing, but the movement did lead in June 1967 to the formation of the North Yorkshire Moors Railway Preservation Society. Track lifting was imminent that autumn but the Society succeeded in delaying the start of work pending a preliminary appraisal of the prospects for acquiring the whole of the line from Grosmont, where the Pickering branch leaves the Whitby–Middlesborough line. It emerged that this stretch of line would cost something like £100,000. Further discussions, carried out by the newly formed North Yorkshire Moors Railway Co., fixed a purchase price of £35,000 for the 6¾-mile section of the line from Grosmont to Eller Beck and a further £7,500 for the railway property between Grosmont and High Mill, near Pickering. The line is double-track as far as Levisham and single from there to Pickering but the negotiated price for the Grosmont–Eller Beck section was for a single line including passing loops.

In March 1971 the Preservation Society and the Company transferred their assets to the North York Moors Historical Railway Trust, which is negotiating with the bodies concerned—the North Riding County Council, BR and the North York Moors National Park Planning Committee—for the purchase of the trackbed south from Eller Beck to High Mill. If they are successful the North Yorkshire Moors Railway could be the second largest standard gauge preserved line in Britain, exceeding even the extended Severn Valley Railway. Members of the Preservation Society have been able to work on the line since the autumn of 1968, making good such decay as had already set in and preventing further deterioration. The Society now has more than 6,000 members and the speed at which it has grown promises well for the ambitious plans which have now been made for the future of the whole Grosmont–

Pickering line. The members include professional railwaymen, groups from the universities of Newcastle, Leeds and Hull and, on the motive power side, the North Eastern Locomotive Group, which owns two of the engines at present on the railway.

There are eight steam locomotives, now located at Goathland station, five of them of industrial origin (see Table 26). The other three were built for the LNER or the Eastern Region of British Railways. The oldest of them is a North Eastern Railway 0-8-0 mineral engine, no. 2238, which eventually became no. 63395 in BR class Q6. Sir Vincent Raven built 120 of them at Darlington between 1913 and 1921 and the example at Goathland was one of the later ones, built in 1918. She was acquired for preservation by the North Eastern Locomotive Group on withdrawal in 1967 and was quickly restored to her original black, lined red livery. Another engine owned by the Group is a J27 0-6-0 no. 2392, built just after the Grouping, in 1923, and the third ex-main line engine is a 2-6-0 K1 class no. 2005, built to BR order by the North British Locomotive Co. at Glasgow in 1949.

Table 26 Steam locomotives at Goathland

Type	Number/name	Where built	Year	Origin
0-4-0ST	'Mirvale'	Hudswell Clarke	1955	Mirvale Chemical Co., Yorks
0-4-0WT	3	Borrows	1898	Wallsend Slipway Co., Northumberland
0-6-0ST	'Salmon'	Andrew Barclay	1942	Stewarts & Lloyds, Harston, Leics
0-8-0	2238	Darlington	1918	NER & BR
0-6-0T	29 'Lambton'	Kitson	1904	NCB Philadelphia
0-6-0T	5	Robert Stephenson & Hawthorns	1909	NCB Philadelphia
0-6-0	2392	Darlington	1923	LNER & BR
2-6-0	2005	North British	1949	BR

21 Lakeside & Haverthwaite Railway

Pettigrew's Furness Railway goods engine

The contract for the construction of the Furness Railway's branch from Ulverston to Newby Bridge was drawn up in 1866 and work began on the line in November that year. The contractors were Benton & Woodwiss and the engineer in charge was a Colonel Strong'i'tharm. Some difficulty was encountered with the terrain, notably a rock face at Haverthwaite, which caused the opening of the line to be delayed for twelve months. The Furness Railway meanwhile decided to extend the line to Lakeside to help them develop their existing interest in the steamer traffic on Lake Windermere. The line opened on 1 June 1869 and shortly afterwards the terminus for the steamer services at the southern end of the lake was moved from Newby Bridge to Lakeside. The Lakeside branch has thus been associated with the Windermere steamers right from the start. The new railway was to establish the cross-platform interchange of traffic between the boats and the trains and create a thriving tourist industry which reached its peak in the inter-war years. Trains were run from all over the country to connect with the steamers at Lakeside, perhaps the most famous of these being the 'Lake Windermere Land Cruises' run from Morecambe and Blackpool during the summer season.

The ironworks at Backbarrow and the gunpowder works at Low Wood and Black Beck brought a certain amount of freight traffic to an otherwise passenger-dominated branch line. Traffic for the ironworks was marshalled in Haverthwaite yard and propelled up a siding half a mile long on to a ramp immediately above the kilns, where the contents of the wagons were discharged into large hoppers. This practice of propelling the wagons up to the ironworks led to the only major accident in the line's history. On 15 July 1932 a train of wagons from the ironworks, loaded with coke, ore and pig iron, proved too heavy for the 2-4-2T on shunting duty at the time and the train ran away down the 1 in 65 gradient into Haverthwaite goods yard and knocked two vans through the stop block onto the main road to Barrow. There were no casualties, the engine's crew having jumped clear before the vans were struck.

The Low Wood and Black Beck gunpowder works were both served by tramways, the former narrow and the latter standard gauge, both horse-drawn. The horses were shod with copper to prevent explosions that could have been caused by sparks from iron shoes. The Low Wood tramway, on which the gauge is believed to have been 3ft 6in., left Haverthwaite yard and plunged by means of a series of reversing points into the valley of the River Leven. After crossing the river by a single-span girder bridge, the tramway turned south-west and fanned out to serve the various mills along its banks. The gunpowder works was closed in 1935 and the track lifted. All that remains of the tramway and the industry along it is five of the original tramway wagons, the river bridge, which is now in a dilapidated and precarious state, and the ruins of some of the mills. Little is known about the Black Beck tramway except that it left the branch at a point between Lady Syke and Haverthwaite known as Dickson's siding. In this case, the traffic was marshalled at Greenodd and was pushed in front of the main train as far as the siding, from where it was drawn by horses up the valley of the Black Beck to the works which was half a mile north-east of the village of Bouth. Little evidence of the tramway remains. The works was closed before the war and its site is now a caravan camp.

After the war, passenger traffic continued to be heavy in summer but winter traffic of all sorts was very light. Closure, however, did not come until 6 September 1965. The last scheduled passenger train from Ulverston to Lakeside was the 12.40 hrs Barrow–Lakeside, hauled by a Fairburn 2-6-4T, no. 42134, of Barrow shed. The same engine worked the last steam-hauled train from Lakeside to Barrow at 19.10 hrs, although not the last train of any sort, which was a three-coach diesel train to Accrington half an hour later. Freight traffic, in the form of a 'pick-up' train three times a week, continued until the closure of the Backbarrow Ironworks early in 1967. Normal traffic ended altogether in April that year.

Plans to preserve the line, however, were well under way before closure. Lakeside Railway Estates Co., Ltd (LREC) was formed in May 1967 with a view to negotiating with British Railways for the purchase of the eight miles of line from Plumpton junction (1½ miles east of Ulverston) to Lakeside. This was supported by a local enthusiasts' club, the Lancashire Railway Circle, which changed its name to the Lakeside (Windermere) Railway Society and later to Lakeside Railway Society. The LREC took over the old BR steam depot at Carnforth in April 1969 and a large collection of locomotives was assembled there ready for work on the branch. The idea at that time was to combine the live museum at Carnforth with providing steam-hauled services on the Lakeside branch. Three or four locomotives would have been sub-shedded at Haverthwaite during the summer season and returned to Carnforth for the winter. The depot and the branch were separated by eleven miles but the combination of works and operating line would have been ideal. Unfortunately, LREC encountered a number of problems, some of which were, and remain, unique. Not the least of them was the then Ministry of Transport's proposals for improving the A590 Levens Bridge–Barrow trunk road, which threatened to truncate the line south of Haverthwaite station. To accommodate the road and the railway, LREC would have to find more than £200,000.

With the prospect of being cut off from the main line, LREC decided to withdraw from the Lakeside branch project and concentrate on transforming Carnforth depot. Three directors of LREC, however, were still interested in the branch and in January 1970 decided to form a new company to proceed with reopening the 3½ miles of line between Haverthwaite and Lakeside. This was the Lakeside & Haverthwaite Railway Co., which is now supported by the Lakeside Railway Society. The Lakeside Railway and Steamtown, Carnforth, are now completely separate ventures.

In June 1970 the LRS was given access to the site at Haverthwaite by BR for the purposes of weeding and generally tidying up. Shortly afterwards, the first item of stock arrived on the railway and more followed in October. These were eight carriages which had been bought by the company from British Railways and two Fairburn 2-6-4Ts. There were more arrivals in November 1970, beginning with the delivery of two Hudswell Clarke saddle tanks by road from Doncaster and, by rail from Accrington, Black 5 no. 44806 and further items of heavy rolling stock. These were just in time, for in May and June 1971 the line between Plumpton junction and Haverthwaite was lifted and the railway isolated from the national network. Experience elsewhere suggests that isolation enhances the attraction of a piece of line but it does create expense and difficulties over the delivery and later the availability outside of locomotives and rolling stock.

The Lakeside & Haverthwaite Railway connects Lakeside, at the southern tip of Windermere, with Haverthwaite, a small village three miles away on the A590 Levens Bridge–Barrow road. Between these points the line follows the west bank of the River Leven and, with magnificent scenery in the background, passes through fields, woodland, rock cuttings and a tunnel. For the first three-quarters of a mile out of

Lakeside the line runs down an avenue of tall trees. From the Haverthwaite end trains face steep gradients as far as Newby Bridge which is the summit of the line. The only substantial engineering features are the two short tunnels at Haverthwaite, cut through solid rock. One of them, the West tunnel, will not normally be used by L&HR trains but locomotives will need to enter it because part of the run-round loop is inside.

Of the three stations on the line Lakeside is the largest but in recent years demolition and track-lifting have reduced its area by about half. It once boasted three platforms, a large office block and clock tower, engine and carriage sheds, water tower and a small turntable: now only the signal box, part of the overall roof, the quayside buildings and two platforms remain. The station is actually owned by Sealink, who now operate the Windermere steamers and the L&HR has had to obtain running rights in order to run its trains into the terminus. Newby Bridge, which was closed in September 1939, consists of a single platform and no station buildings. The third station, Haverthwaite, is the railway's headquarters and with its large goods yard and excellent access it is ideally suited to the purpose. The station has two platforms which stop abruptly at the eastern entrance to the West tunnel and are in the red and yellow brick which is characteristic of the Furness Railway's tourist lines.

Facing north from Haverthwaite towards Lakeside, the railway looks as if it is double-tracked. In fact, the L&HR is single-tracked throughout and the right-hand line which passes through the East tunnel at Haverthwaite is a separate branch which once served the ironworks at Backbarrow. However, all the original earthworks and bridges were built to take double track which could be useful in future if the L&HR finds that traffic on the line warrants a passing loop at, say, Newby Bridge.

The last steam-hauled passenger train to run on the branch was headed by a Fairburn tank and the last train of all by a Black 5. Examples of both these locomotive types are preserved at Haverthwaite today. The Black 5, no. 44806, and the two Fairburns, nos. 42073 and 42085 (now renumbered 2073 and 2085 respectively) were all bought direct from BR and restored to full working order, although their new liveries have attracted some criticism. The two Fairburns have been painted in Caledonian Railway blue (no. 2085) and LNWR 'blackberry black' (no. 2073), while the Black 5 instead of being repainted in the 'mixed traffic black' from which the class got its nickname, is resplendent in BR Brunswick green, normally confined to express passenger locomotives. In some respects this is undoubtedly a dubious practice but is justified by the magnificent results. For lighter work the railway has a Peckett 0-4-0ST, named 'Caliban', which was bought by two members of the LRS from Courtaulds at Preston in 1967 and two Hudswell Clarke 0-6-0STs, nos. 5 and 6, which were acquired very cheaply but will need a great deal of work before they see service on the line. A more recent addition is the Bagnall 0-6-0ST 'Princess' from Preston Docks.

Table 27 Steam locomotives at Haverthwaite

Type	Number/name	Where built	Year	Origin
4-6-0	44806	Derby	1944	LMS & BR
2-6-4T	2073	Brighton	1950	BR
2-6-4T	2085	Brighton	1951	BR
2-6-0	6441	Crewe	1950	BR
0-4-0ST	'Caliban'	Peckett	1937	Courtaulds, Preston
0-6-0ST	—	Hudswell Clarke	1919	Renishaw Ironworks, Yorks
0-6-0ST	—	Hudswell Clarke	1929	Renishaw Ironworks, Yorks
0-6-0ST	'Princess'	Bagnall	1942	Preston Docks

Since serious work began, the Lakeside & Haverthwaite Railway has concentrated on building up a collection of locomotives and rolling stock of a sort to give the best and longest service on the operating railway and little attention has yet been given to the acquisition of rarities or exotic antiques. This policy seems to have been successful. At three and a half miles the Lakeside & Haverthwaite line is among the shorter light railways but the plans to revive it were brought to fruition quickly and efficiently. By reason of its beauty and position in one of the leading tourist areas of Britain, the line should have a successful future.

22 Railway Preservation in Scotland

Killiecrankie viaduct

By the eve of the Grouping the railways of Scotland had coalesced into five companies: Caledonian Railway (CR), Glasgow & South-Western Railway (G&SWR), North British Railway (NBR), Highland Railway (HR), and Great North of Scotland Railway (GNSR). All were highly individualistic and though they have been consumed by successive acts of rationalisation, they evoke a powerful nostalgia and an admiration for a railway system built under intimidating physical and economic conditions.

There had been rail roads in Scotland for two hundred years at the time of the Grouping. The Tranent–Cockenzie Wagonway in East Lothian was opened in 1722 and many others had been built by the end of the eighteenth century. The railway proper was an early arrival north of the border also. The Kilmarnock & Troon Railway was opened in 1812 and on it some of the earliest experiments with steam locomotives took place, in the same decade as the arrival of Matthew Murray's machine on the Middleton Colliery Railway. In 1824 Charles MacLaren averred in *The Scotsman* that by the use of the steam locomotive 'we shall be carried at the rate of four hundred miles per day', that is to say, a day being twelve hours, at an average speed of $33\frac{1}{3}$mph, promising a journey time around twelve hours between London and Edinburgh or Glasgow by comparison with the thirteen and a half days which a good stage coach would have needed in the early nineteenth century over the same distance. MacLaren's estimate was remarkable, prophesying a journey time twelve times faster than anything known in 1824 and one half the average time of the 'Inter City' trains of today.

Locomotives appeared in normal service in Scotland in 1831. In that year the directors of the Monkland & Kirkintilloch Railway decided to work their line with engines built by Murdoch & Aitken of Glasgow. They ran at 6mph and proved more economical than the Stephenson locomotives supplied at about that time to the neighbouring Garnkirk & Glasgow Railway. In the north of Scotland, steam locomotion arrived later and the Dundee & Newtyle Railway was worked by stationary engines and, indeed, by horses, for three years after its opening in 1831. These were parochial developments. Other interests in Scotland were already considering main line links with the south. By 1838, the year in which the London & Birmingham Railway was opened throughout, the Glasgow, Paisley, Kilmarnock & Ayr and the Glasgow, Paisley and Greenock railways had been authorised by Act of Parliament and surveys of routes from Carlisle to Glasgow and Edinburgh had been agreed to and planned. On 15 March 1841 the Royal Commissioners issued their report on the proposed routes between England and Scotland and in the following year the Edinburgh–Glasgow line, later absorbed by the North British Railway, was opened. The Caledonian Railway's Carlisle–Glasgow line followed in 1848, and the west coast main line was thus inaugurated. On the other side of the country, the Great Northern, North Eastern and North British railways established links to form the through route up the east coast from King's Cross to Newcastle and Edinburgh.

By 1876 the railway network of lowland Scotland was established in outline though it continued to develop in detail. The Highland and Great North of Scotland railways meanwhile pressed on northwards, the former reaching Wick, 729 miles from Euston by the west coast route, while the Great North of Scotland line developed on the eastern side of the country. The GNSR had a colourful history. E. L. Ahrons wrote in the *Railway Magazine* (Jan. 1922, p. 55) at the time of the Grouping:

Table 28 Scottish Railway Companies on the eve of the Grouping

Company	Grouped under	Capital £m.	Route miles	No. of locomotives	Locomotive works
North British	LNER	70	1,378	1,107	Cowlairs
Great North of Scotland	LNER	7	334	122	Inverurie
Caledonian	LMS	58	1,114	1,170	St Rollox
Glasgow & South-Western	LMS	17	49	529	Kilmarnock
Highland	LMS	7	506	173	Lochgorm, Inverness
	Totals	159	3,826	3,001	

Once upon a time this was a shocking railway. Why it was ever allowed to be called a railway at all passed comprehension. As a matter of fact part of it, between Aberdeen and Inverurie was not originally a railway, but a canal and the company thoughtfully scooped in the canal, baled it out, and made their line on the remains. After which some people in the district bethought themselves, when it was too late, that the canal would have been infinitely preferable. The stopping trains could not even be

Table 29 Scottish steam locomotives preserved*

Type	Number/name	Builder	Year	Origin
Glasgow Museum of Transport				
4-2-2	123 (LMSR 14010)	Neilson	1886	Caledonian
4-4-0	256 'Glen Douglas' (BR 62469)	Cowlairs	1913	North British
4-4-0	49 'Gordon Highlander' (BR 62277)	North British Loco. Co.	1920	GNSR
4-6-0	103 (LMSR 17916)	Sharp Stewart	1894	Highland
0-6-0	828 (BR 57566)	St Rollox	1899	Caledonian
0-6-0T	9 (LMSR 16379)	North British Loco. Co.	1917	GSWR
Strathspey Railway				
4-6-0	5025 (BR 45025)	Vulcan	1935	LMSR; at present working on the Keighley & Worth Valley Railway
Lochty Private Railway				
4-6-2	4488 'Union of South Africa' (BR 60009)	Doncaster	1937	LNER
Royal Scottish Museum, Edinburgh				
4-4-0	246 'Morayshire' (BR 62712)	Darlington	1928	LNER
Dundee Museum (in store)				
2-6-0	46464	Crewe	1950	BR
Scottish Railway Preservation Society				
0-6-0	673 'Maude' (BR 65243)	Neilson	1891	North British
0-4-4T	419 (BR 55189)	St Rollox	1907	Caledonian
Lytham Motive Power Museum, Lancashire				
0-4-0ST	42 (BR 68095)	Cowlairs	1887	North British

* In addition to these there are various industrial locomotives and such exceptional items as the Royal Scottish Museum's 'Wylam Dilly', described in chapter 1.

dignified by the title 'slow'. They set the pace of a glacier, only the glacier would possibly have got there first.

On 31 December 1922 the individual identity of the five Scottish companies ended and they became part of the LMS or LNER.

Of the 3,001 steam locomotives at work under pre-Grouping companies in Scotland only eight remain, with three post-Grouping or BR engines, and one, entirely English, which it is planned will work on the Strathspey Railway (see Table 29). Another outstanding Scottish locomotive is the Duke of Sutherland's 0-4-4T 'Dunrobin', built by Sharp, Stewart for private use in 1895 and now preserved in the Fort Steele Museum at Cranbrooke, British Columbia.

The activities of the museums, private individuals and the Scottish Railway Preservation Society are complemented by railway preservation schemes in Scotland. Early in 1972, the SRPS was considering a new project in conjunction with the East Lothian County Council. This envisaged taking over the track bed of the old Haddington–Longniddry branch and relaying it by easy stages as funds permit. For the time being, however, the most vigorous railway preservation schemes in Scotland are the Strathspey Railway and the Lochty Private Railway.

Paton and Millar's Cowlairs Incline engine

The Strathspey Railway

The Aviemore region has become the major tourist development area in Scotland, catering for winter sports and summer visitors alike and there has been substantial development over the last ten years to provide the necessary facilities. The attraction of a steam operated railway in comparable settings has been vividly illustrated by the success of the narrow gauge railways of Wales, especially those in Merioneth and Caernarvonshire, not to mention the success of lines through equally alluring if less dramatic areas, such as the Dart and Severn valleys.

Plans for a steam-operated railway in this part of Inverness-shire were first made public in 1967, when the Highlands and Islands Development Board approached the Scottish Railway Preservation Society with a view to exploring the possibility of taking over the line between Aviemore and Boat of Garten, or perhaps beyond. The first plans, indeed, envisaged the outright purchase of the line from Aviemore, through Boat of Garten and thence to Grantown-on-Spey by either the old Highland or Great North of Scotland route, a distance of twelve miles. This very ambitious scheme would have involved several major engineering features and in the event was abandoned in the face of the purchase price alone. A later scheme reduced the proposed route to the Aviemore–Boat of Garten section only with an option to purchase the track bed further north. The cost of putting the five miles of track into operational order was then estimated at £50,000. A proposal that the HIDB should buy the line—the role of the SRPS being limited to that of operating company—was abandoned because it would lead the Board well outside its terms of reference, although they agreed to a substantial loan which would have left the SRPS the comparatively easy job of raising £12,000 capital, apart from its vocational function of providing rolling stock and maintenance and operating staff. Negotiations with both the Board and BR were well advanced, though inevitably subject to delay and frustration, when the Society's offer for the line was withdrawn after the 1971 Annual General Meeting. However, a nucleus of members persevered with the negotiations and formed a new company which by 1972 had contracted to purchase the line for approximately £41,000.

The Aviemore–Boat of Garten line was part of the Inverness & Perth Junction Railway, opened in 1863. It helped to provide a more direct route from Inverness to the south and equally important, a service which avoided the Great North of Scotland Railway, which was then notorious for low standards and missed connections. The line ran north from Perth to Pitlochry and thence through the mountains by way of Blair Atholl, Dalwhinnie, Newtonmore and Kingussie to Forres and then over the last relatively level twenty-four miles into Inverness. When the railway came, Aviemore was an established community but there had been no development at all at Boat of Garten, which was well situated to become a centre for the timber traffic from the surrounding forests. Soon after it had been opened throughout, the I&PJR amalgamated with the Inverness & Aberdeen Railway, which controlled the line along the coast, to form the Highland Railway. In 1866 yet another line was opened to Boat of Garten by the GNSR branch from Craigellachie, which followed the valley of the River Spey. The final section of the branch was actually controlled by the Highland Railway, although north of Boat of Garten there were two independent single tracks for some distance. Relations between the Highland and Great North of Scotland railways were often acrimonious and became litigious over this stretch of line and the exchange facilities at 'The Boat'.

By 1898 the Highland Railway had been encouraged to build a line over the direct route from Aviemore to Inverness by way of Carr Bridge and so Boat of Garten lost its main line status, although through carriages to the south still ran over the line. The GNSR maintained connections at Boat of Garten where there was an engine shed and carriage facilities. During the summer the Speyside branch was much used for excursion traffic from Aberdeen and to a certain extent the same use was made from this direction of the Aviemore line. In post-Grouping and even BR days, circular tours were run from Aberdeen along Speyside to Perth and back by way of Forfar.

Under BR the service from Craigellachie to Boat of Garten and later to Aviemore was taken over by a diesel railbus, an arrangement which robbed 'The Boat' of its interchange importance. In 1964 the through service between Inverness and the south was withdrawn, and in October the following year both lines were closed to passenger traffic and the line over Dava Moor closed altogether. Freight traffic continued between Aviemore and Craigellachie until November 1968 when the branch closed following the running of a special valedictory passenger train from Aberdeen. Track lifting has been completed, except for the section which the Strathspey Railway Co. intends to take over.

Once they are in possession of the line the development of the railway should be comparatively smooth and rapid. The status of the area in Scottish tourism needs no further comment; neither do the scenic splendours of Speyside. The permanent way is in reasonable order; there are no major engineering features and the stations and associated buildings are in good condition, if not always immediately available. The Aviemore engine shed, for example, is a substantial stone structure erected in the days when the station was being developed as a junction and is at present leased to a local firm. However, there are problems in view: BR are unlikely to grant running rights into their own station at Aviemore. A new platform may be erected north of the junction with the Boat of Garten line but the site is likely to be some distance north of the engine shed.

Boat of Garten station is still intact, although some of the siding accommodation needs re-laying. The station here had three platforms, including a central island platform, the eastern face of which was used by GNSR trains. The Strathspey Railway Co. will use only one platform, together with the site of the old locomotive shed and part of the goods yard which will be covered eventually.

There is no shortage of potential native motive power but the only working locomotive earmarked for service on the line at present is Mr

W. E. C. Watkinson's ex-LMS class 5 no. 5025, which has been fully restored and overhauled by the Hunslet Engine Co. at Leeds. It is now running on the Keighley & Worth Valley Railway, whence it will be transferred to Inverness-shire as soon as the line is ready. Appropriately no. 5025, which was one of the first batch of Black 5s built in 1934 at the Vulcan Foundry, Newton-le-Willows, was first based at Inverness for service on the Highland section of the LMS, although most of the rest of its career was passed south of the border. On withdrawal in the summer of 1968, she was the oldest steam locomotive at work on BR. The other locomotives promised for service on the line are the Company's own 0-4-0ST, 'Dailuaine', which is a 'local' engine, although not at present in working order, and the ex-CR 0-6-0 no. 828, which is now in the Glasgow Transport Museum and owned by the Scottish Locomotive Preservation Fund.

The Lochty Private Railway

This 1¼-mile single line from Lochty to Knightsward in Fife is remarkable not only because it is private but because Mr John Cameron, the owner, and his volunteer supporters have created it from nothing more than the track bed of an old railway. The line also provides the most spacious permanent home at present available to a Gresley A4 Pacific, no. 60009, 'Union of South Africa', which, together with an 0-4-0ST from the now dieselised British Aluminium Co. system at Burntisland on the Fife coast, constitutes the steam locomotive stock. The two passenger vehicles are a rebuilt Gresley observation car (SC1719E) and a BR open brake second.

The nostalgia engendered by the end of steam operations on BR was especially powerful along the Glasgow–Aberdeen main line because it was the final home of a number of A4s from 1961 onwards, among them no. 60009. She had worked in Scotland throughout her life, from delivery new from Doncaster as LNER no. 4488 to Haymarket depot, Edinburgh in 1937, where she was stand-by locomotive for the streamlined 'Coronation' service introduced that year. After the war 'Union of South Africa' worked such trains as the 'Elizabethan' and 'Flying Scotsman' on the east coast route from King's Cross to Edinburgh. When that line was largely dieselised she was transferred to Ferryhill depot for service on the new three-hour Aberdeen–Glasgow schedules. She was withdrawn in the summer of 1966 and immediately lost her tender, which was converted for use as the second tender on no. 4472, 'Flying Scotsman'. Otherwise, even though the locomotive was at this time intended for preservation in a museum, little work was required to restore her to first class working order. Her present tender has an interesting history. It was built originally for Gresley's experimental 4-6-4 no. 10000 and was subsequently attached to an A4, no. 60034,

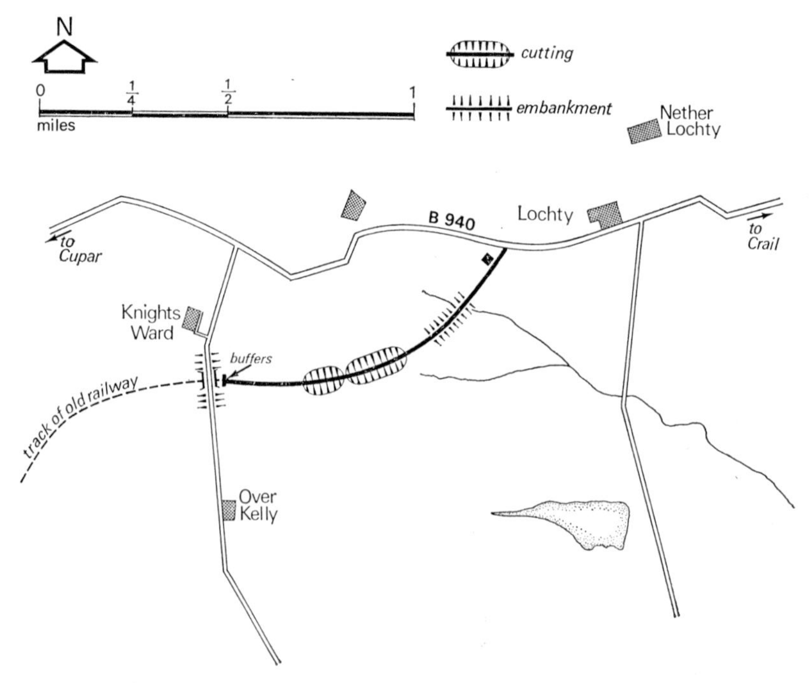

6 Lochty Private Railway

'Lord Faringdon', which was scrapped soon after withdrawal in 1966, the tender alone surviving to serve its present purpose at Lochty.

Mr Cameron bought 'Union of South Africa' with the idea of presenting her to a museum. He changed his plans after he had purchased a farm through which lay the track bed of the railway from East Fife Central Junction to Lochty. The line, which had been exclusively for freight and never operated in competition with the passenger services on the East Fife line from Leven to St Andrews, opened in 1898. Traffic was never heavy and often became so light during summer that it was closed and used for wagon storage. In BR days, most of the stations were classed as 'unstaffed public sidings', although there was a depot at Kennoway. The line remained open until August 1964. When Mr Cameron arrived in 1966 the track had been lifted but restoration, using ex-colliery rails, began immediately and about half a mile of track was soon in place again.

At this time no. 60009 was stored nearby at Thornton, whence it would be transferred by road to Lochty. Meanwhile, she made one more appearance on the main line on 26 March 1967, on a BR rail tour from Edinburgh to Perth, Aberdeen, Speyside, Aviemore, Pitlochry and back to Edinburgh via Perth. The use of 'Union of South Africa' on this trip aroused enormous interest and the size of the train was increased to eighteen coaches, above 700 tons. She worked the Perth–Aberdeen section and the final stretch from Perth to Edinburgh. Because of the weight of the train she was piloted by a Stanier class 5, no. 44997, and the pair reportedly achieved 80mph over parts of the run. The success of this tour confirmed that 'Union of South Africa' would be a great attraction at Lochty and would at least earn her keep there. In her first summer, 1967, no passenger service was provided because of the complete lack of rolling stock but she was steamed up and down the half mile of track on Sunday afternoons.

By 1968 the ex-LNER beaver tail observation car had arrived to provide a civilised means of conveying passengers. This carriage is one of two, the other being on the Keighley & Worth Valley Railway, built for the pre-war 'Coronation' and rebuilt by the Scottish Region of BR in 1957 for services on the West Highland line. In 1971, following the extension of the Lochty Railway as far as Knightsward and the arrival of another passenger coach, nearly 6,000 people travelled on the trains run on Sunday afternoons between June and the end of August. An extension of services is not planned at present but will become inevitable if public interest continues to grow at the rate shown so far.

By comparison with many other preserved, steam-operated railways the scenery along the line is not remarkable, but Lochty does provide the solitary opportunity in this country regularly to ride on a train hauled by an A4 Pacific. Though inhibited by the shortness of the run and other light railway restrictions, the sound of 'Union of South Africa' climbing out of Lochty is authentically redolent of the east coast main line.

23 Ravenglass & Eskdale Railway

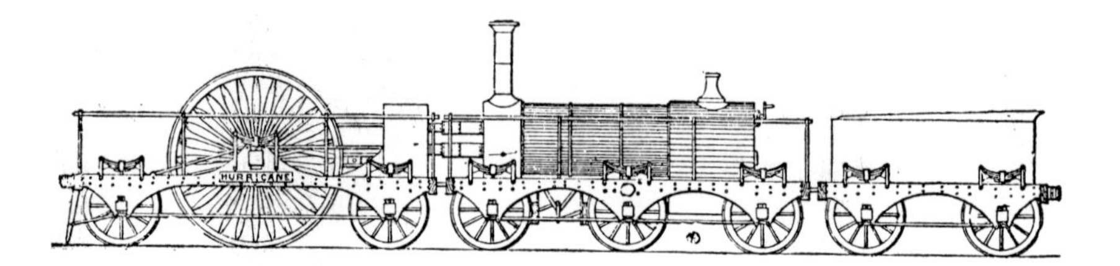

'Hurricane'

Unlike most narrow gauge lines which originated as mineral railways, built after years of frustration and dispute to fill a well-established need, the first Ravenglass & Eskdale Railway was a speculation upon a tenuous and uncertain vein of haematite ore in west Cumberland. As a result, the line has had a more varied and complicated history than any comparable railway.

Iron ore was one of the basic elements of nineteenth-century civilisation. West Cumberland was an ancient source of it, known and exploited by the Romans. Demand for ore fluctuated and reached one of its sporadic peaks around 1870. In Cumberland this led to the formation of Whitehaven Iron Mines Ltd, which took a lease on the deposits around Boot at the head of the valley of the river Esk for twenty-five years from 1873. Early excavations had produced promising results but the cost of transporting the winnings down the valley to Ravenglass, the sea and the Furness Railway was almost prohibitive and the decision to promote a railway was made early in the mining company's life, in 1872. The line was to form a junction with the Furness Railway and would also run down to the foreshore in the hope that the long-silted-up harbour, another feature known and used by the Romans, would one day be opened up enough for use in the shipment of ore. The branch was never built and the harbour never developed in this way, but the Ravenglass & Eskdale Railway Act was passed in 1873. The gauge was not fixed but it was to be between 2ft 9in. and 4ft $8\frac{1}{2}$in. Contemporary accounts conflict as to the gauge actually used but the measurements taken by the late R. C. Clinker, at several places on the line in September 1910, confirm that it was 3ft.

Whitehaven Iron Mines was one of the main shareholders in the railway company, taking up one half of the issued capital of £24,000. The line was built by a new and separate company. This distinction was to have important consequences and prevented the Railway being dragged down when the mining company went into liquidation. The other half of the capital was subscribed by the contractor, A. Oliver, who had previously built the Hemel Hempstead & Boxmoor Railway. Building progressed quickly and the line was ready for opening in April 1875. Perhaps it was designed and built too quickly, for when the company applied for permission to carry passengers the following year, Colonel Yolland's report to the Board of Trade was exceedingly critical and the Railway was declared to be in no condition for passenger traffic. During the remainder of the summer of 1876, the general manager of the line, James Quan, was at work on improvements such as the enlargement of stations in the hope of satisfying Colonel Yolland in time for an opening to passenger traffic on 1 October. He did not arrive to re-inspect until early November but on the ninth reported that the line was 'now in fair order', although he recommended that a speed limit of 10mph should be maintained and that the locomotive should be at least six-wheeled and weigh not more than thirteen tons laden. Yolland also recommended the ultimate sanction in safety for single line working, that only one engine should be in steam at any one time. Thus protected, the first official passengers were carried on the Railway on 20 November 1876.

Soon afterwards the contractor, Oliver, discovered that he was owed £17,000 which the Company was clearly unable to pay and the performance of the Railway over its first eighteen months gave no indication that it would ever be able to do so. Even though it was carrying 15,000 passengers a year, the iron ore traffic was in decline and running expenses were barely covered. Oliver therefore decided to sue for possession of the line and was prevented only by the Whitehaven Iron Mines Company's action, wishing to preserve their outlet, in petitioning the High Court of Chancery for the appointment of a receiver and manager. The man appointed was Henry Copland, secretary of the R&ER, and he worked alongside Quan, who was effectively downgraded to superintendent.

Whitehaven Iron Mines failed in 1882, although they were not finally wound up until 1900. The collapse came, ironically, immediately after general freight traffic on the line had reached a peak and even without the mines there was enough work to enable the line to continue in business after a fashion. The successors to the Whitehaven Co., working under a variety of names, duly resumed mining and even extended

Nab Gill Mine but they, too, abandoned the workings in 1884. Mineral traffic continued to decline and the line was sustained only by local goods and passenger work until the faintest glimmer of a tourist trade began to lighten the gloom. It was a dismal period, especially set against a background of the golden age of railways in general around the turn of the century, while the R&ER sank gradually towards the close of operations. Attempts to revive the mines were bedevilled by natural disasters and the line closed at the end of April 1913. Traffic in fact ceased in December 1912 and the Railway lay in dereliction for three years.

It has already been noted that tourist traffic only began to play any part in the work of the line towards the end. The location and route were definitely an asset from this point of view but although the first Ravenglass & Eskdale Railway would captivate any enthusiast nowadays, in Victorian and Edwardian eyes it was just another narrow gauge branch line. The era of miniature railways as tourist attractions was, however, at hand. Sir Arthur Heywood had pioneered the very narrow 15in. gauge for normal purposes at Duffield Bank twenty-five years before and argued in its favour as the logical development, for appropriate purposes, of existing narrow gauges. Such lines were first taken up by rich enthusiasts in whose eyes they really came within the category of toys, but they developed a solid business and engineering background in the hands of Henry Greenly, W.J. Bassett-Lowke and R. Proctor Mitchell. The last two formed a company, Narrow Gauge Railways Ltd, and began building and working narrow gauge lines in seaside resorts such as Blackpool. They flourished and other railways were built abroad, while in this country the firm eventually owned and worked the Fairbourne Railway (see chapter 27) as well.

Mitchell visited the R&ER early in 1915 and found it in a terrible state, although most of the materials were later re-used for making the new track. A rather curious lease on the line was taken—curious because the grantor had in fact no right to dispose of it—and work on re-laying the track on the new 15in. gauge began before any agreement was signed. The new Railway began operations in the summer of 1915. The locomotives were a Pacific, 'Colossus', from Captain Jack Howey's private railway at Staughton Manor in Huntingdonshire and an Atlantic, 'Sans Pareil' (formerly 'Prins Olaf'), from Narrow Gauge Railway's Oslo line. When the summer passenger service began to develop the following year services were extended up the 1 in 38 gradient to Boot. The engines were unequal to the task and at some point during the season ran off the rails.

After the war the line found a new financial supporter in Sir Aubrey Brocklebank of Irton Hall who was enough of an enthusiast at this time to have a branch from the line on to his estate surveyed. Brocklebank was to be the saviour of the Railway when, in 1924, some irregularities

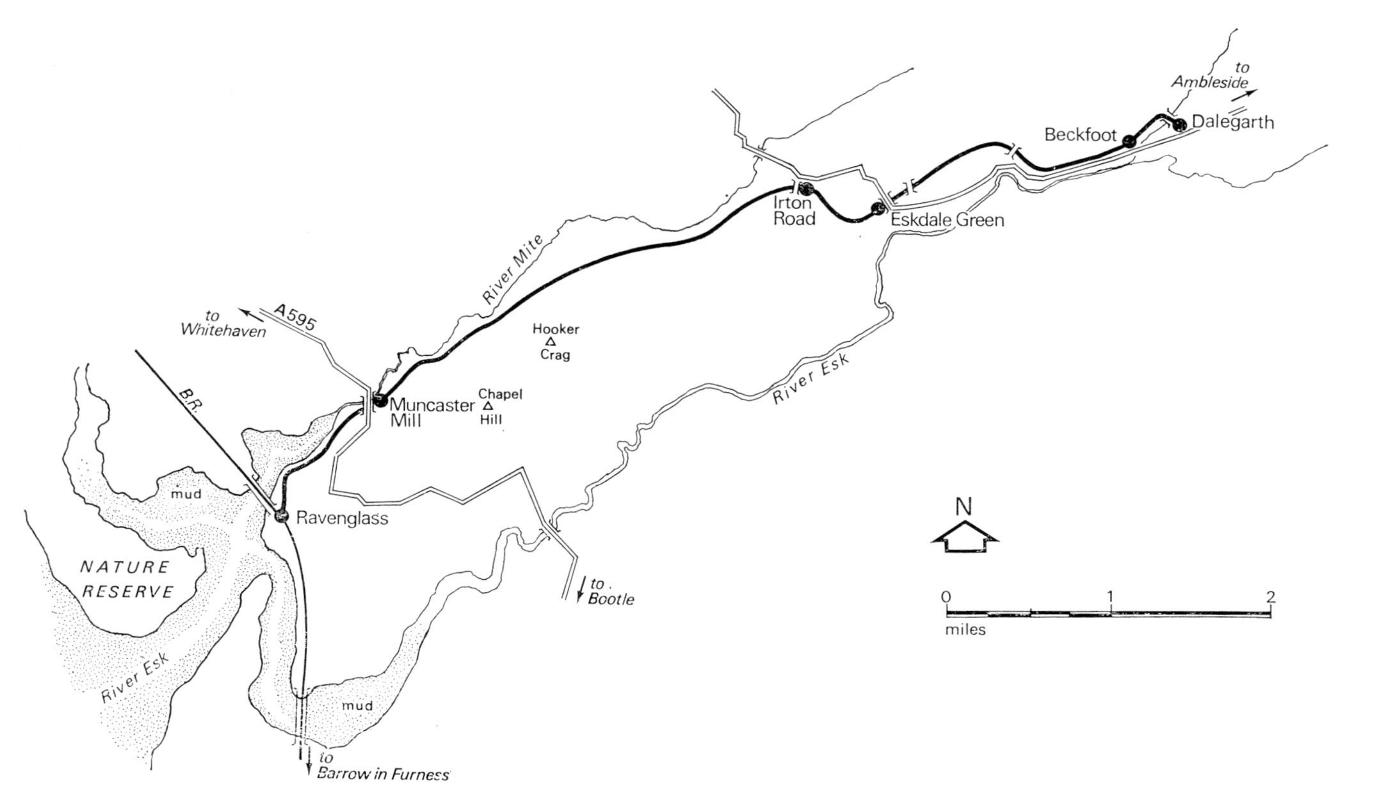

7 Ravenglass & Eskdale Railway

of the new Company's possession of the line began to produce complications. Most appropriately a new Pacific locomotive on the line had already been named 'Sir Aubrey Brocklebank'. Brocklebank also reopened the old granite quarry at Beckfoot, providing a new source of heavy traffic for the line and a crushing plant was built at Murthwaite. New professional management took over in place of the knowledgeable enthusiasts who had reduced the affairs of the Railway to some disorder and the next twenty years were a period of constructive calm. Much work was carried out on the line and for revenue it got by on a mixture of granite and summer tourist traffic.

No advertised passenger services were run during the war and soon after it the quarries and the railway were acquired by the Keswick Granite Co. Quarrying stopped in 1953, four years after the take-over, and the Granite Company did not find that the 40,000 passengers carried each year were enough to keep the line going. They decided to sell and soon advertisements began to appear of which the following, from the *Daily Telegraph* of 4 September 1958, is an example:

> For sale as a going concern by Private Treaty. Ravenglass and Eskdale Miniature Railway. In the Lake District of Cumberland. 7½ miles of 15in. gauge track up beautiful Eskdale. Two model steam and three diesel locomotives. Well-maintained rolling-stock, station buildings, repair shops and wagon sheds. 11 houses, cafe, shop and land comprising the well fenced and wooded permanent way, 3 fields and various open spaces. Inclusive price, £22,500 Freehold. For further information apply to T. Graham, General Manager, Keswick Granite Co. Ltd.

The price for which the complete 'train set' was then available must itself evoke a keen nostalgia fifteen years later among enthusiasts involved in buying or running a standard or narrow gauge railway. No realistic offer was received in response to these advertisements for the line or even part of it. The Granite Company was, in any event, not willing to dispose of the line by lots if this could possibly be avoided, as they wished to see it continue in operation. At this point the Ravenglass & Eskdale Railway Preservation Society, a mixture of lovers of Lakeland and railway enthusiasts, was formed and set about serious fund raising. The line was eventually sold at auction on 7 September 1960 for £12,000 to the Society, backed by a Midlands stockbroker, the late Colin Gilbert, and various substantial residents and landowners in the Ravenglass and Eskdale area. Mr Gilbert became the principal shareholder in the Ravenglass & Eskdale Railway Co. Ltd formed to run the Railway in March 1961 and was later its managing director. Following his death in 1968 control of the line passed to Lord Wakefield of Kendal, formerly Sir Wavell Wakefield, MP for St Marylebone, who was one of those who had supported the Preservation Society's purchase of the line.

Since the new Company took over, with a new general manager and engineer and many former employees, running standards on the Railway have been much improved and the number of passengers now carried each year is approximately a quarter of a million. The enterprise is a happy example of a commercial operation working with a Preservation Society consisting of volunteer helpers. Extensive track re-laying has been accomplished and thanks to Mr Gilbert's generosity, a major realignment of the line through a rock cutting at Holling Head has been carried out. The expansion of operations justified ordering a new locomotive in 1963 and this ('River Mite') is now at work alongside the two veterans of the line. The oldest of these locomotives, 'River Irt',

Table 30 Steam locomotives on the Ravenglass & Eskdale Railway (gauge 15in.)

Type	Number/name	Where built	Year
2-8-2	9 'River Mite'	Clarkson	1966
2-8-2	6 'River Esk'	Davey Paxman	1923
0-8-2	7 'River Irt'	A. Heywood	1894 (rebuilt 1927)

is actually a rebuild, carried out in 1927, of an original Duffield Bank 0-8-0T, 'Muriel'. The Davey Paxman 2-8-2 of 1923, 'River Esk', was originally an articulated 2-8-2-0-8-0, with the second power unit under the tender. No. 9, 2-8-2, 'River Mite', has the distinction of being the most recent steam locomotive in Britain and is a sure portent of the Ravenglass & Eskdale Railway's rewarding future.

24 Isle of Man Victorian Steam Railway

2-4-0T no. 8, 'Fenella'

That the Isle of Man should have been served, and should continue to be served, by a railway system somewhat less than standard gauge is appropriate when one looks at the island, roughly thirty miles by ten miles, on the map. At one time the system was operated by two separate companies, the Isle of Man and the Manx Northern Railways, although the latter was absorbed and one company formed in 1905. As an amalgamated system their total mileage was 46 miles. The Isle of Man Railway had been concentrated in the south of the island, with its lines from Douglas to Peel, on the opposite (west) coast and to Port Erin, at the southern tip. The Manx Northern began at the Foxdale Mines and ran north, crossing and running parallel for a short distance to the Douglas–Peel main line at St John's, and then it headed for the north-west coast of the island at Knocksharry, followed the coast for a few miles and headed for Ramsey by way of Kirkmichael, Ballaugh and Sulby.

The Isle of Man Victorian Steam Railway Co. and its Supporters' Association are concerned with maintaining and operating $15\frac{1}{2}$ miles of the mainly single former Isle of Man Railway line from Douglas to Port Erin, with intermediate stations at Ballasalla, Castletown and Port St Mary. It is a delightful, leisurely railway with fuschias and other vegetation all but brushing the sides of the passing trains at some points on the line as it winds, sometimes within sight of the sea but most of the time further inland, south-west from Douglas round Castletown and Poolvash Bays to Port Erin.

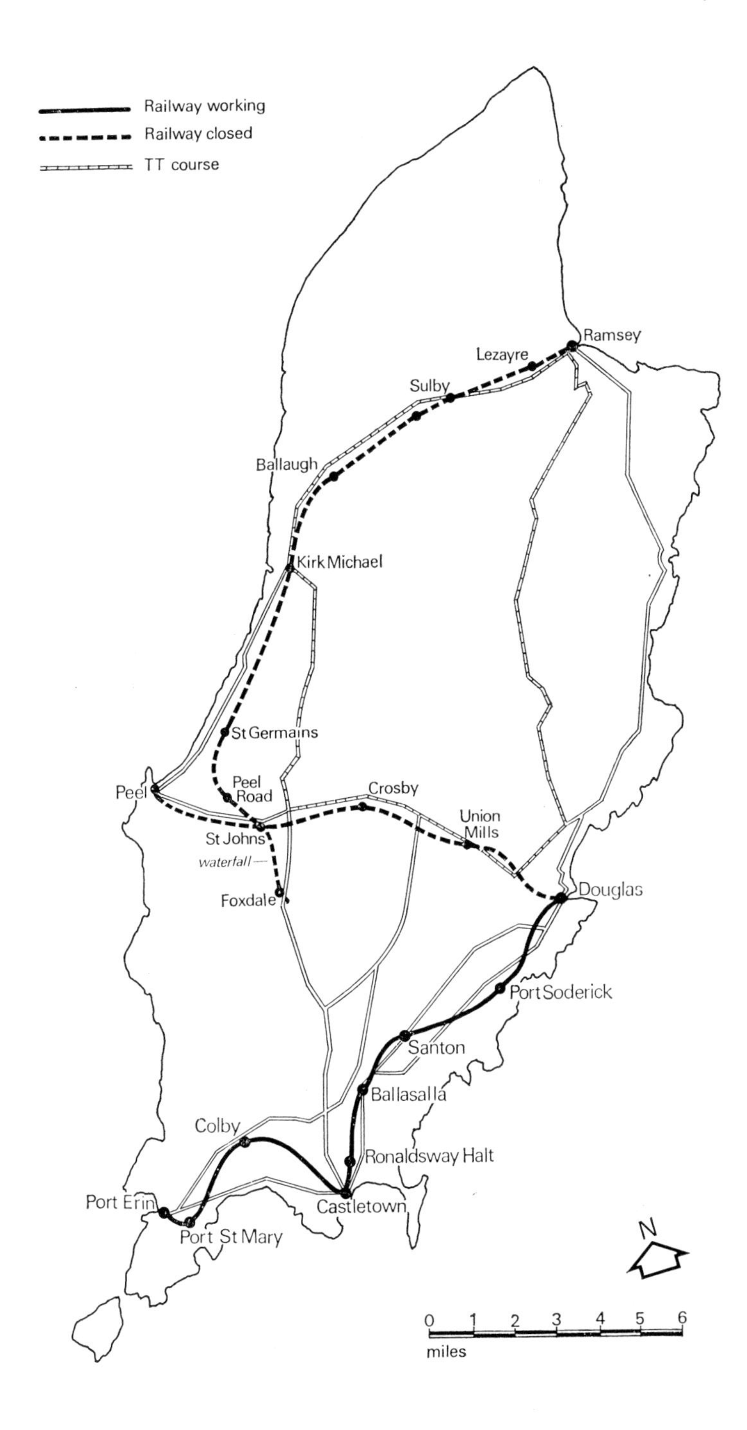

8 Isle of Man Victorian Steam Railway

In the latter months of 1965, substantial sections of the 3ft gauge line were found to be in urgent need of repair. It was decided to close the railway while they were carried out and the last train ran in November. The line did not reopen for the 1966 season. In April 1967, the Marquess of Ailsa took a lease on the whole railway and services started on 3 June that year. Trains were running on the Peel and Ramsey lines but only as far as Castletown on the south (Port Erin) line, although it opened completely the following year. The railway closed down again for 1968 but by the next year the Isle of Man Victorian Steam Railway Co. Ltd had been formed by Lord Ailsa in association with Mr L.T. Salts and Mr T. L. Mylchreest, fortified by a grant from the Tynwald (Manx parliament) for the Port Erin line. This was for three years only, but happily during that period passenger traffic grew at the rate of about fifteen per cent annually and the value of the railway as a tourist attraction has become well enough established to ensure continued official support.

For motive power, as Table 31 shows, the Isle of Man Railway relied on 2-4-0Ts and Beyer Peacock turned out a total of fourteen for the line and one for the Manx Northern. All survive, although not all in working order. The solitary 0-6-0T was built by Dübs & Co. of Glasgow for the Manx Northern line but was always rather too heavy for general use. It is now beautifully restored externally to the Manx Northern dark red livery but is not liked in service because of spreading the track. She was last used in 1968.

Table 31 Steam locomotives on the Isle of Man Victorian Steam Railway (gauge 3ft)*

Type	Number/name	Year	Condition/Origin
2-4-0T	1 'Sutherland'†	1873	Stored
2-4-0T	2 'Derby'	1873	Withdrawn
2-4-0T	3 'Pender'	1873	Stored
2-4-0T	4 'Loch'	1874	In use
2-4-0T	5 'Mona'	1874	Stored
2-4-0T	6 'Peveril'	1875	Stored
2-4-0T	7 'Tynwald'	1880	Withdrawn
2-4-0T	8 'Fenella'	1894	Withdrawn
2-4-0T	9 'Douglas'	1896	Stored
2-4-0T	10 'G. H. Wood'	1905	In use
2-4-0T	11 'Maitland'	1905	In use
2-4-0T	12 'Hutchinson'	1908	In use
2-4-0T	13 'Kissack'	1910	In use
2-4-0T	14 'Thornhill'	1880	ex-Manx Northern Railway; stored
0-6-0T	15 'Caledonia'	1885	ex-Manx Northern Railway; withdrawn
2-4-0T	16 'Mannin'	1926	Stored

* Nos. 1–14 and no. 16 were all built by Beyer Peacock. No. 15 was built by Dübs.

† 'Sutherland', 'Peveril', 'Thornhill', 'Caledonia' and 'Mannin' are restored as museum exhibits and are on show at Douglas.

The Company's locomotives and rolling stock are notably well turned out and the sight of the brown locomotives with their gleaming brass fittings puffing through the beguiling Manx landscape probably comes closer to the railway enthusiast's ideal than anything on the mainland. The fifteen-mile journey from Douglas to Port Erin takes one hour by the five daily trains in each direction on weekdays (there is no Sunday service at present) during the operating season from May to September.

25 Festiniog Railway

Double-ended Fairlie

Of all the narrow gauge railways described in this book, the Festiniog Railway, its history and revival, needs least introduction. The $9\frac{1}{2}$-mile 1ft $11\frac{1}{2}$in. gauge line runs from Portmadoc to Dduallt, with intermediate stations at Boston Lodge, Minffordd, Penrhyn, Plas, Tan-y-Bwlch and Campbell's Platform. A $4\frac{1}{2}$-mile extension to Blaenau Ffestiniog by way of Moelwyn and Tan-y-Grisiau is now under construction.

The line opened for slate trains on 20 April 1836 and ran from the quarries at Blaenau Ffestiniog to Portmadoc, whence the slate could be shipped by sea. The line was constructed on a continually falling gradient so that the loaded wagons would coast down by gravity to Portmadoc. With their load discharged, the empty wagons were then hauled up back to Blaenau Ffestiniog by horse. Traffic on the line increased and by the sixties was such that steam traction was introduced, only, however, for hauling the empties uphill. The loaded wagons continued to descend by gravity even after passenger services had been inaugurated two years later, in January 1865. The line was wholly dependent on the quarries for its existence and these in turn were dependent on building fashions which, by the end of the century, favoured tile over slate. As a result the whole slate-quarrying industry of North Wales went into a decline, dragging with it the way of life which it had created. The Festiniog Railway, deprived of its main source of revenue, struggled on. Passenger services were withdrawn on the outbreak of war in 1939 but goods traffic, including slates, continued until the closure of the line on 2 August 1946.

First moves towards a revival of the line were made by a body known as 'The 1949 Group'. This was followed by the Festiniog Railway Preservation Society and control of the whole enterprise passed to Alan Pegler, now internationally known as the owner of 'Flying Scotsman', in June 1954. Volunteers from the Preservation Society began an organised programme of track clearance and repair with a view to partial reopening in the summer of 1955. Meanwhile the project was threatened by the Central Electricity Generating Board's plans which affected part of the line north of Moelwyn tunnel and meant that if the railway was ever going to run into Blaenau Ffestiniog again, a deviation would be necessary. It is only now, after fifteen years of increasingly successful operation, that the present Company has reached a position from which it is able to undertake this work, so formidable are the problems and costs of railway building, even on a narrow gauge. News of the CEGB plan had first been made known in 1951 at a time when the railway was in the process of being transferred from the original operating company to the preservation body and thus no action was taken until the latter was firmly in command in July 1954. The proceedings then initiated have created a near record for litigation, and judgment, which at the time of writing may still be the subject of an appeal, was not given until December 1971. Under this judgment the Company has been awarded £65,000 of the £153,000 compensation it claimed, though the eventual cost of reinstating the line is estimated at around £250,000.

Nevertheless, the Festiniog Railway Co., powerfully supported by the Festiniog Railway Society, has already turned a moribund railway into a thriving concern, which now carries more than 300,000 passengers annually. The line, although mostly in Merionethshire, starts at Portmadoc harbour on the Caernarvonshire coast. From the station, trains run along the 'Cob', an embankment one mile long built in the early nineteenth century across the Glaslyn estuary, to Boston Lodge, where the locomotive works are situated, and then starts to climb to Dduallt, crossing the Pwllheli branch of BR at Minffordd and into wider and more impressive scenery. The Cei Mawr, a 60ft high dry-stone embankment, precedes the severe curves that lead towards Tan-y-Bwlch, for many years the terminus of the reopened line. More recently trains have travelled through the Garnedd tunnel to Dduallt, an isolated station without road access. The remaining section to Blaenau Ffestiniog will be covered by the deviation now in hand.

Too much has been lost along the line from Portmadoc to Blaenau Ffestiniog to permit the railway to be a purist preservation scheme in the way that some of those described in this book are. What the railway has to offer, however, is uniquely attractive and its collection of

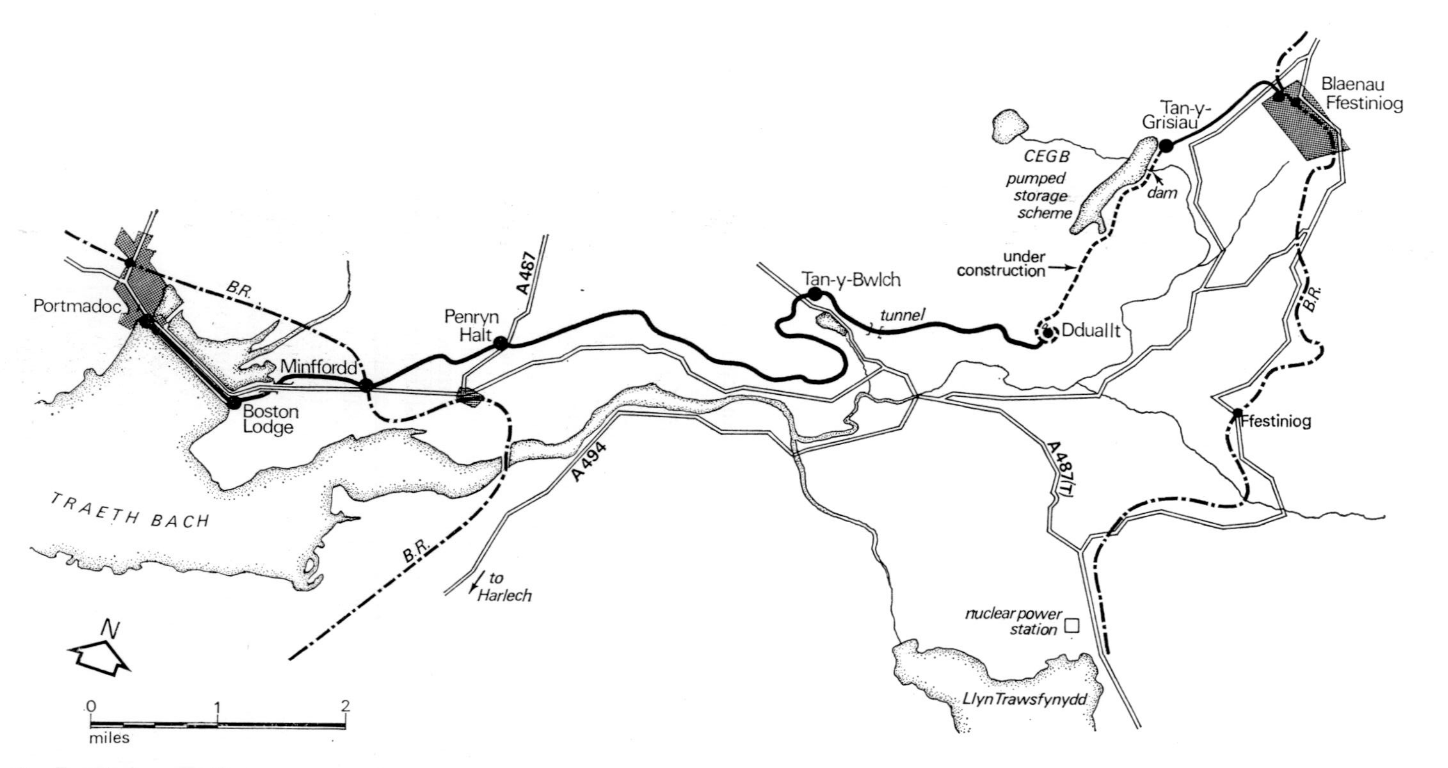

9 Festiniog Railway

locomotives satisfies even the severest critics of the line as a whole (see Table 32).

By far the most distinctive locomotives are the double ended 0-4-40Ts, two of them built by Fairlie and the third by Beyer Peacock. Such was the volume of traffic on the Festiniog Railway in the years following the introduction of steam traction that the management was faced with the problem either of lost production because of delays in drawing empty wagons up from Portmadoc to Blaenau Ffestiniog or with the

Table 32 Steam locomotives on the Festiniog Railway (gauge 1ft 11½in.)

Type	Number/name	Where built	Year	Origin
0-4-0ST	1 'Princess'	George England	1863	
0-4-0ST	2 'Prince'	George England	1863	
0-4-0ST	5 'Welsh Pony'	George England	1867	
0-4-0ST	'Blanche'	Hunslet	1893	Penrhyn Quarry
2-4-0ST	'Linda'	Hunslet	1863	Penrhyn Quarry
2-6-2T	'Mountaineer'	Alco (USA)	1916	Pithiviers Tramway, France
0-6-0ST	—	Peckett	1944	Harrogate Gasworks
0-4-40T	3 'Earl of Merioneth'	Fairlie	1885	
0-4-4-0T	10 'Merddyn Emrys'	Fairlie	1879	
0-4-4-0T	—	Beyer Peacock	1909	Tasmanian Govt Railways

expensive alternative of adding a second line to the railway. Robert Fairlie's double ended locomotive design of 1870 provided a further solution and one which continues to do attractive and reliable service on the line today. Fairlie's engines incorporate two separate boilers with a common firebox in the middle. At one time the Festiniog Railway had four of them, all built at the company's own works at Boston Lodge, no. 10, 'Merddyn Emrys', in 1879 and what is now no. 3 in 1885. The latter engine was originally no. 11, named 'Livingston Thompson'. It received its present number and the name 'Taliesin' in 1932. Ingenious use was made of the many-sided locomotive when it was renamed again in 1962 'Earl of Merioneth' on one side and 'Iarll Meironwydd' on the other. The third 0-4-4-0 engine on the line today is the pioneer of Beyer Peacock's celebrated Garratt compound, which were subsequently built in large numbers on the standard gauge for service all over the world, especially southern Africa. The present Festiniog locomotive was built for Tasmanian Government Railways in 1909, where it remained at work until 1947. On withdrawal, Beyer Peacock acquired her for display at their Gorton works and the Festiniog Railway took her over when the firm closed in 1965.

0-4-0STs nos. 1, 2 and 5 were all built originally with side tanks, later converted to saddles and worked with the distinctive four-wheeled tenders which 'Prince' retains in service today. When George England & Co. built them at New Cross in 1863 they were the first steam locomotives destined for work on so narrow a gauge as the Festiniog's 1ft 11½in. A fourth locomotive of the same class, no. 4, 'Palmerston', spent part of its short working life on the Vale of Rheidol Railway. Of the survivors only no. 2, 'Prince', is in working order at the present time and is the oldest steam locomotive still at work in this country.

'Blanche' and 'Linda' belong to the numerous and well-preserved class of Hunslet 0-4-0 saddle tanks from the Penrhyn Railway, which are fully described elsewhere. 'Mountaineer' was built by the American Locomotive Co. in 1916 for war service in France. She was sold along with many similar locomotives after the war to the Pithiviers Tramway, in France on which she remained until closure in 1964. She is now still at work on the Festiniog Railway.

26 Welsh Highland Railway

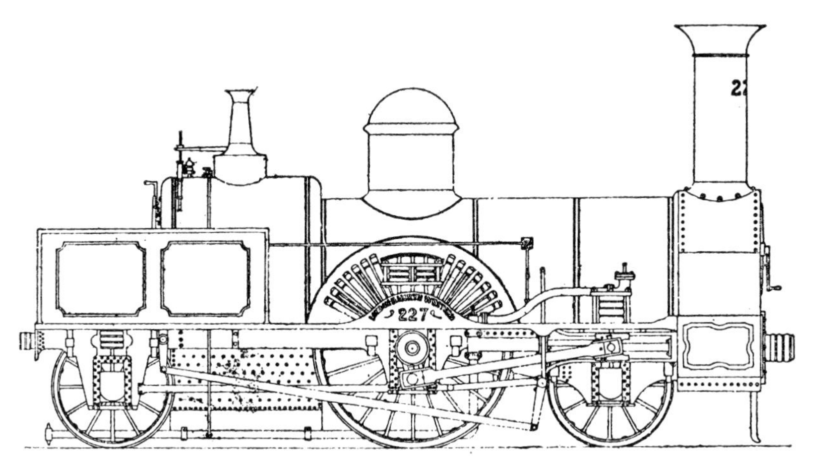

L&NWR no. 227, 'Mac's Mangle'

The Welsh Highland Light Railway (1964) Ltd has one of the most interesting and ambitious schemes to rebuild and operate a part of the former Welsh Highland Railway. The first stage of reopening will comprise the section of line from Beddgelert south through the Aberglaslyn Pass to Nantmor. Eventually it may run on south to Portmadoc, through Hafod-y-Llyn, Hafod Garregog, Ynsfor and Pont Croesor. To the north, it is unlikely that the line will ever be rebuilt beyond Quellyn Lake but redevelopment in this direction would include Hafod Ruffydd, Pitts Head and Rhyd-ddu (South Snowdon). It was the opening of the last named station in 1881, which caused such a threat to the Llanberis-Snowdon tourist trade on the other side of the mountain, that finally toppled such opposition as had prevented the building up to that date of a Snowdon mountain tramroad.

Traffic on the Welsh Highland Railway ceased in 1937 and the track has been lifted. To rebuild and reopen a realistic portion of the 21½-mile railway is a uniquely formidable prospect, comparable only to the Corris Railway Society's more limited plans (see chapter 31). Like all disused railway lines and in particular narrow gauge ones (the Lynton & Barnstaple's heavily overgrown course is an obvious example) the track-bed of the Welsh Highland Railway is full of natural and physical interest, as well as being an important slice of industrial archaeology.

From Nantmor, the line enters a rocky cutting heading north and emerges on to an embankment formed from the rubble of tunnelling of which a great deal was required in building this section of the line. The embankment, indeed, ends suddenly at the entrance to a 300-yard tunnel at the beginning of Aberglaslyn Pass. Fallen rocks, intrusive vegetation and running water at the tunnel entrance are evidence of the sort of work which the Welsh Highland's preservers will have to do. Inside, the tunnel is curved and fairly dry and the line emerges on to a high ledge above the River Glaslyn. The line continues along the stone ledge through two short tunnels, one thirty-seven yards long, the other, at seventeen yards, short enough to have the look and feel of a flying buttress supporting the steep slope of the Aberglaslyn Pass. These, like the longer tunnel further south and the forty-seven yard one near Beddgelert, are unlined and have stood up splendidly to years of neglect, even though the continuous dripping apparent as one walks through them may suggest otherwise to the uninitiated. Beddgelert station, which was situated some way from its village, is then reached by way of a continuation of the stone ledge, a lattice girder bridge over the river and an overgrown cutting.

The course of the railway is easy to follow on foot and it is immediately clear that on the whole surprisingly little work will be needed to re-lay the line. The walk from Nantmor to Beddgelert is already an evocative exercise. Under steam, with the NWNGR locomotive 'Russell' barking energetically at the precipitous walls of the Pass, the journey will be one of the most nostalgic available to steam enthusiasts.

The locomotives and rolling stock of the Welsh Highland Light Railway (1964) Ltd are at present kept at Kinnerley in Shropshire and consist primarily of an ex-industrial 0-6-0T, 'Gertrude', built by Andrew Barclay in 1918, and a genuine ex-Welsh Highland Railway 2-6-2T built by the Hunslet Engine Co. in 1906. 'Russell', as the latter engine is called, has had a varied career, beginning working life on the WHR's predecessor, the North Wales Narrow Gauge Railway, and remaining on the system until it closed in 1937. 'Russell' was then stored at Dinas for four years until she was sold to the Brymbo Steel Co. at Wrexham and thereafter passed through the hands of a succession of industrial users, most recently Messrs Fayles of Corfe Castle, Dorset. When the railway system there closed, the engine was acquired by the Birmingham Locomotive Club and exhibited in the Narrow Gauge Railway Museum at Towyn, pending the opportunity of being prepared for a working preservation. 'Russell' has since been restored, partly by her builders, the Hunslet Engine Co., and partly at Steamtown, Carnforth.

27 Fairbourne Railway

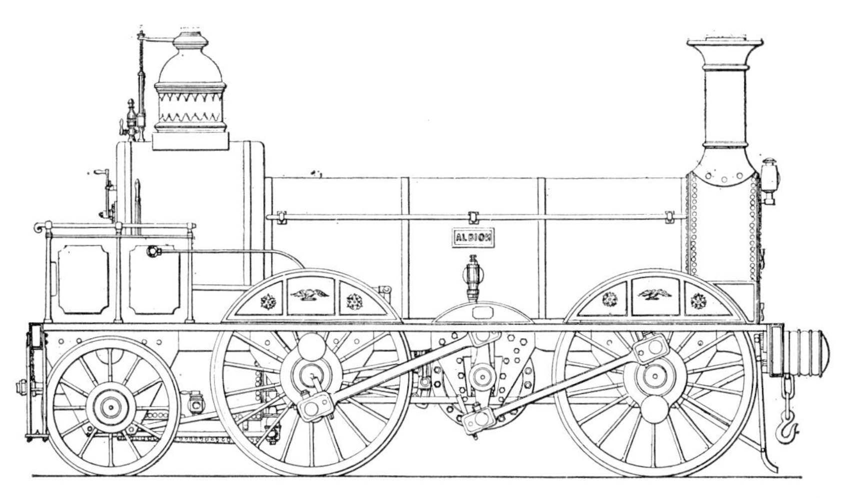

Cambrian system locomotive 'Albion'

The Fairbourne Railway began life in 1890 as a 2ft gauge horse tramway, initially for the carriage of building and construction materials but soon for passengers as well. The line was converted to its present 15in. gauge and to steam traction in 1916 and has been in operation ever since, apart from a period of abandonment during and immediately after the war. The two-mile single track with passing loops runs from Fairbourne to Penrhyn Point at the tip of a tapering sandy spit known as Morfa Henddol, facing Barmouth across the Mawddach Estuary. The area is a low-lying shelf at the foot of the Cader Idris range and, although now protected by a sea wall, has been liable to serious flooding, notably in 1927 and 1943.

Until the arrival of the Cambrian Railways' standard gauge line in the sixties, it was a deeply introverted rural area, in spite of being on the coast. When the railway reached Barmouth Junction in 1865 the surrounding area began to develop as a holiday resort. Although the railway crossed the estuary to Barmouth itself by way of Barmouth bridge in 1867, no station opened in Fairbourne until 1897. Nevertheless, the building firm of Solomon Andrews & Son began to develop the area around the southern end of the railway bridge towards Arthog, very soon after it was opened. Two miles away in Fairbourne, Sir Arthur McDougall (of 'self raising flour' fame) was soon active in the same field as Andrews. By 1890 he had built a brickworks near the main line in Fairbourne and was concentrating on building along the

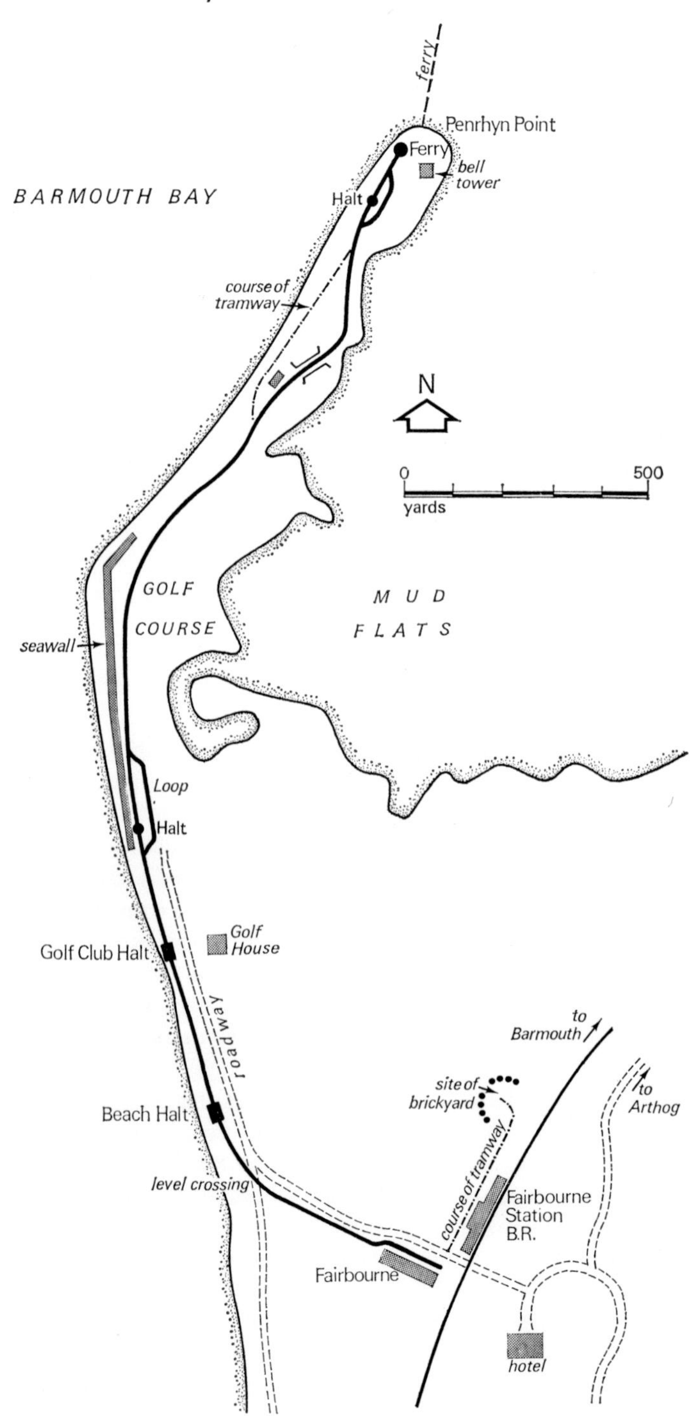

10 Fairbourne Railway

promontory in the direction of Penrhyn Point. The horse tramway was made to carry materials for this building activity and once the developments were inhabited, he invested in two passenger wagons to carry people. The line continued to be worked by horse and the wagons were drawn from the side, a practice inherited from the more hazardous business of hauling, or more precisely stopping, a train of heavy contractors' vehicles.

McDougall sold his Fairbourne estate in 1916 and very soon afterwards Narrow Gauge Railways Ltd, who were pioneer operators of 15in. gauge railways whose enterprises, apart from lines in seaside resorts like Blackpool and Rhyl, included by this date the Ravenglass & Eskdale Railway, were at work on the line converting the tramway to the narrower gauge, using the original materials. Operations began in the summer of 1916 with a new 4-4-2 locomotive, 'Prince Edward of Wales', designed by Henry Greenly and built at Northampton by Bassett-Lowke. Other early locomotives on the line were an 0-4-0T, 'Katie', designed and built by Sir Arthur Heywood, the protagonist of the very narrow gauge, at Duffield Bank, near Derby. 'Katie' had been built in 1896 originally for the Duke of Westminster's private miniature railway at Eaton Hall in Cheshire but neither there nor at Fairbourne was she ever a very satisfactory performer and was scrapped in 1926. By that time, the line had been fortunate in acquiring another Bassett-Lowke locomotive designed by Greenly and built in 1912. This was an Atlantic named 'Count Louis' and is part of the line's present motive power. The engine had been destined at one time for the private railway of Count Louis Zborowski, one of the builders of the Romney, Hythe & Dymchurch Railway. Zborowski was killed very soon after the engine had been delivered to his house near Canterbury and so it never ran there. The Count's other locomotive, 'Northern Chief', was taken over by his partner on the Romney, Hythe & Dymchurch venture, Captain Jack Howey, and is still at work there but 'Count Louis' was returned to Bassett-Lowke and was available to rescue the Fairbourne line and to replace 'Katie'.

In 1927, following a flood, the line was leased to Sir Peter Peacock and services continued up and down the beach for ten peaceful years. By the late thirties, however, various troubles began to build up. The Railway's general manager, who had come to the line from the Ravenglass & Eskdale soon after the conversion of gauge, retired through ill health in 1936; in 1939 'Count Louis' had to be withdrawn from service because of a fractured connecting rod; and then on the outbreak of war not only were many of the staff called up but the area was marked for intensive use for military training. The line did not reopen after the 1939 season and for the next seven years underwent such ravages that in parts little trace of the line was apparent when it was inspected in 1945. Quite apart from the years of neglect and military occupation, there had been damaging floods in 1943. Fortunately the three Midland businessmen who now took the line over were not put off and set to work on comprehensive restoration and re-laying, including provision for the physical developments which had taken place, such as the tidal channel which had appeared in the sand up towards Penrhyn Point and had to be bridged.

By 1948, 'Count Louis' was back in action ready for the re-opening of the line. Since then, to meet the ever growing traffic, a collection of four steam and five diesel engines has been built up (see Table 33). For a while the G&S 4-6-0, 'Prince Charles', was borrowed from Dudley Zoo, as in the first place was one of the railway's present engines, 4-6-2, 'Ernest W. Twining', built in 1949 and named after its designer. Twining also designed the unique 2-4-2, 'Katie', and 'Siân', both carrying special protective devices against sand which is a menace to locomotives on this line.

Table 33 Steam locomotives on the Fairbourne Railway (gauge 15in.)

Type	Name	Where built	Year
4-4-2	'Count Louis'	Bassett-Lowke	1912
4-6-2	'Ernest W. Twining'	G&S	1949
2-4-2	'Katie'	Guest	1950
2-4-2	'Siân'	Guest	1963

28 Snowdon Mountain Railway

0-4-2T no. 3, 'Wyddfa'

The Snowdon Mountain Railway, although in no sense a preservation line, deserves mention as the only rack railway in Britain and as an exemplar of a type of steam traction which is now unique in this country. In origin the line was an entirely private affair and neither an Act of Parliament nor a Light Railway Order was obtained to build it. The 2ft 7½in. gauge line, built on the Abt (staggered rack) system, was opened on 6 April 1896. It climbs from Llanberis, 353ft above sea level, to the summit of Snowdon, 3,540ft, in 4¾ miles by gradients which, at the steepest, reach 1 in 5½.

Opening a new single track branch from Caernarvon to Llanberis in 1869 the chairman of the LNWR, Sir Richard Moon, had said that 'the next extension must be to the top of Snowdon'. The fame of Snowdonia, the growth of tourism and the comparative gentleness of the slopes of Snowdon itself, seen beside the opening of the Mount Washington Rack Railway in the United States and of the Rigi Railway in Switzerland in 1871, brought this prospect well within the bounds of possibility. Somewhat precipitous conventional narrow gauge railways were not new to the area where the Dinorwic and Penrhyn quarry systems had long fed the Padarn Railway at the foot of the mountain. These quarries, like most of the area, including Snowdon, were owned by Mr W. A. Assheton Smith who, together with a powerful body of somewhat un-Victorian conservationists, was opposed to any assault on the mountain. Attempts to scale Snowdon by rail were considered from the more arduous side, the south-west, running from the railway line which was eventually to become the Welsh Highland Railway. It thus became clear that Snowdon would be violated from one direction or another and Assheton Smith and his colleagues decided to do so themselves, forming the Snowdon Mountain Tramroad & Hotels Co. in 1893.

The engineers appointed were Sir Douglas Fox and Francis Fox. There were two basic questions to be settled before work could proceed beyond the first survey: what form of motive power to use and which rack rail system. The choice between steam and electricity as the source of motive power was resolved simply. The use of electricity for such purposes was still largely experimental and the installation of the necessary equipment would have been very expensive. Steam thus triumphed over electricity as it was to do on the Vale of Rheidol line two years later.

The question of which of the several rack rail systems which had proved themselves in various parts of the world would be most suitable for Snowdon was much more complicated. The working of conventional railways depends on the adhesion of smooth wheels and smooth rails and this will work on gradients up to 1 in 15 but no steeper. Beyond this point a rack rail is needed. On railways which are a mixture of steep, slight and level gradients a mixture of rack and adhesion rails can be used. Locomotives for work on such lines are built with separate engines, sharing one boiler, with the adhesion and rack drive independently controlled. Such locomotives may either push or pull their train but when pulling they are usually supported by a banking engine to obviate a breakaway. Pure rack railways, on the other hand, as the name implies, make no use of adhesion and are the kind used for real mountain railways like that up Snowdon. The flanged wheels are used only to guide and sometimes to help with braking. Engine and train are kept together by gravity whether going up or downhill, that is, pushing upwards, and preceding the train downwards. In this case the danger of a breakaway is guarded against by the independent emergency braking system usually fitted to the trains. Rack rail locomotives can also, of course, run on the level and indeed Matthew Murray's Middleton colliery engine of 1812 belonged to this class. Of the two main types of rack, the Riggenbach system is in the shape of a ladder and the Abt system consists of two separate racks, side by side, with their teeth staggered. The Abt system was quite early shown to be both smoother and safer than the Riggenbach, particularly on the very steepest gradients, and was adopted by the promoters of the Snowdon Mountain Tramroad. The rack rail was supplied by the British firm of Richard Cammell & Co. and the contractors for the rest of the work were Holme & King. The locomotives were built by the Swiss Locomotive & Machine Co. (SLM) of Winterthur, which accounts for the somewhat eccentric (for Wales) gauge of 800mm (2ft 7½in.).

Midland Railway Project, plate 92

92 (above) Johnson 'Spinner', 4-2-2, no. 173, near Ambergate

Middleton Railway, plates 93–5

93 (below) Murray Blenkinsop locomotive (1812) with a train at the Leeds coal staith, *c.* 1830. The print has two curious errors of draughtsmanship: the inclination of the crosshead guide tie bars is impossible, and a mill chimney, one of several in the background, has been swept round and incorporated in the locomotive in addition to its own chimney

94 (above) NER 0-4-0T, no. 1310, with a train about to leave Dartmouth yard for the BR exchange sidings. On the right is Mersey Docks and Harbour Board 0-6-0ST, no. 21, since 'combined' with 'Swansea'

95 (below) Hudswell Clarke 0-4-0ST, 'Henry de Lacy II', at Moor Road

Keighley & Worth Valley Railway, plates 96–102

96 (above) Midland Railway class 4F 0-6-0 no. 3924 at Haworth, is the only tender locomotive of MR origin in working order

97 (below) Ex-US Army, Southern Railway and BR 0-6-0T no. 72 approaching Haworth

42700
2700

98 (opposite above) Ivatt class 2, no. 41241, with a six-coach rake accelerating up the 1 in 60 gradient between Haworth and Oxenhope

99 (opposite below) Ex-LMS Horwich 'Crab', 2-6-0 no. 2700 as re-painted

100 (above) 0-6-0T no. 69023, 'Joem', built at Darlington in 1951, leaving Haworth. On the right is one of the many worsted mills once served by the railway

WORTH VALLEY
RAILWAY
RE-OPENING SPECIAL
41241
K W V R

101 (opposite above) No. 41241, built at Crewe in 1949, double heading no. 72 on the special reopening train, 29 July 1968

102 (opposite below) Lancashire & Yorkshire Railway 0-6-0 no. 957, built by Beyer Peacock in 1887, as she appeared in the film *The Railway Children*, on Mytholmes viaduct with a train emerging from the northern end of the tunnel

Yorkshire Dales Railway, plate 103

103 (above) Locomotives on shed at Embsay

Nº 5

North Yorkshire Moors Railway, plates 104–7

104 (opposite above) Ex-Lambton Railway 0-6-2T no. 5, climbing towards Goathland with a three-coach train from Grosmont

105 (opposite below) Ex-Lambton Railway 0-6-2T no. 5, near Darnholm

106 (above) Ex-NER 0-8-0 Q6 no. 3395, at Moorgates, seen through an arch underneath the original (1836) route

107 A general view of Goathland, with three fully operational steam locomotives

Lakeside & Haverthwaite Railway, plates 108, 109

108 (above) Ex-LMS & BR 'Black 5', no. 44806, arriving at Lakeside with a six-coach train on 31 May 1971

109 (below) BR Fairburn 2-6-4T no. 2085, restored to full Caledonian Railway livery of blue with maroon undercarriage and company arms on the side tanks

Scottish Railway Preservation Society, plate 110

110 (above) Ex-Caledonian Railway 0-4-4T no. 419 (BR no. 55189) built at St Rollox in 1907, at Falkirk, September 1971

Lochty Private Railway, plate 111

111 (below) 'Union of South Africa' as BR no. 60009 leaving Lochty with the ex-LNER beaver-tail design 'Coronation' observation car

Strathspey Railway, plate 112

112 (above) Mr W. E. C. Watkinson's 'Black 5', no. 5025, is planned to work on the Strathspey Railway, although at present located on the Keighley & Worth Valley Railway

Ravenglass & Eskdale Railway, plates 113–15

113 (below) 3ft gauge days: 'Devon' at the original Boot terminus, c. 1905

114 (above) 2-8-2 'River Esk' heads a train for Dalegarth near Gilbert's Cutting

115 (below) 0-8-2 'Rivert Irt' at Ravenglass

Isle of Man Victorian Steam Railway, plates 116–18

116 (above) No. 11, 'Maitland', on the cliff-top at Gob-y-Deigan (Devil's Mouth) with a Ramsey-bound train, July 1967

117 (below) The Royal Train, hauled by no. 11, 'Maitland', entering Kirk Braddan station on Sunday 7 July 1963

118 (above) Glen Mooar viaduct on the Ramsey line. The rails are 75ft above river level, July 1967

Festiniog Railway, plates 119–23

119 (opposite above) Oiling 'Linda' after the first official run of the season, March 1971

120 (opposite below) 'Britomart', a privately owned locomotive kept at Boston Lodge, about to leave for Portmadoc

LINDA

BRITOMART
3

121 (opposite) Double-ended Fairlie 0-4-4-0T, 'Earl of Merioneth'/ 'Iarll Meironwydd', in store at the end of Boston Lodge shed, November 1971

122 (above) 'Blanche', with a late evening train between Tan-y-Bwlch and Dduallt

123 (below) 'Mountaineer' leaving Portmadoc station with a train for Dduallt and, *left*, double-ended Fairlie coming to a stand before following with a works train

GERTRUDE

RUSSELL

Welsh Highland Railway, plates 124–6

124 (opposite above) Barclay 0-6-0T, 'Gertrude', when new in 1918

125 (opposite below) Ex-North Wales Narrow Gauge Railway 2-6-2T, 'Russell', has been fitted with a new boiler by the Hunslet Engine Co. who built her in 1906, ready for service when part of the line is reopened

126 (above) Tunnels in Aberglaslyn Pass

Fairbourne Railway, plate 127

127 (opposite above) 'Sian' with a train just outside Fairbourne station

Snowdon Mountain Railway, plates 128–31

128 (opposite below) 'Wydffa' climbing towards the first loop at Hebron

129 (right) No. 7, 'Aylwin', raising steam outside Llanberis shed

130 (below) Near the summit

131 'Snowdon' approaching Afon Hwch viaduct and the first gradient. The Dinorwic quarries are visible in the background

Building progressed quickly. It was completed in January 1896, thirteen months after it had begun, having progressed at an average rate of 120 yards rising to a maximum of 350 yards a day. The season delayed the inspection by the Board of Trade until March 1896 but Major Francis Marindin judged that the railway was fit to be used as a public carrier, although he recommended that services should be suspended under certain weather conditions, notably of wind. The public opening followed ten days later, on Easter Monday. Locomotives nos. 1 and 2, 'Ladas' and 'Enid', hauled the first trains. Unfortunately it was also no. 1's last, for on the return journey at Clogwyn, the steepest part of the line, she left the rails and plunged to destruction far down the mountain. 'Ladas' was not, of course, coupled to her train which was soon brought to a halt by the automatic brake without danger to the passengers, except for the two who leapt out in panic, one of whom later died of his injuries. The engine crew jumped clear and were not injured.

It was a disastrous opening and public services had to be suspended for the rest of the season while the accident was investigated and the necessary alterations carried out. The cause was found to be subsidence following the settling of the road bed. 'Ladas' had come adrift from the rack and all control had been lost immediately on the very steep section of line at Clogwyn. This particular defect was eliminated once the line had settled permanently but as a further insurance against a similar mishap rack girders (guard rails) were placed on either side of the rack and the locomotives were fitted with grippers.

By the time the line was fully reopened in April 1897 three more locomotives, also from SLM ('Wyddfa', 'Snowdon' and 'Moel Siabod') had been delivered, although no. 1 was never replaced. The present locomotive stock is completed by three more, 'Padarn' (originally 'Sir Harmood'), 'Aylwin' and 'Eryri', delivered in 1922–3 (see Table 34).

The 'hotel' part of the Tramroad Company once consisted of the Summit Hotel and of two hotels in Llanberis. The last of them was sold in 1953. Since then the Company, which was renamed Snowdon

Table 34 Snowdon locomotives (gauge 800mm, 2ft 7½in.)

Type	Number/name	Where built	Year
0-4-2T Rack	2 'Enid'	SLM	1895
0-4-2T Rack	3 'Wyddfa'	SLM	1895
0-4-2T Rack	4 'Snowdon'	SLM	1896
0-4-2T Rack	5 'Moel Siabod'	SLM	1896
0-4-2T Rack	6 'Padarn'	SLM	1922
0-4-2T Rack	7 'Aylwin'	SLM	1923
0-4-2T Rack	8 'Eryri'	SLM	1923

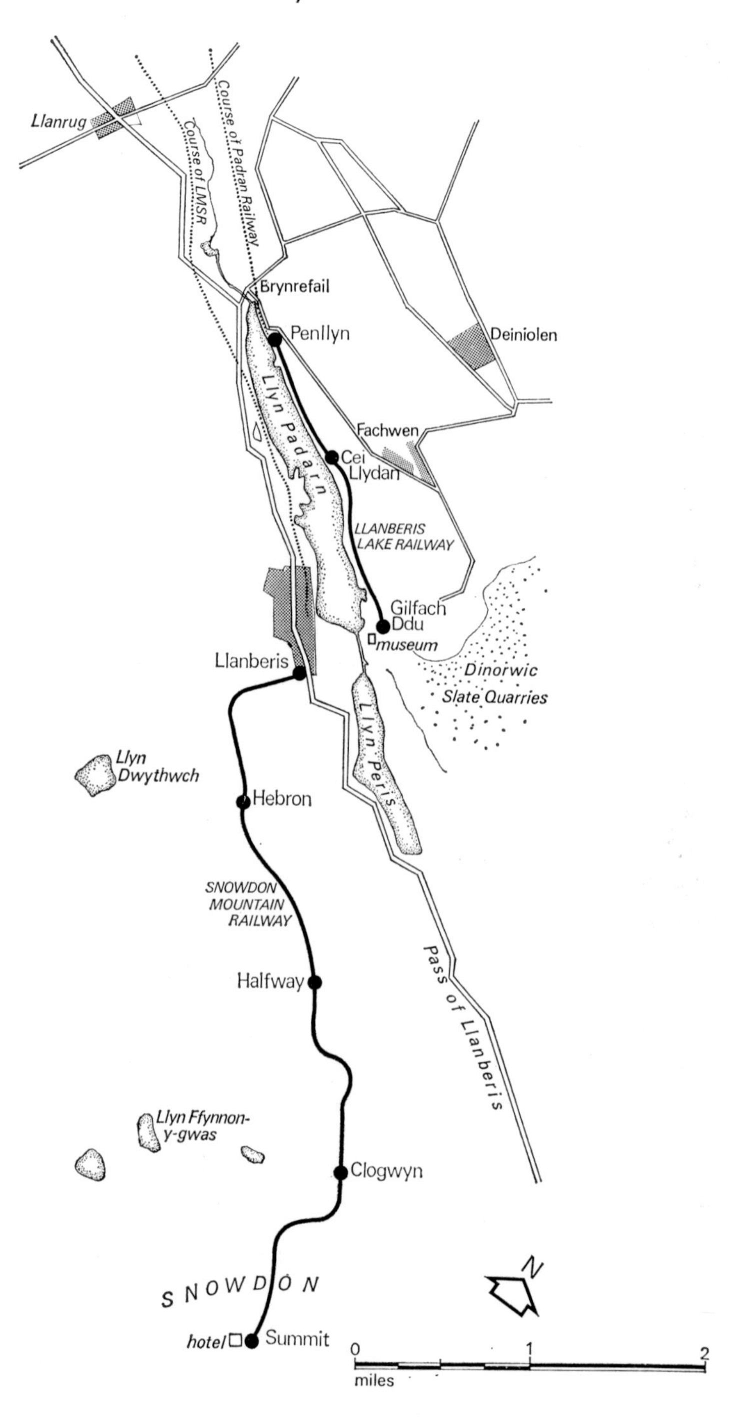

11 Snowdon Mountain Railway and Llanberis Lake Railway

Mountain Railway Ltd as long ago as 1920, has been wholly concerned with running the railway.

The 4¾-mile journey from Llanberis to the summit takes between sixty and seventy minutes. The running of trains between March and October is subject to weather conditions and trains do not, as a rule, run with less than twenty-five return passengers aboard at the start. The summit cannot be seen from Llanberis station, which is situated on the southern edge of the town. The first stage of the journey is the 1 mile 8 chains and 616ft to Hebron. After a quarter of a mile or so of meadows the railway reaches the first short, steep gradient just before crossing the fourteen-arch Hafon Hwch viaduct. The smaller Upper Viaduct a little further on passes close to the Ceunant Mawr waterfall which plunges for over a hundred feet in two stages into the gorge. The summit is now visible, as no more than a small peak, for the first time over the receding ridges in the foreground. Soon the enclosed arable landscape begins to change to the rougher, open grazing land of the lower and middle slopes. From Hebron station Llyn Padarn is a strip of water narrowing from the middle to the far distance, and beyond the comparatively gentle country on its northern shores the Menai Strait and Anglesey can sometimes be seen.

The next part of the journey is a 2½-mile 572ft climb to Halfway and begins with 23½ chains of straight track, the longest such section on the railway. The ground is peat, unlike the rock on which most of the rest is built and this part of the line thus needs a great deal of maintenance. Just before Halfway, the line passes through the only rock cutting on it, which reaches a depth of about twenty feet. Engines usually take water at Halfway ready for the very exacting second half of the journey. Throughout the 1 mile 9 chains from Halfway to Clogwyn the gradient, with curves to match, seldom eases from 1 in 6·6. The distance climbed in this short section to Clogwyn, 2,556ft above sea level, is 915ft. The surrounds of Clogwyn are less slatey than Halfway but far more dramatic, with a 2,000ft drop into the Llanberis Pass. The summit is reached after another 1 mile and 18 chains and a climb of 952ft over gradients as steep as 1 in 5·5.

The summit of Snowdon is the second highest point in Britain and the Mountain Railway, fulfilling Sir Richard Moon's prediction, takes passengers to within sixty feet of it. Although there have often been plans for a similar rack railway up Ben Nevis they have come to nothing and the Snowdon Mountain Railway remains unique.

29 Llanberis Lake Railway

Bury's 'Liverpool', the first engine with inside cylinders

The tourist value of a steam-operated railway has long been recognised and this is especially evident with narrow gauge lines in areas of great natural beauty which may not be otherwise accessible except on foot. The Snowdon Mountain Railway is the outstanding example and its success has not passed unnoticed by the inhabitants of the opposite (north-west) shore of Llyn Padarn. The Caernarvonshire County Council is actively planning the further development of the area for recreational purposes and the local people have capitalised on this prospect by founding and financing their own narrow gauge railway: Rheilffordd Llyn Llanberis, the Llanberis Lake Railway.

The line, though dependent to a certain extent on voluntary labour, is run on commercial principles and the shares, owned in amounts ranging from £10 to £500, have been bought by local residents and tradespeople as well as enthusiasts from outside. The line opened on 19 July 1971 and in its first week carried 6,200 passengers. This fully justified the expectations of investors after the start of operations had been postponed for two months, for reasons which are explained later.

The railway and line are new but the route follows the course of part of the Padarn Railway. This system was built in the 1830s on the 4ft gauge. It and the Glasgow District Subway were the only lines constructed to this specification on the mainland of Britain. The railway linked the Dinorwic Slate quarries, once the largest in the world, with the shipping outlets and LNWR at Port Dinorwic on the Menai

Strait. A similar line linked the nearby Penrhyn quarries with Port Penrhyn. Within both quarries and ports the main line was served by a 1ft 10¾in. system from which wagons were loaded in fours on to the 4ft gauge transporter wagons, thus avoiding the hazards and delays of transhipment. Of the locomotives which worked on this gauge a Horlock 0-4-0 of 1848, 'Fire Queen', survives in the National Trust Railway Museum at Penrhyn Castle, Bangor, together with a 'velocity car', rail velocipede and an 1896 coach. There is also one transporter wagon in the Narrow Gauge Museum at Towyn. The line closed in October 1961 when it was bought by a scrap merchant who, after trying and failing to sell it as a complete railway system for industrial use, broke up the three Hunslet 0-6-0 tank engines which had worked on the line since the 1880s and lifted the track. The Dinorwic quarries closed in July 1969, although small-scale slate workings continue in the area. Well before closure the dispersal of the narrow gauge railway equipment had begun, much of it being sold to the Gwynedd River Authority. The remainder was sold at auction in December 1969 when much of it was acquired by the founder of the present Company, Mr Alan Porter. The quarry was bought by McAlpines in June 1970 and the workshop area and undeveloped land by the County Council, who intend to set up an industrial museum in due course.

The tourist potential of the route of the Padarn Railway had been appreciated for many years. For two and a quarter miles from Gilfach Ddu to Penllyn the line lay along a stone shelf at the very edge of the lake, giving magnificent views of the Snowdon range. Early plans to exploit it envisaged a line about 4½ miles long running right round the lake, and making use of the course of the LMS branch to Llanberis as well as the Padarn trackbed. This was cut to a shorter line over part of the latter only, on land leased from the Gwynedd River Authority and the Caernarvonshire County Council.

The stock bought by Mr Porter in 1969 included three 1ft 10¾in. gauge Hunslet 0-4-0 saddle tanks: 'Elidir' (originally 'Red Damsel'), 'Wild Aster' and 'Dolbadarn'. Of these only the newest, 'Dolbadarn', was in service in the opening season, 1971. 'Elidir' and 'Maid Marian', the latter newly arrived from Bressingham, joined her in 1972 and 'Wild Aster' was scheduled for restoration during the winter of 1972–3, before entering service. Most trains on the Llanberis Lake Railway are steam hauled, although the company also owns four diesels. The steam locomotives are listed in Table 35. All are ex-Dinorwic 1ft 10¾in. locomotives and 'Maid Marian' had originally been preserved in that gauge at Bressingham. The chance of building the new Llanberis line in what would then have been a unique gauge was abandoned because greater quantities of stock in the 1ft 11½in. gauge had been acquired from elsewhere and so the Dinorwic engines were altered. Nevertheless, the Hunslet 0-4-0 saddle tanks have done well from the point of view of

Table 35 Steam locomotives on the Llanberis Lake Railway (gauge 1ft 11½in.)

Type	Number/name	Where built	Year
0-4-0ST	1 'Elidir'	Hunslet	1889
0-4-0ST	2 'Wild Aster'	Hunslet	1904
0-4-0ST	3 'Dolbadarn'	Hunslet	1922
0-4-0ST	'Maid Marian'	Hunslet	1903

preservation, both working and inert. Thirty of them, with their extraordinary names such as 'Cackler', 'Lady Madcap', 'Holy War' and 'Rough Pup', survive in various parts of the world.

Building the new railway began in December 1969. For a line that had been raised and abandoned six years before, the course of the Padarn Railway was in good condition. Few obstacles, apart from the encroachments of nature, were encountered. For the most part 40lb per yard quarry rail in chairs was used, although there is also some flat-bottomed 45lb and 60lb per yard rail, some of which was previously used on the Lynton & Barnstaple railway in Devonshire.

For its opening season, 1971, the mile or so of line from Gilfach Ddu to Cei Llydan was operational and trains ran at forty-five minute intervals, allowing time for Snowdon to be contemplated from the northern end. In 1972 services were half-hourly and ran as far as Penllyn, another mile up the lakeside. The 18- and 24-seat carriages were built on the site at Gilfach Ddu and were the cause of the postponement of the opening in 1971. They were originally six feet wide and it was found that at certain stages of loading there was some small risk of derailment, although settlement of the track at the time of testing may have been equally responsible, In any event, before commercial operations began the width of the carriages was reduced to 4ft 6in. and the suspension modified, since when their performance has been flawless

The Llanberis Lake Railway is uniquely part of the Caernarvonshire community. One may hope that residents of other areas likely to benefit from a steam-operated railway, including places where a preservation society is already at work, will be equally far-sighted in supporting its financial development when they have the chance to buy shares.

30 Talyllyn Railway

The 2ft 3in. gauge Talyllyn Railway was built by James Swinton Spooner and opened to passenger and freight traffic in 1866. It was planned to transport slate and labour from the Bryn Eglwys quarries near Abergynolwyn down to the Merionethshire coast at Towyn, seven miles away. In the sixties these quarries were employing up to 300 men and doing a little to alleviate the position of the area as one of the most backward in Wales. At the same time there was a minor gold rush in progress, which attracted entrepreneurs from outside. These included William McConnel, a cotton magnate from Manchester who, although he had owned an estate in the area since 1859, had previously had no business interests there. With the cotton trade suffering from the after-effects of the American Civil War he began to look for alternative avenues of exploitation and founded the Aberdovey Slate Co. in 1864, primarily to look for gold, in an area which included the Bryn Eglwys quarries. The slate quarries on the other side of the hill at Upper Corris had been served by a tramroad since 1858 and it was not long before the new management at Bryn Eglwys was planning one too.

Slate was the foundation of the railway's business. Although passengers were also carried from Towyn as far as Abergynolwyn with intermediate stops at Rhydronen, Brynglas and Dolgoch, the line's future was threatened as soon as the quarries closed in 1948. It survived because of the dedication and tenacity first of Sir Henry Haydn Jones and second of the Talyllyn Railway Preservation Society.

Henry Haydn Jones was a native of Towyn, born in 1863. He sat in Parliament as a Liberal for Merioneth for thirty-five years from the crisis election of December 1910, precipitated by the peer-baiting Budget of his fellow countryman, David Lloyd George. Jones, however, was a traditional rather than a radical Liberal. He rose from obscure origins to a position of some wealth and great local repute. He bought the business from McConnel's successor in 1910 and was general manager of the railway from 1911 until June 1950 when he died at the age of eighty-six. He kept his promise that the railway would continue to run during his lifetime and a limited passenger service was maintained during the two years between the closure of the quarries and his death. Thereafter, his executors planned to sell the land and lift the railway and its fittings, understandably, because only Jones's inspiration had kept it going so long. Happily a group of enthusiasts intervened to make the Talyllyn the first railway successfully revitalised and preserved, and to inspire the preservers of other lines, narrow gauge at any rate.

The Talyllyn Railway Preservation Society was formed in October 1950 following a meeting in Birmingham to discuss the future of the line. As a result, a new, non-profit-making company was formed with directors drawn from the Society and from the former operating company. This is basically the arrangement which continues today. The evidence of the last summer of passenger operations suggested that the line could be viable, especially with volunteer support. The preservationists were very fortunate in being able to acquire, at short notice, the two former Corris Railway locomotives nos. 3 and 4, together with rolling stock which arrived at Towyn in March and July 1951. Since then the Railway has been an unimpeded success and has begun to build an extension ¾-mile long over the bed of a former mineral tramway to the foot of a rope-worked incline in the Nant Gwernol ravine, which should be open by 1975.

The present line, in use today, begins at Wharf station, Towyn, at right angles to the former Cambrian Railways station. Officially this station was for slate traffic only but in practice passengers used it, in addition to Pendre station a quarter of a mile up the road, and by the turn of the century timetables were pointing out that trains left Wharf station five minutes before arriving at Pendre, although no such implied invitation was extended to down passengers who were still encouraged to alight at Pendre. The Narrow Gauge Railway Museum at Wharf (originally King's) station is housed in a building which stands between the narrow gauge station and the standard gauge railway line. The journey uphill and inland begins with a 1 in 10 climb through a cutting lined with trees. Although the gradient eases quite soon it is an exacting start. The rest of the journey to Pendre station is over one of the easiest sections on the whole line. Pendre ('the end of the town') station

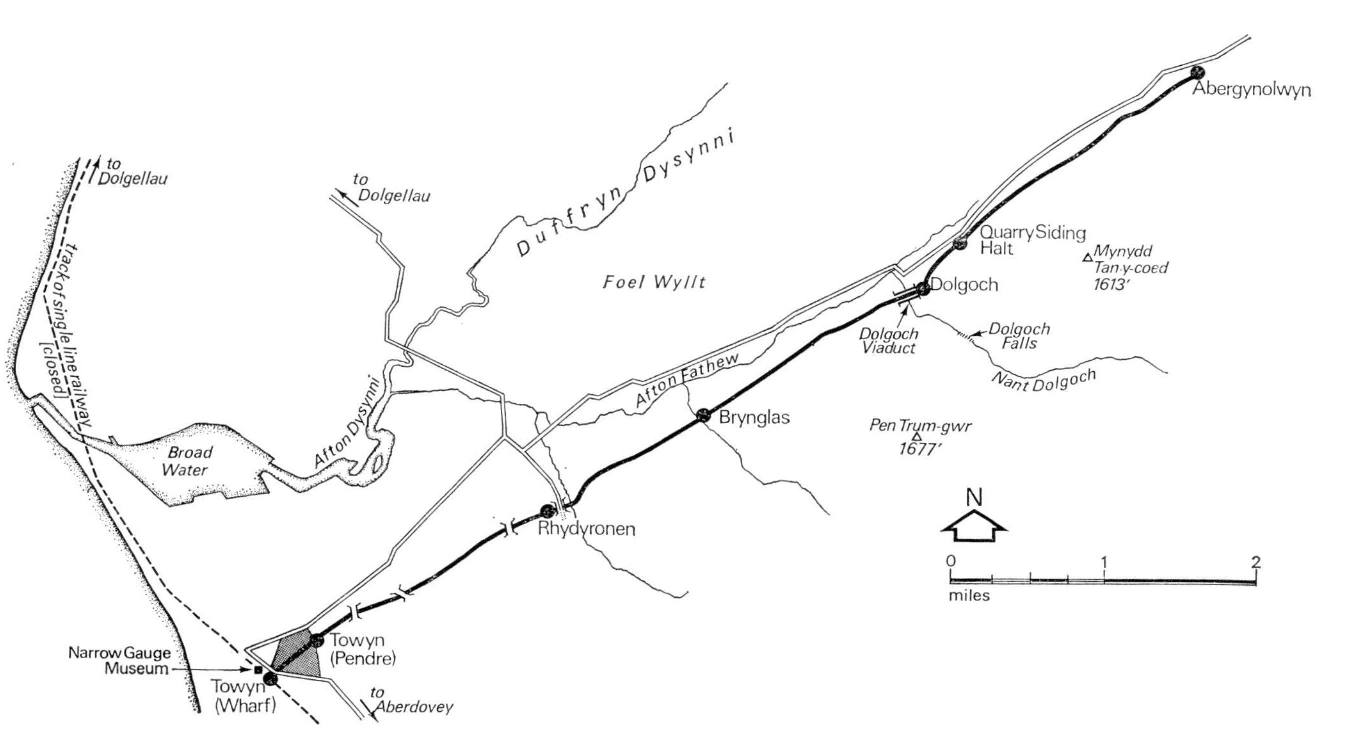

12 Talyllyn Railway

with its single platform, shelter and cottage opposite, is unchanged from McConnel's days.

As its name suggests, Pendre station is on the outskirts of Towyn and the railway now climbs from a short level towards Hen-dy halt, with a prospect of Cardigan Bay beginning to unfold behind. The next steep gradient is a stretch at 1 in 79 between Fach Goch halt and Cynfal, which is ninety-one feet above sea level, representing a climb of fifty-one feet in the 1 mile and 69 chains from Towyn, Wharf. The next stopping place is Rhydronen, one of the earliest stations on the line, opened in 1867, like Brynglas a mile further on past Tyn-y-llyn-Hen halt. Soon, some impression of height begins to develop as the line creeps up the side of the valley, over some of the notorious curves towards the woodlands that precede Dolgoch. After more curves and denser woods the line emerges on to the splendid Dolgoch viaduct, which is the Railway's major engineering feature, fifty-one feet above the Nant-Dolgoch gorge.

Once the line has emerged from the woods the nature of the country has changed from that of the easy coastal lowlands to the slopes of the crueller mountain interior of Wales, precipitous and heavily afforested. Before Abergynolwyn, the present terminus, is reached the valley has become almost oppressively narrow although the station itself, rebuilt three times, the present one dating from 1968, is in an open setting. Another Preservation Society addition, dating from 1964, is a siding at the east end built to hold the 'Tea Van'. The run-round loop too has been extended and beyond this lies the extension along the Nant Gwernol ravine already mentioned.

In addition to the five steam locomotives listed in Table 36, the

Table 36 Steam locomotives on the Talyllyn Railway (gauge 2ft 3in.)

Type	Number/name	Where built	Year	Origin
0-4-2ST*	1 'Talyllyn'	Fletcher, Jennings	1864	
0-4-0WT	2 'Dolgoch'	Fletcher, Jennings	1866	
0-4-2ST*	3 'Sir Haydn'	Hughes	1878	Corris Railway
0-4-2ST	4 'Edward Thomas'	Kerr Stuart	1921	Corris Railway
0-4-0WT†	6 'Douglas'	Andrew Barclay	1918	RAF Calshot

* Originally 0-4-0ST.
† Originally 2 ft gauge.

Talyllyn Railway has, since 1969, possessed an Andrew Barclay 0-4-0WT built in 1949 for the Bord na Mona (Turf Board) of the Republic of Ireland. It has been numbered 7 in the Talyllyn stockbook and is named 'Irish Pete'. The engine's original gauge was 3ft but it is in the process of being converted to a 2ft 3in. 0-4-2T for work on the line.

The five steam engines listed are all classics of their kind and all have a history worthy of the line on which they now work. No. 1 'Talyllyn', for example, built by Fletcher, Jennings at the Lowca Engine Works, Whitehaven, in 1864 has been at work on the line throughout its life, apart from nine years from 1950 between withdrawal and restoration by members of the TRPS to full working order. After some years of running, the locomotive's wheel arrangement was changed from 0-4-0 to 0-4-2 which is generally more suitable for work on some of the difficult curves on the line. 0-4-0WT no. 2, 'Dolgoch', is also a pure Talyllyn engine, built by Fletcher, Jennings. She was temporarily known as 'Pretoria', in patriotic deference to the British capture of that city during the Boer War. Although her dimensions are very similar to those of no. 1, she is probably slightly more powerful. 'Dolgoch' did not re-enter service until June 1963 after an absence of nearly ten years in the Midlands, while she was completely rebuilt at Oldbury.

Nos. 3 and 4, 'Sir Haydn' and 'Edward Thomas', are the two former Corris Railway locomotives which played such a vital part in facilitating the reopening of the Talyllyn. They were named by their present owners, no. 3 commemorating the patriarchal ownership and management of the line of Sir Henry Haydn Jones for nearly forty years. No. 4, most appropriately, commemorates Edward Thomas's managership of the Railway over the same period. 0-4-2ST no. 3, like no. 1 originally an 0-4-0, was built by the Hughes Locomotive & Tramway Engine Works of Loughborough in 1878. She has retained her Corris number (no. 3) under the GWR, which worked the line from 1930 until nationalisation, very briefly under BR—the Corris line being closed in 1948—and now on the Talyllyn. No. 4, 'Edward Thomas', is much newer, built by Kerr Stuart for the Corris Railway in 1921. Neither locomotive was in working order when they were moved from Machynlleth, where they had been in store since the Corris Railway closed, to Towyn in March 1951 but at £25 apiece they were an excellent buy, if only for scrap. Their repair and renewal went hand in hand with that of the track and both have now done good service over it.

0-4-0WT no. 6, 'Douglas', was built for the Admiralty in 1918 by Andrew Barclay. She was stationed first at Manston Aerodrome, Kent, and was transferred in 1921 to the Calshot RAF Railway which is on the 2ft gauge. The engine was presented to the TRPS in April 1953 by Abelson & Co. of Birmingham and has been successfully converted to the Talyllyn's gauge, proving a most reliable worker as well as being a striking machine to look at.

The Talyllyn has most of the characteristics which an ideal preserved line should have: a worthwhile history, a beautiful route, interesting and valuable locomotives and rolling stock, and a reputation among enthusiasts and casual tourists which ensures that it is never short of passengers during the operating season from Easter to October. Indeed, pressure of traffic is so great on the Talyllyn that the Company is actively planning the provision of more trains at more frequent intervals over the 45-minute $6\frac{3}{4}$-mile journey from Towyn to Abergynolwyn. Most enviably of all, from the point of view of others engaged in the operation of a light railway, the Talyllyn is a viable and profitable enterprise and an inspiration to preservationists everywhere, whether on narrow or standard gauge lines.

31 Corris Railway

In the summer of 1965 a small group of members of the Talyllyn Railway Preservation Society began to take an interest in the remains of the Corris Railway, over the hill in the Dulas Valley. The remaining units of the Corris rolling stock had been running for some years on, and in the ownership of, the Talyllyn Railway. It was the knowledge of those engines (0-4-0STs nos. 3 and 4, 'Sir Haydn' and 'Edward Thomas'), whose availability in 1951 saved the railway from extinction, that inspired the exploration of their former home and the idea of trying to do something to revive it.

The first step was the formation of a study group to discover the scope of the subject, to formulate precise objectives and to consider ways of achieving them. The Corris Society emerged from these deliberations with the declared aim of collecting all relics which could be acquired for display in a museum housed in a building on the line. The Society was also to have a programme of research into the history both of the railway and of the industrial and social history of the area it served. The museum too was envisaged as a comprehensive neighbourhood museum, covering such fields as the local slate industry and other activities which fed the line with traffic and, indeed, caused it to be built in the first place.

The Corris, Machynlleth and River Dovey Railway or Tramroad Company was incorporated in 1858 primarily to carry slate from the mines and quarries of the Corris area to the old port of Derwenlas

(Quay Ward). All traffic over the eleven-mile line was horse-drawn until 1879, when three steam locomotives were introduced. They were built at the Falcon Works of the Hughes Engine Co. of Loughborough. Before that, in 1864, the name of the 2ft 3in. gauge line was changed to the Corris Railway and the section of line from Machynlleth to Derwenlas abandoned. Slate was transhipped to the standard gauge line at Machynlleth whence trains could run to Aberdovey for loading on to far larger ships than could come up the estuary to Quay Ward. Some of the branches of the railway, however, continued to be worked by horse traction until they ceased operation. This was mainly because of the light wooden bridges by which they crossed the River Dulas. Only the branch to the largest quarry, at Upper Corris, leaving the main line at Maespoeth Junction, had anything more substantial and on this the gradient was too much for steam.

In 1878 some tram-like carriages were purchased, initially to be hauled by horses. Five years later, in spite of opposition from the quarry owners who thought that it would interfere with their traffic, a regular steam-hauled passenger service was introduced, with first class, second class and parliamentary fares. For some years the railway thrived on both passenger and freight traffic but inevitably road transport became competitive after World War I. The line became part of the GWR in 1930. From 1878 it had been part of the Imperial Tramways Co. of Bristol, which was associated with the Bristol Tramways & Carriage Co. Just before the former company was wound up in 1930, the Corris Railway was transferred to the BT&C Co., in which the GWR had a stake. The Great Western purchased it and entered into possession on 4 August 1930. The brass plate outside the Imperial Tramways Company's office in Clare Street, Bristol, also carried the words 'Corris Railway Company, Registered Office'.

To the usual post-war difficulties were added flood damage, which in 1948 caused erosion of the south approach embankment of the Dovey bridge. Repairs were considered to be uneconomic and it was decided to close the line permanently. The last train ran on 20 August 1948 and thereafter a lorry service was provided for such goods traffic as remained. At the time of the closure the line was worked by two locomotives. One of them, no. 4, was already laid up on a siding behind Machynlleth station with a condemned firebox, while no. 3 did such work as there was to do. She was shedded at Maespoeth and ran down to Machynlleth daily to haul the up morning goods, although after the threat to the Dovey bridge she, too, was kept at Machynlleth and worked the last train from there. Both remained under nothing more than sheets at Machynlleth station until acquired for the Talyllyn Railway in 1951. Within a few months of closure the Dovey bridge and the track were dismantled and the various buildings associated with the line were allowed to fall into disrepair. However, Machynlleth Low Level station has been in use as a store and the Forestry Commission have used the former locomotive shed as a workshop. The passenger carriages had been scrapped with the exception of two, which found their way to Gobowen as summer houses. One of them has been purchased by the Talyllyn and fully rebuilt. The other has more recently been donated to the Corris Society whose members will restore it in due course as a workable museum exhibit.

Since its foundation, the Society had been looking for a suitable building to use as its museum. Machynlleth station was considered but the price required proved unrealistic. Meanwhile the local council demolished Corris station, leaving only the former coach house and stable. Parts of the site were surrendered for car parking and part of the track bed dug up to accommodate a new sewer but the Society has helped to convert the coach house and stable for its museum, ready for opening on a limited scale in 1970. Although Corris station has been lost, the Society is actively engaged in preserving the two small stations at Llwyngwern and Escairgeiliog which are currently in use as bus shelters and will continue in this role as far as is possible.

Across the yard from the museum at Corris is the start of the line. Here, at the original station approach, where the tracks fanned out into the loop and shed roads, the new railway is being constructed on top of the old. The original rails, rolled at Dowlais steelworks in 1858, have been used for the first few yards of line but new ones have been, and will be, required for the remaining half mile down to Maespoeth. Beyond that point, the railway runs between the road and the River Dulas, through woods and a gorge to Escairgeiliog and Llwyngwern and the re-laying of this section will depend entirely on costs and the availability of land. After twenty-three years of decay and change, re-laying the track is not a simple operation. The new sewer at Corris, for example, has involved negotiating manhole covers and other points of access, and the road surface of a level crossing just over one hundred yards from the start had been raised by two feet. This latter hazard has demanded a formidable amount of infilling and the original 1 in 100 gradient has been considerably steepened for some hundreds of yards beyond the crossing.

The Society intends to uphold the original Corris Railway's reputation for the quality of its track and also to ensure that visitors' rides in unsprung vintage vehicles are not too uncomfortable.

32 Vale of Rheidol Railway

The eleven and three-quarter mile, 1ft 11½in. gauge railway up the Vale of Rheidol from Aberystwyth to Devil's Bridge in Cardiganshire represents British Railways' last working interest in steam traction and, indeed, the narrow gauge.

The first plans for a line along the Rheidol Valley were authorised by the Manchester & Milford [Haven] Railway Act of 1861. This was for a branch from the main line at Devil's Bridge to Aberystwyth but the promoting company never itself got anywhere near either Milford Haven or Manchester, declined into a local Welsh line, and the powers obtained for the construction of branches, the Rheidol Valley among them, were never taken up. None of the promoters either in the eighteen-sixties or later on thought that traffic from the lead mines in the valley would be heavy enough to sustain the railway by itself. When, therefore, the idea of building the line revived in 1895 it was with passenger and tourist traffic to the beauty spot of Devil's Bridge in mind. As coastal resorts burgeoned in response to the growing popular habit of seaside holidays, the narrow gauge railways of the Welsh coast and highlands took on a commercial importance beyond their prosaic mineral origins. By 1896 the Snowdon Mountain Railway was open and even a small resort such as Fairbourne had a tramway along the beach. The outlook for Aberystwyth which, apart from plans for a cliff lift, had nothing of this sort to offer, looked bleak.

It was thus with tourists as well as lead in mind that a Bill for a railway up the valley was deposited in 1896. The Vale of Rheidol Light Railway Company was incorporated on 6 August 1897, with an authorised capital of £39,000 in 3,900 shares of £10 each. The Act provided for two railways: from Aberystwyth to what was to become Devil's Bridge station and from near the Aberystwyth terminus to the town harbour. With the consent of the Board of Trade the gauge of the line could be increased to standard.

Building began in the spring on 1901 and the line was ready for freight traffic sixteen months later. Passenger services began in December 1902 and were very much used by the local people from the beginning, in spite of the fact that some of the ticket holders on the inaugural train were so unnerved by the precipitousness of parts of the line on the outward journey from Aberystwyth, that nothing would induce them to return other than on foot. The lead mines at Lefel Fawr, Erwtomau, Dyffryn Castell, Ystumteun and Cwmystwyth, together with the timber industry in the area, in general provided a hard core of regular passengers as well as freight traffic and at one time the Railway was used by as many as three hundred season ticket holders. Stations, apart from the termini at Devil's Bridge and Aberystwyth, were at Llanbadarn, Capel Bangor, Nantyronen and Aberffrwd. The Company maintained a sensibly flexible attitude towards the opening of additional halts and within three years of opening, Rheidol Falls, Glanrafon and Rhiwfron were thus served. From 1910 onwards an army summer camp and a territorial army camp at Lovesgrove led to an enormous increase in the number of passengers carried and to the opening of a halt at Lovesgrove for military use.

Traffic in these summer months in the three or four years before World War I was so heavy that the management had to borrow the Festiniog Railway's locomotive 'Palmerston' for a few months in 1912. This development, together with the independent considerations of novelty and possibly economy as well, caused the management to consider, not for the first time, converting the line's source of power to electricity. In the mountainous parts of Wales where electricity was, potentially at any rate, to be readily available such a possibility had been considered from very early on. The promoters of the Snowdon Mountain Railway had been severely tempted in this direction and were put off only by the expense of installing the necessary equipment and the caution that a rack railway would be novelty enough by itself. The Vale of Rheidol Railway was nearly lost to steam before it even opened, for in 1899 the Company had applied for and been granted powers to work the line by electricity.

Unlike many late branch lines, run at a loss by one of the large companies as a public service until superseded by more versatile and economical buses, the Vale of Rheidol line in these years was not only viable but a commercially attractive enterprise from the point of view of outside investors. Thus the Cambrian Railways assumed control on 1 August 1913; but the branch had only twelve months of prosperity left. The war brought great confusion to freight services and virtually stopped passenger traffic while line, locomotives and rolling stock deteriorated. After the war, when passenger services revived a little, the management again had to borrow an engine but this time because of the derelict condition of its own, rather than to meet exceptional traffic requirements. Soon after the Grouping, when the GWR took over, the nature of the line changed with the withdrawal of freight services which had been run down following the closure of the lead mines soon after the war. In 1924, the branch to Aberystwyth Harbour was closed.

When the GWR took over the line at the beginning of 1922, considerable renovation of the track, buildings and equipment was carried out. Buses having taken away most of the local, non-tourist passengers, the service was withdrawn in winter from 1 January 1931, but such freight traffic as there was continued by rail until 26 September 1937, when collection and delivery was made by GWR lorries based on Aberystwyth. As previously mentioned, the locomotive stock was in need of immediate attention. The Vale of Rheidol Railway had begun operations in 1902 with three locomotives, two of them new. These were Davies & Metcalfe 2-6-2Ts, no. 1, 'Edward VII', and no. 2, 'Prince of Wales'. No. 1 was thoroughly overhauled and partly rejuvenated in 1923 but was withdrawn in 1932 and scrapped three years later. The third engine at work when the Railway opened was a Bagnall 2-4-0T of 1896 named 'Rheidol'. She had been bought second hand by the contractors, Pethick Brothers, from the Hafan & Talybont Tramway for use during the construction of the line and continued in service after it was finished and open. She was the only engine permitted to work on the branch to Aberystwyth Harbour but was scrapped in 1923, before it was closed. The steam locomotives on the line at present consist of one of the 1902 originals and two others built by the GWR in 1923 (see Table 37). Although never required to work mineral trains on the line, the Swindon-built 2-6-2Ts of 1923 were made slightly more powerful than their predecessors and continue to be ideally suited for their function which is now unique within the nationalised railway system. 'Prince of Wales' was drastically overhauled in 1924 and rebuilt to the same standard as its new stable-mates.

Table 37 Steam locomotives on the Vale of Rheidol Railway (gauge 1ft 11½in.)

Type	Number/name	Where built	Year
2-6-2T	7 'Owain Glyndwr'	Swindon	1923
2-6-2T	8 'Llywelyn'	Swindon	1923
2-6-2T	9 'Prince of Wales'	Davies & Metcalfe	1902

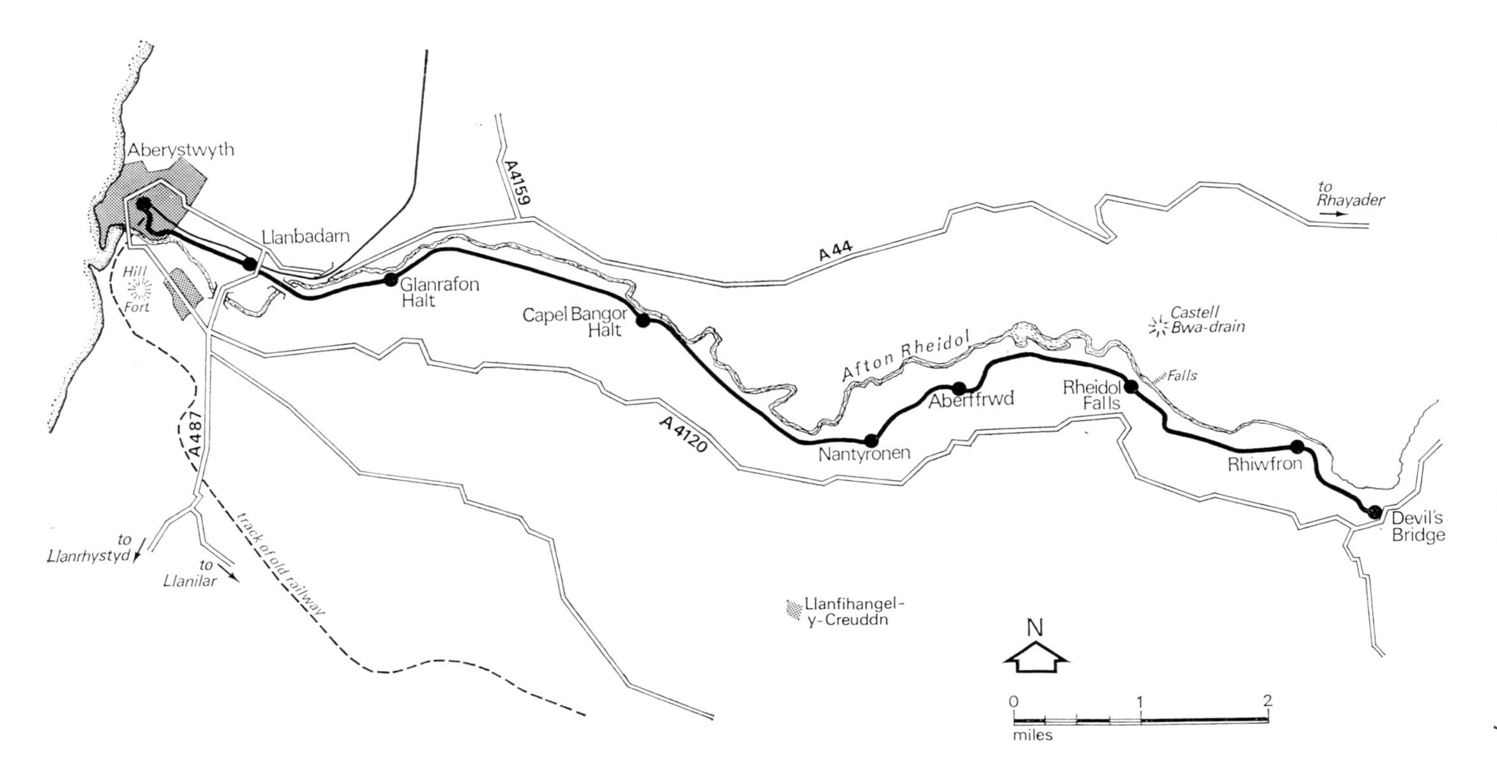

13 Vale of Rheidol Railway

As from 31 August 1939 the line was closed altogether during World War II and after re-opening, for passengers only, in the summer months from July 1945, viability declined drastically afterwards. While the Railway was sinking towards permanent closure, however, it was transferred from the Western to the London Midland Region of BR and in the opinion of the chairman and general manager of the Region, (Sir) Henry Johnson (chairman, BRB 1968–71), was not beyond hope. He initiated a policy of energetic publicity and enlisted the help of organisations such as the Welsh Tourist Board, with the result that passenger journeys rose from their post-war nadir of 15,000, to 84,064 in 1967 and 117,772 in 1970, which is rapidly approaching the line's record of 126,358 in 1910.

The Vale of Rheidol Railway has all the natural advantages of the other 'little railways of Wales'. Indeed, the line was aimed by its promoters specifically at a well-known beauty spot, Devil's Bridge, where Wordsworth wrote of Mynach Falls in 1824:

> There I seem to stand,
> As in life's morn; permitted to behold,
> From the dread chasm, woods climbing above woods,
> In pomp that fades not; everlasting snows;
> And skies that ne'er relinquish their repose;
> Such power possess the family of floods
> Over the minds of Poets, young or old!

The journey from Aberystwyth to Devil's Bridge may be divided up in several ways. From Aberffrwdd, for example, the line climbs nearly five hundred feet in just under four miles at an unrelenting 1 in 50. The real half-way mark, however, is at a point just west of Capel Bangor, where the Rheidol Valley narrows dramatically and the line, robbed of any natural bed, begins to climb through a succession of alternating levels and stiff gradients, perched on a ledge clinging to the side of the gorge.

By Capel Bangor, the line has climbed about eighty feet in 4½ miles. The station, corrugated iron buildings and no platform, as throughout the line, lies immediately south of the Afon Rheidol and once had a carriage shed. After an easy half mile, the climb to Nantyronen begins with two very steep gradients, one of them the steepest on the line at 1 in 48, followed by an almost equally exacting climb to Aberffrwd and the famous left-hand curve. The latter part of the line runs through heavily wooded country.

Near Aberffrwd also is the power station of the Central Electricity Generating Board's Rheidol hydroelectric scheme. Each of the three stages of the scheme consists of a reservoir, an aqueduct and a generating station. The whole complex has added considerably to the splendours of the area, complementing the natural magnificence of the Plynlimon plateau, which surrounds the head of the Rheidol valley.

33 Welshpool & Llanfair Railway

Not all narrow gauge lines originated as mineral railways in mountainous areas. In 1896, the year of the emancipation of the motor-car from the 'man in front' law, the Light Railways Act was passed with the intention of improving general passenger and freight movement in rural areas. There had been earlier Acts, in 1864 and 1868, and a Tramways Act in 1870 with similar aims but as these carried no powers of compulsory purchase they were comparatively ineffective. The 1896 Act was more thorough. It emerged from the deliberations of a conference in 1894–5 under the chairmanship of James Bryce, the historian, who was then President of the Board of Trade. Many of the lines built after it became law were no more than tramways but among the true railways were the Rother Valley and Welshpool & Llanfair lines.

Railways were no novelty in the Welshpool area of Montgomeryshire when work on the line began in May 1901. An Act authorising the Newtown branch of what became the Shropshire Union Canal had been passed in 1794, with the usual provisions for small railways to serve it. The canal opened to the outskirts of Welshpool in 1797 and the first of the small railways followed in 1818. This was a horse-worked tramway, known as the Welshpool Rail Road, built by the second Earl of Powis to serve his Stondart (stone) quarry. The quarry remained in existence until 1939, though the Rail Road was closed in 1854 and road surfaces were built over it later. Some of the rails excavated during works in 1878 and 1937 were sent to the Science Museum in London. Needless to say, the area was not unaffected by the railway 'mania' thirty years after Lord Powis's iron road but the more grandiose schemes for penetrating the centre of Wales came to nothing and only Welshpool benefited from the Oswestry & Newtown Railway, opened in the town in 1860. Further plans for lines west from Welshpool followed close behind.

The first of them was proposed in July 1862 by Captain R. D. Pryce, later chairman of the Cambrian Railways Company, to link Llanfair Caereinion with the new main line at Welshpool. Much of its course, particularly at the eastern end, lay through the land of the third Earl of Powis who objected to the scheme in general and the use of the Black Pool Dingle, so it was abandoned in favour of another route further to the south following the course of the Luggy brook. An appeal to the local people to invest in their own future met with little response and this scheme failed too. The next plan was proposed by Abraham Howell of Welshpool, with the support of David Davies, a railway builder who had worked with Thomas Savin on much of the Cambrian Railways system, and, in the hope of financial support from the Potteries, with support from the Shrewsbury & North Wales Railway (known as 'The Potts'). It was to be a 2ft 3in. line over the Luggy brook route from Welshpool to Llanfair, with an additional line north-west from there to the GWR at Bala. A Bill incorporating these plans was actually placed before parliament but in the face of continuing opposition from Lord Powis and the waning interest of the promoters it got nowhere and was allowed to lapse. Two further schemes, one of them for a 3ft line, were introduced in parliament in the 1870s and 1880s but were abandoned.

Although renewed efforts to make progress might have been expected when the third Earl of Powis died in 1891, nothing happened immediately. The next initiative, indeed, followed the first sessions of the President of the Board of Trade's conference on light railways and tramways, which had been attended by various officials and dignitaries from Montgomeryshire. Local meetings welcomed the conference and its findings and exhorted the government to act upon them. Lines constructed under a Light Railway Order could be of any gauge, follow the natural contour and operate with simplified signalling and road crossings, though at restricted speeds. Equally important for Welshpool and Llanfair were the Act's financial provisions. The Light Railway Commissioners, the Earl of Jersey, Col. Boughey and Mr G. A. R. Fitzgerald, sat at Llanfair Caereinion on 3 and 4 August 1897. They had to decide whether the needs of the area would be served better by a line through Castle Caereinion to the Cambrian Railways' line at Welshpool or by one further north through Meifod to Arddleen. A month later they reported in favour of the Castle Caereinion–Welshpool line. It was two years before the Order was actually made, when the Board of Trade imposed the very common requirement for light railways, that it should be operated by an existing company. The Cambrian Railways Co. was the natural candidate for this job and they accordingly leased the line for ninety-nine years from March 1900, in return for 60 per cent of the gross receipts. The operating company was to indemnify the light railway against accident losses and to maintain and renew rolling stock provided by it. The Treasury grant of £17,500 amounted to one-third of the estimated capital cost; the local inhabitants subscribed £15,065 in ordinary shares; and a few local councils advanced fifty-year loans. In 1901 a Light Railway (Amendment) Order increased the amount that local authorities could subscribe and authorised the Cambrian Railways Co. to do so as well. The enterprise had the active support of the fourth Lord Powis, who was on the board from the start and he, together with other local dignitaries, gave much of the land required.

The 2ft 6in. gauge used for the railway was unusual in this country. It was popular with military-railway builders at the end of the nineteenth century—the Admiralty's Chattendon & Upnor Railway at Chatham, from which the Welshpool & Llanfair Preservation Co. got much of its stock, was built on it—and much used in the colonies. Others in this country were the Leek & Manifold Valley Light Railway and the St Austell & Pentewan Railway but only the Bowater system at Sittingbourne, now operated by the Locomotive Club of Great Britain, survives. Among the advantages of the gauge was the fact that standard gauge goods wagons could be carried on 2ft 6in. transporter wagons, thus avoiding transhipment at interchange stations, but although the light railway terminus at Welshpool was constructed with this in mind, the facility was not used.

The Board of Trade allowed three years for building the line. This was carried out by Messrs Strachan of Cardiff under the supervision of successive Cambrian Railways' resident engineers, to normal light specifications. Obstruction by the owners of small pieces of land not donated at the outset, together with unforeseen engineering difficulties, inflated the cost to double the estimates. By February 1903 the line was ready for inspection by Major Druitt of the Board of Trade and although he ordered a number of minor modifications the Board's certificate was issued on 4 March. Goods traffic started five days later. The inaugural passenger train on 4 April was accompanied by the usual ceremonial and was hauled by one of the railway's present engines, 'The Countess', which had arrived from the Beyer Peacock foundry at Gorton in September 1902.

The line from Welshpool to Llanfair involves some of the most severe gradients on the former Cambrian and Great Western systems. Within 9 miles and 4 chains it climbs from 230ft to 600ft at the summit of the Golfa incline, descends to 300ft at the River Banwy and climbs back to 380ft at Llanfair. Welshpool itself lies in typical Severn-side 'marcher'

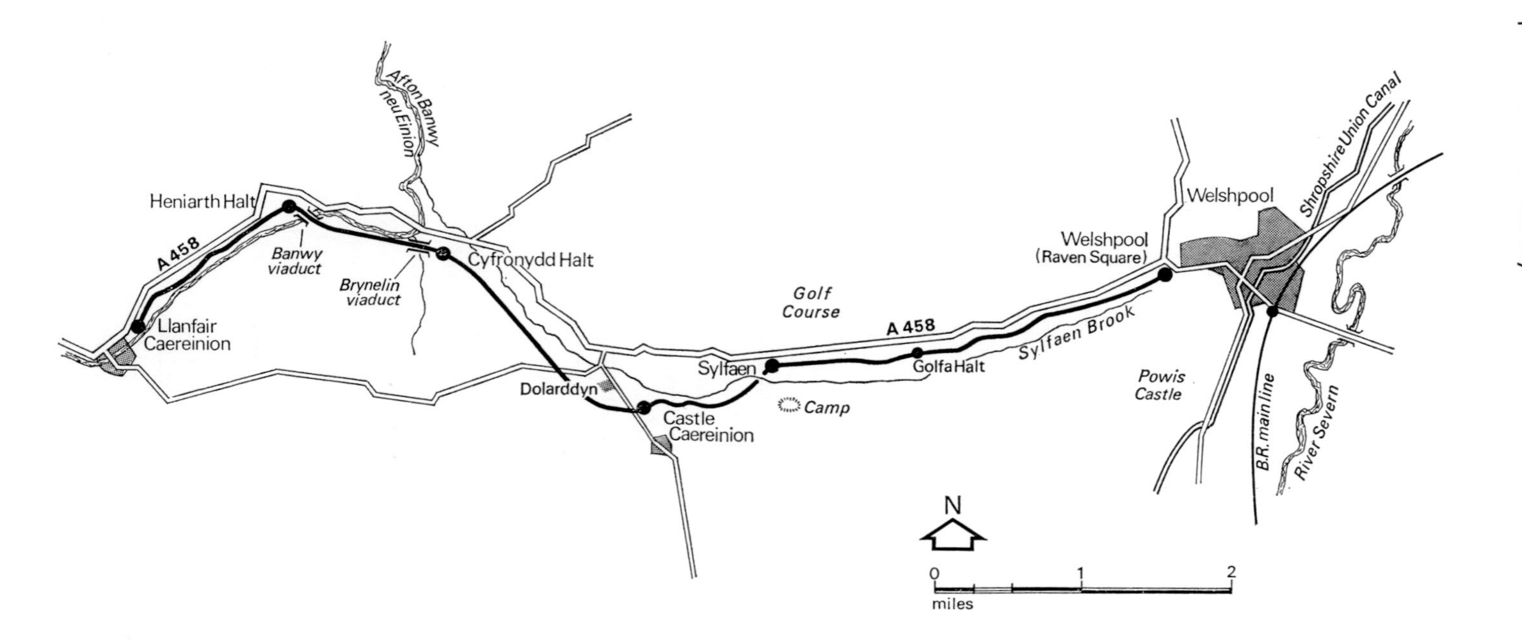

14 Welshpool & Llanfair Railway

country, with the Welsh hills rising in the west. Passengers at the station there were always less well-provided for than goods and while the latter enjoyed a transhipment shed, passengers had neither platform nor the corrugated-iron station buildings provided further up the line. A climb of 1 in 33 begins immediately in order to carry the line over the Montgomeryshire Canal. By the time the railway has covered the course of the Rail Road through Seven Stars, past the Stondart quarry to the preservation company's terminus at Raven Square, the line has climbed 100ft in just over a mile. The long haul up the north slope of the Golfa pass then begins and is sometimes as steep as 1 in 29. By the time the peak is reached, which can be clearly felt in the train, there is clear sky behind the train. On the decline to Sylfaen enough momentum is gathered to carry the train up the steep rise which follows before the fall to Castle Caereinion. The fall continues to Dolarddyn where the line turns north-west giving open views towards the mountains of North Wales. The Brynelin viaduct crosses the River Cwmbaw beyond Cyfronydd and Banwy viaduct is crossed a little further on. From Heniarth the line is almost level all the way to Llanfair.

From the start of operations there was a natural bias in goods traffic from the Welshpool end, though the Stondart quarry provided some until it closed just before World War II. Most of the trains were in fact mixed goods-and-passenger trains but neither the Cambrian Railways nor the GWR ever ran any on Sundays. Like so many branch lines, the Welshpool & Llanfair Railway never quite broke even and never paid a dividend. Competing road carriers charged less for freight and after the GWR had absorbed the Cambrian Co. in the wake of the 1922 Grouping the new operators, in accordance with their policy towards branch lines, introduced a bus service. Soon afterwards, moves towards closing down passenger services began and though there was an influential outcry, supported by the Rt Hon. Clement Davies, QC, MP, for Montgomeryshire and later leader of the Liberal Party, they succeeded, and the passenger service was withdrawn in February 1931. The railway still had an important role to play in the carriage of goods and the scheduled service of one train a day in each direction was supplemented by others as required. Nevertheless, a permanent staff of nine—driver, fireman, guard, three permanent-way staff, porter-in-charge at Llanfair and two transhipment porters at Welshpool—was needed and quite apart from considerations of economy such personnel were not easy to find by the 1950s. Neither, in the immediate post-war period, was coal and for these reasons the line was often closed for days on end at that time. The line was thus a natural candidate for closure long before Lord Beeching's rationalisation. The possibility had been actively considered from very soon after the war and, in spite of intelligent and persistent opposition, led to the withdrawal of freight services in October 1956.

Inspired by the success of the Talyllyn and Festiniog railway preservation schemes, a Welshpool and Llanfair Preservation Society was formed within a month of the line's closure. National publicity in advance of the end of services had stirred interest in the future of the line far beyond the locality. Negotiations with British Railways were soon in progress but it was not until the summer of 1959 that work on the restoration of the line began. As the Preservation Society advanced towards possession of the line, it grew into a guarantee company—the Welshpool & Llanfair Light Railway Preservation Co., Ltd—in January 1960 and possession was effected by the British Transport Commission (Welshpool & Llanfair Light Railway Leasing and Transfer) Order, dated 3 October 1962. This authorised the lease or transfer of the line from Llanfair Caereinion to Welshpool, Raven Square. The section of line from Raven Square to Welshpool standard gauge station, over the right of way established by Lord Powis's Rail Road of 1818, was surrendered to the Borough Council's plans for the redevelopment of the ancient but decrepit part of the town known as Seven Stars, and the use of it ended in August 1963. The company's lease on the line runs for twenty-one years from 25 December 1962, at an annual rent of £100, rising to £250 after ten years.

The line from Llanfair to Castle Caereinion was reopened by the Earl of Powis on 6 April 1963. In its first season, the Preservation Company's services carried over 10,000 passengers. An extension of a little over a mile to Sylfaen halt in June 1964 brought the length of operational line to 5 miles 31 chains. Three miles remain to be opened to Raven Square where Royal Engineers reservists have constructed a buffer and run-around loop now threatened by road improvements. This section, which includes the Golfa incline, cannot be operated until the trains have been fitted with continuous braking and until further restoration has been carried out on the track and a more suitable terminal site acquired.

The Preservation Company has had to overcome one major set-back. On 11 and 12 December 1964 there were rainstorms which led to flooding along the Banwy. One of the main piers of the railway viaduct was tilted by the flood waters and a dangerous dip thus developed in the track. The necessary repairs were a depressing burden on the Company which could not be readily met in financial terms, quite apart from equipment. However, a repair fund launched by the then chairman of the Company, the late Sir Thomas Salt, and the assistance of the Railway Unit of the Royal Engineers from Longmoor, met both aspects of the challenge and in spite of hostile weather conditions during repair work the viaduct was reopened on 14 August 1965. Earlier in the season a limited service had been run between Llanfair and Heniarth.

The railway is worked by six steam locomotives, supported by four diesels. The steam engines are listed in Table 38.

Table 38 Steam locomotives on the Welshpool & Llanfair Railway (gauge 2ft 6in.)

Type	Number/name	Where built	Year
0-6-0T	1 'The Earl'	Beyer Peacock	1902
0-6-0T	2 'The Countess'	Beyer Peacock	1902
0-4-4-0T	6 'Monarch'	Bagnall	1953
0-4-0WT	8 'Dougal'	Barclay	1946
0-8-0T	10 'Sir Drefaldwyn'	SFB France	1944
0-6-2T	12 'Joan'	Kerr Stuart	1927

At the time the line was completed in 1903, the company could not afford proper signalling. Other economies included making do with two instead of three locomotives. Nevertheless, these two, named 'The Earl' and 'The Countess' in honour of Lord and Lady Powis, have been on the line throughout their working lives. They were specially designed by S. E. Garratt and built at the Beyer Peacock foundry in Gorton at a price of £1600 each. At the time, the firm had built comparatively few narrow gauge engines for railways in Britain, apart from those on the Glyn Valley Tramway and the Isle of Man Railway. However, the Welshpool & Llanfair locomotives were built on a model which later became almost standard, with outside frames, cylinders and valve chests. After 1923, their numbers were changed from 1 and 2, to 822 and 823 and their Cambrian Railways livery of black with red and yellow lining was replaced by Swindon green. They were completely overhauled at Swindon in 1929 and 1930 when they acquired their present copper-capped chimneys in place of the plain stove pipes with which they were built. During World War II, both reverted to black and 'The Earl' remained so afterwards. In 1956 the engines were removed to the BR works at Oswestry with the idea that one of them should eventually be preserved in the Narrow Gauge Museum at Towyn. In the event, they were condemned and while neither was broken up they were left in a neglected condition until they were acquired for the Preservation Society. Both were back at Welshpool by October 1962 fully overhauled, and have since been restored, 'The Earl' to Swindon green and 'The Countess' to Cambrian black.

The other locomotives on the line today have all been acquired since the Preservation Company began operations. No. 6, 'Monarch', was built by Bagnall at Stafford in 1953 and is a Meyer articulated locomotive, specially designed for work on tight curves, in this case the Bowater railway at Sittingbourne. No. 8, 'Dougal', was built by Barclay at Kilmarnock in 1946 for the Provan gasworks, Glasgow. No. 5, 'Nutty', arrived in May 1966 on loan from the Narrow Gauge Museum at Towyn. This was originally a 2ft 11in. gauge locomotive built by Sentinel at Shrewsbury for the London Brick Co. As the permanent couplings did not match those otherwise in use on the Welshpool & Llanfair line and as she lacked braking power, she was used mainly on light engineering trains such as the weed-killing train with which she is seen in Plate 151. She was returned to Towyn in the autumn of 1971.

No. 12, 'Joan', is a Kerr Stuart 0-6-2T built in 1927 for the Antigua Sugar & Estates Development Board Railway in the West Indies. She spent her entire working life there. She is the first example of a British colonial locomotive class to be re-imported by a Preservation Society. 'Joan' arrived at Liverpool in November 1971 and was safely delivered to Llanfair Caereinion at the end of the month.

The Welshpool & Llanfair Railway is linked with other 2ft 6in. gauge railways in Melbourne, Australia, and in Austria. One of the locomotives of the Zillertalbahn in Austria has been named 'Castle Caereinion'. The Welshpool & Llanfair Railway acquired four coaches of 1900–1 from it and also a locomotive built in France in 1944 for German military use and now re-named 'Sir Drefaldwyn'.

34 Sittingbourne & Kemsley Railway

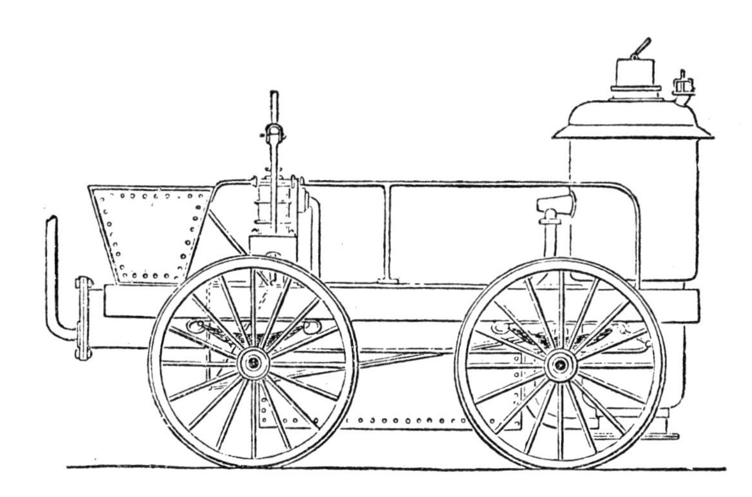

'Novelty'

The Sittingbourne & Kemsley Railway is a two-mile stretch of the 2ft 6in. gauge Bowater Light Railway from Sittingbourne (Wall) to Kemsley Down station, leased from Bowaters (UK) Paper Co. Ltd by the Locomotive Club of Great Britain in 1969.

Around the turn of the century Milton creek, running south from the Swale to Sittingbourne in Kent, began to silt up. Sittingbourne had previously enjoyed direct, navigable access to Milton creek and through it the Edward Lloyd paper mill depended for the supply and delivery of its materials and products. To ensure continued access to the Swale for the expanding output of their paper mill at Sittingbourne the Company built a 2ft 6in. gauge railway to Grovehurst Dock at Kemsley. This was in operation by 1908 but the dock soon became too small for Lloyd's requirements and by 1914 another bigger one was under construction at Ridham, further up the Swale near Kingsferry. The railway followed, although it was to be in Admiralty service for two years before becoming Lloyd's principal outlet in 1919. Then, as now, the line was worked by Kerr Stuart 0-4-2Ts, added to over the years as loadings have increased, by heavier and more versatile engines like the Barclay 0-4-4-0 'Monarch' of 1953, sold by Bowaters to the Welshpool & Llanfair Light Railway in 1966.

By 1924, Lloyd's had opened another mill at Kemsley. In 1948, the Company became part of the Bowater organisation. This Company, founded in 1881, now employs over 30,000 people and the mills at

Sittingbourne and Kemsley remain among their principal plants. Under the management of Bowaters a first class maintenance depot and workshops were built at Kemsley in 1954 to service the unique 2ft 6in. gauge line and its stock, which were in service for twenty-four hours a day. Until 1968, the railway also provided a passenger service for staff.

When Bowaters decided to replace the railway with even more flexible methods of transport between Sittingbourne and Kemsley and Ridham Dock, there was little question of lifting the line which had long been a source of much interest to railway enthusiasts from outside as well as within the organisation. The Company therefore approached the Association of Railway Preservation Societies for guidance about the line's future and in particular for advice as to whom to approach as a possible operator of the railway as a preservation line.

The Locomotive Club of Great Britain, which was consulted as a result of these negotiations, was founded in 1949 with the intention of encouraging interest in railway history and operations and includes among its members a good proportion of professional railwaymen. The Sittingbourne & Kemsley Railway was handed over to the LCGB on 4 October 1969, having been in the service of the paper mills until the very last minute. From the following spring, the line has been in operation with a regular service of up to ten trains a day in each direction, Sittingbourne to Kemsley, at weekends and Bank Holidays between April and September.

Table 39 Steam locomotives* on the Sittingbourne & Kemsley Railway

Type	Name	Where built	Year
0-4-2ST	'Premier'	Kerr Stuart	1904
0-4-2ST	'Leader'	Kerr Stuart	1906
0-4-2ST	'Melior'	Kerr Stuart	1924
0-6-2T (Fireless)	'Unique'	Bagnall	1924
0-6-0T	'Alpha'	Bagnall	1932
0-6-0T	'Triumph'	Bagnall	1934
0-6-0T	'Superb'	Bagnall	1940

* All acquired from Bowaters (UK) Paper Co. Ltd

35 Romney, Hythe & Dymchurch Railway

'Black Prince' (now 'Dr Syn') with an original Vanderbilt tender

The Romney, Hythe & Dymchurch Railway was planned and built both as a 'toy' and to fill a definite transport need. However, its originators, the racing enthusiasts Captain J. E. P. (Jack) Howey and Count Louis Zborowski, had most of the mechanical details settled in outline before the site and route were chosen. Count Zborowski was killed in a racing accident in 1924 before work had begun but Captain Howey carried on, built the line and remained in control until his death in 1963. The New Romney–Hythe route was chosen because the area was in need of additional transport facilities and because that part of the Kent coast was developing rapidly as a holiday area in the 1920s and the line would thus be well-placed as a tourist attraction. The ground was comparatively easy for railway building and the line was in good narrow gauge company, with the independent Rye & Camber Railway, opened in 1895, a few miles along the coast. The Southern Railway welcomed the New Romney–Hythe line, which linked its termini in these places, $8\frac{1}{4}$ miles apart.

Building began in 1926, and the New Romney–Hythe section was opened in July the following year. The railway's 15in. gauge had been much favoured by light railway theorists such as Sir Arthur Heywood but was very little used on public railways until the conversion of the Ravenglass & Eskdale and Fairbourne Railways during World War I. The first section of the Romney, Hythe & Dymchurch Railway was double track but the $5\frac{1}{2}$-mile extension west to Dungeness, built in

1928–9, is single track only. A further extension north from Hythe to the SR's Ashford–Folkestone line at Sandling junction was surveyed but abandoned on grounds of difficulty and expense. This part of the line would have been severely graded and the only legacy of the project is the two 4-8-2 locomotives of 1927, 'Hercules' and 'Samson', which had been ordered to work it.

During the war the Railway was literally in the front line and was taken over by the army in June 1940. It was extensively used in troop and armament movements and played a prominent part in exercises such as Operation PLUTO—the laying of a pipeline from Littlestone-on-Sea to the coast of France. The depredations of war were made good before the line returned to civilian use in March 1946 but over the years since then the circumstances and functions of the line have changed very substantially. The immediate environs of the railway are now rather populous and other forms of transport for both passengers and freight are readily available. As a result the Railway has long ceased to carry goods, and passenger services are run only between Easter and the end of September. Since Captain Howey's death, control of the Railway, which has always been operated by a public company, has changed hands twice but in spite of crises in the summer of 1971 the line seems to have an assured future.

The cost of working a train on the line has reached an average of 70p per mile. The number of passengers carried during each season has been consistently over 300,000 in recent years but in order to stabilise costs the increased numbers are carried in heavier trains, now often up to the fifteen- or sixteen-coach maximum, rather than in extra ones. As a result, the Railway continues to operate at a small profit. From the point of view of maintenance costs, the line is an economical one. Although, at nearly fourteen miles, it is one of the longest light railways in Britain, there are neither major engineering features nor severe gradients on the line and much of the permament way, especially on the New Romney–Dungeness section, is laid directly on the shingle.

Including the terminals and two halts the line is served by nine stops. As soon as the train has begun to move one of the line's distinctive features becomes apparent from the sound and feel of the ride, namely that the rails are laid with the joins staggered, rather than opposite one another, as is the usual practice in this country. The maximum speed permitted is 30mph but in the interests of comfort trains do not exceed 25mph for normal running, which means that the journey time, excluding a five-minute stop at New Romney, is sixty-five minutes from one end of the line to the other. Hythe is the only terminus and because of the loop at Dungeness the RH&DR is in the unique position of being able to run a non-stop train from Hythe to Dungeness and back. In recent years it has been the custom to do this on the last Saturday of the season.

Llanberis Lake Railway, plates 132–5

132 'Dolbadarn' raising steam prior to working the first public passenger train on 19 July 1971. Gilfach Ddu station buildings are in the background

133 (above) The line from Gilfach Ddu to Penllyn is on a stone shelf at the very edge of Llyn Padarn

134 (below) Horlock 0-4-0, 'Fire Queen', built in 1848 for the 4ft gauge Padarn Railway. Now in the Penrhyn Castle Museum, Bangor

135 (above) 'Dolbadarn' at work in the Dinorwic quarries in the early 1960s

Talyllyn Railway, plates 136–42

136 (below) A double-headed train passing Quarry siding. The group on the left are volunteers resting from digging out ballast

137 (opposite) No. 6, 'Douglas', taking water at Dolgoch

138 (above) Wharf station, Towyn, in the late 1950s with No. 3 'Sir Haydn' (*left*), and 'Douglas'

139 (below) 'Sir Haydn' with a down train near Pendre

No 4

THIRD CLASS
THIRD CLASS
REFRESHMENTS

140 (opposite above) No. 4, 'Edward Thomas', with a train entering Rhydronen station

141 (opposite below) 'Douglas' with a train including the tea van near Abergynolwyn

142 (above) No. 2, 'Dolgoch', on Dolgoch viaduct

Corris Railway, plates 143–5

143 (below) Hughes locomotive and train on the original Dovey bridge, *c.* 1900

144 (left) Maespoeth junction in 1939. The engine shed and signal box are in the fork of the long-abandoned branch to Upper Corris

145 (below) Nos 3 and 4, the surviving locomotives, with some wagons at Machynlleth after the closure of the line

Vale of Rheidol Railway, plates 146–9

146 (opposite) No. 7, 'Owain Glyndwr', approaching Devil's Bridge station through the rock cutting

7

LLYWELYN
8

147 (opposite above) No. 9, 'Prince of Wales', on the curves near Aberffrwd

148 (opposite below) No. 8, 'Llywelyn', in the former GWR locomotive shed at Aberystwyth

149 (below) 'Owain Glyndwr' approaching Aberffrwd

Welshpool & Llanfair Railway, plates 150–2

150 (above) Ex-GWR 0-6-0 'The Earl' crossing the reb Banwy viaduct

151 (left) Vertical boilered Sentinel 0-4-0T, 'Nutty', wi a weedkilling train at Golfa station. The engine has nov been returned to the Narrow Gauge Museum at Towyn

152 (opposite above) 'Sir Drefaldwyn' on Brynelin viaduct, September 1970

Sittingbourne & Kemsley Railway, plates 153–5

153 (opposite below) Kerr Stuart 0-4-2ST, 'Premier', climbing Milton Bank

154 Bagnall 0-6-2T, 'Triumph', at Sittingbourne

155 'Premier' preparing to leave Kemsley Down

Romney, Hythe & Dymchurch Railway, plates 156–9

156 (above) Because of the loop at Dungeness, the RH&DR is in the unique position of being able to run a non-stop train from Hythe to Dungeness and back. In recent years it has been the custom to do this on the last Saturday of the season. No. 10, 'Doctor Syn', is here seen piloting 'Winston Churchill' with such a train, near Burmarsh Road crossing

157 (below) The same train just before rejoining the main line at the end of the Dungeness loop, with the power station in the background

158 (above) 4-8-2 no. 5, 'Hercules', at New Romney station

159 (below) 4-6-2 no. 1, 'Green Goddess', built by Davey Paxman in 1925, is a contemporary scale model to 15in gauge of a Gresley A1 Pacific

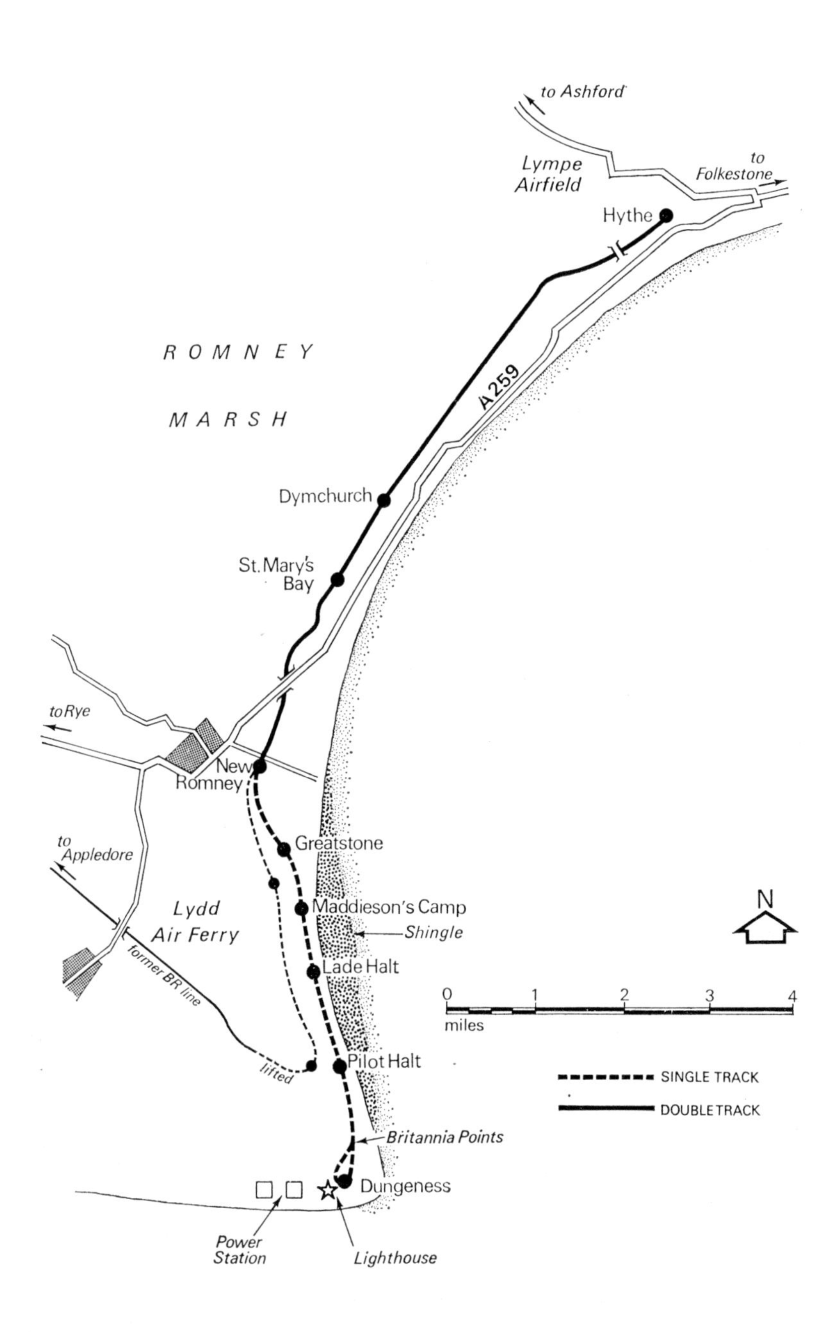

15 Romney, Hythe & Dymchurch Railway

Hythe station is the largest on the line, with four roads and a fifth in the middle to enable locomotives to be detached from their trains and turned round. Near the end of the south platform is one of the two signal boxes (the other is at New Romney) which now control the line. A third box at Dymchurch has been removed now that the colour-light system there is operated from the station building and the single track section from New Romney to Dungeness is run on a staff and ticket system. From Hythe the line heads south-west, parallel to the Royal Military Canal but at the beginning of Romney Marsh within a mile of the start they veer south and north, the railway following the coast and the canal clinging to the foot of the Downs. As the line proceeds towards Dymchurch the view of the Downs recedes over an ever wider expanse of marsh and although the railway is very close to the sea throughout this section, the sea wall hides any sight of it.

Dymchurch station, five miles from Hythe and 8·8 miles from Dungeness, has two platforms and a bay on the down (i.e. east/south) side. Near the station, as indeed throughout this part of the line, are the remains of Martello Towers which, like the Royal Military Canal, are remnants of the threat of invasion in Napoleonic times. From Dymchurch the line passes into the thick of the holiday-camp area around St Mary's Bay, across a drainage canal by a fifty-six foot long bridge, rebuilt in 1968, and soon into The Warren, a shallow cutting, which constitutes one of the few earthworks on the line.

New Romney is the administrative headquarters of the Railway and also has the main engine shed. The station, 8·3 miles from Hythe and 5·5 miles from Dungeness, is on two levels, the higher of which was the terminus of the railway when it first opened. The SR standard gauge terminus stood opposite the entrance on the other side of the Littlestone road but this was closed in March 1967 and the track was lifted soon afterwards. The other half of the RH&DR station consists of two platforms serving the through lines. It was built at a lower level because it was necessary to tunnel under the Littlestone road, although this was somewhat half-hearted and the bridge over the line has a decided hump back. Beyond New Romney is a small area of lush countryside before the line plunges into the desert of shingle and coastal development which culminates in the Dungeness Power Station. Half a mile before the railway station at Dungeness the loop begins at Britannia points, where the single track divides. These points are spring-loaded to ensure that down trains carry straight on into Dungeness station. On leaving Dungeness, trains continue round the loop and once past Britannia points become up trains on the return journey to New Romney, Dymchurch and Hythe.

The RH&DR locomotives are unique (Table 40). The missing number, no. 4, was formerly carried by the Railway's original locomotive, much used in the building of the line, an 0-4-0T built at Munich in 1926 and named 'The Bug'. This engine was very little used once the line was in operation and was eventually sold to the Bellevue Miniature Railway in Belfast, who renamed her 'Jean'.

'Green Goddess', 'Northern Chief' and 'Southern Maid' were all designed by Henry Greenly, basically as replicas of Gresley's first GNR Pacifics of 1922. However, they are by no means mere models and have many claims to represent a design entirely their own. 'Green Goddess' worked for a while on the Ravenglass & Eskdale Railway in 1925. Nos. 7 and 8, 'Typhoon' and Hurricane', were also built by Davey Paxman of Colchester to Greenly's design and are identical in all respects to nos. 1, 2 and 3, except in so far as they originally had three instead of two cylinders. However, they were converted to two-cylinder engines in the thirties. 'Hurricane', which was called 'Bluebottle' during and immediately after the war, was the engine chosen to haul the Royal Train during the visit by the Queen on 30 March 1957 and now carries commemorative plates on the cab sides.

Table 40 Steam locomotives on the Romney, Hythe & Dymchurch Railway

Type	Number/name	Where built	Year	Colour
4-6-2	1 'Green Goddess'	Davey Paxman	1925	LNER green
4-6-2	2 'Northern Chief'	Davey Paxman	1925	Napier green
4-6-2	3 'Southern Maid'	Davey Paxman	1927	GNR green
4-8-2	5 'Hercules'	Davey Paxman	1927	maroon
4-8-2	6 'Samson'	Davey Paxman	1927	dark blue
4-6-2	7 'Typhoon'	Davey Paxman	1927	Malachite green
4-6-2	8 'Hurricane'	Davey Paxman	1927	Caledonian blue
4-6-2	9 'Winston Churchill'	Yorkshire Engine Co.	1931	black
4-6-2	10 'Doctor Syn'	Yorkshire Engine Co.	1931	black

The Railway's two eight-coupled locomotives, 'Hercules' and 'Samson', were built by Davey Paxman in preparation for work on the planned extension of the line to Sandling junction in 1927. When this project was abandoned the new engines, with their long, rigid wheelbases, were unsuitable for work on the existing line and fell into some decay. However, progressive modification of the track in the years leading up to the war made it possible to bring them into full service.

Nos. 9 and 10, 'Winston Churchill' and 'Doctor Syn' (originally 'Doctor Syn' and 'Black Prince' respectively), are both Pacifics and the Railway's newest locomotives, built by the Yorkshire Engine Co. at Sheffield in 1931. Basically, they are similar to the other Pacifics on the line and like them were designed by Henry Greenly. Externally, however, they were built to look like Canadian Pacific engines, complete with cow-catchers which the Ministry of Transport at one time suggested could be fitted to all locomotives on the line. Fortunately, this was never done; neither has the management of the RH&DR been inspired to emulate 'Flying Scotsman' which has been fitted with a cow-catcher during its peregrinations of North America. The RH&DR 'Canpacs' are splendid and reliable engines. When no. 9 was new Captain Howey fitted it with an American chime whistle which Sir Nigel Gresley liked so much that Howey gave him the similar one which had been intended for no. 10. Gresley fitted the whistle to the first of his P2 class 2-8-2s, 'Cock o' the North', and subsequently had similar ones made for his A4 Pacifics. There are now two of these A4 whistles on RH&DR locomotives. The one on 'Hurricane' was a gift from Sir Nigel Gresley to Captain Howey and the other, on 'Doctor Syn', was salvaged from no. 4491, 'Commonwealth of Australia'.

Appendices

Appendix I British main line locomotives extant in England, Scotland, Wales and the Isle of Man

Compiled by R. N. Pritchard*

Pasey's compressed air locomotive, 1852

1 Locomotives in Barry Scrapyard

Type	Class	Number/name	Where built	Year	Company of origin
4-6-2	8P	71000 'Duke of Gloucester'	Crewe	1954	BR
4-6-0	5	73082 'Camelot'	Derby	1955	BR
4-6-0	5	73096	Derby	1955	BR
4-6-0	5	73129	Derby	1955	BR
4-6-0	5	73156	Doncaster	1956	BR
4-6-0	4	75014	Swindon	1951	BR
4-6-0	4	75069	Swindon	1955	BR
4-6-0	4	75078	Swindon	1956	BR
4-6-0	4	75079	Swindon	1956	BR
2-6-0	4	76017	Horwich	1953	BR
2-6-0	4	76077	Horwich	1956	BR
2-6-0	4	76079	Horwich	1957	BR
2-6-0	4	76080	Horwich	1957	BR
2-6-0	4	76084	Horwich	1957	BR
2-6-0	2	78018	Darlington	1954	BR
2-6-0	2	78019	Darlington	1954	BR
2-6-0	2	78022	Darlington	1954	BR
2-6-0	2	78059	Darlington	1956	BR
2-6-4T	4	80064	Brighton	1953	BR
2-6-4T	4	80072	Brighton	1953	BR

* Hon. Publications Officer, Worcester Locomotive Society, November 1971.

I Locomotives in Barry Scrapyard—*cont.*

Type	Class	Number/name	Where built	Year	Company of origin
2-6-4T	4	80078	Brighton	1954	BR
2-6-4T	4	80080	Brighton	1954	BR
2-6-4T	4	80097	Brighton	1954	BR
2-6-4T	4	80098	Brighton	1954	BR
2-6-4T	4	80100	Brighton	1955	BR
2-6-4T	4	80104	Brighton	1955	BR
2-6-4T	4	80105	Brighton	1955	BR
2-6-4T	4	80135	Brighton	1956	BR
2-6-4T	4	80136	Brighton	1956	BR
2-6-4T	4	80150	Brighton	1956	BR
2-6-4T	4	80151	Brighton	1956	BR
2-10-0	9F	92085	Crewe	1956	BR
2-10-0	9F	92134	Crewe	1957	BR
2-10-0	9F	92207	Swindon	1959	BR
2-10-0	9F	92212	Swindon	1959	BR
2-10-0	9F	92214	Swindon	1959	BR
2-10-0	9F	92219	Swindon	1960	BR
2-10-0	9F	92240	Crewe	1958	BR
2-10-0	9F	92245	Crewe	1958	BR
2-8-0	2800	2807	Swindon	1905	GWR
2-8-0	2800	2857	Swindon	1918	GWR
2-8-0	2800	2859	Swindon	1918	GWR
2-8-0	2800	2861	Swindon	1918	GWR
2-8-0	2800	2873	Swindon	1918	GWR
2-8-0	2800	2874	Swindon	1918	GWR
2-8-0	2884	2885	Swindon	1938	GWR
0-6-0PT	5700	3612	Swindon	1939	GWR
0-6-0PT	5700	3738	Swindon	1937	GWR
2-8-0	2884	3802	Swindon	1939	GWR
2-8-0	2884	3803	Swindon	1939	GWR
2-8-0	2884	3814	Swindon	1940	GWR
2-8-0	2884	3817	Swindon	1940	GWR
2-8-0	2884	3822	Swindon	1940	GWR
2-8-0	2884	3845	Swindon	1942	GWR
2-8-0	2884	3850	Swindon	1942	GWR
2-8-0	2884	3855	Swindon	1942	GWR
2-8-0	2884	3862	Swindon	1942	GWR
2-6-2T	5101	4110	Swindon	1936	GWR
2-6-2T	5101	4115	Swindon	1936	GWR
2-6-2T	5101	4121	Swindon	1937	GWR
2-6-2T	5101	4141	Swindon	1946	GWR
2-6-2T	5101	4144	Swindon	1946	GWR
2-6-2T	5101	4150	Swindon	1947	GWR
2-6-2T	5101	4156	Swindon	1947	GWR
2-6-2T	5101	4160	Swindon	1948	GWR
2-8-0T	4200	4247	Swindon	1916	GWR
2-8-0T	4200	4248	Swindon	1916	GWR
2-8-0T	4200	4253	Swindon	1917	GWR
2-8-0T	4200	4270	Swindon	1919	GWR
2-8-0T	4200	4277	Swindon	1920	GWR
2-6-2T	4500	4561	Swindon	1924	GWR
0-6-0PT	5700	4612	Swindon	1942	GWR
4-6-0	Hall	4920 'Dumbleton Hall'	Swindon	1929	GWR

Type	Class	Number/name	Where built	Year	Company of origin
4-6-0	Hall	4930 'Hagley Hall'	Swindon	1929	GWR
4-6-0	Hall	4936 'Kinlet Hall'	Swindon	1929	GWR
4-6-0	Hall	4942 'Maindy Hall'	Swindon	1929	GWR
4-6-0	Hall	4953 'Pitchford Hall'	Swindon	1929	GWR
4-6-0	Hall	4979 'Wootton Hall'	Swindon	1930	GWR
4-6-0	Castle	5029 'Nunney Castle'	Swindon	1934	GWR
4-6-0	Castle	5043 'Earl of Mount Edgcumbe'	Swindon	1936	GWR
4-6-0	Castle	5080 'Defiant'	Swindon	1939	GWR
2-6-2T	5101	5164	Swindon	1930	GWR
2-6-2T	5101	5193	Swindon	1934	GWR
2-6-2T	5101	5199	Swindon	1934	GWR
2-8-0T	5205	5224	Swindon	1924	GWR
2-8-0T	5205	5227	Swindon	1924	GWR
2-8-0T	5205	5239	Swindon	1924	GWR
2-6-2T	4575	5521	Swindon	1927	GWR
2-6-2T	4575	5526	Swindon	1928	GWR
2-6-2T	4575	5532	Swindon	1928	GWR
2-6-2T	4575	5538	Swindon	1928	GWR
2-6-2T	4575	5539	Swindon	1928	GWR
2-6-2T	4575	5541	Swindon	1928	GWR
2-6-2T	4575	5542	Swindon	1928	GWR
2-6-2T	4575	5552	Swindon	1928	GWR
2-6-2T	4575	5553	Swindon	1928	GWR
0-6-2T	5600	5619	Swindon	1925	GWR
0-6-2T	5600	5637	Swindon	1925	GWR
0-6-2T	5600	5643	Swindon	1925	GWR
0-6-2T	5600	5668	Swindon	1925	GWR
4-6-0	Hall	5952 'Cogan Hall'	Swindon	1935	GWR
4-6-0	Hall	5967 'Bickmarsh Hall'	Swindon	1937	GWR
4-6-0	Hall	5972 'Olton Hall'	Swindon	1937	GWR
4-6-0	King	6023 'King Edward II'	Swindon	1930	GWR
4-6-0	King	6024 'King Edward I'	Swindon	1930	GWR
0-6-2T	5600	6619	Swindon	1928	GWR
0-6-2T	5600	6634	Swindon	1928	GWR
0-6-2T	5600	6686	Armstrong Whitworth	1928	GWR
0-6-2T	5600	6695	Armstrong Whitworth	1928	GWR
4-6-0	Mod. Hall	6960 'Raveningham Hall'	Swindon	1944	GWR
4-6-0	Mod. Hall	6984 'Owsden Hall'	Swindon	1948	GWR (BR)
4-6-0	Mod. Hall	6989 'Wightwick Hall'	Swindon	1948	GWR (BR)
4-6-0	Mod. Hall	6990 'Witherslack Hall'	Swindon	1948	GWR BR)
4-6-0	Castle	7027 'Thornbury Castle'	Swindon	1949	GWR (BR)
2-8-2T	7200	7200	Swindon	1930*	GWR
2-8-2T	7200	7202	Swindon	1930*	GWR
2-8-2T	7200	7229	Swindon	1925†	GWR
4-6-0	Manor	7802 'Bradley Manor'	Swindon	1938	GWR

* Rebuilt 1934 † Rebuilt 1935

I Locomotives in Barry Scrapyard—*cont.*

Type	Class	Number/name	Where built	Year	Company of origin
4-6-0	Manor	7812 'Erlestoke Manor'	Swindon	1939	GWR
4-6-0	Manor	7819 'Hinton Manor'	Swindon	1939	GWR
4-6-0	Manor	7820 'Dinmore Manor'	Swindon	1950	GWR (BR)
4-6-0	Manor	7821 'Ditcheat Manor'	Swindon	1950	GWR (BR)
4-6-0	Manor	7822 'Foxcote Manor'	Swindon	1950	GWR (BR)
4-6-0	Manor	7828 'Odney Manor'	Swindon	1950	GWR (BR)
4-6-0	Mod. Hall	7903 'Foremarke Hall'	Swindon	1949	GWR (BR)
4-6-0	Mod. Hall	7927 'Willington Hall'	Swindon	1950	GWR (BR)
2-6-0	4300	9303	Swindon	1932	GWR
0-6-0PT	9400	9466	Robert Stephenson & Hawthorn	1952	GWR (BR)
0-6-0PT	5700	9629	Swindon	1946	GWR
0-6-0PT	5700	9681	Swindon	1949	GWR (BR)
0-6-0PT	5700	9682	Swindon	1949	GWR (BR)
2-6-2T	2P	41312	Derby	1952	LMSR (BR)
2-6-2T	2P	41313	Derby	1952	LMSR (BR)
2-6-0	'Crab'	2765	Crewe	1927	LMSR
2-6-0	'Crab'	2859	Crewe	1930	LMSR
2-6-0	5F	2968	Crewe	1934	LMSR
0-6-0	4F	4123	Crewe	1925	LMSR
0-6-0	4F	4422	Derby	1927	LMSR
4-6-0	5	4901	Crewe	1945	LMSR
4-6-0	5	5163	Armstrong Whitworth	1935	LMSR
4-6-0	5	5293	Armstrong Whitworth	1936	LMSR
4-6-0	5	5337	Armstrong Whitworth	1937	LMSR
4-6-0	5	5379	Armstrong Whitworth	1937	LMSR
4-6-0	5	5491	Derby	1943	LMSR
4-6-0	Jubilee	5690 'Leander'	Crewe	1936	LMSR
4-6-0	Jubilee	5699 'Galatea'	Crewe	1936	LMSR
2-6-0	2F	46428	Crewe	1948	LMSR (BR)
2-6-0	2F	46447	Crewe	1950	LMSR (BR)
2-6-0	2F	46512	Swindon	1952	LMSR (BR)
0-6-0T	'Jinty'	7279	Vulcan Foundry	1924	LMSR
0-6-0T	'Jinty'	7298	Hunslet	1924	LMSR
0-6-0T	'Jinty'	7324	North British	1926	LMSR
0-6-0T	'Jinty'	7406	Vulcan Foundry	1926	LMSR
0-6-0T	'Jinty'	7493	Vulcan Foundry	1927	LMSR
2-8-0	8F	8151	Crewe	1942	LMSR
2-8-0	8F	8173	Crewe	1943	LMSR
2-8-0	8F	8305	Crewe	1943	LMSR
2-8-0	8F	8431	Swindon	1944	LMSR
2-8-0	8F	8518	Doncaster	1944	LMSR
2-8-0	8F	8624	Ashford	1943	LMSR
4-6-0	B1	1264	North British	1947	LNER
4-6-0	S15	499	Eastleigh	1920	LSWR

Type	Class	Number/name	Where built	Year	Company of origin
4-6-0	S15	506	Eastleigh	1920	LSWR
2-8-0		89	Robert Stephenson	1925	SDJR
0-6-0	Q	541	Eastleigh	1939	SR
4-6-0	S15	825	Eastleigh	1927	SR
4-6-0	S15	828	Eastleigh	1928	SR
4-6-0	S15	830	Eastleigh	1928	SR
4-6-0	S15	841	Eastleigh	1936	SR
4-6-0	S15	847	Eastleigh	1936	SR
2-6-0	U	1625	Ashford	1929	SR
2-6-0	U	1638	Ashford	1931	SR
2-6-0	U	1806	Brighton	1925*	SR
2-6-0	N	1874	Woolwich Arsenal	1925	SR
4-6-2	WC	21C107 'Wade-bridge'	Brighton	1945	SR
4-6-2	WC	21C110 'Sidmouth'	Brighton	1945	SR
4-6-2	WC	21C116 'Bodmin'	Brighton	1945	SR
4-6-2	WC	21C127 'Taw Valley'	Brighton	1946	SR
4-6-2	WC	21C128 'Eddystone'	Brighton	1946	SR
4-6-2	WC	21C139 'Boscastle'	Brighton	1946	SR
4-6-2	WC	21C146 'Baunton'	Brighton	1946	SR
4-6-2	BB	21C153 'Sir Keith Park'	Brighton	1947	SR
4-6-2	BB	21C158 'Sir Frederick Pile'	Brighton	1947	SR
4-6-2	BB	21C159 'Sir Archi-bald Sinclair'	Brighton	1947	SR
4-6-2	BB	21C167 'Tangmere'	Brighton	1947	SR
4-6-2	BB	21C170 'Manston'	Brighton	1947	SR
4-6-2	BB	34072 '257 Squadron'	Brighton	1948	SR (BR)
4-6-2	BB	34073 '249 Squadron'	Brighton	1948	SR (BR)
4-6-2	BB	34081 '92 Squadron'	Brighton	1948	SR (BR)
4-6-2	WC	34101 'Hartland'	Eastleigh	1950	SR (BR)
4-6-2	WC	34105 'Swanage'	Brighton	1950	SR (BR)
4-6-2	MN	21C5 'Canadian Pacific'	Eastleigh	1941	SR
4-6-2	MN	21C6 'Peninsular & Oriental S.N. Co.'	Eastleigh	1941	SR
4-6-2	MN	21C9 'Shaw Savill'	Eastleigh	1942	SR
4-6-2	MN	21C10 'Blue Star'	Eastleigh	1942	SR
4-6-2	MN	21C11 'General Steam Navigation'	Eastleigh	1944	SR
4-6-2	MN	21C18 'British India Line'	Eastleigh	1945	SR
4-6-2	MN	35022 'Holland-America Line'	Eastleigh	1948	SR (BR)
4-6-2	MN	35025 'Brocklebank Line'	Eastleigh	1948	SR (BR)
4-6-2	MN	35027 'Port Line'	Eastleigh	1949	SR (BR)

* Rebuilt 1928

II Locomotives now in Industrial Service

Type	Class	Number/ name	Where built	Year	Company of origin	Present operator
4wVBT		12	Sentinel	1926	GWR	Thos E. Gray Ltd
0-6-0PT	5700	7714	Kerr Stuart	1930	GWR	National Coal Board
0-6-0PT	5700	7754	North British	1930	GWR	National Coal Board
0-6-0PT	5700	9600	Swindon	1945	GWR	National Coal Board
0-6-0PT	5700	9792	Swindon	1936	GWR	National Coal Board
0-6-0ST	J94	8078	Barclay	1946	LNER	National Coal Board
0-6-0ST		'Margaret'	Fox Walker	1878	NPFR	J. & P. Zammit Ltd

III Locomotives stored by British Railways for eventual display

Type	Class	Number/name	Where built	Year	Company of origin
2-10-0	9F	92220 'Evening Star'	Swindon	1960	BR
2-8-0	8K	102	Gorton	1911	GCR
0-6-0	G58	1217	Stratford	1905	GER
0-6-0	4F	4027	Derby	1924	LMSR
4-6-0	5	5000	Crewe	1934	LMSR
2-6-2	V2	4771 'Green Arrow'	Doncaster	1936	LNER
0-8-0	G2	485	Crewe	1921	LNWR
2-4-0WT	0298	0298	Beyer Peacock	1874	LSWR
0-4-4T	M7	245	Nine Elms	1897	LSWR
0-8-0	T3	901	Darlington	1919	NER
4-6-0	LN	850 'Lord Nelson'	Eastleigh	1926	SR
0-6-0	Q1	C1	Brighton	1942	SR
4-6-2	BB	21C151 'Winston Churchill'	Brighton	1946	SR

IV Locomotives in National or Local Authority museums

Type	Class	Number/name	Where built	Year	Company of origin	Museum
0-4-0		'Sans Pareil'	Hackworth	1829	B&LR	Science
4-2-2		123	Neilson	1886	CR	Glasgow
0-6-0	812	828	St Rollox	1899	CR	Glasgow
0-4-0		3	Bury Curtis & Kennedy	1846	FR	Clapham
0-6-0T	5	9	North British	1917	G&SWR	Glasgow
4-4-0	11F	506 'Butler-Henderson'	Gorton	1919	GCR	Clapham
0-6-0T	S56	87	Stratford	1894	GER	Clapham
2-4-0	T26	490	Stratford	1904	GER	Clapham
4-2-2	A1	1	Doncaster	1870	GNR	York
4-4-2	C1	251	Doncaster	1902	GNR	York
4-4-2	C1	990 'Henry Oakley'	Doncaster	1898	GNR	York
4-4-0	F	49 'Gordon Highlander'	North British	1920	GNSR	Glasgow
2-2-2		'North Star'	Swindon	1925	GWR	Swindon
0-4-0ST		921	Brush	1906	GWR	Leicester
0-6-0	2301	2516	Swindon	1897	GWR	Swindon
2-8-0	2800	2818	Swindon	1905	GWR	Bristol*
4-4-0	City	3717 'City of Truro'	Swindon	1903	GWR	Swindon
4-6-0	Star	4003 'Lode Star'	Swindon	1907	GWR	Swindon
4-6-0	Castle	4073 'Caerphilly Castle'	Swindon	1923	GWR	Science
0-6-0PT	9400	9400	Swindon	1947	GWR	Swindon
4-6-0	'Jones Goods'	103	Sharp Stewart 1894	1894	HR	Glasgow
0-2-2		'Rocket'	Robert Stephenson	1829	L&MR	Science
0-4-2		'Lion'	Todd Kitson & Laird	1838	L&MR	Liverpool
0-6-0T	A1	82 'Boxhill'	Brighton	1880	LBSCR	Clapham
0-4-2	B1	214 'Gladstone'	Brighton	1882	LBSCR	York
4-6-2	Coronation	6235 'City of Birmingham'	Crewe	1939	LMSR	Birmingham
2-6-0	2F	46464	Crewe	1950	LMSR (BR)	Dundee*
0-6-0T	'Jinty'	7237	North British	1926	LMSR	Derby Corporation*
0-6-0T	'Jinty'	7357	North British	1926	LMSR	Derby Corporation*
0-6-0T	'Jinty'	7445	Hunslet	1927	LMSR	Derby Coporation*
4-4-0	D49	246 'Morayshire'	Darlington	1928	LNER	Edinburgh*
4-6-2	A4	4468 'Mallard'	Doncaster	1938	LNER	Clapham
2-2-2		49 'Columbine'	Crewe	1845	LNWR	York
2-4-0	Precedent	790 'Hardwicke'	Crewe	1873†	LNWR	Clapham
0-4-0ST		1439	Crewe	1865	LNWR	Shugborough
2-2-2		3020 'Cornwall'	Crewe	1847‡	LNWR	Clapham
4-4-0	T3	563	Nine Elms	1893	LSWR	Clapham
0-4-0STT		Wren	Beyer Peacock	1887	LYR	Clapham
4-2-2	115	118	Derby	1897	MR	Leicester
2-4-0	156	158A	Derby	1866	MR	Leicester
4-4-0	4	1000	Derby	1902	MR	Clapham
0-6-4T		5 'Cecil Raikes'	Beyer Peacock	1885	Mersey Rly	Liverpool*
4-4-0T	A	23	Beyer Peacock	1866	Met. R.	Clapham
4-4-0	K	256 'Glen Douglas'	Cowlairs	1913	NBR	Glasgow

* Stored † Rebuilt 1892 ‡ Rebuilt 1858

IV Locomotives in National or Local Authority museums—*cont.*

Type	Class	Number/name	Where built	Year	Company of origin	Museum
2-2-4T		66 'Aerolite'	Kitson Thompson & Hewitson	1851*	NER	York
2-4-0	901	910	Gateshead	1875	NER	York
0-6-0	1001	1275	Dübs	1874	NER	York
2-4-0	1463	1463	Darlington	1885	NER	York
4-4-0	M1	1621	Gateshead	1893	NER	York
0-6-2T		2 (2271)	Stoke	1923	NSR (LMS)	Shugborough
4wWT			Aveling & Porter	1872	O&AT	Clapham
4-4-0	D	737	Ashford	1901	SECR	Clapham

* Rebuilt at Gateshead 1902

V Other preserved locomotives

Type	Class	Number/name	Where built	Year	Company of origin	Location
0-4-0ST		'Trojan'	Avonside	1897	AD&R	GWS Didcot
0-6-0ST		2 'Pontyberem'	Avonside	1900	BPGVR	GWS Taunton
4-6-2	7	70000 'Britannia'	Crewe	1951	BR	Severn Valley Rly
4-6-2	7	70013 'Oliver Cromwell'	Crewe	1952	BR	Bressingham
4-6-0	5	73050	Derby	1954	BR	Peterborough Loco. Soc.
4-6-0	4	75027	Swindon	1954	BR	Bluebell Railway
4-6-0	4	75029	Swindon	1954	BR	Stored
2-6-4T	4	80002	Derby	1952	BR	Keighley & Worth Valley Rly
2-6-4T	4	80079	Brighton	1954	BR	Severn Valley Rly
2-10-0	9F	92203	Swindon	1959	BR	Stored
0-4-4T	439	419	St Rollox	1907	CR	Scottish RPS, Falkirk
0-4-0ST		5	Kitson	1898	Cor. Rly	Bleadon & Uphill
0-4-2ST		3	Hughes Locomotive & Tramway	1878	Cor. Rly	Talyllyn Rly
0-4-2ST		4	Kerr Stuart	1921	Cor. Rly	Talyllyn Rly
0-4-0		'Invicta'	Robert Stephenson	1830	CWR	Canterbury
0-4-0ST		18	Sharp Stewart	1863	FR	George Hastwell Training Centre, Barrow in Furness
0-4-0ST		25	Sharp Stewart	1865	FR	Stone Cross Special School, Ulverston
0-4-0STT		1 'Princess'	G. England	1863	Fest. Rly	Festiniog Rly
0-4-0STT		2 'Prince'	G. England	1863	Fest. Rly	Festiniog Rly
0-4-4-0T		3 'Taliesin'	Boston Lodge	1885	Fest. Rly	Festiniog Rly
0-4-0STT		5 'Welsh Pony'	G. England	1867	Fest. Rly	Festiniog Rly
0-4-4-0T		10 'Merddin Emrys'	Boston Lodge	1879	Fest. Rly	Festiniog Rly
0-4-0ST		0229	Neilson	1876	GER	Fairfield Mabey Ltd, Chepstow
0-6-0	Y14	564	Stratford	1912	GER	North Norfolk Rly
0-6-2T	K89	7999	Stratford	1924	GER (LNER)	Neville Hill (Leeds)
4-6-0	S69	8572	Beyer Peacock	1928	GER (LNER)	North Norfolk Rly
0-6-0ST	J13	1247	Sharp Stewart	1899	GNR	Tyseley

Type	Class	Number/name	Where built	Year	Company of origin	Location
0-6-2T	N2	1744	North British	1921	GNR	Keighley & Worth Valley Rly
0-6-0ST	1361	1363	Swindon	1910	GWR	GWS Bodmin
0-6-0PT	1366	1369	Swindon	1934	GWR	Dart Valley Rly
0-4-2T	1400	1420	Swindon	1933	GWR	Dart Valley Rly
0-4-2T	1400	1442	Swindon	1935	GWR	Tiverton Museum
0-4-2T	1400	1450	Swindon	1935	GWR	Dart Valley Rly
0-4-2T	1400	1466	Swindon	1936	GWR	GWS Didcot
0-6-0PT	1500	1501	Swindon	1949	GWR (BR)	Severn Valley Rly
0-6-0PT	1600	1638	Swindon	1951	GWR (BR)	Dart Valley Rly
0-6-0	2251	3205	Swindon	1946	GWR	Severn Valley Rly
4-4-0	3200	3217 'Earl of Berkeley'	Swindon	1938	GWR	Bluebell Rly
0-6-0PT	5700	3650	Swindon	1939	GWR	GWS Didcot
4-6-0	Castle	4079 'Pendennis Castle'	Swindon	1924	GWR	GWS Didcot
2-6-2T	4500	4555	Swindon	1924	GWR	Dart Valley Rly
2-6-2T	4500	4566	Swindon	1924	GWR	Severn Valley Rly
2-6-2T	4575	4588	Swindon	1927	GWR	Dart Valley Rly
4-6-0	Hall	4983 'Albert Hall'	Swindon	1931	GWR	Tyseley
4-6-0	Castle	5051 'Earl Bathurst'	Swindon	1936	GWR	GWS Didcot
2-6-0	4300	5322	Swindon	1917	GWR	Caerphilly
2-6-2T	4575	5572	Swindon	1928	GWR	GWS Taunton
0-6-0PT	5700	5764	Swindon	1929	GWR	Severn Valley Rly
0-6-0PT	5700	5775	Swindon	1929	GWR	Keighley & Worth Valley Rly
0-6-0PT	5700	5786	Swindon	1930	GWR	H. P. Bulmer Ltd, Hereford
4-6-0	Hall	5900 'Hinderton Hall'	Swindon	1931	GWR	GWS Didcot
4-6-0	King	6000 'King George V'	Swindon	1927	GWR	H. P. Bulmer Ltd, Hereford
2-6-2T	6100	6106	Swindon	1931	GWR	GWS Didcot
0-6-0PT	6400	6412	Swindon	1934	GWR	Dart Valley Rly
0-6-0PT	6400	6430	Swindon	1937	GWR	Dart Valley Rly
0-6-0PT	6400	6435	Swindon	1937	GWR	Dart Valley Rly
0-6-2T	5600	6697	Armstrong Whitworth	1928	GWR	GWS Didcot
4-6-0	Mod. Hall	6998 'Burton Agnes Hall'	Swindon	1949	GWR (BR)	GWS Didcot
4-6-0	Castle	7029 'Clun Castle'	Swindon	1950	GWR (BR)	Tyseley
0-6-0PT	5700	7715	Kerr Stuart	1930	GWR	Quainton Rly Society
0-6-0PT	5700	7752	North British	1930	GWR	Tyseley
0-6-0PT	5700	7760	North British	1930	GWR	Tyseley
4-6-0	Manor	7808 'Cookham Manor'	Swindon	1938	GWR	GWS Didcot
4-6-0	Manor	7827 'Lydham Manor	Swindon	1950	GWR (BR)	Dart Valley Rly
0-6-0PT	5700	9642	Swindon	1946	GWR	NCB Maesteg
2-4-0T		1 'Sutherland'	Beyer Peacock	1873	IMR	Isle of Man Victorian Steam Rly
2-4-0T		2 Derby	Beyer Peacock	1873	IMR	IMVSR
2-4-0T		3 Pender	Beyer Peacock	1873	IMR	IMVSR
2-4-0T		4 'Loch'	Beyer Peacock	1874	IMR	IMVSR
2-4-0T		5 'Mona'	Beyer Peacock	1874	IMR	IMVSR

V Other preserved locomotives—*cont.*

Type	Class	Number/name	Where built	Year	Company of origin	Location
2-4-0T		6 'Peveril'	Beyer Peacock	1875	IMR	IMR
2-4-0T		7 'Tynwald'	Beyer Peacock	1880	IMR	IMVSR
2-4-0T		8 'Fenella'	Beyer Peacock	1894	IMR	IMVSR
2-4-0T		9 'Douglas'	Beyer Peacock	1896	IMR	IMVSR
2-4-0T		10 'G. H. Wood'	Beyer Peacock	1905	IMR	IMVSR
2-4-0T		11 'Maitland'	Beyer Peacock	1905	IMR	IMVSR
2-4-0T		12 'Hutchinson'	Beyer Peacock	1908	IMR	IMVSR
2-4-0T		13 'Kissack'	Beyer Peacock	1910	IMR	IMVSR
2-4-0T		16 'Mannin'	Beyer Peacock	1926	IMR	IMVSR
0-6-0T	A1X	40 'Brighton'	Brighton	1878	LBSCR	Butlins Pwllheli
0-6-0T	A1X	46 'Newington'	Brighton	1876	LBSCR	'Hayling Billy', Hayling Island
0-6-0T	A1X	50 'Whitechapel'	Brighton	1876	LBSCR	Tenterden Rly
0-6-0T	A1X	55 'Stepney'	Brighton	1875	LBSCR	Bluebell Rly
0-6-0T	A1X	62 'Martello'	Brighton	1875	LBSCR	Bressingham
0-6-0T	A1X	70 'Poplar'	Brighton	1872	LBSCR	Tenterden Rly
0-6-0T	A1X	72 'Fenchurch'	Brighton	1872	LBSCR	Bluebell Rly
0-6-0T	A1X	78 'Knowle'	Brighton	1880	LBSCR	Butlins Minehead
0-6-0T	E1	110	Brighton	1877	LBSCR	Chasewater Light Rly
0-6-2T	E4	473 'Birch Grove'	Brighton	1898	LBSCR	Bluebell Rly
2-6-2T	2P	41241	Crewe	1949	LMSR (BR)	Keighley & Worth Valley Rly
2-6-2T	2P	41298	Crewe	1951	LMSR (BR)	Quainton Rly Society
2-6-4T	4P	42073	Brighton	1950	LMSR (BR)	Lakeside & Haverthwaite Rly
2-6-4T	4P	42085	Brighton	1951	LMSR (BR)	Lakeside & Haverthwaite Rly
2-6-4T	4P	2500	Derby	1934	LMSR	Bressingham
2-6-0	'Crab'	2700	Horwich	1926	LMSR	Keighley & Worth Valley Rly
2-6-0	4F	43106	Darlington	1951	LMSR (BR)	Severn Valley Rly
4-6-0	5	4767	Crewe	1947	LMSR	Carnforth
4-6-0	5	4806	Derby	1944	LMSR	Lakeside & Haverthwaite Rly
4-6-0	5	4871	Crewe	1945	LMSR	Carnforth
4-6-0	5	4932	Horwich	1945	LMSR	Carnforth
4-6-0	5	5025	Vulcan Foundry	1934	LMSR	Keighley & Worth Valley Rly
4-6-0	5	5110	Vulcan Foundry	1935	LMSR	Severn Valley Rly
4-6-0	5	5212	Armstrong Whitworth	1935	LMSR	Keighley & Worth Valley Rly
4-6-0	5	5231	Armstrong Whitworth	1936	LMSR	Carnforth
4-6-0	5	5305	Armstrong Whitworth	1937	LMSR	Albert Draper & Son Ltd, Hull
4-6-0	5	5407	Armstrong Whitworth	1937	LMSR	Carnforth
4-6-0	5	5428 'Eric Treacy'	Armstrong Whitworth	1937	LMSR	Tyseley
4-6-0	Jubilee	5593 'Kolhapur'	North British	1935	LMSR	Tyseley
4-6-0	Jubilee	5596 'Bahamas'	North British	1935	LMSR	Dinting
4-6-0	Royal Scot	6100 'Royal Scot'	Derby	1930	LMSR	Bressingham
4-6-0	Royal Scot	6115 'Scots Guardsman'	North British	1927	LMSR	Dinting
4-6-2	Princess	6201 'Princess Elizabeth'	Crewe	1933	LMSR	Ashchurch

Type	Class	Number/name	Where built	Year	Company of origin	Location
4-6-2	Princess	6203 'Princess Margaret Rose'	Crewe	1935	LMSR	Butlins Pwllheli
4-6-2	Coronation	6229 'Duchess of Hamilton'	Crewe	1938	LMSR	Butlins Minehead
4-6-2	Coronation	6233 'Duchess of Buccleuch'	Crewe	1938	LMSR	Bressingham
2-6-0	2F	46441	Crewe	1950	LMSR (BR)	Carnforth
2-6-0	2F	46443	Crewe	1950	LMSR (BR)	Severn Valley Rly
2-6-0	2F	46521	Swindon	1953	LMSR (BR)	Severn Valley Rly
0-6-0T	'Jinty'	7383	Vulcan Foundry	1926	LMSR	Severn Valley Rly
2-8-0	8F	8233	North British	1940	LMSR	Severn Valley Rly
4wVBT	Y1	59	Sentinel	1933	LNER	Middleton Rly
2-6-0	K4	3442 'The Great Marquess'	Darlington	1938	LNER	Neville Hill (Leeds)
4-6-2	A4	4464 'Bittern'	Doncaster	1937	LNER	Neville Hill (Leeds)
4-6-2	A3	4472 'Flying Scotsman'	Doncaster	1923	LNER	North America*
4-6-2	A4	4488 'Union of South Africa'	Doncaster	1937	LNER	Lochty Private Rly
4-6-2	A4	4498 'Sir Nigel Gresley'	Doncaster	1937	LNER	NCB Philadelphia
0-6-0ST	J94	8077	Barclay	1947	LNER	Keighley & Worth Valley Rly
4-6-2	A2	60532 'Blue Peter'	Doncaster	1948	LNER (BR)	Neville Hill (Leeds)
4-6-0	B1	61306	North British	1948	LNER (BR)	Carnforth
2-6-0	K1	62005	North British	1949	LNER (BR)	Neville Hill (Leeds)
0-6-2T	'Coal Tank'	1054	Crewe	1888	LNWR	Penrhyn Castle Museum
0-4-0STT		'Pet'	Crewe	1865	LNWR	N. G. Museum, Tywyn
0-4-0T	B4	96	Nine Elms	1893	LSWR	Stored
0-4-0T	B4	102	Nine Elms	1893	LSWR	Bressingham
4-4-0	T9	120	Nine Elms	1899	LSWR	Tyseley
0-4-4T	02	209	Nine Elms	1891	LSWR	Haven St (I.o.W.
2-4-0WT	0298	314	Beyer Peacock	1874	LSWR	Quainton Rly Society
4-4-2T	0415	488	Neilson	1885	LSWR	Bluebell Rly
4-4-2T	79	80 'Thundersley'	Robert Stephenson	1909	LTSR	Bressingham
0-4-0ST	21	19	Horwich	1910	LYR	Keighley & Worth Valley Rly
0-4-0ST	21	68	Horwich	1901	LYR	Keighley & Worth Valley Rly
0-6-0ST		752	Beyer Peacock	1881	LYR	Keighley & Worth Valley Rly
0-6-0	25	957	Beyer Peacock	1887	LYR	Keighley & Worth Valley Rly
2-4-2T	5	1008	Horwich	1889	LYR	Tyseley
0-6-0	27	1300	Horwich	1896	LYR	L. Fairclough Ltd, Adlington, Lancs.
0-6-0T	1	1418	Derby	1880	MR	Keighley & Worth Valley Rly
0-6-0	4F	3924	Derby	1920	MR	Keighley & Worth Valley Rly
0-4-4T	E	1	Neasden	1898	Met. Rly	Quainton Rly Society
2-4-0T		3	Beyer Peacock	1880	MNR	I.O.M. Victorian Steam Rly

* On tour

V Other preserved locomotives—*cont.*

Type	Class	Number/name	Where built	Year	Company of origin	Location
0-6-0T		4	Dübs	1883	MNR	IMVSR
0-4-0ST		42	Cowlairs	1887	NBR	Lytham Motive Power Museum
0-6-0		673 'Maude'	Neilson	1891	NBR	Scottish RPS Falkirk
0-6-0	CI	876	Gateshead	1889	NER	Stored
0-4-0T	H	985	Darlington	1923	NER (LNER)	Stored
0-4-0T	H	1310	Gateshead	1891	NER	Middleton Rly
0-8-0	T2	2238	Darlington	1918	NER	North Yorkshire Moors Rly
0-6-0	P3	2392	Darlington	1923	NER (LNER)	North Yorkshire Moors Rly
0-6-0T	EI	69023	Darlington	1951	NER (BR)	Keighley & Worth Valley Rly
0-6-0T	75	116	Bow	1880	NLR	Bluebell Rly
2-6-2T		'Russell'	Hunslet	1906	NWNGR	Stored
0-6-0ST		26	Hudswell Clarke	1901	PTR	Severn Valley Rly
0-6-0T	USA	64	Vulcan Iron Works	1943	SR	Bluebell Rly
0-6-0T	USA	65	Vulcan Iron Works	1943	SR	Tenterden Rly
0-6-0T	USA	70	Vulcan Iron Works	1943	SR	Tenterden Rly
0-6-0T	USA	72	Vulcan Iron Works	1943	SR	Keighley & Worth Valley Rly
4-6-0	N15	777 'Sir Lamiel'	North British	1925	SR	Tyseley
4-4-0	V	925 'Cheltenham'	Eastleigh	1934	SR	Tyseley
4-4-0	V	928 'Stowe'	Eastleigh	1934	SR	Montagu Motor Museum
2-6-0	U	1618	Brighton	1928	SR	Stored
4-6-2	WC	21C123 'Blackmore Vale'	Brighton	1946	SR	Bluebell Rly
4-6-2	WC	34092 'City of Wells'	Brighton	1949	SR (BR)	Keighley & Worth Valley Rly
4-6-2	MN	35028 'Clan Line'	Eastleigh	1948	SR (BR)	Ashford
0-4-0		1 'Locomotion'	Robert Stephenson	1825	S&DR	Darlington Station
0-6-0		25 'Derwent'	Kitching	1845	S&DR	Darlington Station
0-4-2WT		1	Dodman	1893	S&MR	Longmoor Army Camp
0-4-0WT		'Shannon'	G. England	1857	Sandy & Potton Rly	GWS Didcot
0-4-0VBT		151 'Tiny'	Sara	1868	SDR	Newton Abbot Station
2-8-0		88	Robert Stephenson	1925	SDJR	Radstock
0-6-0	01	65	Ashford	1896	SER	Ashford
0-6-0T	P	27	Ashford	1910	SECR	Bluebell Rly
0-6-0T	P	178	Ashford	1910	SECR	Bluebell Rly
0-4-4T	H	263	Ashford	1905	SECR	Ashford
0-6-0T	P	323	Ashford	1910	SECR	Bluebell Rly
0-6-0T	P	556	Ashford	1909	SECR	Tenterden Rly
0-6-0	C	592	Longhedge	1902	SECR	Bluebell Rly
0-6-2T	01	28	Cardiff	1897	TVR	Caerphilly
0-6-2T	02	85	Neilson Reid	1899	TVR	Keighley & Worth Valley Rly
0-6-0T		1 'The Earl'	Beyer Peacock	1903	W&LLR	Welshpool & Llanfair Light Rly
0-6-0T		2 'The Countess'	Beyer Peacock	1903	W&LLR	W&LLR

Appendix II Railway and locomotive preservation bodies described in this book

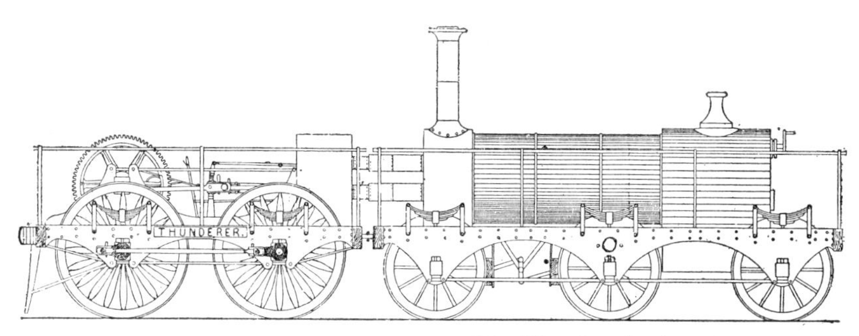

The 'Thunderer', a broad gauge engine

A4 Locomotive Society Ltd,
50, Parkland Crescent,
Leeds, LS6 4PR.

Association of Railway
Preservation Societies,
34, Templegate Road,
Whitkirk,
Leeds, LS15 0HE.

Bahamas Locomotive Society,
23, Malton Road,
Heaton Moor,
Stockport, SK4 4DE.

Bluebell Railway
Preservation Society,
Sheffield Park Station,
Uckfield, Sussex.

Bressingham Steam
Engine Museum,
Bressingham Hall,
Diss, Norfolk.

Corris Railway Society,
53, Main Street,
East Leake,
Loughborough,
Leics., LE12 6PF.

Dart Valley Light
Railway Ltd,
Buckfastleigh Station,
Buckfastleigh,
Devonshire.

Dean Forest Railway
Preservation Society,
15, Sudbrook Way,
Gloucester,
GL4 9QP.

Dowty Railway
Preservation Society,
c/o Dowty Mining
Equipment Ltd,
Ashchurch,
Tewkesbury,
Glos., GL20 8JR.

Fairbourne Railway Ltd,
Beach Road,
Fairbourne,
Merioneth.

Festiniog Railway Co.,
Harbour Station,
Portmadoc,
Caernarvonshire.

Foxfield Light Railway
Society Ltd,
100, Drubbery Lane,
Blurton, Longton,
Stoke-on-Trent,
Staffs.

Glasgow Museum of
Transport,
Albert Drive,
Eglinton Toll,
Glasgow, S2.

Great Western
Railway Museum,
Faringdon Road,
Swindon, Wilts.

Great Western
Society Ltd,
196, Norwood Road,
Southall, Middx.

Isle of Man Steam
Railway Supporters'
Association,
11, Stanley Place,
Douglas, I.O.M.

Lakeside Railway
Society,
230, Ribbleton
Avenue,
Preston, Lancs.

Llanberis Lake
Railway Co. Ltd,
Gilfach Ddu,
Llanberis,
Caernarvonshire.

Lochty Private
Railway,
nr Cupar, Fife.

Main Line Steam
Trust Ltd,
Loughborough
Central Station,
Loughborough,
Leics.

Middleton Railway,
18, Inglewood Drive,
Otley,
Leeds, LS21 3LD.

Midland Railway Project,
c/o Derby Museum,
The Strand, Derby.

Midland Railway Society,
Shackerstone Station,
Nuneaton,
Warwickshire.

Museum of British Transport,
Clapham High Street,
London, S.W.4.

North Norfolk
Railway Co. Ltd,
Sheringham Station,
Sheringham, Norfolk.

North Yorkshire Moors
Railway,
12, Staindrop Drive,
Middlesbrough,
Teesside, TS5 8NX.

Quainton Railway
Society Ltd,
Quainton Road Station,
Aylesbury, Bucks.

Railway Museum,
Queen Street,
York.

Ravenglass & Eskdale
Railway Preservation
Society Ltd,
The Retreat,
Ravenglass,
Cumberland.

Romney, Hythe &
Dymchurch Light
Railway Co.,
New Romney,
Kent.

Royal Scottish Museum,
Chambers Street,
Edinburgh, EH1 1JF.

Science Museum,
Exhibition Road,
South Kensington,
London, S.W.7.

Scottish Railway
Preservation Society,
Oakley,
Arthurlie Drive,
Uplawmoor,
Glasgow.

Severn Valley Railway
Co. Ltd,
Railway Station,
Bridgnorth,
Shropshire.

Sittingbourne & Kemsley
Light Railway Ltd,
85, Balmoral Road,
Gillingham, Kent.

Snowdon Mountain
Railway Ltd,
Llanberis,
Caernarvonshire.

Standard Gauge Steam
Trust,
74, Ferndown Road,
Solihull, Warwickshire.

Steamtown,
68, Marine Drive,
Hest Bank,
Lancaster.

Stour Valley Railway
Preservation Society,
9, Ousden Close,
Cheshunt,
Herts.

Talyllyn Railway,
Wharf Station,
Towyn, Merioneth.

Tenterden Railway Co.,
Tenterden Town Station,
Tenterden, Kent.

Transport Trust,
138, Piccadilly,
London, W.1.

Vale of Rheidol Railway
Supporters' Association,
Room 3,
Divisional Manager's
Office,
British Rail,
Station Road,
Stoke-on-Trent,
Staffordshire.

Welsh Highland Light
Railway (1964) Ltd,
57, Sherriff Street,
Rochdale,
Rochdale, Lancs.

Welshpool & Llanfair
Light Railway Preservation
Co. Ltd,
37, Langford Road,
Cockfosters, Herts.

West Somerset Railway
Co. Ltd,
16, Elm Grove,
Taunton,
Somerset.

Worcester Locomotive
Society,
24, Cecilia Avenue,
Worcester, WR2 6EN.

Yorkshire Dales
Railway Co. Ltd,
Embsay Station,
Skipton, Yorks.

Note: This list of addresses is included to indicate sources of further information about the organisations described in the book. In most cases, these are NOT the headquarters of the railways and societies concerned.

Appendix III By-laws of the Severn Valley Railway Company Limited

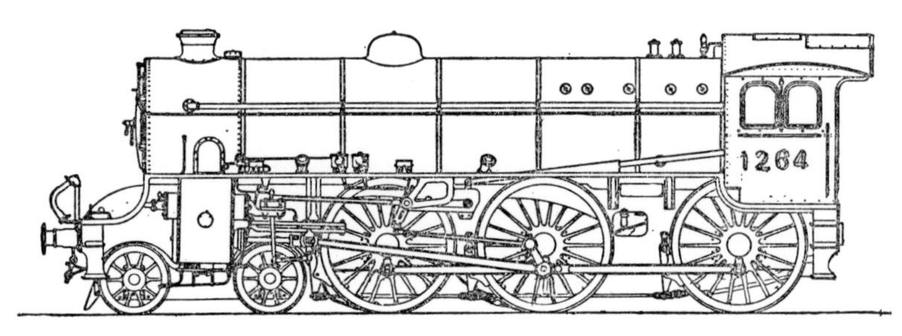

4-6-0 LNER class B1 no. 1264, now in Barry scrapyard

By-laws

Made under Section 67 of the Transport Act 1962 as applied by Section 84(3) of the said Act by The Severn Valley Railway Company Limited and confirmed by the Minister of Transport for regulating the use and working of, and travel on, its Railway, the maintenance of order on its Railway and railway premises, and the conduct of all persons on those premises.

1 In these By-laws unless the context otherwise requires the following expressions shall have the meanings hereby respectively assigned to them:

(*a*) 'the Company' means The Severn Valley Railway Company Limited.

(*b*) 'vehicle' means any railway vehicle (including locomotives) on the Railway and includes any compartment of any such vehicle.

(*c*) 'the Railway' means the railways and railway premises of The Severn Valley Railway Company Limited, including stations and the approaches to stations, and

(*d*) 'authorised person' means any officer, employee or agent of The Severn Valley Railway Company Limited (whether on the permanent or volunteer staff) acting in the execution of his or her duty on or in connection with The Severn Valley Railway Company Limited.

2 Any person offending against any of the following By-laws numbered 8, 9, 10, 12, 14, 15 and 19 shall be liable for every such offence to a penalty

not exceeding Twenty-five Pounds. Any person offending against any of the said By-laws numbered 5, 6, 7, 11, 13, 16, 17, 18, 20, 21, 22, 23, 24, and 25 shall be liable for every such offence to a penalty not exceeding Ten Pounds. Any person offending against any of the said By-laws numbered 4, 7, 8, 11, 12, 16, 17, 18, 20, 21, 22, 23, 24 and 25, and failing to desist or quit, or failing to comply with the By-law, as the case may be, when requested so to do by an authorised person may be removed from the Railway or any part thereof or any vehicle by or under the discretion of any authorised person without prejudice where any penalty is described as aforesaid for the contravention of any such By-law to such penalty.

3 These By-laws will come into operation in accordance with the provisions of the Transport Act, 1962. Upon coming into operation of these By-laws, any By-law previously made in relation to the Railway shall be repealed without prejudice, however, to the validity of anything done thereunder or to any liability incurred in respect of any act or omission before the date of the coming into operation of these By-laws.

4 No person other than an authorised person shall enter any vehicle for the purpose of travelling unless he or she or someone on his or her behalf obtains from the Company or from an authorised person a ticket or other authority entitling him or her to travel therein.

5 No person with intent that the Company shall be defrauded or prejudiced, shall:

(*a*) alter, deface, mutilate or destroy any ticket, or

(*b*) knowingly and wilfully use or attempt to use any ticket which shall have been in any respect materially altered, defaced, or mutilated.

6 No person, with the intent that the Company shall be defrauded or prejudiced, shall transfer, tender, or deliver up a ticket to another person with intent to enable any person to travel on the Railway without having previously paid his or her fare.

7 When a vehicle contains the full number of passengers which it is constructed to carry, no additional person shall enter or remain therein if requested by an authorised person not to do so.

8 No person other than an authorised person shall mount or attempt to mount on any vehicle except on such part or parts as are provided for the carriageway of passengers.

9 No person except an authorised person shall operate, move, work or tamper with any mechanical or electrical appliance upon the Railway, or any switch, lever, or other device operating or controlling any mechanical or electrical appliance upon the Railway.

10 Except in case of accident or other emergency, no person, except an authorised person, shall open the door, or stand or attempt to stand on the step or foot-board of any vehicle whilst it is in motion or between stations, or enter or leave or attempt to enter or leave any vehicle whilst it is in motion.

11 No person in a state of intoxication shall enter or remain upon the Railway, and no person who is in an unfit or improper condition to travel by passenger train or whose dress or clothing is in a condition liable to soil or injure the linings or cushions of any carriage, or the dress or clothing of any passenger, shall enter or remain in any vehicle, except with the permission of an authorised person.

12 No person shall at any time while upon the Railway:
(*a*) use any threatening, abusive, obscene, or offensive language, or
(*b*) behave in a riotous, disorderly, indecent, or offensive manner, or
(*c*) write, draw or affix any abusive, obscene, or offensive word, representation, or character upon, or wilfully soil or defile, the Railway or any vehicle, or
(*d*) molest or wilfully interfere with the comfort or convenience of any passenger or person in or upon the Railway.

13 No person shall take or cause to be taken on to, or cause or allow to remain upon, the Railway, if requested not to do so by an authorised person, any animal, article, or thing which by reason of its nature is in the opinion of such authorised person likely to cause or in fact does cause annoyance or damage to any passenger or property. If any person in charge of such animal, article, or thing fails when requested by an authorised person immediately to remove the same from the Railway, the same may be removed therefrom by or under the direction of such authorised person.

14 No person shall take or cause to be taken upon, or place or cause to be placed upon, the Railway or, while upon the Railway, have in his or her possession or discharge, as the case may be, any loaded or offensive weapon of any kind or any inflammable, explosive, or corrosive gas, spirit, liquid, substance, or matter, or any article or thing which is or may become dangerous to any person or property. Provided that nothing in this By-law shall apply to small quantities of film or of spirit or liquid carried for the personal use of such a person and not for the purpose of trade or business, provided that all due precautions are taken for the prevention of accident or injury therefrom. If any person offending against this By-law fails to remove from the Railway immediately upon request by an authorised person, any article or thing to which this By-law relates, the same may be removed therefrom by or under the direction of an authorised person.

15 No person shall wilfully, wantonly, or maliciously:
(*a*) move or set in motion or stop or attempt to stop any vehicle, or
(*b*) break, cut, scratch, tear, soil, deface, or damage any vehicle, or any of the fittings, furniture, decorations or equipment thereof, or any notice, advertisement, number plate, number, figure, or letter therein or thereupon, or remove therefrom or detach any such article or thing, or
(*c*) deface or damage any part of the Railway or any property upon the Railway.

Any person offending against this By-law shall be liable to the Company for the amount of the damage done to any part of the Company, without prejudice to any penalty incurred by the contravention of this By-law.

16 No person, while upon the Railway shall, to the annoyance of any other person, sing, perform on any musical or other instrument or use any gramophone, record player, tape recorder, or portable wireless apparatus.

17 No person while upon the Railway shall, except by permission of an authorised person:
(*a*) display or exhibit any printed, written, or pictorial matter or any article for the purpose of advertising or publicity, or distribute any book, leaflet, or other printed matter or any sample or other article, or
(*b*) sell or expose for sale any article or goods, or

(*c*) tout, ply for, or solicit alms, reward or custom or employment of any description.

18 No person shall loiter or remain upon the Railway after having been requested by an authorised person to depart, unless such person is lawfully entitled so to remain.

19 No person shall deposit, or throw or wilfully drop on or from any vehicle, on the Railway any article or thing whatsoever capable of injuring, damaging or endangering any person or property.

20 No driver or person in charge of any motor car, public service vehicle, cab, carriage, wagon, bicycle or other conveyance or of any animal in or upon the Railway shall leave or place any such conveyance or animal in or upon the Railway:

(*a*) in any manner or place so as to cause an obstruction or hindrance to the Company or to persons using the Railway, or

(*b*) otherwise than in accordance with any reasonable direction of an authorised person, or

(*c*) where parking or waiting is prohibited.

No such driver or person in charge shall leave or place any such conveyance or animal in or upon the Railway for a period longer than necessary for such person to transact any lawful business upon the Railway. Any conveyance or animal so left or placed in breach of this By-law may be removed by or under the direction of an authorised person.

21 No person shall:

(*a*) spit upon the floor or in, upon, or against any part of any vehicle upon the Railway, or upon the platform or the permanent way at any station of the Company, or in, upon, or against any hall, office, waiting room, public room, or public passage at any station of the Company, or

(*b*) place or throw any litter upon the Railway except into receptacles expressly provided for that purpose.

22 The Company may establish queues on the Railway for the purpose of regulating the access to services and facilities provided on or in the immediate vicinity of the Railway, and every person desirous of availing himself or herself of any such service or facility shall, upon notice or request by the Company or an authorised person, take up position in the rear of one of such queues and move forward in an orderly and regular manner, and obey the reasonable instructions of an authorised person regulating such queues.

23 No person shall occupy or use any vehicle, compartment, or seat on the Railway, upon which or in relation to which notice has been fixed or given by the Company that such vehicle, compartment or seat is reserved, except the person or persons for whom the Company has made the reservation.

24 Any person who is reasonably suspected of committing or attempting to commit any offence against any of these By-laws shall give his or her name and address to any authorised person when requested to do so.

25 The guard or other authorised person in charge of a passenger train may require passengers to travel in a particular vehicle or to change the vehicle in which they are travelling. Passengers must obey the reasonable instructions of the guard or other authorised person requiring them to do so.

Bibliography

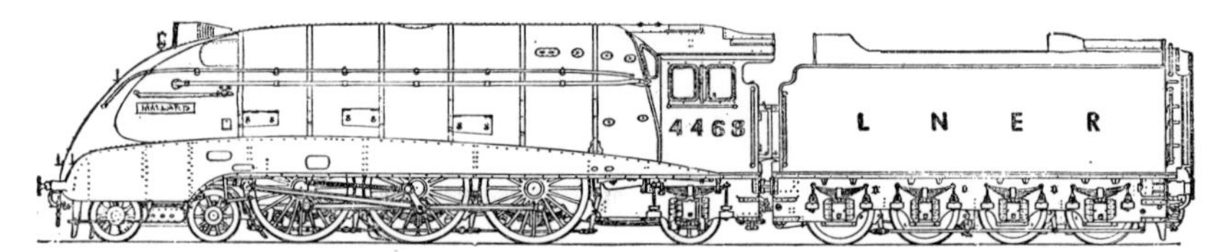

Gresley A4 Pacific no. 4468, 'Mallard', now in Clapham Museum

(*For addresses of Societies mentioned, see Appendix II*)

Ahrons, E. L., *British Steam Railway Locomotive, 1825–1925* (Locomotive Publishing Co., 1927).

Bloom, Alan, *Steam Engines at Bressingham* (Faber & Faber, 1970).

Body, Geoffrey (ed.), *Light Railway Timetables and Guide, 1971* (David & Charles, published annually).

Body, Geoffrey (ed.), *Railway Enthusiasts' Handbook. 1971–72* (David & Charles, published annually).

Boyd, James I. C., *Isle of Man Railway* (Oakwood Press, 1967).

Boyd, James I. C., *Festiniog Railway* (Oakwood Press, Vol. I, 2nd ed., 1965, Vol. II, 1962).

Boyd, James I. C., *Narrow Gauge Railways in Mid-Wales* (Oakwood Press, 2nd ed., 1970).

Casserley, H. C., *Preserved Locomotives* (Ian Allan, 2nd ed., 1969).

Cole, Terry, *Bluebell Railway—Steaming On!* (from Bluebell Railway Preservation Society, 2nd ed., 1971).

Cooke, D. N. & Williams, D. C., *Severn Valley Railway Guide* (from Severn Valley Railway Co., Ltd, 1971).

Cox, J. A., *Keighley & Worth Valley Railway Stockbook* (from Keighley & Worth Valley Railway Preservation Society, 1970).

Cox, J. A., *Worth Valley Railway Guide* (from Keighley & Worth Valley Railway Preservation Society, 1969).

Crew, Peter, *Snowdon Mountain Railway: Travelogue* (Snowdon Mountain Railway, Ltd, 1971).

Dart Valley Railway (Ian Allan, 1969).

Davies, W. J. K., *Light Railways* (Ian Allan, 1964).

Davies, W. J. K., *Vale of Rheidol Light Railway* (Ian Allan, 1970).

Davies, W. J. K., *Ravenglass & Eskdale Railway* (David & Charles, 1968).

Dumbleton, F., *Locomotives and Rolling Stock of the Great Western Society, 1971* (from Great Western Society, Ltd.).

Fairbourne Railway (Narrow Gauge Railways of Wales Joint Marketing Panel, 1971).

Garrett, S. R., *The Kent & East Sussex Railway* (Oakwood Press, 1972).

Joy, David, *Whitby and Pickering Railway* (Dalesman Books, 2nd ed., 1971)

Lee, Charles E., *The Welsh Highland Railway* (Welsh Highland Railway Society and David & Charles, 1962).

Leithead, R. H., *Stockbook of Light Railways, Miniature Railways, Preserved Locomotives and Tramcars*, 1971 edn. (from R. H. Leithead, 18, Rannoch Rise, Arnold, Nottingham, published annually).

Light Railways Acts 1896 and 1912.

Locomotives of the LNER, Part I, Preliminary Survey (Railway Correspondence and Travel Society, 1963).

Middleton Colliery Railway, Leeds, 4th ed., 1970 (from 1758 Middleton Railway Trust).

Morgan, Bryan, *Railway Relics* (Ian Allan, 1969).

Morgan, Bryan, *Transport Preserved* (British Railways Board, 1963).

Nabarro, Sir Gerald, *Severn Valley Steam* (Routledge & Kegan Paul, 1971).

Nock, O. S., *British Steam Railway Locomotive, 1925–1965* (Ian Allan, 1966).

Nock, O. S., *Kings & Castles of the GWR* (Ian Allan, 2nd ed. 1969).

Nock, O. S., *LNER Steam* (David & Charles, 1969).

Nock, O. S., *Locomotives of Sir Nigel Gresley* (Railway Publishing Co./Longmans, Green, 1945).

Nock, O. S., *Pocket Encyclopaedia of British Steam Locomotives in Colour* (Blandford Press, 1964).

Nock, O. S., *The Railway Enthusiast's Encyclopaedia* (Arrow Books, 1970).

Oxley, J. Stewart, *Light Railways, Procedures, Reports and Precedents* (P. S. King & Son, vol. 1, 1901, vol. 2, 1903).

Povey, R. O. T., *History of the Keighley & Worth Valley Railway* (from Keighley & Worth Valley Railway Preservation Society, 3rd ed., 1970).

Price, J. H., 'Llanberis Lake Railway', *Modern Tramway*, October 1971.

Pritchard, R. N., Worcester Locomotive Society, 'Preserved Locomotive Checklist', 1970 (from Worcester Locomotive Society).

Quainton Railway Society Stocklist, 1971 (from Quainton Railway Society, Ltd.),

Railways Act 1921.

Ransome-Wallis, P., *Snowdon Mountain Railway* (Ian Allan, 5th ed., 1969).

Ransome-Wallis, P., *World's Smallest Public Railway* (Ian Allan, 6th ed., 1970).

Rolt, L. T. C., *The Railway Museum, York* (British Railways Board, 2nd ed., 1968).

Rolt, L. T. C. (ed.), *Talyllyn Adventure* (David & Charles, 1971).

Scott, E. Kilburn (ed.), *Matthew Murray, Pioneer Engineer* (Jowett, 1927).

Scottish Railway Locomotives (Glasgow Museums and Art Galleries Department Art Gallery & Museum, Kelvingrove, Glasgow, 1967).

Sellick, Roger, *The West Somerset Mineral Railway* (David & Charles, 2nd ed., 1970).

Smith. D. J., *The Severn Valley Railway* (Town & Country Press, 2nd ed., 1970).

Smith, D. J., *The Welshpool and Llanfair Railway* (Town & Country Press, 2nd ed., 1969).

Smith, John L., *Rails to Tenterden* (Lens of Sutton, 1967).

Smith, S. W., 'Midland Revival', *Railway World*, November, 1971.

'Taunton to Minehead Railway' (Minehead and District Round Table, 2nd ed., 1971).

Thorndike, A. E., and Russell, R. T., *The Welshpool & Llanfair Light Railway* (David & Charles, 1972).

Tyseley Story: A Unique Venture (Ian Allan, 1970).

'Vale of Rheidol, its Railway and its Industries' (The Powysland Club, July, 1967).

Walsh, B. D. J., *The Stour Valley Railway*, 1971 (from Stour Valley Railway Preservation Society).

Williams, D. C., *Severn Valley Railway Stockbook, 1971–72* (from Severn Valley Railway Co., Ltd).

Woodford, C. G., *Stockbook of the Dart Valley Railway*, 1971 (from Dart Valley Railway Association).

Acknowledgments and Permissions

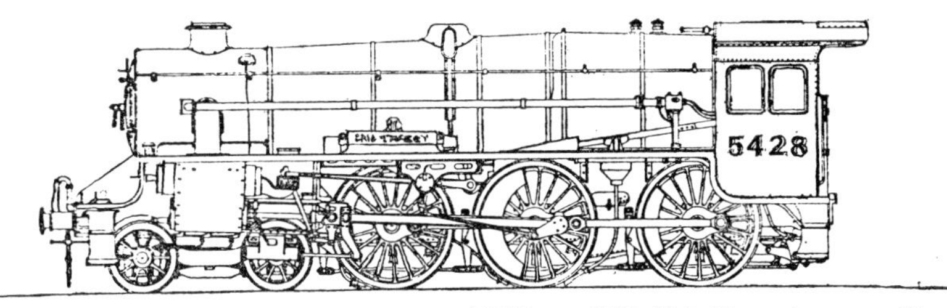

LMSR no. 5428, 'Eric Treacy', now at Tyseley

For general advice I would like to thank Mr William Broadbent, Viscount Garnock, Mr Richard Dunn, MBE, TD, Sir Gerald Ley, Bt, TD, Maj-Gen. E. H. G. Lonsdale, CB, MBE, and Mr J. N. Slater, Editor of *Railway Magazine*. For assistance with individual sections of Part 1, I wish to thank Mr Alan Bloom of Bressingham, Mr J. T. Webb of the Transport Trust, Mr M. D. Crew of the Association of Railway Preservation Societies, Mr John Scholes, Curator of Historical Relics, British Railways Board, Mr F. K. Burton of the York Railway Museum, the BRB Archivist Mr E. H. Fowkes, Dr B. S. Bryant and Mr J. R. Hillier of the Bahamas Locomotive Society, Mr Kevin R. McCormack of the Great Western Society, Mr A. A. Harland and Mrs Anthea Hanscomb of the Quainton Railway Society, Mr P. B. Whitehouse, OBE, of the Standard Gauge Steam Trust, Dr P. L. Beet and Mr G. W. Keen of Steamtown, Mr David Wood of the Worcester Locomotive Society, Mr S. A. Mourton of the Dowty Railway Preservation Society, Mr David Billmore of the Brockham Museum Association, Mr Julian Riddick of the A4 Locomotive Society, Mr Robert Kirschling of the National Railroad Museum, Green Bay, Wisconsin, and Mr Robert A. Linney of the Canadian Railway Museum, St Constant, Quebec.

Turning to the standard gauge railways described in chapters 5 to 22 I would like to thank Mr Terence Holder of the Dart Valley Railway, Mr Douglas Fear of the West Somerset Railway, Mr James Crawford, Mr Alan G. Dixon and Mr John Snewin of the Kent & East Sussex

Railway, Mr John Potter, Mr T. Cole and Mr R. T. Price of the Bluebell Railway, Mr A. E. G. Butcher of the Stour Valley Railway, Mr R. W. Turner of the Dean Forest Railway, Mr Arthur Rogers of the Foxfield Railway, Mr David Pratley of the Midland Railway Society, Mr S. W. Smith of the Midland Railway Project Group, Mr Richard Willis of the Main Line Steam Trust, Mr David Morgan of the North Norfolk Railway, Mr John Bushell and Mr T. Apperley of the Middleton Railway, Mr M. Goodall of the Keighley & Worth Valley Railway, Mr E. Black of the Yorkshire Dales Railway, Mr David Calvert of the North Yorkshire Moors Railway and Mr W. D. Ballard of the Lakeside & Haverthwaite Railway. Mr Keith G. Jones assembled all the material on railway and locomotive preservation in Scotland, with the help of Mr John Hume, Mr Ian N. Fraser, Mr Donald Storer and Mr Andrew Boyd. I am also grateful to Mr Neil Sinclair for additional information for chapter 22 and to Mr W. E. C. Watkinson for reading and correcting it.

For guidance in the fascinating and highly individualistic field of narrow gauge railways I am indebted to Mr Douglas Ferreira, Mr J. E. Hodgson and Mr William Morrison of the Ravenglass & Eskdale Railway, Mr Anthony Beard of the Isle of Man Victorian Steam Railway, Mr F. Clifton Sherriff of the Welsh Highland Railway, Mr Hugh Sykes of the Fairbourne Railway, Mr Ninian Davies of the Snowdon Mountain Railway, Mr V. J. Bradley of the Llanberis Lake Railway, Mr Richard Hope of the Talyllyn Railway, Mr E. A. Meaden of the Corris Railway Society, Mr A. E. Thorndike and Mr R. I. Cartwright of the Welshpool & Llanfair Railway, Mr R. Ratcliffe of the Sittingbourne & Kemsley Railway and Mr W. H. McAlpine of the Romney, Hythe & Dymchurch Railway.

I am pleased to acknowledge here the kind permission of the following for the use of photographs:

Mr Terence Cuneo for the frontispiece, which is from an original oil painting by him '"Clun Castle" on Campden Bank'; Mr H. C. Casserley for nos 1–4, 7, 9; Mr R. C. Riley for nos 5 and 6; Mr R. J. Buckley for no. 8; the Royal Scottish Museum for no. 10; Mr Ian N. Fraser for no. 11; Mr G. N. Heathcote for no. 12; Mr John Hume for nos 13, 15, 16 and 110; the Auchlochan Collection for no. 14; Mr Michael Warren for no. 17; Mr E. N. Kneale for nos 18, 119–23, 127–9, 131–3, 135, 146 and 148–9; British Railways for nos 19, 40 and 41; BR, London Midland Region for no. 147; Mr Alan Bloom for no. 20; Mr R. A. Bolger for no. 21; Mr J. R. Hillier for no. 22; Great Western Society Ltd for nos 23–7; Quainton Railway Society Ltd for nos 28 and 29; Rail Pictorial for no. 30; Mr T. E. Williams for no. 31; the Rt. Rev. Eric Treacy for nos 32 and 50; Mr C. M. Whitehouse for no. 33; Mr P. B. Whitehouse for nos 34, 36 and 37; Times Newspapers Ltd for no. 35; Dr P. L. Beet for no. 38; Mr Leslie Stringer for no. 39;

Worcester Locomotive Society for no. 42; Mr D. R. G. Nowell for nos 43, 44 and 53; *Railway Magazine* for no. 45; Mr F. R. Hebron for no. 46; Mr W. Lawson Kerr for no. 47; Real Photographs Co. Ltd for nos 48 and 56; Mr J. Binks for no. 112; Ravenglass & Eskdale Railway Co. Ltd for nos 113–15; Mr Hank Lefebvre for no. 49; Yorkshire Post Newspapers Ltd for no. 50; Mr J. Scrace for no. 51; Mr Kenneth Leech for no. 54; Mr C. W. Howell for no. 55; Mr Grenville R. Hounsell for nos 57, 58 and 104; Mr John Adams for nos 60, 136, 138–40 and 142; Mr John M. Boyes for nos 59 and 61; Locomotive and General Railway Photographs for nos 62 and 92; Mr J. L. Smith for nos 63–5; Mr D. A. Idle for nos 66–70, 80, 81, 83, 105–7 and 156–9; Mr Peter Le Neve-Foster, ARPS, for nos 71 and 72; Mr R. H. Marrows for no. 73; Mr S. Trigg for no. 74; Mr Roger W. Norfolk for no. 75; Mr D. C. Williams for nos 77 and 79; Mr Miles Macnair for no. 82; Mr T. D. A. Civil for no. 84; Mr D. R. Donkin for no. 85; Mr J. W. Jacques for nos 86 and 88; Mr J. Alsop for nos 87 and 89; Mr Michael J. Chapman for nos 90 and 91; Horner for no. 93; Middleton Railway Trust for nos 94 and 95; *Halifax Courier* for no. 78; Mr R. Higgins for nos 96–100 and 102; Mr D. N. Scott for no. 101; Mr Peter Weightman for no. 103; Mr Bill Ballard for nos 108–9; Mr W. S. Sellar for no. 111; Mr D. J. Mitchell for nos 116 and 118; Manx Press Pictures for no. 117; Welsh Highland Light Railway (1964) Ltd for nos 124–6; J. Salmon Ltd for no. 130; Mr K. A. Jaggers, of the Penrhyn Castle Museum, Bangor, for no. 134; Rimmer for nos 137 and 141; Photomatic Ltd/Corris Railway Society for nos 143–5; Welshpool & Llanfair Light Railway Preservation Co. Ltd for no. 150; Mr R. I. Cartwright for nos 151 and 152; and Mr Brian Stephenson/LCGB for nos 153–5.

Index

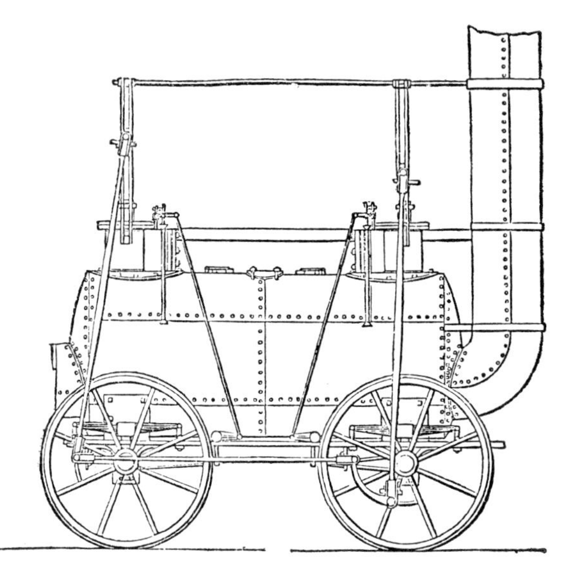

A Stephenson engine fitted with steel springs